Sacred Science

Also by John Heron

Practical Methods in Transpersonal Psychology
Experience of the Subtle Realms
Cosmic Psychology
The Facilitators' Handbook
Helping the Client
Feeling and Personhood
Group Facilitation
Co-operative Inquiry

Sacred Science

Person-centred Inquiry into the Spiritual and the Subtle

John Heron

PCCS BOOKS
Ross-on-Wye

First published 1998
Reprinted 2003

PCCS BOOKS
Llangarron
Ross-on-Wye
Herefordshire
HR9 6PT
UK
www.pccs-books.co.uk

Sacred Science: Person-centred Inquiry into the Spiritual and the Subtle

ISBN 1 898059 21 7

British Library Cataloguing in Publication data

A catalogue record for this book is available from the British Library

Library of Congress catalog record available

Cover design and type-setting by John Heron

Printed in Great Britain by Bookcraft,
Midsomer Norton, Wiltshire, UK

Contents

Preface

I am most grateful to all the co-inquirers - from Australia, Germany, Holland, New Zealand, UK, USA - who have participated in the several co-operative inquiries reported in this book, for their creative colleagueship and redoubtable integrity in researching the spiritual and the subtle. I also appreciate the notes, comments and reports which many of them have made available to me, and which I have included as citations in the text, or as corrections, amendments and additions to my writing.

Over sixty percent of my co-inquirers have been women, and under forty percent have been men. I am appreciative of the influence this ratio has had on my beliefs about a fully human, bigendered spirituality. In this regard, I have learnt from so many, including Anne Bailey, Louise Belcher, Dave Breuer, Julian Briggs, Jill Calveley, Nicola Campbell, David Colbourne, Graham Colbourne, Mary Corr, Liadon Cotter, Kim Gosden, Jennie Harris, Richard Horrocks, Dale Hunter, Katy Jennison, Quentin Jones, Don Joyce, Peta Joyce, Barbara Langton, Evelyn Marsden, Rex McCann, Glenn McNicoll, Pam Michell, James Nichol, David Petherbridge, Jenny Pinder, Kate Reed, Val Regan, Niek Sickenga, Roberta Skye, Joke Stassen, Nick Thompson and Annie Wheeler. Barbara Langton read a late draft of the book and I am grateful for her wisdom in raising my consciousness about key points, which has led to important revisions in the text of Part 1.

Outside the field of co-operative inquiry, I owe a special debt of gratitude to Jorge Ferrer for providing me with a large number of relevant references, the study of which has enabled me to portray my ideas on a wider canvas than would otherwise have been the case; also for a detailed critical commentary, on an early draft of Part 1 of the book, which alerted me to several issues needing more thoroughgoing attention. He is, of course, in no way responsible for the ideas which I have expressed as a result of his critique.

I also wish to give my warm thanks to Maggie Taylor-Sanders of PCCS Books for her strong, supportive response to the original proposal, and for her co-operative and flexible approach to working with me throughout the publishing process.

The book is in three parts. Part 1 is about the beliefs and perspectives based on my own lived inquiry into the spiritual and the subtle, and which have led me to the practice of co-operative inquiry in this same field. Part 2 presents eleven reports of co-operative inquiries which I have initiated, most of them in recent years. Part 3 elaborates beliefs about participatory research and participatory theology.

Part 1 includes a discussion of basic matters to do with spiritual inquiry. A certain proportion of this consists of a critique of other commentators, principally Ken Wilber, whose current standing in the field of transpersonal studies I can only honour by making clear the many respects in which I find his views unsound. The issues thrown into relief by this sort of disagreement I regard as a fruitful outcome of dialogue between radically differing perspectives.

The guiding ideas behind my belief in and practice of co-operative inquiry in the spiritual and subtle field are that the human person:

- Is a distinct spiritual presence in, and nonseparable from, the given cosmos; and as such is not to be reduced to, or confused with, an illusory, separate, contracted and egoic self with which personhood can become temporarily identified.
- Emerges from and is grounded in immanent spiritual life; and is informed and illuminated by a transcendent spiritual consciousness.
- Participates, through immediate experience - the very process of being in a world - in divine presence.
- Has her or his own original relation to and revelation from divine creation.
- Has spiritual authority within as inner life and inner light.
- Has freedom to co-create, with immanent spiritual life, an innovative spiritual path.
- Manifests the creative process of divine becoming as an autonomous spiritual being, embedded in connectedness, and engaged in co-operative, transformative relations with other persons similarly committed.

In an earlier book, *Feeling and Personhood* (Heron, 1992), I suggested that there are various states of personhood, which I called primal, spontaneous, compulsive, conventional, creative, self-creating, self-transfiguring and charismatic; and looked at various possible relations between them, and possible patterns of personal development in which they figure. The self-transfiguring person I portrayed as one who:

> ...has embarked upon the realization of their subtle energies, psychic capacities and spiritual potentials. They are busy with transformations of ordinary perception and action, extra sensory development and access to other realities, ritual, meditation, prayer, worship, and living in the now. And all this is integrated with a creative, expressive life in the world. (Heron, 1992: 61)

The present book is about some of the options available to the self-transfiguring person: participating in a self-generating spiritual culture, adopting a path of lived inquiry, and joining in occasional co-operative inquiries into the spiritual and the subtle. Of all this there is more in the pages which follow.

Neither I nor my co-inquirers make excessive claims for the co-operative inquiries presented in Part 2 of this book. They are short-term pioneer forays into a new field. We commend them for the transformations they yield, the liberation of their method, and as an invitation to others to go much further.

John Heron
San Cipriano

Part 1: Perspectives of lived inquiry

1

Introduction and background

This opening chapter sets the scene. It introduces the kind of sacred science this book is about, looks at some contemporary trends, defines some basic terms, sketches in some key components of the philosophy involved, introduces the inquiry methods used and the warrants they provide. It gives some personal history, summarizes various strands of thought and experience that contribute to the story, presents two introductory diagrams, and says a little about the International Centre for Co-operative Inquiry.

The first page of Contents shows the several sections within this chapter, thus providing an overview of it and a road map for navigating your own idiosyncratic journey around it.

A pioneer approach

There is a huge contemporary field of spiritual studies. It includes theology, philosophy of religion, history of religion, comparative religion, phenomenology, psychology, anthropology and sociology of religion, studies of mysticism, studies of transpersonal therapy, studies based on running transpersonal workshops.

Transpersonal psychology and inquiry draw on all these strands, focusing particularly on typologies of spiritual and subtle experiences and of their sequential stages. In the last analysis many of these typologies rest, in part or whole, on appeals to the authority of one or more established spiritual traditions and ultimately to the charismatic authority vested in some spiritual teacher.

Some work also been done to develop a natural history of religious experience based upon surveys and questionnaires sent to samples of a given population, and to categorize the range of altered states of mind entered by people who have ingested psychedelic drugs. Varieties of subtle experience, such as extrasensory perception and telekinesis, have been studied by conventional forms of psychical research.

What is so far unknown is a form of sacred science in which human beings cooperate together to inquire in a rigorous manner into the nature of their own spiritual and subtle experience, without prior allegiance to any existing school. Part 2 of this book is an account of the first pioneer work using co-operative inquiry in this way. While the collaborative research reported here is rudimentary, it nevertheless represents a breakthrough in spiritual and subtle studies. It commends a form of spiritual inquiry which:

- Departs from appeals both to the authority of spiritual traditions and teachers, and to the authority of academic researchers specializing in the field.
- Vests authority in the critical subjectivity and inner discrimination of group of co-inquirers who use the full range of their sensibilities to explore their relationship with being.
- Practises a form of democratic experiential and applied theology and parapsychology.
- Affirms the primacy of personhood, grounded in immanent spiritual life, as the foundation of religious knowing,

Part 1 of the book reflects my own lived inquiry in the spiritual and subtle field, and in this respect goes well beyond the content of the conjoint research. However, it is this individual experiential research which has led to my engagement with co-operative inquiry as a form of sacred science. So it is a crucial and important part of the story. And this personal exploration continues on, the individual process fed and reinforced by the co-operative. The interaction between the two has developed the transpersonal map which I use for a preparatory journey of opening prior to the start of an inquiry, and which I present in Chapter 6.

A self-generating spiritual culture

Let me make clear at the outset of this book that I do not believe that co-operative inquiry all on its own is the best way to carry out experiential spiritual inquiry. I believe it is a very useful short-term complement to the long-term process of individual lived inquiry, my version of which I describe later in this chapter. An increasing number of spiritually-minded people are currently busy with their own lived inquiry, and are seeking open and constructive dialogue about it. I call this social phenomenon a newly emerging and self-generating spiritual culture. It is a loose, informal network of individuals and groups who are creating their own spiritual path from a diversity of ancient and modern sources. It involves a growing and significant minority of people across the planet.

This culture is born from the post-war boom of adult and continuing education, of people-centred and peer self-help movements of all kinds, of the democratization and laicization of knowledge-acquisition, of health care, of psychological and soul growth. There has been, in the second half of the twentieth century, a growing deprofessionalization of the skills of taking care of body, mind and spirit. At the same time a vast proliferation of methods of self-care has mushroomed, from innumerable diets to every kind of spiritual practice. The human race stirs itself to fulfil the legacy of the Renaissance: the idea of the free and self-determining human person, active in all spheres of human endeavour.

What this means is a doctrine of *universal* political rights. This is an advance on the widely accepted right of any person to political membership of their community, that is, to participate in the framing and working of political institutions. The universal version expands such participation so that every social situation of decision-making is regarded as political. Then we have the all-pervasive right of persons to participate in any decision-making that affects the fulfilment of their needs and interests, the expression of their preferences, values and, above all, the inner life of their spirit. This right to political participation in the universal sense is on an unidentified march throughout the world, claiming attention not only in political institutions, but, in piecemeal fashion, in the family, in education, in medicine, in industry, in research, and, finally, in religion. It is the emergence of personhood as the *imago dei:* each human a responsible co-creator of their domain within the universal estate, in relation with others similarly engaged.

Religious authority has for centuries been the linch-pin which has kept in place the whole wheel of authoritarianism in society. Traditional religious institutions, East and West, are still today major bastions of the restriction of rights, for example, the spiritual rights of women. Religious authoritarianism, as we shall see, makes its continuing bid for control, even in modern transpersonal theory and practice. Yet people on every hand are bursting out of this ancient containing chrysalis of the free human spirit.

Emerging self-determination in the religious sphere is, in my worldview, the sign of immanent spiritual life at work at a breakthrough level, not as in the past when this or that religious innovator started a modified version of Christianity or Buddhism or some other traditional creed, but in large numbers of ordinary people generating their own lived inquiry into religious practice and deep inner transformation. My sense of it is that there are three interrelated criteria which, applying in varying degrees to any one individual, identify people in this self-generating spiritual culture:

- They affirm their own original relation to the presence of creation, find spiritual authority within and do not project it outward onto teachers, traditions or texts.
- They are alert to the hazards of defensive and offensive spirituality, in which unprocessed emotional distress distorts spiritual development, either by denying parts of one's nature, or by making inflated claims in order to manipulate others.
- They are open to genuine dialogue about spiritual beliefs and to collaborative decision-making about spiritual practices undertaken together.

Co-operative inquiry into the spiritual would not be possible without the pre-existence of this culture, and is continuously nourished and supported by it, since it is where long-term lived inquiry occurs. Equally, the nature, challenge and discipline of such long-term lived inquiry is brought into relief, honed and refined by the periodic use of co-operative inquiry, which thus intermittently serves to enhance its emerging cultural ground and develop more fully collaborative spiritual practice within it. The important points contained in this brief section are elaborated in Chapters 2 and 3. And I say more about co-operative inquiry and lived inquiry later in this chapter.

Gender-laden perennialism

This emerging self-generating spiritual culture, incidentally, is not at all the same as the current field of transpersonal studies, which is dominated by male theorists, some of whom uphold the dubious notion of a perennial philosophy, which seeks to elevate and universalize one traditional strand, Hindu-Buddhist nondualism, and make it the controlling paradigm for all past, present and future spiritual belief and experience (Coomaraswamy, 1943; Guenon, 1945; Huxley, 1945; Schuon, 1984; Smith, 1976, 1982; Wilber, 1977, 1983, 1995, 1997). This elevation has rightly been questioned on and off for some years and from a variety of standpoints (Zaehner, 1957, 1958; Katz, 1978; Gimello, 1983; Dean, 1984; Rothberg, 1986; Winkelman, 1993; Wright, 1995; diZerega, 1996; Heron, 1992, 1996b, 1997a: Kremer, 1996a; Hanegraaff, 1998; Kelly, 1998a, 1998b; for a searching critique of perennialism in general and Wilber's structuralist version in particular, see Ferrer, 1998a).

It does not at present permit, at the level of practice, any genuine experiential spiritual inquiry. It only allows experiential training within a traditional school of practice, frequently a Buddhist one among western transpersonalists, in which controversial, antique assumptions about the human condition are built into the protocols of meditative practice. These assumptions are in fact never questioned, but held firmly in place by benignly authoritarian and invariably male teachers. The teacher's controlling and directive role, especially strong in Zen, is insisted on in all eastern traditions. The result is that some of those pursuing the practice over many years start to enact, experientially, an indoctrinated, dubious and gender-laden worldview. I discuss this issue further in Chapter 2, and at the end of Chapter 7.

What is particularly gendered about accounts of the supposed *end-state* of such practice is that the traditional, typically male, practitioner claims to have become spirit as spirit, without remainder, the whole all-inclusive suchness, the original emptiness which is one with all form of any sort anywhere. He claims that any kind of self, subject or personhood has been annihilated, so that he has become reality, and is not other than the entire ground of being (Wilber, 1997: 47).

This, to use Wilber's terms, and to apply them where he would not, is supremely alienated and inflated agency, a man wanting only to be the whole of reality, and in no sense whatsoever a part of it or a participant in it. It is an artefact of the highly *agentic* achievement of long-term meditation, involving not only the subtle and disciplined control of awareness, but also a sustained dissociation, within spiritual practice, from the autonomous, dynamic impulses of immanent spiritual life. It talks of spirit exclusively in terms of consciousness, emptiness and form to the exclusion of spirit as life, fullness and process. It is the striking, yet very one-sided, voice of a small elite of male high spiritual achievers. While a radical transformation of consciousness undoubtedly occurs, the problems lie with its nature, the way it is defined and the imperialistic use to which that definition is put.

Religious feminism

However, my impression is that many people, especially women, in the emerging spiritual culture to which I refer, intuitively sense that the above kind of transpersonal perennialism is biased, oppressive and improperly controlling, locked in a closed experiential circuit of authoritarian indoctrination, and sensibly let it go.

In this regard, feminist philosophers of religion raise issues of gender, power and authority in relation to mysticism. Jantzen refers to:

> ...current areas in philosophy of religion (and beyond it) where concepts are bandied about as though they were objective and universally applicable when in fact they are products of particular, gendered, constellations of authority. What power relations are concealed, for example, in philosophical discourses about religious pluralism and interreligious dialogue in which there may also be an appeal to a mystical core of religion? (Jantzen, 1994: 203-4)

Raphael says that, within western religious feminism:

> The presentation of male sacral experience as generic of the 'innermost essence' of human religious experience has been recognized...as a falsification of many women's religious experience. (Raphael, 1994: 525).

Women's religious experience varies from that of men (Sinclair, 1986). Affirming their inherent *spiritual* experience of connectedness with nature, their empathic ecological permeability, they question the Wilber/Buddhist/male notion of the self as, ultimately, nothing but illusory separateness (Wright, 1995). They question the relevance of male ideals of emptiness or no-self as relevant to women's spiritual development (Allione, 1984; Saiving, 1992). Rather than becoming empty, they become full, 'a grounding of selfhood in the powers of being' (Christ, 1980: 19). They talk about present wholeness, rather than a goal of enlightenment (Kornfield, 1990). Instead of a linear, hierarchical model, they look for alternative web-like models that reflect an orientation toward wholeness, rather than transcendence (Gilligan, 1982).

Wright points out that, in the disciplines and traditions, East and West, on which transpersonal psychology is based, women have been oppressed and their views have been excluded. And that these traditions have pursued, inimical to women, a detached, ascensional spirituality at the expense of human bodies, senses, sexuality, generativity, and the earth itself.

> Any model that is based on traditions that have marginalized women is bound to be vulnerable in the context of women's scholarship and lived experience. (Wright, 1995: 3)

They complain of 'hierarchically invidious monism', the idea of one universal perennial sort of transcendence, one dominant male and intolerant viewpoint that downgrades all other perspectives and prioritizes enlightenment at the expense of women's other goals (Minnich, 1990). They question the male preoccupation with enlightenment via solitary meditation, and doubt its effectiveness in reflecting a fully developed human, in improving one's life and relationships, noting that skilled meditation masters may exhibit greed, hatred and neurosis (Kornfield, 1990), not to mention serious sexual and financial abuse (Lachs,1994; Crook, 1996).

Years ago, Valerie Saiving wrote:

> It is just possible that the unheard testimony of that half of the human species which has for so long been rendered inarticulate may have something to tell us about the holy which we have not known. (Saiving, 1976: 197)

When women have become articulate, men become restive, and put a stop to it. In the high and late Middle Ages, there were many women visionaries, including

Gertrude the Great, Mechthild of Helfta, Mechtild of Magdeburg, Hadewijch of Antwerp, Bridget of Sweden, Catherine of Siena, Julian of Norwich and Teresa of Avila. However, the male ecclesiastical authorities became increasingly wary of them, tightened the controlling criteria and in the final mediaeval and early modern periods executed thousands of women as heretics, often on charges of false mysticism (Jantzen, 1994).

On average, well over sixty percent of the participants in the co-operative inquiries in which I have been involved have been women. In listening to them give voice to their spirituality, it has become clear to me that a contemporary, bigendered account of the sacred, and of sacred practice, has not yet, so far as I am aware, emerged upon this planet. Wilber's recent analysis (1997: 186-202) of 'integral feminism' and 'female spirituality' is subordinated to his overall patriarchal, hierarchical model, as I discuss in Chapter 5. It simply prolongs the old story of men defining women's spirituality for them. Wilber dogmatically insists that a woman's 'permeable self is not, in itself, a spiritual self at all', except at the highest levels of the one-way ascensional system he promotes (1997: 198).

Part 1 of this book does not give my account of women's spirituality, nor does it present a bigendered account of the sacred. It offers a provisional, male account of a bigendered model. It is a limited contribution to future dialogue.

The nature of the self

One current transpersonal and archaic view is that the self is, without remainder, illusory, separate, narcissistic, contracted and knotted, and remains so in more and more refined, expanding and elevated ways, through an ascending sequence of stages of development, until final enlightenment, when the last knot disappears in the nondual state of being (Wilber, 1997). This Hindu-Buddhist view, from Shankara and Nagarjuna, and the practices and training schools which support it, are, as I have suggested, expressions of an exclusively male and rigidly authoritarian oriental system - in which 'masters' have an all-powerful role - imported into the West. I think it is highly dubious metaphysically. It is dubious too in the way it is used to legitimate spiritual power over people, by telling them what an impossible, unregenerate mess they are in without direction from those who claim to know the road to liberation. Authoritarian abuse has run amok with the spread of Buddhism in the UK and USA, and I discuss this further at the end of Chapter 7.

This view of the self bears no relation to my immediate present experience, which is already a diunity. Let me explain. I find that my everyday self is always and inalienably immersed in divinity simply by virtue of its way of being in a world. The process of my perceiving - visual, auditory, tactile, kinaesthetic imaging - is relational, interactive, interdependent and correlative. There is no gap, no separation between I the imager, the imaging, and the imaged. This unitive process enacts a local world with infinite, unlimited horizons without, and emerges from a generative infinitude within. The enactment is tacitly continuous with these dipolar infinities. I am engaged with cosmic imagination: 'The living power and prime agent of all human perception and a repetition in the finite mind of the eternal act of creation in the infinite I AM' (Coleridge).

Moreover, my perceiving is not only imaging, it is at the same time a felt mutual resonance with what is being imaged. This tells us that we, the entities present, in the totality of our reciprocal relations, constitute the sheer vibrant presence of Being here and now. I call this, simply, immediate present experience. This is already a religious experience: the diunity of self and world within the embrace of Being.

Without this going on all the time, there is no world for the everyday self. At the same time my self can get dissociated and distracted from its necessary participatory nature. It can get constricted in the illusory separateness of an alienated ego structure: by childhood wounding; by the exigencies of survival and social life; by the way the concepts that come with language separate subject from object, imager from imaged, bury the participative transaction of imaging, and distract attention from felt resonance (Heron, 1992).

However, by paying attention to these three factors, and by learning how to disperse their constricting impact, I can uncover what has been going on all the time - interactive imaging and resonance within the presence of Being here and now. This uncovering and coming to my senses reveals a real person in relation with other centres of reference. As such

- I am unique by having a standpoint and viewpoint, an enactive perspective. Whereas the self as contracted ego is to do with illusory separateness, the self as emergent person is to do with a distinct perspective within real unity.
- I am constituted by participatory and mutual engagement with others in a world.
- I am capable of extensive and intensive unfoldment by virtue of an inherent opening onto an infinite actuality without and beyond, and an infinite potential within. I can creatively transform my world, and be a catalyst to transfigure myself.

This immediate present experience, this being one of the here and now Many-in-relation-in-the-One, is the locus and foundation of personhood. In the current jargon of the trade, it is not prepersonal, not prior to verbal and conceptual mastery. I have called it post-linguistic and post-conceptual (Heron,1992, 1996a), to mean simply that it follows from deconstructing the subject-object split that language-use imposes on the process of perceiving. It is a person participating intentionally in local, temporal divine presence, and poised at the interface between transcendent spiritual consciousness and immanent spiritual life. From this here and now, the ongoing spiritual process is one of rhythmic expansion, increasing the present wholeness through a spiralling inclusion of hitherto immanent and transcendent spirit, with various intermittent phases of consolidation and reactive contraction.

If someone tells me that this account of immediate present experience is really this or that stage in the developmental map of some ancient or modern spiritual authority, I respectfully request: 'Please affirm your own inner spiritual authority and tell me about your own equivalent or related type of experience, so that we can dialogue on the basis of present revelation. Why tell me what someone else thinks is valid spiritual experience, based on summaries of what yet other people say is the case?'

Sacred science

A sacred science, I believe, is grounded in this immediate present experience of a world that is sacramental. The world is known as an *epiphany,* that is, an embodiment, a manifestation, an integrated revelation of the divine.

Lincoln and Denzin in the concluding chapter of their *Handbook of Qualitative Research* explore emerging trends in qualitative social science. They comment that the human disciplines since the turn of the century have been on a journey to join science and the sacred, citing many writers from Durkheim to Mary Douglas. They point to a contemporary range of sacred 'happenings and rituals' which 'suggest that concerns of the spirit are already returning to the human disciplines'.

> A sacred science is certain to make its effects felt within the emerging discourses of qualitative research. (Lincoln and Denzin, 1994: 583)

They also cite a seminal article by Peter Reason on sacred science, in which he argues that a secular science is inadequate for our times and points to the pressing need to resacralize our experience of ourselves and our world. He commends a sacred and collaborative human inquiry based on love, beauty, wisdom and the inquirers' commitment to practical engagement with healing their lives and their worlds (Reason, 1993). The present book present several reports of inquiries that are rudimentary instances of this approach.

A basic quaternary of terms

I find it helpful to distinguish between the spiritual, subtle, the phenomenal and the divine. Here is how, grounded in my lived inquiry, I shall use these key terms:

- By the *spiritual* I mean a comprehensive, all-pervasive, dipolar consciousness-life that appears to include human consciousness-life, to be beyond it and to be within it. Note here that I am bearing witness to spirit in two complementary and interdependent modes: spirit as transcendent and present consciousness and spirit as present and immanent life. By spirit as life I mean a moving, vitalizing principle that is anterior to our normal distinction between the animate and the inanimate. For my taste, spirit as consciousness and spirit as life are too often conflated, life usually being ignored or reduced to consciousness. So only consciousness is mentioned as 'the proper subject matter of transpersonal psychology' (Cortright, 1997: 49). Transpersonal experience is viewed only as transpersonal states of consciousness (Hunt, 1995).
- By the *subtle* I refer to extrasensory capacities in humans, and to energies, domains, presences and powers to which those capacities may bear witness. At one level it is far beyond the phenomenal realm, at another level it permeates it. At the latter level, the subtle has often been called the psychical, as in the field of psychical research.
- By the *phenomenal* I mean the manifest human world, which, among other things, includes the physical, biological, psychological and cultural spheres.
- By the *divine* I refer to an integrated One-Many reality including the spiritual, the subtle and the phenomenal.

The subtle and the phenomenal may be regarded as complementary kinds of content of the consciousness-life that is the spiritual. The divine is a wider and more inclusive term than the spiritual. It is the spiritual, the subtle and the phenomenal as a total epiphany, a sacred manifestation. I experience the divine as the *presence* of what there is here and now. I also call the divine the presence of Being. A simple diagram symbolizes the divine, as in figure 1.1.

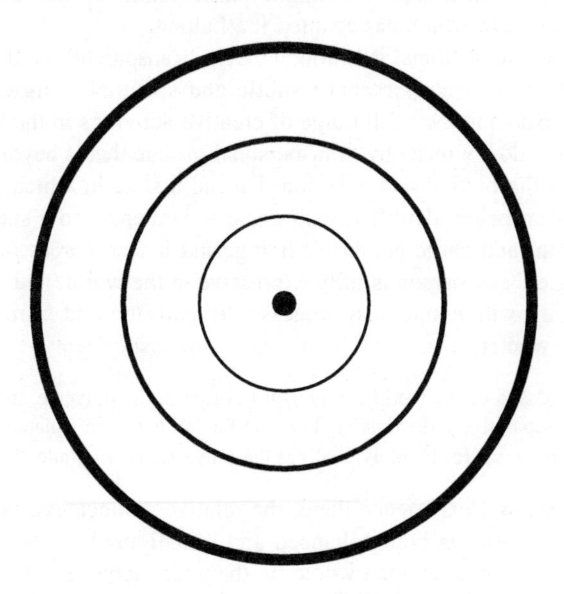

Figure 1.1 *The divine*

The circumference represents spirit as the infinitude beyond, a transcendent consciousness, which informs everything with the archetypes of creation. The centre represents spirit as the infinitude within, an immanent life, which moves everything with indwelling potential. The inner circle represents the phenomenal, the intermediate circle the subtle. All these four together symbolize the divine. The point about the phenomenal circle of human experience is that it can open both to the circumference and to the centre, in qualitatively different dipolar practices. The whole model is an experiential conjecture, a working hypothesis, not a dogma.

The transpersonal, ego and person

'Transpersonal' is a term much in vogue for designating the spiritual and subtle. Since I use it myself in this book I need to explain what connotation I give to it.

The Latin prefix 'trans' in transpersonal is highly ambiguous and has several meanings. It can mean 'beyond', as in 'transcend'. Or it can mean 'from one state to another', as in 'transform' or 'transfigure'. This is the ambiguity. Some writers use it to refer to what is beyond the person, as if personhood is something transcended and left behind, or discarded like a dead skin. They confuse the person with the limiting ego, and so mistakenly kill off both at the same time.

By the word 'transpersonal' I refer to the person changing from one state to another, emerging from identification with egoic separateness into intrinsic personhood: distinctness of being within a wider and deeper unity. In this sense 'transpersonal' means 'transforming'. Personhood is not left behind. On the contrary, it enters into its true estate, unique participation in here and now divine presence, the heritage which has awaited it all along.

Another meaning of 'trans' is 'through', as in 'transparent'. And this is another meaning I attach to 'transpersonal': subtle and spiritual energies manifesting through the person and their full range of creative activities in the world.

In summary, I do not mean by 'transpersonal' a state that is beyond personhood and implies its dissolution and negation. I mean a state in which personhood is transformed from being identified with egoic separateness to a state of resonant attunement with, and participation in, Being; and is transparent for psychic and spiritual energies. The person is fully expressive in the world, and celebrates distinctness of being within unitive awareness. This calls to mind Aurobindo's 'gnostic individual' who is:

> ...in the world and of the world...universal but free in the universe, individual but not limited by a separative individuality. The true Person is not an isolated entity, his individuality is universal for he individualizes the universe. (Aurobindo, 1970: 972-73)

In unitive states, as I experience them, the relative distinctness, uniqueness, autonomy of each entity is both enhanced and transfigured by their participative relations with each other and the whole. In the wider scheme of things, I hypothesize, there is a divine integration of the spiritual, the subtle and the phenomenal uniquely within each being and universally within the totality.

Personhood, autonomy and process theology

A person on my view, then, is an embodied spiritual presence, one of the real Many within the divine One, whose distinctness of being within the unity of the whole is more fundamental than any of her or his temporary and illusory states of egoic alienation and separateness. To add a crisper line to the account given in the earlier section on the nature of the self, a distinct person is one who:

- Participates reciprocally in the presence of other beings, human and non-human, within the presence of Being.
- Images their forms of appearing.
- Makes discriminatory judgements about their status and significance.
- Chooses to act in relation to them (Heron, 1992, 1996a).

The distinctness of a person is to do with him or her being one unique focus, among many, of the whole web of interbeing relations. Personal autonomy is grounded in this unique presence, participating resonantly in an unitive field of interconnected beings, within the presence of Being; and in the individual perspective necessarily involved in imaging a world. It is manifest as the individual judgement inalienably required for a person to appraise what is valid and valuable; and as individual responsibility in choosing to act.

This is not the personal autonomy of the Cartesian ego, an isolated, self-reflexive consciousness independent of any context - what Charlene Spretnak calls the Lone Cowboy sense of autonomy. It is, rather,

> The ecological/cosmological sense of uniqueness coupled with intersubjectivity and interbeing...One can accurately speak of the 'autonomy' of an individual only by incorporating a sense of the dynamic web of relationships that are constitutive for that being at a given moment. (Spretnak, 1995: 5)

This web or context has two layers. There is the superficial linguistic, cultural context within which autonomy is exercised and by which it is socially defined. And there is the deeper primary, extralinguistic and extracultural, context of *conscious* mutual participation with other presences in given Being, within which autonomy can also be intentionally exercised and by which it is, so to say, divinely defined.

Theologically, I take the buoyant view that personal autonomy, interdependent with its connectedness, is a form of divine expression. A person, *grounded awarely in these two contexts,* judging that some state of being is a valid spiritual experience and choosing to act accordingly, reveals their divine status in and through this very process. Thus final spiritual authority resides within the court of personal autonomy, yet always in relation to the two settings, so its expression is never immaculate. It is maculate, fallible and temporary, limited by and relative to the superficial and deep ground of its utterance. There is always an unacknowledged wider context, at each of these levels, which, once it is identified, calls for a radical revision of that utterance. I develop this view in Chapter 3.

This is the thrust of my provisional process theology. While one pole of the divine is transcendent, both beyond all manifestation and informing it, the other pole is temporal process in our world, the innovative, emergent becoming of divine immanence. Through its dynamic unfolding new contexts within established contexts, divine becoming is always transcending its current manifestation, notably as self-directing personhood. I think here of Nikolai Berdyaev's affirmation of human personhood as the creative process of divine spirit: self-determining subjectivity engaged in the realization of value and achieved in true community (*sobornost*) (Berdyaev, 1937).

This kind of dipolarity, which affirms the divinity of temporal process, breaks down the distinction between the sacred and the profane, a distinction which feminist writers have opposed (Daly, 1991; Goldenberg, 1979). Feminist theology is 'strongly immanentist: a woman's embodied finitude is holy in that it belongs to the intramundane processes of divine creativity' (Raphael, 1994: 519). Mothers in particular, through the experience of pregnancy and giving birth, enter a profound spiritual knowledge of divine developmental immanence; and their voice has been shockingly absent from traditional religious texts (Miller-McLemore, 1985).

Within the temporal dynamic of divinity, of which we are all part, relevant revelation is always now, the living, spiritual impulse of the present context, manifest in our lived and shared inquiry. There is an evolutionary process afoot 'by which each experience of Truth and Reality is a function of a dialogue between the temporal and the eternal' (McDermott, 1988: 37). We cannot know from past forms of divine becoming what its innovative future holds in store. The attempt to extract from the past a primordial tradition of universal religious truth holding for all contexts in the future, is a vain denial of the inherent unpredictability of the divine womb of time. Any candidate put forward - currently a Hindu-Buddhist account - is a maculate revelation only relevant to its original ancient context. The most that traditionalists can do is to view their task

> ...not as the attempt of one tradition or strand to legitimize itself as the one universal truth that always was, but as an invitation to dialogue among the many revelational traditions in the name of that which yet may come. Such dialogue is not the one-sided advocacy of the absolute certainty to be found in the 'already answered questions' of one particular tradition or type of spirituality; it is a shared community of questioning, a co-thinking on Being. (Dean, 1984: 216)

Personal experience as inclusive

Now a further account of the participatory nature of human knowing. Personal experience, I believe, is always inclusive, never exclusive. In other words, when I open fully to the process, an experience is never an experience *of* someone or something entirely external to that experience, but always an experience *with* someone or something. It is participative, shared. When I meet you, I never have an experience exclusively of you, but only and always inclusively and intersubjectively with you. Similarly with the more-than-human world: I don't experience a tree out there over against me, I experience reciprocal, participative engagement with the tree. Subjectivity is always contextually engaged.

Sensorial reality in my regard is subjective-objective. There is a given cosmos which I meet, encounter, become acquainted with, *participate in,* and through such meeting I know that it is there. At the same time as I meet it and participate in it, I shape it in terms of my own sensibilities, sensory, imaginal, conceptual and practical. To meet is also to shape or enact. The *meeting* gives immediacy of relationship with what is other, the sense of being engaged by it. The *shaping* of this engagement mediates the encounter in subjective-objective form. And the conceptual aspect, in particular, of this shaping derives substantially from the intersubjective context of culture and language within which I am embedded.

I take my stand here on a participatory theory of knowing, which has its precursors in Goethe, Coleridge and Emerson (McDermott, 1993), and more recently in Merleau-Ponty (1962), Bateson (1979), Reason and Rowan (1981), Spretnak (1991), Heron (1992), Varela et al. (1991), Skolimowski (1994), Reason (1994a), Abram (1996), Kremer (1997). For more on this and the subjective-objective account of reality, see Chapter 21 on the participative inquiry paradigm.

The spiritual and the subtle are likewise subjective-objective. I do not believe we have purely subjective experience of transpersonal realities, in the sense that it is other than them and leads to knowledge *of* them. Rather, such experience is knowing by acquaintance, by participation. It is already experiential knowledge *with.* It is subjective-objective, mediated-immediacy.

There are three points I would make about the subjective-objective nature of transpersonal experience. Firstly, we enter into such experience from an intersubjective culture, a field of discourse, which purveys the beliefs and practices of a spiritual school or a tradition or an eclectic amalgam drawn from several schools. This shared cultural context contributes a lot to the subjective shaping of transpersonal experience. Without it, we couldn't have raised our consciousness enough to enter into, and identify, experiences as transpersonal. But if we stay too much within it, we may well misrepresent our idiosyncratic experience at both its subjective and objective poles. Hence it is important to make the case for personal autonomy, including critical subjectivity or, in other terms, internal spiritual authority. I elaborate a model for this in Chapter 3.

Secondly, the subjective-objective structure of transpersonal experiences is highly fluidic. What is subjective in one type of experience may be objective in another, and vice versa (Ferrer, 1998c). There are many different realms, mansions, ways of being-in-a-world, with different allocations within each of them to its subjective and objective poles. However, my belief is that the subjective-objective format is a constant, like the properties of a figure that are invariable throughout different sections and projections in projective geometry.

Thirdly and relatedly, the subjective component in well-developed spiritual experience may be profoundly transfigured and re-allocated. I doubt whether it is ever the case that, in this human world, it is done away with, in the sense that at the highest levels of transpersonal experience, it becomes the same as given, divine objectivity. To do away with it, is to reduce the Many to the One, to emasculate a dipolar reality into a monopolar one, to plunge into ontological incoherence, and to make inflated experiential claims.

It is improbable to suppose that any human being, embodied in a physical organism, and embedded in a prevailing culture, as well as in a local subtle ambience, can at the same time be totally absent as a knowing subject and only be present as the One reality. This oriental view that each person can, in principle, with due application, become nothing but the One, is as unlikely as the Christian view that God can be fully manifest, without remainder, through one and only one person, Jesus Christ, at one particular point in space and time. At any rate, it does not tally with my experience of consciousness-world union.

So again I find that the claim that there is a perennial mystical philosophy, which holds good for past, present and future, and whose central tenet is that all the top mystics experience the absolute identity of subject and object, self and world in one transcendent consciousness, is nothing but untenable special pleading on behalf of an old monopolar Hindu-Buddhist practice. This meditative practice flees, and dissociates from, the Many; and supposes that any sort of subjectivity can be annihilated so that one becomes, *in toto,* the One all-inclusive 'nondual' ground of everything.

Transpersonal theorists who put forward this central tenet don't ground it unambiguously in full reports of their own spiritual life, often don't tell us clearly whether or not they have had any relevant transformations, yet are clear, first, that very few people indeed ever fully and properly reach this state, and, second, that the experiences of mystics they have never met, and only read about, confirm it. This looks like spiritual projection at work, a process I discuss in Chapter 2.

By contrast, I take the view that the more real the Many the more real the One, the greater the diversity the greater the unity of the whole, the more irreducible subjectivity to objectivity and vice versa, the greater their inseparable interdependence and the more variable their allocations, the more supreme in majesty the divine Many-One. And this, so far as it goes, is my contextually engaged, subjective-objective experience: not of a duality, nor of a nonduality, but of a diunity.

There is, indeed, a deep anomaly in the term 'nondual'. To say something is 'not two' is to affirm the duality while ostensibly rejecting it. The term is attached to a denied two at the same time as claiming it has been transcended. So I prefer to use 'diunity', to affirm the distinctness of the inseparable two - Many and One, manifestation and spirit, subject and object - within the one.

A final point in this section about personal experience. The notion that it is always contextually engaged entails a view about spiritual development. Simply stated, my contextual engagement with the transpersonal calls me to inner transformation, and my contextual engagement with the phenomenal realm of culture and nature calls me to aesthetic, social, political, economic and ecological transformation. My experiential knowing in these complementary contexts is consummated in my practical knowing how to engage in the relevant transformations and their integration. I pick up this theme again at the end of Chapter 6 and the opening of Chapter 7

Mediated-immediacy and inquiry

Postmodern 'incredulity toward metanarratives' (Lyotard, 1984) rejects any absolutist, universally true story about human beings and their place in history and the cosmos, on the grounds that such a story can have no tenable warrants and has, by virtue of its claim to be valid for everyone, an oppressive, totalitarian impact and *intent.* This postmodern view cannot itself be put forward as universally true without self-contradiction. But it can be put forward as a perspective, relative to the context of its utterance, which has a general bearing upon the human condition.

Some transpersonalists promote a universal story about human spiritual development in terms of a preordained sequence of historical stages (Wilber, Engler, Brown, 1986). However, since they are writing from within the confines of the current stage, their story is relative to the limiting structure of that stage. A stage-relative story is not a universal story. It is a contextually shaped perspective on hypothetical general features of human spirituality. Its claim to say something universal is relative to the stage within which it is uttered.

This kind of modified perspectivism is the way I go. It derives from a participatory view of reality as subjective-objective and truth as relative-universal, a view which by self-definition is also only a perspective. Such perspectivism can only offer context-relative views with some limited to claim throw light on what is universal. Hence it calls for shared inquiry at the level of practice, for active collaboration with others and their perspectives.

Thus to say that mystical experience is in transfigured subjective-objective form, is mediated-immediacy, is not to lapse into the shifting sands of absolute relativism or absolute constructivism. My experience is subjective and mediated because I shape it within my context, including my intersubjective social context and my participation in nature and cosmos - the field of interbeing. It is objective and immediate because through it I meet and touch what there is, given Being. Provided I have followed sound procedures for having a well-grounded experience, then my account of that experience is not only subjective and relative to its context. For it can at the same time lay claim to be a relatively valid perspective on what is objective and universal.

In a critique of Katz, Wilber (1995: 599-605) acknowledges the mediate-immediate nature of all experience, but then makes too much of the immediate 'touching' component, and implies it is this which entitles us to make universal and objective validity claims. In my view, this argument overreaches itself: for the other, mediate, contextual component only allows us provisionally to claim that we have a limited view from a local standpoint on a universal vista.

The views put forward in Part 1 are relative-universal in this sense. They represent the perspective born of my lived inquiry, including launching many co-operative inquiries, and are relative to my critical subjectivity and its context. They also lay claim to being well-grounded in directly touching what there is, given Being, and so to disclosing a worthy-to-be-considered perspective on what is universal.

But because they are only a relative subjective perspective on what is universal, they call for dialogue with others, for the sharing and overlapping of several individual perspectives. Above all, they call for exploring, in collaboration with others, *agreed practices* that may enrich a shared, more comprehensive and intersubjective perspective on what is universal. Kremer has already proposed that we need to go beyond rational discourse to resolve issues of spiritual validity, and to adopt 'concourse' (Kremer, 1992a, 1992b, 1994, 1996b). As well as reasoned discussion, concourse brings in 'challenges from all other human dimensions of experience - somatic, sexual, emotional and spiritual' (1994: 33). There may be ritual, silence, stories, humour, spiritual practices, theatre, dancing, other arts - any or all of which can be involved in the search for consensus. People who explore interreligious dialogue have also found it fruitful to ground rational discussion in spiritual practices and rituals (Walker, 1987).

These multidimensional, collaborative forms of spiritual inquiry are a close relative of the systematic interaction of reflection and experience in what I call co-operative inquiry. However, Rothberg, in commending these forms for the future, points out that two kinds of setting require radical transformation before such forms can be adopted and applied. Current schools of spiritual practice are too hierarchical and authoritarian to tolerate democratic and collaborative inquiry. And academic institutions are still closed to the integration of intellectual learning with experiential and practical learning.

> This suggests that to take the idea of multidimensional inquiry seriously (and playfully) in a particularly contemporary way demands critical transformations of the present ideas of spirituality, scholarship, and educational institutions....In this sense, the exploration and understanding of spiritual inquiry is only at a beginning. (Rothberg, 1994: 10)

So I wish to say that, however polemical my discussion in this book of perspectives with which I disagree becomes, I am, after an appropriate amount of rational discourse, open to engage in mutually agreed forms of experiential practice in order to deepen and extend the range of further discussion and understanding.

Co-operative inquiry

Now I believe that the account of personhood so far given, or something like it, is implicit in the idea of person-centred research into the spiritual and the subtle. Part 2 of this book is about people using one form of it, *co-operative inquiry,* to explore together their spiritual and subtle experiences and the relation of these to the rest of their lives. A group of people come together and devise a do-it-ourselves inquiry into experiences of their own extended and deepened reality, making sense of it according to their own lights. Co-operative inquiry is a very simple idea, however challenging it is to practise. I have defined it as:

> ...two or more people researching a topic through their own experience of it, using a series of cycles in which they move between this experience and reflecting together on it...It is a vision of persons in reciprocal relation using the full range of their sensibilities to inquire together into any aspect of the human condition with which the transparent body-mind can engage. (Heron, 1996a: 1)

In these cycles, the inquirers are moving between fours ways of knowing: conceptual, practical, experiential, and imaginal. These are, respectively: (i) knowing in words and concepts; (ii) knowing how to do something; (iii) knowing by meeting and engaging with Being and with beings - a person, place, process or entity; and (iv) knowing aesthetically, by intuitive apprehension of a pattern as a whole.

I'll use these same numbers to define one whole cycle of inquiry. The inquirers (i) conceptually define a topic for their inquiry and devise a method of exploring it in action, then (ii) they practically apply that method in their own actions, and in so doing (iii) engage experientially with the domain of practice. Next, they review this phase of action and experience, first (iv) grasping the whole pattern of it intuitively, then (i) appraising it conceptually, re-evaluating their starting topic in the light of it, and planning another and modified phase of action and experience in order to deepen their knowing. And so the process goes on for several cycles of inquiry, so that these four ways of knowing become more comprehensively engaged with the topic and its domain, and more congruent with each other, both within each inquirer and, with due allowance for individual perspectives, within the group as a whole.

The citation above is from *Co-operative Inquiry: Research into the Human Condition,* which gives a full account of this participative form of research and of the inquiry paradigm underlying it. In writing the present work, I am assuming that some readers will be familiar either with this previous book or with a range of other books and papers which introduce the basics of the method (Reason, 1988, 1994a; Reason and Heron, 1995; Heron and Reason, 1997). However, if you are not so familiar, see the description at the start of Chapter 21, the outline of inquiry stages in Chapter 8; and the account of the inquiry paradigm in Chapter 21.

Here is a recent comment from a regular co-operative inquirer into the spiritual and subtle:

> I have found the shared enquiry into transpersonal states very enriching. Without making too big a deal of it, what seems to be happening is a spurt of development of intuitive functioning, a subtle flowering. And I think that has been hastened by the natural alchemy which occurs when we hold a question in a genuine spirit of inquiry. This process seems to sharpen any existing capacities for active reflection, and heightens/deepens that essential connection with our capacity to witness our own experience in a neutral way. It demands as a prerequisite, a willingness and capacity to release our grip on favourite conceptual maps, or at least hold them very loose, and to develop subtle discernment in order to avoid self deception: the cooking up of imaginary altered states. (Glenn McNicoll)

Lived inquiry

Part 1 of the book is about the fruits of my own lived inquiry in the realm of the spiritual and the subtle, which has led me to the importance and practice of co-operative inquiry in the transpersonal field. For the past twenty five years it has both included and been interdependent with such practice. By lived inquiry I mean simply the active, innovative and examined life, which seeks both to transform and understand more deeply the human condition. It seems to me that many spiritually-minded people are busy with their own version of lived inquiry, and I have already suggested, earlier in this chapter, that they constitute a newly emerging self-generating spiritual culture.

The examined life, as I construe it, involves several interwoven strands:

- Being open to the here and now immediate revelation of being-in-a-world, of participating in the great field of interbeing, its *sheer presence* of Being, and all its powers and presences on many different levels.
- Being open to inner living impulses to creative action and exploration, and to their felt sense of fit within the field of interbeing.
- Exercising a finely-tuned critical discrimination and awareness with regard to experiences of the spiritual and the subtle, both one's own and others', and to their affirmation in everyday living.
- Being committed to creative and disciplined spiritual practice, devising innovative practices, adapting traditional practices.
- Taking time out for more considered reflection on the issues, moving to and fro in irregular cycles between spiritual activity and reflection, reflecting on ancient and modern transpersonal maps, and drawing out and modifying one's own maps.
- Being committed to deconstruct spiritual projection.
- Being committed to the disciplined passion of inquiring engagement with the subtle and phenomenal worlds, especially in respect of human relationships (rooted in emotional healing, emotional and interpersonal competence), the creation of knowledge, of art, of social justice and of planetary transformation.

- Engaging in dialogue and active co-operation, including short-term formal inquiries, with others on a similar path.
- Being critically informed of relevant trends of thought and practice in the prevailing culture and in past cultures.

The bottom line of all this is that, for the examined life, revelation is here and now; and spiritual authority is within. Such authority is relative to its context and unfolding, never final, and always open to spiritual deconstruction. I discuss this more fully in Chapter 3. Lived inquiry as I here describe it has significant overlaps with action inquiry (Torbert, 1991), experiential research (Cunningham, 1988) and radical practice (Heron, 1996a) all of which involve a person being intentional about living as inquiry, and all of which include the importance of dialogue with others.

Ralph Waldo Emerson championed his own account of lived spiritual inquiry, for which revelation is now. For Emerson, each person is the source of his or her own true religion.

> Why should not we also enjoy an original relation to the universe? Why should not we have a poetry and a philosophy of insight and not of tradition, and a religion by revelation to us, and not the history of theirs? Embosomed for a season in nature, whose floods of life stream around and through us, and invite us, by the powers they supply, to action proportioned to nature, why should we grope among the dry bones of the past? (in McDermott, 1993)

The Buddha, too, urged people not to be led by tradition, nor by the idea of having a teacher, but to follow what 'you know for yourselves' to be 'wholesome and good' (Rahula, 1974: 2-3). It is ironical that Buddhism today, in its western outposts, is riddled with unhealthy authoritarianism, a matter I discuss further in Chapter 7.

Inquiry warrants

Lived inquiry as I define it is not solipsistic: it is not locked up alone within the self. It is inherently participative within the cosmos; and in society, involved in active dialogue and practice with other persons and in cultural learning. It is not narcissistic: the self is not contracted round the content of experience to the exclusion of openness to the presence of Being (Almaas, 1996). For the inquiring person is awarely engaged with the enveloping field of interbeing as the immediacy of divine presence (see the earlier section on the nature of the self). More strictly and modestly speaking, the inquiry itself attends to and manages the rhythmic sequence of contracted and open states.

> Where one sees oneself seeking or motivated to seek, one inquires of oneself directly: 'Avoiding relationship?' By this inquiry, rooted in understanding, one founds oneself in the awareness of what always already is, prior to avoidance...Where there is understanding, Narcissus does not arise. (Da Avabhasa, 1992: 396, 423)

Spiritual narcissism, 'the illegitimate misuse of spiritual practices...to bolster...self-centred ways of being' (Ferrer, 1998c), is a hazard on any spiritual path, whether autonomous or traditional. It might be thought that a self-directed path of lived inquiry is, by definition, more prone to spiritual narcissism than a traditional path. I take the opposite view. The autonomous inquirer, through the practice of openness to Being, is far less at risk than established practitioner-teachers in traditional hierarchical schools. These people invariably fall foul of the spiritual narcissism involved in the authoritarian direction of the spiritual practices and lives of their students; and seem quite unaware that such direction is a rock solid form of self-centredness. I develop this point further in Chapter 2, and at the end of Chapter 7

The lived inquiry, which is the foundation for Part 1 of this book, involves alert discrimination, innovation, discipline, healing and reflection, and provides a warrant for the views advanced in it. They are not the fruit of idiosyncratic and arbitrary preference, any old off-the-cuff methodology, spasmodic and incoherent application, pathological defensive pursuits. Indeed the outcomes of rigorous lived inquiry provide the only warrant which any so-called 'master' of the spiritual life has to offer for his claims and teachings. I am simply proposing the full democratization of this principle within the self-generating spiritual culture which is currently emerging.

At the same time the warrant provided by lived inquiry is limited. It gives substance only to a personal perspective, and to a limited claim that this perspective has a general bearing on what there is, has some degree of universal relevance. It commands, not belief by others, but only a respectful and considered hearing as part of a responsible dialogue of mutual inquiry. But then, as we shall see in Chapters 2 and 3, any spiritual view put forward by anyone anywhere, has at root no more than the warrants of that person's lived inquiry, however much his or her view may be dressed up in appeals to some spiritual tradition or authority, cross-cultural consensus and so on. All of us inescapably stand upon our own original relation to the presence of creation. It is the maculate nature of that stance which calls for the enhancements and rigours of dialogue, and the challenge of inquiring into shared practice.

Co-operative inquiry, in its full-blown form, takes us beyond just one person's lived inquiry in the scope of its warrants. And it brings to a sharper focus the status of presumed warrants implicit in beliefs prevailing in the self-generating spiritual culture out of which its co-inquirers emerge. Yet co-operative inquiry is in too rudimentary a stage of development, grappling with the basics of method and content, to provide really substantive warrants for the wide-ranging content of Part 1 of this book. Furthermore, the warrants it does provide are relative to the procedures and context of the inquiry group that generates them.

The findings they support do not hold absolutely for everyone, but are illuminative pointers toward themes that may enrich the individual and co-operative inquiries of others, or practices in the wider self-generating spiritual culture. Their limited claim to validity does not warrant any wholesale prescription to others. At most, it commends them to the attention of others to explore on their own terms. They are promising approaches to transformations of being and practice, which others will reconsrue and apply in their own way.

Ferrer makes a related point, that the validity of spiritual knowledge is grounded on its emancipatory and transformative power of self and world, and that this validity is relative to the spiritual culture that generates the knowledge (Ferrer, 1998b). It is also important to distinguish what views can be grounded in a co-operative inquiry and what are presupposed by the inquiry method. Thus details of the dipolar map and the diverse sorts of practices presented in Chapter 6 are substantial content which calls for further co-operative inquiry. Whereas, as I see it, the participative worldview, the process theology and the whole notion of the authority within, are part of the inquiry paradigm, a worldview about knowing and being that is presupposed by the method itself, and to which the method gives expression. It is the use of the method by many different people over a long period of time, rather than the outcomes of any particular inquiry, which start to throw into relief the special strengths and shortcomings of the worldview to which that method gives expression. There is more on this in Chapter 7 (the section on method, metaphysic, and acting out) and in Chapter 21.

A little bit of personal history

My explicit religious life began at twelve years old when I became a devout High Anglican, enjoying mystical ardour as an acolyte at the high altar. At the age of fifteen I came upon the Everyman edition of the works of Swedenborg. I was impressed by the fact that he was an eminent scientist of the day and was also a ghost-seer, as Kant called him, writing lucid accounts of his visionary experiences of people in heavenly worlds. Two years later I moved on to the books and reported lectures of Rudolf Steiner, who earlier in his career became an authority on the scientific work of Goethe, before going public as a seer of higher worlds and the founder of Anthroposophy. Steiner believed in the idea of spiritual science, thought of himself as a spiritual scientist, and made several practical proposals for opening natural science into the subtle realms which he claimed to see.

Both these seers purveyed versions of esoteric Christianity, so my studies of them had a tenuous link with the Anglo-Catholicism which I had left behind. Another influence at this time was provided by the lectures and pamphlets of the Guild of Pastoral Psychology, a forum for progressive clergy and spiritually minded psychotherapists building on the work of C. G. Jung. I soon found any form of the Christocentric theology unconvincing and divisive, and abandoned any allegiance to Christian doctrine whether exoteric or esoteric.

At the age of twenty, I went to live in the country with the English disciple of an Indian guru. This man supported me in developing meditative concentration as a form of psychic and spiritual integration. He taught me the philosophy and practice of his Indian guru's version of raja yoga. I stayed with him several months and became sufficiently inwardly organized, under his supervision, to leave his retreat and continue my journey. A little later I complemented his work with some sessions with an eclectic psychotherapist, trained by Dr. Hadfield, who had written an excellent book on dreams and nightmares.

My next main step was to join an esoteric school which combined a deep religious mysticism with powerful ritual, and individual transformative practice. I worked intensively within the spiritual craft of this school for fourteen years, coinciding with marriage and raising three children. I found this work truly profound.

While originating in modern times, it was consonant with western mystical and occult tradition. It affirmed the reality of the unseen universe as a forum of divine manifestation and avoided the ancient oriental error of regarding it as little more than a subtle, subjective distraction on the way to total spiritual release.

However, the school was founded in the earlier decades of the twentieth century, and carried the limitations of its social context. It paid no attention to emotional, interpersonal, group or organizational processes. It had no engagement with any significant forms of social change. It was unawarely involved in patriarchal beliefs. It had no interest in developing modern forms of spiritual inquiry. I progressively withdrew from association and eventually resigned. Meanwhile I took a degree, launched myself on an academic career, my own psychological healing, and a professional involvement with the human potential movement. This involved founding the Human Potential Research Project at the University of Surrey.

My spiritual practices at this time were a combination of inner prompting, creative innovation, alert discrimination and the adaptation of methods from traditional and modern sources, both eastern and western. In the next section but one I review some of the sources that contributed to this process. It was an exploratory path of lived inquiry from which I evolved progressively a series of experiential transpersonal maps, which charted the inner options and the possible relations between them. From 1972 I started to run experiential workshops on transpersonal psychology using a simple method of experiential inquiry into early versions of these maps of meditative and altered states.

From 1978 onwards the transpersonal psychology workshops became explicit co-operative inquiries, primitive in form, eleven of which are reported in this book. Though rudimentary, I believe they are important pioneer adventures. Nowadays my own inner path of spiritual and subtle inquiry and development is closely interwoven with themes from recent and ongoing co-operative inquiries.

An early version of one of my transpersonal maps was published in 1975 as *Practical Methods in Transpersonal Psychology* by the Human Potential Research Project at the University of Surrey. The map I currently use is given in Chapter 6. A precursor to the current map and the first form of it appeared in my *Cosmic Psychology,* published by the Endymion Press, London, in 1988, and has undergone much lived inquiry and development since.

A simple map

There is another map, figure 1.2 below, which I use these days, rooted in my lived inquiry and the quaternary of terms mentioned earlier. It is simple map of divinity, which overlaps with the more elaborate one in Chapter 6, and also goes beyond it, because it is not only a crude map of being, but also a map of primary options for creating a path. Each of the four quadrants on the map is interrelated with every other. The design is not meant imply that there is some exclusive connection between the transcendent and the subtle, or the immanent and the everyday.

As a map of being, of what there is, it conjectures that:

- There is a spiritual consciousness informing everything and also beyond everything, ineffable splendour.

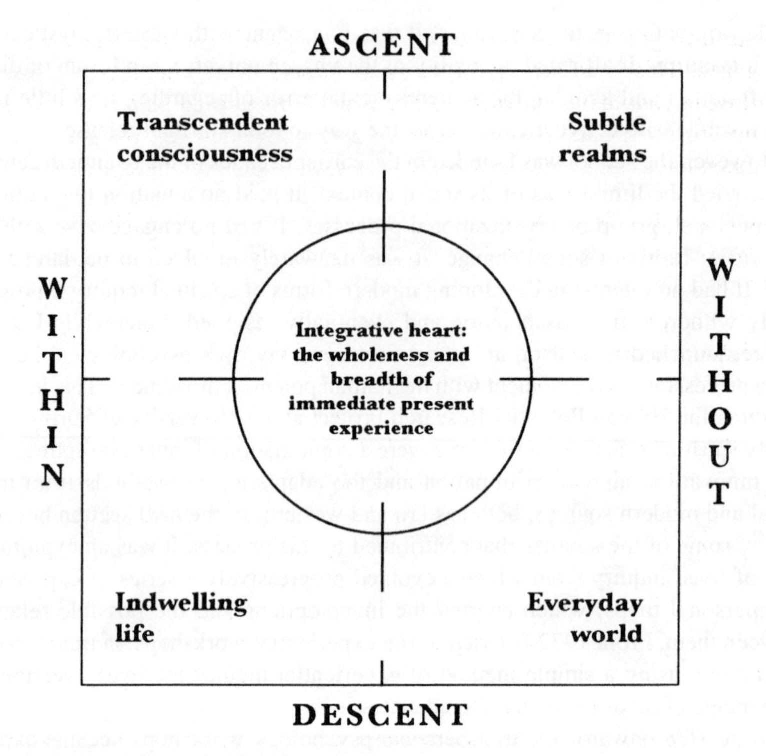

Figure 1.2 *Fivefold path of integrative heart*

- There is a spiritual life within everything as its interior source, its pregnant depth and ground. By spiritual life, as I said earlier, I mean a vitalizing principle that is anterior to our normal distinction between the animate and the inanimate.
- There are subtle realms of invisible powers and presences.
- There is the world of human society, nature and the visible cosmos.
- There is divinity which is the integrated One-Many totality of these four modes of being.

These modalities also generate a practical working hypothesis, another set of categories whose directions provide the creative options for a self-directed and comprehensive journey for the soul.

- Inward ascent to the heights of spiritual awareness beyond all name and form.
- Inward descent to the depths of spiritual life within, the ground of all manifestation.
- Outward ascent to engage creatively with the presences and energies of higher worlds.
- Outward descent to become actively involved in social change and planetary transformation.
- The transformation of these four processes within present breadth and wholeness, within the ever-present reality of immediate present experience, through

> our own growth in divine autonomy in co-operation with others similarly engaged. This is an activity of the heart through which the four processes can flow in continuous interaction. The map of the unified path is thus five-fold: inward ascent and descent, outward ascent and descent, integrated through autonomous heart into an expansion of immediate present experience.

All maps of this sort are provisional. They have a triple destiny. They are grounded on lived inquiry. They provide a tentative framework to guide such inquiry, both individual and co-operative. They are in principle open to revision by such inquiry.

Spiritual and subtle currents in contemporary culture

I will mention here some of the streams of influence, during my lifetime, which I have found it important to take account of, either positively or negatively or both. This is a selective sketch, not a complete or comprehensive account. It gives more context to the little bit of personal history above.

Liberal theology

One stream has been the progressive liberalization of Christian theology. Karl Rahner writes of 'unthematic experience', the relation of every individual, prior to all education, to infinite divine horizons (Kelly, 1993). Paul Tillich speaks in a fruitfully inconsistent way of god both as being itself and as the ground of being (Tillich, 1951-63). John Hick redefines the nature of Christ to remove the divisiveness of exclusive salvation (Hick, 1973). Matthew Fox gives Christianity an affirmative cosmic perspective and takes the world-negation out of it (Fox, 1983). All these moves appear to be headed in a direction which will sooner or later make any reference to historical Christianity largely redundant. Any form of Christocentric theology seems to me to be inherently implausible.

Process philosophy and personalism

Another important and related influence has been process philosophy and theology, originating with A. N. Whitehead (1929) and Charles Hartshorne (Hartshorne and Reese, 1953). This offers a dipolar theism or panenthesim: god in different aspects both includes the world and transcends it, is both contingent and necessary, both temporal and eternal. An independent but resonant strand is that of European personalism. Nikolai Berdyaev, as mentioned earlier, affirms human personhood as the creative process of divine spirit: self-determining subjectivity engaged in the realization of value and achieved in true community (*sobornost*) (Berdyaev, 1937).

What I take from all this is the notion that the temporal process of evolution, including human agency and society, is a basic, irreducible pole of divine reality, within which chaos, order and innovation creatively interact. This view, as I have already said, properly followed through exposes the perennial philosophy fallacy that selected past mystics have uncovered the basic format of future spiritual development (see also chapters by Slater, Wyschograd, Lee and Gadamer in Olson and Rouner, 1981).

Existentialism and phenomenology

Existentialism, influential for both Tillich and Berdyaev, has affirmed usefully the irreducibility of individual agency, of the choice and commitment of the will, of the first-person, the 'real subject' in Kierkegaard's phrase. Heidegger sees Being and primordial or revelatory truth as temporal and unfolding. While phenomenologists like Merleau-Ponty have affirmed a truly radical empiricism, the irreducible ground of meaning of the lived-through world found in unrestricted perception, the consciousness-world union that is anterior to every distinction, including that of mind and nature. Merleau-Ponty's work spearheads the participatory worldview, affirming the reciprocal engagement of subject and object in a unitive field (Merleau-Ponty, 1962). It demystifies the absolute nondual state and makes it relatively accessible as the diunity of immediate perceptual experience.

Poststructuralism

What I find important in poststructuralist and deconstructionist critiques of the subject, the Cartesian ego, is the view that the self 'can only describe itself through its placing in language, culture, history, text, gender and the variety of discourses both emerging from and constituting such contexts'; and is only known through its contextual relation with the other (Bleakley, 1996). What this means is that the claims of personal experience, of the autonomous subject, are always immersed in the hermeneutic situation (Heidegger 1962, Gadamer, 1976), are always relative to their linguistic and cultural context.

However, this does not mean, as some poststructuralists seem to think, that such claims have no truth or meaning. It means only that truth and meaning are context-bound, and that context is boundless, infinitely extendable (Culler, 1982; Heron, 1996a). Moreover, any cultural context of meaning is itself grounded in a wider and deeper context of non-linguistic ecological meaning, the primary meaning of our participative, sensorial, immediate and reciprocal engagement with our world (Abram, 1996; Spretnak, 1995; Heron, 1996a). I sketched in these ideas earlier in this chapter, and develop them further in Chapter 3.

The human potential movement

The birth of humanistic psychology in the 1960s and its practical proliferation in numerous centres offering workshops on various aspects of personal and professional development has been a major influence. I have been involved in this kind of work for over 25 years, through the Human Potential Research Project at the University of Surrey, the British Postgraduate Medical Federation at the University of London, and for the past ten years as an international consultant and at my centre in Italy. One of the central themes in this work has been that of emotional competence or emotional intelligence.

For me, this means a person being aware and in charge of their own emotional processes. These include their distresses and woundedness, with the distortions and compulsions to which these give rise, their delights and celebrations, their loving, their self-esteem, their felt values and preferences. And all this as a foundation for interpersonal sensitivity and skill, and spiritual development. Human emotion, in my worldview, is not some primitive level of the human ego to be transcended on a path of spiritual ascent, but a self-transfiguring touchstone of the spiritually distinct person, one of the divine Many.

Religious studies

Over the years I have made diverse forays into this very large field of religious studies. Most relevant in transpersonal psychology and philosophy have been typologies of subtle and spiritual states. The studies that come particularly to mind are those of W. T. Stace (1961), more recently Stan Grof's classification based on the clinical use of LSD and holotropic breathwork (Grof, 1976, 1988), and Washburn's model of the ego and the dynamic ground (Washburn, 1995). Claims like those of Huxley (1945), Wilber (1995) and others to derive from the writings of past sages and mystics a perennial philosophy which is a valid guide to spiritual development today and for the future, seem to me, as I mentioned earlier, to be quite untenable (Heron, 1996b). Ancient cartographies of the spiritual realms are probably as unreliable as those of the physical planet. They are deeply interesting and fruitful, but by no means conclusive, sources. I discuss this in more detail in Chapter 2.

Wilber's hierarchical map is primarily a contemporary reworking of ancient views, mainly of Advaita Vedanta Hinduism and Madhyamika Buddhism. It is intermittently enlightening here and there in some of its parts. But I do not find it persuasive, either experientially or theoretically, as a total scheme, which is too monopolar and patriarchal. Also Wilber's use of it is hegemonic: he tries to convert just one strand of our religious legacy, the old Hindu-Buddhist model, into a controlling paradigm that defines the religious path for all time. His attempt to dress this strand up in modern theoretical clothes is elaborate, and unconvincing, special pleading for his strong personal allegiance to a very traditional path. I have criticized his approach extensively in other places (Heron, 1992, 1996b, 1997a), and cover many of the important points in Chapters 2 and 5. I have learnt a lot through clarifying the several respects in which I find it unsatisfactory.

Hindu and Buddhist teachers

However, I have found useful, both theoretically and experientially, a selective approach to oriental religions. The selection includes: the account of Tibetan Buddhism given by Govinda (1960); an encounter with Tarthang Tulku and his version of Nyingma Buddhism; the *shaktipat* and siddha yoga of Muktananda, before stories circulated about his erotic abuses; some forms of Tantra; and Taoism. I also have strong reservations about each of these particular items, and about ancient eastern religion in general.

There has been an invasion from the east, in postwar decades, of mystics and masters seeking a following in the west. Streams of Hindu and Buddhist teachers have been a feature of the transpersonal landscape throughout my adult life. They seem to have influence in the west because of a range of factors:

- Their teachings avoid the Christocentric exclusiveness and divisiveness of Christianity, yet share with it a sustained negativity about the world and the self.

Thus familiar and ingrained religious neurosis can readily be transferred across, when someone abandons the western tradition in favour the eastern.

- They seem to offer some respite from the anomie of western materialism.
- They can both dissociate one from, and reinforce, emotional repression and its effects.
- They offer experiential, meditative alternatives to the Christian liturgy of prayer and praise.
- They offer both ancient and modern spiritual heroes whom one can appoint as external authority figures.
- They allow people to affirm their spirituality in a distinctive, counter-cultural way.

The problem with both traditions is that, however much they are up-dated and brought into relation with the idiom of contemporary life, they carry the blight of world-denial from their ancient and problematic cultures. Their monism and pantheism is of the acosmic variety. They are pre-occupied with *moksha*, release from the world, its sorrows and perplexities. They are in flight to god from the works of god. They flee the Many, via dissociative meditation, to find the One, and can only reinstate the Many as passive perceptual forms presumed to be identical with quietist absorption in the One. Their primary injunction is to be not attached to any single thing, with the result that they become attached to, and inflated by, this very injunction.

They have no adequate concept of repression, of its effects and what to do about it. They have an entirely undeveloped relation to the social and natural worlds, having no autonomous ethics, politics, human and natural sciences. In their traditional forms, they are constitutionally incapable of the transformative affirmation of culture and nature. They lack rigour about given reality, with a tendency to reduce the subtle unseen universe to high level distraction from absorption in the One.

They have no affirmative notion of the person as a real spiritual presence in the world, but reduce the embodied person, without remainder, to an illusory separated self-sense composed of fear, attachment and misplaced desire. They have an entirely authoritarian, patriarchal approach to the development of the spiritual life. They are gender-biased, and devoid of any grasp of an authentic feminine spirituality.

Encounters with the after-life

This is an area with regard to which many current transpersonalists seem to be short on ontological robustness. They are evasive, or dismissive in a rather superior way, or reduce the matter to the Buddhist intermediate *bardo* state between death and reincarnation. It is for me a truism that human beings survive the death of their physical bodies with the selfsame personal identity. I find this to be so because of my encounters with people in the post-death realms in my out-of-the-body experiences, and my strong awareness of them at different times and under different sorts of conditions when I am in my body.

Modern spiritualism was born suddenly with the rappings associated with the Fox sisters in Hydesville, USA, in 1848. It had strong impact, via trance mediumship, throughout the second half of that century, attracted the attention of several major thinkers, led to the emergence of psychical research to try to authenticate its claims to give evidence of an after-life, then faded dramatically from view into a backwater of interest until its resurgence as channelling in the USA and elsewhere in the second half of the twentieth century. It is now again a potent influence in emergent forms of new age religion.

I have encountered three kinds of spiritualism. The first is to do with making contact with the recently deceased, to provide solace and promote belief among their partners, relatives and friends still on earth. Spiritualist churches and mediums in private practice largely attend to these needs. There are fraudulent mediums, hit and miss mediums and a few deeply committed and reasonably reliable mediums (Cummins, 1967). The best mediums are still beset by the severe problem of refraction. This is the way in which information from people in another realm of being is distorted as it is passed through the medium's emotional, mental and cultural field (Heron, 1987: 171-79).

The second kind is to do with people in the other world who purport to be of greater education and development than the recently deceased, and who claim to offer some kind of teaching for the enlightenment and benefit of human kind. The human channel receives this teaching by trance mediumship, by automatic or telepathic writing. The distorting effects of refraction are even more severe with this kind of information. Apart from this, the discarnate teachers may be phoney or deluded or misinformed. The medium may have dubious motives, if not deliberate, then the fruit of unprocessed repressed emotion. The followers of the 'teacher' may lack discrimination and suspend critical judgement in favour of a sensationalistic kind of credulity.

The problem is that both parties in the transmission can and do disclaim full responsibility for what is said. The mediums claim they are trying to get mentally out of the way to give a voice to the unseen teachers, who in their turn frequently say how difficult it is adequately to convey their teachings through the limitations inherent in earthly language. The ambiguity of utterance that can emerge from this melange gives full scope for followers to read into it whatever they will. This is not entirely to discredit this kind of spiritualism, just to suggest that its aims and conditions of occurrence require far more stringent examination than they usually receive (Klimo, 1987).

The third and, in my view, highest and most interesting kind is to do with communion with high-raised and exalted presences, in meditation and ritual, for purposes of personal and planetary transformation. This is an important aspect of the realm of the high subtle, an interior association which is deeply valuable for processes of spiritual transfiguration. It tends to be ignored or reduced to the high subjective by transpersonal theorists, such as Huxley and Wilber.

All human beings, I believe, are unconscious mediums to a greater or lesser degree, their minds busy refracting and receiving influence, at one or more of these levels, from the great host of deceased people, whose emotional and mental states are like waves of a vast ocean constantly breaking on the subliminal fringes of human consciousness. Our materialistic culture regards this idea as an embarrassing nonsense. Such denial is a useful defense in an age committed to gain increasing competence in managing the natural world. It conveniently simplifies the issues, keeps the mind focused on material tasks, eliminates any tendency to become consciously dependent on unseen 'guidance', and generally enhances human autonomy to a degree.

Religious traditions have not gone in for outright denial, but for declaring the whole field off-limits, forbidden and dangerous territory. The Christian approach, apart from its notion of the communion of saints, has been to regard the occult as the work of the devil. Oriental mysticism has regarded the unseen and its inhabitants as a distraction from attending to the absolute. This kind of dismissive proscription keeps the devotee focused on the heart of the religious and mystical quest, but at the expense of discounting serious inquiry into what is probably the greater part of divine creation. It is analogous to the attitude of mediaeval clerics who regarded the pursuit of any kind of natural science as impiety.

Both materialistic denial and religious dismissal only partially keep at bay the incoming tide of discarnate influence. It flows into human affairs, under, over and through these barriers, unchecked and unabated, is never acknowledged for what it is, and is never brought within the aegis of human measure and control. The human race can never claim to be autonomously in charge of its cosmic estate, to respect and honour the whole field of creation, until it turns about to deal intelligently with discarnate presences and powers by developing a science, a politics and an ethics of the unseen. I continue this theme in the next section.

The spiritual and the subtle

As I said earlier, by the spiritual I mean a dipolar reality, a comprehensive consciousness-life that appears to include human consciousness-life, to transcend it and to be immanent within it. By the subtle I refer to extrasensory capacities in humans and to energies, domains and presences beyond, or immanent within, the physical, psychological and cultural spheres, to which those capacities may bear witness. I generally take the view that, ontologically, nothing spiritual goes on without concomitant subtle events, whether notice is taken of them or not; and vice versa.

However, I find it important to distinguish, psychologically, between subtle capacity and spiritual capacity, since it is my impression that either can function in apparent dissociation from the other, and can then get confused with each other. Subtle capacity addresses the subtle dimensions of this world and the subtle realms in their own right, sometimes divided into lower and higher. It is involved in unfolding the imaginal mind into the wider reaches of manifest being. Spiritual capacity addresses divine consciousness-life as such in its several modalities.

To elaborate further on a point raised in the previous section, the subtle realms, in all their majesty and vastness, have been:

- Dismissed as non-existent.
- Subjectivized - that is, regarded as purely psychological in character.

- Castigated as distractions on the way to the Absolute.
- Feared as the work of the devil.
- Simply left out of account.

Materialistic science holds the first of these views, Aldous Huxley (1945) is a good example of the second, Zen espouses the third, Christianity has often put forward the fourth, and Evelyn Underhill (1927) in her sensitive study of the supernatural is an interesting example of the fifth. None of these views do justice to my experience.

No competent modern transpersonal theorist that I know of would be so foolish as to dismiss physical science as an irrelevance. In the same way the time has come for the subtle worlds to be respected by forms of inquiry that are appropriate to them, and for this we need developed subtle competence. So the self-transfiguring person (Heron, 1992) is one who is unfolding both subtle and spiritual capacities, is becoming both adept and priest, both occultist and mystic.

> The renaissance of religion will come from the union of a genuine mysticism with the rediscovery and reapplication of the immensely powerful principles of a true spiritual science. (Hyde, 1949: 195)

International Centre for Co-operative Inquiry

This is a large Tuscan farmhouse situated on an isolated promontory of land that projects out over surrounding fields which curve steeply down into deep ravines. The neighbours, to north, east, south and west are a long way away, their farmhouses visible on crests and hills across the ravines. It is a ravishing landscape, graced by inhabitants who have taken the measure of its form and framed its sacramental beauty with human scale.

The farmhouse is halfway between Pisa and Siena, along the base of a triangle of which the apex is Florence. This triangle defines the birthplace of the Renaissance, which Skolimowski defines as 'the civilization that did not make it', being overtaken and ousted in the seventeenth century by the mechanistic-materialistic worldview that emerged from the work of Bacon, Galileo, Descartes and Newton. The Renaissance was an 'awakening of the senses'. Its artists rediscovered 'the lushness, beauty and exuberance of nature'. But, says Skolimowski, they did not just reproduce nature in a humdrum manner.

> They brought sanctity to nature. Renaissance landscapes are alive precisely because the are infused with spiritual energy. Beneath the visible currents of the sensuous forms of life, a deep process of re-sacralization is going on. (Skolimowski, 1994: 130)

The artists of the Renaissance showed through their achievements that the human being is a co-creator of the world as imaginal reality. They affirmed not just the person as the measure of all things, but the person as the measure of a sacral reality, of a world that is the spiritual artefact of the depths of the imaginal mind.

The landscape here provides a setting where I and others, through lived inquiry and co-operative inquiry, continue the process of re-sacralization. What this contemporary re-affirmation adds to the highly individual accomplishments of the

Renaissance in forms of art, is the collaborative accomplishment of lived inquiry as an art-form that sacralizes the world in and through a participative awareness shared with others. Within the grounds there are several distinctively named and appointed sacred spaces, including a Sun Temple and a Moon Temple.

> The place I was most strongly drawn to, felt an intuitive resonance with, was the Moon Temple. I felt enfolded, enclosed by it. It represented the womb of creation, the cauldron of rebirth, the Underworld, chthonic forces, the ground of being. It also felt motherly, to do with the female principles of birth and bringing forth… I lit candles and brought in flowers, as did others, and I felt that I had for the first time become aware of myself as an emerging spiritual being. (Katy Jennison)

2

Spiritual inquiry and projected authority

Here is the first of two chapters that deal with a range of basic issues about person-centred spiritual inquiry, both individual and co-operative. This chapter examines the role of authoritarianism in religious traditions and its consequences, presents a perspective on the spiritual projection that feeds it, puts forward a model of initiation by inquiry instead of initiation by authority, and exposes the appeal to authority lurking within two fallacies, one being the idea of a perennial philosophy, and the other the idea that traditional mystical schools practise transcendental science. It concludes with a discussion of the relations between indoctrination, training and inquiry.

Spiritual studies

There has been a long modern tradition of spiritual studies, the various forms of which I outlined at the start of Chapter 1. All these studies ultimately refer back, whether by first-hand, second-hand or multiple-hand reports, to the personal witness of mystics, ecstatics, religious practitioners themselves, revealed through their words, their deeds and their presence.

Spiritual innovation and tradition

Mystics engage in an inner journey, which includes a necessary element of experiential inquiry, since subtle discrimination needs to be exercised at critical points. But the journey is also set within a given spiritual tradition and guided by a living teacher. So the inquiry component is severely limited and constrained. The exercise of inner discrimination is subordinate to the categories, claims, definitions and demands of the tradition. Indeed, in oriental traditions the capacity for such discrimination is subjected to long periods of scriptural indoctrination and conditioning, before any meditative practice commences. The neophyte is taught what experiential distinctions to make prior to having any relevant experience.

> In most traditions - such as Advaita Vedanta and many Buddhist schools - a period, usually lasting several years, of rigorous study of the spiritual scriptures and 'right views' is regarded as a prerequisite for meditative practice and experiential enactment of the teachings. The immersion in experiential practices without an appropriate understanding of the teachings is regarded not only as premature, but also pointless and potentially problematic. (Ferrer, 1998c)

The result of this sort of thing is that budding practitioners, within established religious traditions both east and west, have the kinds of experiences that they have been taught to have.

Some mystics, however, are primitive and solitary pioneers of a more authentic spiritual inquiry. They apply to the mystical quest a limited version of lived inquiry (see Chapter 1) together with careful phenomenological reporting. They rise out of the immediate constraints of local religious tradition, eastern or western, and originally define or redefine the territory of spiritual experience. Such revision, however, is still limited. It is necessarily restricted to an innovative rearrangement of traditional elements, with some fruitful additions. It inescapably bears the limiting hall marks of the prevailing culture and Zeitgeist.

The authoritarian blight

Furthermore, the mystic innovators usually become authoritarian when they start a teaching career to pass on their realizations; and their followers will in any case rapidly turn them into authority figures. This is because the only model of spiritual education and training the world has ever known is authoritarian. Thus a sectarian culture is formed, and what is taught within it is given a warrant of authority via an appeal to a combination of some of the following:

- The teacher's intuitive and experiential certitude or faith.
- Divine revelation.
- Instruction from the gods/angels/ancestors/entities.
- Sacred scriptures.
- Established doctrine and practice.
- A lineage of gurus, teachers or priests within the sect.
- An ancient or modern innovative sage or religious founder.

Religious training everywhere, from the remote past to the immediate present, means believing-and-doing what an authority prescribes. A warrant of authority means that when an inquirer asks why they should believe-and-do what is taught, the teacher's reply is, 'Because the tradition of which I am a representative says so. And if you follow its teaching, as I have, you will find that it is correct'. This appeal to the weight of established thought and practice proves that it is durable. It does not show that it is valid. Equally, of course, it does not show that it is invalid. It just doesn't answer the inquirer's question. It is beside the point, for the question is an early sign of the inquirer's spiritual autonomy stirring from its life-long slumber. The question cannot be answered from without, but only from the full awakening and alertness of divine autonomy within.

The universal authoritarian tendency within the diverse religious schools, ancient and modern, of our planet, is presumably to do with the remarkable call of the religious quest, which initially throws up a great deal of insecurity. No better way to put a stop to the upsurge of such shakiness - and the underlying challenge of finding an inner source of guidance - than by capping it with allegiance to an external source of certitude. This is the process of spiritual projection, which I discuss in the next section. The institutionalization of this process has had a range of unfortunate consequences *within* each school that maintains it. Let me overstate the case, but only somewhat, in outlining these consequences in the remainder of this section.

- Little attention is paid to the psychopathology of current authority figures within the sect, to the impact of unprocessed emotional distress on their motivation, their practices, their teachings and their relations with their followers. Thus sexual hypocrisy and perversion is routine for religious authority figures, from Roman Catholic cardinals, bishops and priests, through Muslim mullahs and imams, to Hindu and Buddhist meditation masters.

  It is only very recently that a working distinction has been made between a truly transformative spirituality and a false, psychologically unhealthy, spirituality, of which two kinds can be distinguished. There is repressive spirituality, in which spiritual beliefs and practices are used to reinforce the denial of whole parts of oneself. There is oppressive spirituality, in which inflated spiritual claims are made in order to manipulate, constrain and dominate others to support and follow the claimant (Battista, 1996). And the oppressive kind is itself rooted in the underlying repressive kind. It is a major issue as to the extent to which all past spirituality is riddled with these pathologies.
- Relatedly, little attention is paid to the way current authority figures elicit and subtly or brazenly exploit what is unwittingly projected on to them by their followers. Authoritarian abuse of power by leaders and teachers is an invariable consequence of such projection, and there is widespread evidence of abuse in current spiritual movements, whether of ancient or recent origin, whether eastern and western. The spread of Zen and Tibetan institutions in the USA provides a telling example (Lachs, 1994).
- Little attention is paid to the limiting impact, on doctrine and practice, of the worldview of the culture and Zeitgeist prevailing at the time of the origination of a religious tradition by its founder. And, even more so than with current authority figures, the pathological elements in the spirituality of founding sages and 'heroes' go unnoticed.
- Little attention is paid to generating criteria to evaluate the overall soundness of a school: its beliefs, practices, teaching methods, initiation procedures, social and political structure, financial basis, claims of its founder, personal behaviour of current authority figures, and so on. It is only very recently that information on the relevant kind of criteria to apply to spiritual schools and cults has had any impact, especially via the internet.
- No attention is paid to the unseen ambience, the spiritualistic context, of what goes on in a spiritual school or church, that is, to the influence - benign, murky or malign - of discarnate persons on its activities. As long as this kind of influence is ridiculed, denied, occluded and hence unknown, no sect can have any proper claim to understand fully what is going on within its culture. Before going to a week-end retreat with Muktananda, I once saw clairvoyantly a host of associated minions in the next world seeking psychically to prompt humans into attending the event.

- Where a cult is based on channelling from some discarnate entity, the status of the entity will become the peg for unaware projections, rather than a focus of critical scrutiny.
- Most fundamentally, perhaps, no really serious attention is paid to the ground of discriminating spiritual authority within each student, disciple, or church follower. Any school or tradition that claims any kind of established authority for its teachings and practices will not encourage a full flowering of the autonomous spiritual judgement of each of its followers. Critical subjectivity, individual discriminating practice, independent judgement, inner-directed unfoldment, personal freedom of spirit in defining spiritual reality and in choosing and shaping the spiritual path - all this is discreetly side-stepped or blatantly suppressed or seductively hijacked or, at the very best, affirmed only to be contained within carefully prescribed limits.

The last point calls for some further discussion. It points to the inescapable logic of spiritual projection, the displacement of internal authority on to an external source.

Spiritual projection and authority

If you claim that spiritual authority resides in some other person, being, doctrine, book, school or church, you are the legitimating author of this claim. You choose to regard it as valid. No authority resides in anything external unless you first decide to confer that authority on it. Nothing out there is accredited and definitive until you first elect it to be so. All explicit judgements that illumination resides without, rest upon a prior and much more basic tacit light within. When it is made explicit, this is the internal authority of which your own discriminating judgement is the expression. Individual human judgement, with its inner spiritual ground, is the legitimating source of all external spiritual authority. The religious history of the human race appears to involve the slow and painful realization that this is indeed the case.

> We have to realize that every revelation must finally be appropriated by the individual soul. The very term 'revelation' implies the existence of the minds by which it is received. And it is on the attitude of such minds that everything in the end depends. The last word is with the interior monitor. The process is not completed until the divine which appears without is acknowledged by the divine which is enthroned deep within. And no amount of ingenious sophistry can do away with this ultimate fact. In other words the individual must take his stand upon the witness of the inner light, the authority within his own soul. This principle was clearly formulated by the Cambridge Platonist, Benjamin Whichcote, who ventured on the statement: 'If you have a revelation from God, I must have a revelation from God too before I can believe you'. (Hyde, 1949: 39)

When you are aware that the final court of spiritual authority resides within, and that any authority you have vested in anyone or anything external has derived from the imprimatur of that inner court, then you are spiritually centred and will not in the future become improperly subservient to any religious school or teacher. But when you are not aware of this, then you are busy with spiritual projection, and are spiritually off-centre. The spiritual authority that resides within is not known for what it is, is in some sense suppressed and denied, and is then unawarely projected on, invested in, *and inevitably misrepresented and distorted by,* what is without.

On the view that all realities are subjective-objective, as proposed in the Chapter 21, any view that reality is independently objective has a suppressed and unacknowledged subjective component which is prior, and which is inevitably misrepresented by the purely objective account. So in perceiving a world, if the subjective process of visual imaging is displaced and projected out as an objective image, then the subject is misrepresented as a dissociated Cartesian ego peering out at an independent world, instead of being known as a presence in mutual participative engagement with other presences in a shared world. In the same way, if my internal authorising of a spiritual teacher is displaced and projected out as an external authority residing in that teacher, then my inner authority is misrepresented as nescience seeking illumination from another, instead of being affirmed as my inner knowing seeking dialogue with the inner knowing of another.

Now both sorts of projection, the perceptual and the spiritual, yield benefits up to a point, but sooner or later break down because they try to make a half-truth represent a whole-truth. The critical turning point is when the process of projection becomes conscious and the subject reclaims the personal power within. This doesn't put a stop to the projective process, but it thoroughly reduces it and brings it within the aegis of critical subjectivity. It can now be monitored and modified.

There is no doubt that the process of spiritual projection has been virtually the sole means of spiritual development both for the great mass of mankind and for many of the small minority with serious mystical intent. Indeed, eastern mysticism makes an explicit virtue of it. The guru without represents the guru within, and the guru within is only developed by full allegiance to, and identification with, the guru without. Today, however, in a world of mass communication and planetary information exchange, the competing claims of innumerable spiritual authorities of all kinds stand revealed as a composite Tower of Babel, a noisy confusion of tongues which are missing the inner point.

Spiritual authorities, who are themselves off-centre, have no authentic spiritual autonomy as a basis for real religious co-operation with each other. Their continued spiritual projection - their allegiance to the authority of traditional belief and practice - keeps them apart. There is no co-operation among those who believe, by virtue of traditional indoctrination, that they are one of the god-realized of their respective traditions. An ecumenical movement among eastern-style perfected masters is not only unheard of, it is in the nature of the case impossible. There are, of course, exceptions among more modest claimants, such as the Dalai Lama (1996). Christian creeds, all of which keep more of a distance from god, keep having a go at ecumenical togetherness, but their different traditional allegiances permit only the attempt at, not the substance of, religious co-operation.

Four stages of projection

Here is my working hypothesis about the process of spiritual projection, based on my own involvement with it in different contexts, discussions with friends and colleagues about their inner journey, and on reflections on spiritual psychology.

There appear to be four stages in the process, from total projection to its substantial, but not total, withdrawal:

- **Intolerance.** When the projection is blind and wholly unaware, the devotee is dogmatic and intolerant, outlawing and attacking all other creeds. The spiritual ground within is severely repressed and denied, and the resultant frustration is displaced into the spiritual oppression of alien beliefs.
- **Toleration.** When there is limited awareness of the projection, we have the anomaly of (1) personal allegiance to the authority projected onto one's own school or church, combined with (2) religious toleration and freedom as between different creeds. In other words, you respect and accept the fact that what is authoritative for you is not so for other people with their diverse beliefs, but fail fully to grasp that this is so because you and they are still busy projecting inner authority outward.

  The most extreme version of this anomaly is when you both respect fully the right of other people to vest authority in any creed they choose, and at the same time vest your own authority in a cult that continually denigrates the exercise of your autonomous spiritual judgement.
- **Collusion.** When there is rather more awareness of spiritual projection, we have an unfortunate anomaly much practised by contemporary authoritarian spiritual teachers, and colluded with by their followers. The teachers repetitively define and prescribe things spiritual, while also repeatedly affirming that authority lies within each follower, who is exhorted to take nothing on teacher say-so but check it out through personal experience. The effect is hypnotic and seductive. The follower comes to believe that what he or she is being taught is also being confirmed from within. But what is within the follower is never encouraged, in it own terms and on its own terms, to define or direct anything spiritual. All definition and direction remain firmly in the hands of the teacher. At the same time as inner discrimination is being encouraged, the person is being told what to believe and to do, and is thus lulled seductively into acquiescent projection.

  This anomaly has its degenerate apotheosis in the case of the advanced conventional practitioner, the supposed enlightened one who uncritically directs all his practice and construes all his experience in the terms of tradition with which he has been indoctrinated and which he has internalized, and which has long since usurped the voice of authentic inner discrimination. What he has thus internalized may lead him to believe that he is now one of the god-realized, at an end-stage of enlightenment. Such a person will be benignly and inescapably autocratic in ruling the roost in his or her school of practice, while ostensibly encouraging disciples to make rigorous experiential tests of what is taught.
- **Freedom.** When you are fully aware of spiritual projection so that it can be substantially withdrawn and undone, then the spiritual path itself is based on internal authority through the continuous exercise of your own discriminating judgement and its spiritual ground; and this in association with others simi-

larly engaged. Divine becoming emerges as the living spiritual ground of human autonomy and co-operation. And the divinity thus manifest will be significantly different, I believe, in terms of beliefs and practices, from all divinities defined by external authorities. However, there are three very important caveats about all this, the second being the crucial one.

First, such withdrawal is not an all or nothing phenomenon. It may involve a variety of hybrids. These include:

- **Sequential projection** A person projects for a period on one spiritual school, then withdraws it and projects on to another, going through several over a number of years. This process may become quite intentional, in the sense that the person consciously goes along with the authoritarian tendency of a school in order to benefit from its teachings and practices, and pulls out when that tendency becomes too spiritually restricting.
- **Partial projection** A person stays constantly within one tradition in allegiance to certain strands of it, while radically reappraising other strands.
- **Intellectual freedom** The intellect appears to exercise a lot of freedom, for example, with respect to transpersonal theory, but practice remains firmly wedded to a traditional school. The theoretical outcome will then include veiled special pleading for the practical allegiance.
- **Discreet freedom** A person remains within one tradition for purposes of the support found within its spiritual community, otherwise picks and chooses among its beliefs and practices, refracting them through the prism of the internal monitor.

Second, and crucially, I do not think there is any such thing as a final end to, a total freedom from, spiritual projection. There is certainly a critical point when it is raised into consciousness and radically withdrawn as personal power is reclaimed. But this reclamation, this radical reappraisal of one's spirituality, necessarily includes elements drawn from past and present spiritual practitioners and thinkers. So the reappraisal weeds out past projections while relying, in part, on new ones in order to do so. The difference, of course, is in the awareness that this going on. Hence the critical subjectivity of a reframing mind, which continually deconstructs presumed internal authority to uncover the projections at work within it. The authority within is never final, always provisional and fallible. I return to this theme in the next chapter.

Thirdly, the substantial withdrawal of spiritual projection from traditional schools certainly does not mean that one ceases to take account of them and learn anything from them. I have on occasion been criticized on the grounds that my approach to spiritual inquiry is to eliminate from consideration almost everything which has been written on the subject up to now. This is a gross misrepresentation, and quite the opposite of what I believe, which is that the beliefs and practices of the various mystical traditions constitute a huge data-bank, a massive resource which, when treated with due caveats, can be drawn upon, modified and revised in framing the maps which guide the examined life and co-operative spiritual inquiry.

I have learnt a great deal from this legacy. I totally ignore it at my peril, just as I unawarely project on to it at my peril. This is an interesting knife-edge. I need to remember that I do not really know for sure what the ancient mystics meant by what they wrote, and that when I read them (often already via a translation) it is how I make sense of them - my inner knowing in dialogue with the text - that is central.

If I project this inner knowing out and claim that such and such is what the mystic meant, and claim further that this meaning is a traditional guide to spiritual wisdom, then I am sorely lost in the process of spiritual projection. I am hiding my own light behind the sage's robe to the rear of which it is displaced. I have lost faith with myself. The whole of the current perennial philosophy business seems to me to be beset by this kind of *mauvais foi.*

The distortions of spiritual projection

When the spiritual authority that resides within is projected on and invested in some external authority, it inevitably becomes misrepresented and distorted. To disown, deny and be unaware of the inner presence is to damage its formative power and this disfiguration is reflected in the teaching of the outer authority that replaces it. From the other side of the equation, if you want to become a spiritual authority for others, then you need a perverse doctrine that invalidates and undermines their intrinsic inner spirit, and will thus lock in with their disfigured projection of it.

The Christian religion maintained its authority for centuries primarily by the corrupt doctrine of original sin, which proposed that human nature is congenitally tainted and depraved, with a proclivity to sinful conduct. The essence of original sin for Augustine (354-430), the most influential figure in Western Christianity, lay in concupiscence, meaning desire in general and sexual lust in particular. He regarded humanity as 'a mass of sin, waited upon by death'. He identified the 'great sin' that lay behind such misery with sex and sexual intercourse. This catastrophic assault on human eroticism deeply undermined people's faith in their own inner life.

It is not surprising that the last twenty years of Augustine's life were dominated by his controversies against the Pelagians, and as a result of his determined opposition, Pelagianism was condemned by the church as a heresy. Pelagius had rejected the idea of original sin as an inherited defect which impaired the freedom of the will. He believed in a true freedom of the will as the highest human endowment, and held that persons are responsible for and capable of ensuring their own salvation. This optimistic account of human nature, had it spread widely, would have drastically undermined the authority of the early church.

The authority of spiritual schools and lineages in oriental religions rests on the denigrating view that human personhood, far from being a spiritual presence within divine being, reduces to a selfhood which is lost in illusory separateness. At the ordinary, everyday level, the self is nothing but a mass of congealed fear and clinging, all knotted up. At its very highest level, the soul is still *nothing but* a knot, a contraction, which must die to itself, to become absolute spirit (Wilber, 1997: 47). The spiritual teacher who has undone the knot and transcended separateness is the only one to judge whether the contracted disciple has attained any measure of enlightenment. The disciple surrenders to the guru and identifies with the guru to attain *moksha,* spiritual release and liberation from the illusion of selfhood and the bondage of mortal existence. Indeed, the Zen master subjects his students to physical and mental abuse in order to destroy the illusions in which they are imprisoned (Katz, 1978: 44).

So western spiritual authorities invalidate the erotic roots of personal life and eastern spiritual authorities undermine personal consciousness. Both of them are misrepresenting, denying and oppressing, the spiritual potential of personhood which, honoured in fullness, has its flower in personal autonomy and comprehensive connectedness. Between them, they inflict much damage. For spiritual practices based on negative views of human nature, by repressing positive potential, will cause a distorted return of the repressed. Thus the practice, by denying potential good and thus turning it into actual bad, appears to confirm the negative view on which it is based. This is the ancient corruption of patriarchal priestcraft. The priests put about beliefs and practices, and organize their hierarchy in ways, which generate the sins they claim the power to redeem.

The Christian religion tends toward a modified dualism. It regards the human world as a fallen creation outside god, although he is intimately connected with it. And it regards its priests as appointed by god with authority to mediate in Christ's name on behalf of fallen humanity.

Eastern religions tend toward acosmic monism: the world and the human are illusory save when known to be identical with absolute spirit. And the enlightened who know this have absolute authority with regard to the salvation of the unenlightened, who are too identified with the illusion to effect self-liberation. What we see at work, both west and east, is the classic autocracy of spiritual patriarchy. There is no hint of, no interest in, the sacral reality of womankind: embodiment as a primary source of sacrality (Raphael, 1994: 519-20).

The authoritarian spiritual teacher is also busy, of course, in suppressing some aspects of his or her own authentic inner light and inner life. The resultant subtle frustrations are displaced, acted out, not only in controlling the spiritual path for other people, but also in more or less frequent episodes of verbal, physical, sexual, power-play, and financial abuse of followers.

> The behaviour of teachers, both Oriental and Western, participating in the dramatic spread of Zen and Tibetan institutions in America has often fallen severely short of the ethical ideal. (Crook, 1996: 15)

The stories are legion, and likely to be found in all authoritarian spiritual schools, ancient and modern, eastern and western. They are hushed up for as long as possible, and rationalized by devotees as consciousness-raising tests and challenges. But sooner or later they demand understanding in terms of what they are: evidence of distortions stemming from a neglected spiritual process within the directive teacher. Such distortions exhibit gross and crude forms of spiritual narcissism in the very process whereby the teacher claims he is interrupting it in others.

Initiation old and new

Traditional schools of spiritual practice, and their current representatives, take the view that spiritual development requires a long period of guided initiation. An established teacher, competent in theory and advanced in inner experience, must design and supervise a curriculum of study and practice for the aspiring student. The following quotation is typical of current views on the subject.

> It is necessary for whomever is genuinely interested in being trained in awareness strategies to approach a teacher who has been trained within the particular contemplative tradition, and who is authorized by the tradition to give instruction in the practice of meditation. (De Wit, *Contemplative Psychology,* 1991: 112)

The model of this sort of recommended instruction is basically one of benign unilateral control on the part of the teacher and necessary spiritual surrender on the part of the student. The teacher directs the spiritual learning, experiential and theoretical, of the student, who does not have any say in designing his or her curriculum. The teacher also assesses the student's spiritual progress. Once the student has achieved a level of development approaching that of the teacher, the teacher's role has finished. The student has become spiritually mature, it is supposed, and can be a teacher for other students.

On this view, the spiritual teacher is an external authority for the student, prescribing the student's development. This conservative account of spiritual education as control of the process by an authority figure, is just the same as R. S. Peters' conservative model of ordinary university education as the initiation of students into the culture of a discipline by a teacher who is competent in it and who directs and assesses the students' learning of it (Peters, 1966).

This authoritarian model of university education is deeply flawed, as staff development units all over the planet are nowadays gently pointing out. It presupposes that you can educate a student to be self-directing within the culture of a discipline, by a process that is other-directed by the staff. It is preoccupied with teaching things at, to and into students. It overlooks the fact that all the deep aspects of learning - its processes, motives and purposes - are necessarily self-generated. Only much of the content, what is learned, comes from the culture, from without.

It is also preoccupied with unilateral assessment of students by staff. It overlooks the fact that you cannot produce properly self-assessing graduate professionals by excluding them from all assessment of their undergraduate work. So the notion of the teacher as directive authority is being slowly replaced by that of the teacher as the facilitator of self-managed learning and collaborative assessment. Students are encouraged and supported, in a bilateral dialogue with staff, to unfold and assess from within, their engagement with the cultural content without (Boud, 1988; Boud and Miller, 1996)).

Just so, the authoritarian model of spiritual education is deeply flawed. Spiritual development that is other-directed by authoritarian spiritual teachers is unwittingly distorted by the spiritual projection which such direction elicits. Students are directed to adopt spiritual practices shaped by negative worldviews, which are not questioned, and which then become experientially enacted by the sustained practice that is always under the control of the teachers. Students 'graduate' and become teachers themselves when the resultant warp has become endemic and ingrained.

The distortion is then sustained by generations of authoritarian teachers as authentic spiritual practice. Indeed, they come to regard both their lineage and their authority as guarantors of the authenticity of the practices they promulgate. They also hold that the spiritual development of the novitiate is critically dependent on inner surrender to that authority. Wilber has even maintained that this kind of thing represents a genuine transcendental science, a fallacy which I attend to later in this chapter.

For my taste, a more up-to-date model of spiritual education goes as follows. Spiritual development is an inward process that is necessarily self-generated by inner light and inner life. The critical opening and surrender is to what is within, not to what is without. Support for this is in the form of empowering facilitation, not directive discipline. Moreover it is not just a matter of learning the content of some pre-existent spiritual culture. It goes beyond learning some established set of practices and beliefs into a self-directed inquiry into the innovative emergence of immanent divinity as this self-reflexive and self-determining person in relation with other persons and beings here and now in this place and time.

My own conclusion from all this is that there is a new kind of initiation afoot. It is not the other-directed initiation of learning, sanctioned by external authority, about how to be proficient within a pre-existent spiritual culture. Rather it is a self-directed initiation of inquiry, grounded in internal authority, a lived inquiry that is both individual and co-operative, an inquiry about the emergence of temporal divine process as an innovative self-generating and self-transforming culture.

The spiritual history of humankind appears to be a continual attempt to break out of authority-laden initiation into inquiry-oriented initiation. Thus some school of spiritual practice and belief, whether oriental or occidental, only has to become relatively well established, for some innovative practitioner to thrust away from it with some variation, small or large, in the original system. The bolder spirits within the school, who have not been totally conditioned by its authoritarianism, insist on bearing witness to their inner light and inner life, and so enlarge the repertoire of spiritual know-how. Yet they too fall foul of the inveterate historical propensity of humans for spiritual authoritarianism, so a new school is founded, until the next generation of bold spirits insist on bearing witness to their inner light and inner life - and so the process goes on.

But today, at the end of the twentieth century, this whole process has reached almost hysterical, fever pitch. The proliferation of schools, ancient and modern, eastern and western, each invoking the exclusive imprimatur of this or that or the other authoritative source, is both remarkable and absurd. It is absurd because the exclusive claims to authority break down and collapse in confusion when, for the intelligent observer, they are lined up side by side in the stalls of some great exhibition of current cults and creeds. All this is surely evidence of the human impulse to spiritual inquiry about to break out of its long-standing authoritarian chrysalis and capsule.

Lived inquiry, intermediate projection and a self-generating spiritual culture

And of course the impulse has already broken out among an increasingly large minority of people over the last one hundred and fifty years. Today there is the widespread appearance of the independent inquirer, and of the informal network of such inquirers, to whom Marilyn Ferguson alluded in *The Aquarian Conspiracy* (Ferguson, 1980). This network I have already described as a self-generating spiritual culture, introduced in Chapter 1. It consists of people who put together their own programme of spiritual development, and are busy with their own version of lived inquiry, the examined life - my version of which I also outlined in Chapter 1.

They do this, in part, by charting a self-directed course among a range of different spiritual schools, consciously putting out a bit of spiritual projection within each school in order to get some benefit from what it has to offer, then withdrawing the projection before moving on to the next. Or they creatively shape an amalgam of methods from different traditions, with innovative additions of their own. The network is constituted by encounters and discussions among these inquirers at innumerable conferences, workshops, seminars, retreat centres, ashrams, institutes, study groups, and in other more everyday locations. This is a huge, loose, rambling, all-over-the-place, immensely fruitful and utterly unstructured shared inquiry into the creatively chaotic propensities of emergent divinity, out of which new kinds of spiritual order may take form. One of its current manifestations is the proliferation of hyperlinked spiritual websites on the internet.

The people in this free-form network are not lost in wholesale spiritual projection. They seem to be deconstructing varying degrees of projection, with greater or lesser awareness, with more or less explicitness, more or less of the time. Thus a person may grow spiritually, immersed in a series, or a concurrent mix, of differing schools, ancient and modern, benefiting from their insights, practices, environments, the modelling of teachers, while (1) adding creative innovations, (2) using critical subjectivity, the authority within, as the final arbiter for spiritual matters (Ferrer, 1998d), and (3) being in open dialogue with other such inquirers, who are perhaps immersed in a different series or mix.

What distinguishes such dialogue, at its best, is that no participant pushes the authoritative claims of any tradition they currently use, but share it as a perspective from which they benefit and whose presuppositions they are inwardly free to question and do question.

I suggested in Chapter 1 that there are three interrelated criteria which identify participants in this culture:

- They affirm their own original relation with creation, find spiritual authority within and do no project it outward onto teachers, traditions or texts.
- They are alert to the hazards of defensive and offensive spirituality, in which unprocessed emotional distress distorts spiritual development.
- They are open to genuine dialogue about spiritual beliefs and collaborative decision-making about spiritual practices undertaken together.

In such a self-generating culture, the spiritual traditions of the past are a fruitful secondary resource, the primary resource being the autonomous spiritual creativity and inner authority involved in putting each individual pattern together.

The formally structured, short-term method of co-operative inquiry is a complement to the long-term lived inquiry of persons within the informal processes of this newly arising culture. It is a way of bringing such processes temporarily to a sharper focus. It may deepen individual lived inquiry. It may lead to the development of collaboratively devised and shared practices within the new culture. In turn, it is, from its inception and continuously thereafter, supported and nourished by this wider culture.

Those who are wedded to traditional authority-based forms of spiritual training will insist that this is all an evasion of the serious challenge of long-term, sustained transformative practice. As an autonomous inquirer I assert that traditional practices are based exclusively on one-sided views, those of the male half of the human race, and are headed down a well-established, authoritarian and monopolar cul-de-sac. I mention complexity theory, which tells us that organic and social systems need to get to the edge of chaos prior to reorganizing themselves at higher and more comprehensive levels of innovative order. I suggest that traditional practitioners are stubbornly avoiding this challenge.

Fallacy of the perennial philosophy

It is a popular view among transpersonal theorists that there is such a thing as the perennial philosophy, a basic common denominator of belief, practice and spiritual development to be found among mystics of any time and place. Aldous Huxley popularized the idea in modern times (Huxley, 1945). He boiled the common denominator down to four doctrines which, simply put, are: there is an all-inclusive divine ground; humans can have direct experiential knowledge of it; humans have not only an everyday self but an inner spirit which is the same as, or of like nature with, the divine ground; the sole purpose of human life is to come to unitive knowledge of the divine ground.

There is a brace of other theorists, currently more influential, who go further than Huxley's four doctrines and hold that the core of the perennial philosophy is an hierarchical, tiered account of both the world and the self (Nasr, 1981; Schuon, 1984; Smith, 1976, 1982; Wilber, 1977, 1980, 1983, 1990, 1995, 1997; Wilber, Engler, Brown, 1986). In this model, the higher hierarchical levels are more real, more potent and more valuable than the lower levels generated from them. And human destiny is to ascend from the lowest level to the highest where self and world coincide. The force of the term 'perennial' is to suggest that not only is this model, *and the predetermined path of ascent it prescribes,* applicable to past and present mystics, but is valid for all future mystics as well. Indeed, Wilber is quite explicit in affirming this last point (Wilber, 1995).

I must say I find it astonishing that such a notion can be taken seriously. The perennial philosophy theory, especially in its current hierarchical and prescriptive form, looks to me like a favourite vehicle for unaware spiritual projection, a highly generalized displacement of inner spiritual authority outward. It certainly is a massive appeal to the external authority of a supposed universal tradition. As I mentioned in Chapter 1, for a cogent critique of perennialism in general and Wilber's structuralist version in particular see Ferrer (1998a).

It is quite plausible to say that there is among some members of the human race a perennial propensity for mystical aspiration, and to imply that this may well hold into the far-flung future. It is also reasonable to suggest that the expression of this aspiration may include some sort of inner training, certain ethical and other guidelines, and a sense of the sacred.

It is entirely implausible to say that a consensus about spiritual development among past mystics is a sufficient basis for predicting the basic structure of all spiritual development for all future time. In fact, the very idea of such a consensus has severe internal problems. For it all rests on the *texts:* without preserved texts, and in the absence of long-standing and diverse oral traditions, it is not possible to claim that there is a perennial philosophy.

- The first problem with the consensus claim is that it is based on the recorded religious experience of a very minute fraction of the human race over a short time span of less than 3000 years (Camphausen,1992). This textual data base is perilously small for the monolithic claim about the whole human race, past, present and future, which it is used to justify.
- Secondly, the consensus claim is based on an even smaller selection from the small number of extant religious texts. There are criteria for deciding which texts are to be included for the analysis, and which excluded. These criteria are taken *to* the selection. They are necessarily prior to and independent of the texts. They derive from the collator's religious beliefs, beliefs ultimately based on personal preference, practice and reflection, and encounters with living teachers. These criteria determine the selection of texts. Thus a monist like Aldous Huxley will throw the theists out (Huxley, 1945). The criteria also determine what will be read into the chosen texts. Consensus does not just sit out there in the texts waiting to hit you in the face, but, like all 'evidence' it is identified in terms of prior theory. It is already theory-laden, criteria-laden, when it is served up.

  So the claim that there is textual consensus is in reality a veiled form of special pleading for views held on other grounds. And the more insistently the textual consensus claim is pushed, the more we may suppose that there is an unacknowledged, unidentified and radical insecurity about the unstated grounds on which those views are held. Otherwise why not state those grounds on their own and leave it at that? The real consensus is not a consensus among mystics from diverse times and places. After all, they never met each other and so cannot properly be said to agree about anything. It is a consensus among a small group of male scholars that the religious texts they have selected reflect back to them the beliefs that determined the selection.
- Thirdly, the consensus claim is massively *under*determined by the supposed evidence for it. This is because the interpretation of ancient texts is itself notoriously problematic. Ancient writings are embedded in and emerge from ancient cultural and linguistic contexts. Each such context is a set of mutually

shared values and meanings, some of them explicit and some implicit. The meaning of an ancient text is inseparable from this ancient intersubjective set of meanings, at both its explicit and its implicit levels. Translating this meaning into a modern language whose usage is embedded in its own intersubjective context of cultural values and meanings, is a precarious matter. Even Christians have questioned the very possibility, in some cases, of finding modern equivalents for biblical meanings (Mudge, 1983).

- Fourthly, the meaning of an ancient text is subjective-objective. If a text sheds light on your experience, the meaning of the words without are shaped by an illumination from within. To attribute this illumination exclusively to the text or its author is to engage in immediate spiritual projection. Since no reader can be sure - in the mystical field more than any other - what the author really experienced and meant, it is more prudent to garner the harvest within, give due credit to the text for seeding it, and resist the temptation to project the harvest out and become an expert in the experiential realizations of the author.
- Fifthly, even if it could be said to exist, a textual consensus among mystics, per se, would confer no validity on its content. It could mean that all those concerned are in deluded morphic resonance, to use Sheldrake's theory (Sheldrake, 1981). It would certainly mean that they are bound within cultural and other constraints that affect the whole human race for a 3000 year period, and don't apply in the future. As we have seen, the dynamics of repression is a very recent discovery, a discovery which makes possible full body-mind integration. There is no evidence that mystics of the last 3000 years ever got to grips with it. Hence their supposed consensus could be, in part, evidence of their shared pathology, that is, of a mixture of repressive and oppressive spirituality, as defined in Chapter 2. More generally, it could at best be evidence of a culturally relative and incomplete account of human spirituality.

My view is that the mysticism of the last 2500 - 3000 years has been by and large, in its *practices,* monopolar, that is, aspiring towards a transcendental spiritual consciousness at the expense of realizing the complementary pole. In other words, the unfolding and flowering of embodied immanent spiritual life has been subordinated to, and sacrificed for, this single transcendental aim. Hence there has an element of repression and denial of the full developmental claims of the immanent pole; and a corresponding inflation of the transcendent pole with a concomitant tendency toward the authoritarian manipulation and constraint of other souls. The perennial philosophy approach is itself a continuation of this process; and in my view a misguided continuation. Donald Rothberg gets to the core of the matter:

It is certainly historically true that most of even those exponents of the great metaphysical and religious traditions identified as embodying most closely the core perennialist thesis of a hierarchical ontology (with, to be sure, some significant exceptions) link such an ontology to the devaluation of the body, sexuality and nature, and to patriarchal and class-based social relations...Affirming the hierarchical ontology alone may be a one-sided and potentially dangerous mode of expression, stressing, as it were, the more 'masculine' qualities of differentiation, ascension to the heights, activity and movement, and transcendence. What may be most needed, more than a resumption of a classical hierarchical ontology alone, is an exploration of the corresponding, more 'feminine' qualities: integration and relationship, awareness of the 'ground', receptivity and openness, and immanence, the 'always already' quality of enlightenment and liberation. (Rothberg, 1986: 23-26)

- Finally, a past consensus among mystics, were it to exist, would have no prescriptive or predictive relevance for the present or the future spiritual experience of mankind. Past agreement about any kind of human experience, especially the mystical kind, cannot and should not either provide a final standard for judging its present occurrence, or provide a formula for its future development. The claim that past spiritual experience is an unalterable bench-mark for the present and the future of human spirituality is a form of religious conservatism rooted in an appeal to the binding authority of tradition. It is an indefensible form of oppressive absolutism: it cannot possibly serve the liberation of postmodern spirituality. It is also, of course, incompatible with any genuine theory of the unpredictable, emergent, *innovative* evolution of the human spirit as the expression of divine becoming.

Tradition and inquiry

There is another view which I find very obviously mistaken and unacceptable. This is the notion that traditional spiritual schools such as Zen are busy with a kind of transcendental science, which offers a verification procedure for spiritual experiences, and is based on similar injunctions to those followed in natural science.

Wilber makes this error (1990: 39-81;1995: 265, 273-76; 1998). He says that transcendental inquiry, like ordinary scientific inquiry, has three simple steps: a practical instruction of the form 'To know this, do this'; immediate experience which follows from acting on the instruction; consensual validation by checking, with others who have also gone through the first two steps, to see whether you have indeed had the right experience. This last he calls communal confirmation or refutation in a community of peers (1995: 274), in which 'bad data are rebuffed' (1995: 276). Wilber illustrates this procedure in terms of Zen training. He thinks that Zen and similar spiritual traditions are sound and valid forms of transcendental inquiry (1990: 59-61).

This account is mistaken because it confuses inquiry with training. All the examples Wilber gives of his three inquiry steps presuppose that established knowledge is already built in to the practical instruction of step one. So in ordinary science, he says, if you want to know that a cell has a nucleus, take sections, stain the cell and look at it under a microscope (1995: 273). Similarly, in transcendental inquiry, if you want to know that there is a Buddha Nature, take up the practice of zazen (1990: 60). What this means is that the checking of step three is to make sure that you have followed the instruction properly and have had the experience that pre-existent knowledge says you are supposed to have had. This kind of checking is no more than the assessment of experiential training within an established field of practice and discourse.

The whole procedure only becomes inquiry when presuppositions built into the instructions for step one are questioned. That is, when you ask whether the nucleus of a cell does in fact have this or that function ascribed to it; or whether the Buddha Nature is what tradition holds it to be. And this is precisely what many traditional spiritual schools don't like and can't handle. They will often dismiss it as egoic resistance. Any serious attempt to introduce genuine inquiry into such schools would rapidly show up the teachers' narcissistic attachment to their positions of spiritual authority.

Wilber has recently tried to claim that Popper's falsifiability principle - that genuine scientific knowledge must be open to empirical disproof - applies to his third step of communal confirmation or refutation (Wilber, 1997: 87; 1998). This claim is spurious. No Zen master, or any other authoritarian spiritual teacher in a traditional school, is going to permit students to set up experiential tests to see if traditional doctrine is falsifiable.

> In contemporary spiritual settings, there frequently remain hierarchical social structures and authoritarian relationships often at odds with the contemporary democratic spirit (if not reality) of inquiry. (Rothberg, 1994: 10)

Furthermore, the falsifiability principle has been thoroughly discredited within science in general (Klee, 1997), and in its application to religious experience in particular (Ferrer, 1998b).

Wilber's account tries to disguise training in a hierarchical spiritual school as peer spiritual inquiry. He presents what is in fact teacher-run experiential training as if it were peer group experiential inquiry, and teacher assessment of skills as peer validation of data. The teacher in experiential *training* tells you what experiences you are able to have, tells you how to have them and checks whether you have had them. The peers in an experiential *inquiry* ask whether a defined experience is what it claims to be, enter the experience in ways that are open to reframing the definition, then check with each other to see whether their experiential data does or does require such reframing.

What Wilber calls consensual validation by checking with others is really teacher-dominated assessment of training outcomes. And this is not at all the same as confirmation or refutation in a peer community of inquiry. It is important to note that the peers, in such an inquiry, do not validate experiential data. That is, they do not confirm or refute their experiences in the light of the original idea - that is peer assessment of learning. They do the opposite: they confirm or reframe the original idea in the light of their experiences - and that is peer inquiry.

Wilber refers to Zen as an example of trascendental inquiry. Zen, however, is a *training* run by a Zen teacher who has himself had ten to twenty years of training within a very strong, long-standing and traditional lineage. This powerful tradition has both cognitive and technical authority: it defines both what experiences mean and how to have them. Zen is training people to grasp the notion of satori, then ungrasp it and have the experience of satori, and is then assessing whether they have had the experience - an assessment dominated by the Zen master. The only 'bad data' that are rebuffed are experiences that are not in line with traditional experiential claims.

Zen training, in its traditional oriental form, is not a collaborative inquiry as to whether satori is indeed what it claims to be. It is an hierarchical not a peer process. It is not practising openness to experiential data that could lead to a reconceptualization of the satori claim. In short, to say that it is a valid form of inquiry is rather like saying that a government training course on the basics of communism in the old Soviet Union provided a valid education in political science.

If the structure of the spiritual path were really based on transcendental inquiry involving consensual validation in a community of peers, then we should expect to see this at work among those who claim to be spiritually accomplished, the so-called spiritual masters. Current masters of the same and different schools would meet regularly and engage in ecumenical dialogue and experiential inquiry. This would parallel what goes on in ordinary science, where leaders in any field are in regular peer exchange to review the validity of each other's work and try it out experimentally. But of course spiritual masters are notorious for each becoming a law unto himself. They sedulously avoid acknowledging the existence of other masters. The authority each master claims for himself - as a basis for eliciting spiritual projection in devotees - precludes any kind of peer relationship with any other. There are important exceptions to this tendency, such as the Dalai Lama, who need to be honoured:

> I suggest that we encourage meetings between people from different religious traditions who have had some deeper spiritual experiences...genuine practitioners who come together and share insights as a result of religious practice. According to my own experience, this is a powerful and effective means of enlightening each other in a more profound and direct way. (Dalai Lama, 1996: 42)

Indoctrination, training and inquiry

I take the view that experiential training and experiential inquiry are always to some degree involved in each other. They range along a spectrum between theoretical extremes of all training at one end and all inquiry at the other. In experiential *training,* the training component is greater than the inquiry component, and this occurs when the trainer gives more technical (how to do it) and conceptual (what it means) shape to the trainees' experiences than the trainees do individually and co-operatively.

When the degree of the trainer's combined technical and cognitive authority is very high, and that of the trainees' very low, then, in the spiritual field, the training is equivalent to experiential indoctrination. Trainees have been indoctrinated when what they do and what it means to them are entirely derived from, and justified exclusively by appeal to, the external authority of the trainer and his or her tradition.

When, however, the trainer's combined technical and cognitive authority only carries a little more weight than that of the trainees, then spiritual training is close to, but not yet, a spiritual inquiry. In such a training, the trainees will justify what they do and what it means to them by an appeal to their own technical and cognitive internal authority in close second place to the external authority of their trainer and her or his tradition. Where the trainees note a disparity between inner and outer authority, they will tend to defer to the latter, although there always seem to be some trainees who quietly give more credence to the inner voice than to the outer.

In experiential *inquiry,* the inquiry component is greater than the training component, and this is the case when the 'trainees', now co-inquirers, individually and co-operatively, give more technical and conceptual shape to their own experiences than the 'trainer', now the initiating inquirer, does. Authority lies within them, as individuals and as a critical collective. The element of training in such a co-operative inquiry is provided by the initiating inquirer who introduces the co-inquirers to a co-operative method of research. Her or his authority is methodological and short-lived: it seeks to empower the co-inquirers to give technical and conceptual shape to their own experiences for the purposes of inquiring into them. Once the co-inquirers have internalized the method, modified it and made it their own, the originating authority of the initiating researcher becomes very secondary to his or her ongoing parity.

A spiritual training, then, within any given school, has a strong propensity for indoctrination, if it has a weak subordinate dimension of self and peer inquiry and gives little scope for the technical and cognitive internal authority of its trainees. I have little doubt that the training within many an ancient oriental spiritual lineage is still today closer to experiential indoctrination than it is to experiential inquiry. The spirit of the teacher's authority pervades such a lineage, not the spirit of inquiry. It is an established experiential tradition, based on a strong appeal to external authority, precisely because it doesn't have a methodology of experiential in quiry and will invariably resist such inquiry.

The experiential claims of oriental spiritual schools such as Zen or Siddha Yoga are based on established spiritual tradition, a lineage of trainers, whose technical and cognitive authority always has more weight than that of the trainees. Such a spiritual tradition is a set of experiential claims waiting for an inquiry-based validity warrant. These claims become warranted, or otherwise, when their tradition-and-guru-based experiential training is transformed into co-operative inquiry (Heron, 1996a). In such an inquiry, the technical and cognitive authority of the co-inquirers is internal and primary. And for such an inquiry, the technical and cognitive authority of any spiritual lineage is a contributory external and secondary resource. Thus cartographies of subtle and spiritual states, drawn from diverse lineages, and subject to modification in the light of contemporary experience and newly emerging paradigms of reality, can at best provide provisional orientation for co-operative inquiries.

3

Spiritual inquiry and the authority within

The discussion of basic issues in person-centred spiritual inquiry continues in this chapter with my model of the nature of the spiritual authority that resides within, in terms of inner light, inner life, discourse with the other, and spiritual deconstruction. I then propose some of the advantages gained by the use of co-operative inquiry in the spiritual field, mention some likely precursors, and explore relevant attitudes of mind. The chapter ends with an outline of the dipolar theology and dipolar spiritual path, which is grounded in lived inquiry, and which I use to launch the preparation for a co-operative inquiry into the spiritual. This outline is elaborated in the dipolar map in Chapter 6.

Internal spiritual authority

What is internal spiritual authority? And who, indeed, can say what it is for anyone else but themselves? Neither John Heron nor any other person can set themselves up as an external authority who defines the nature of internal authority for other people. It is logically impossible to be authoritarian about the nature or the practice of internal authority, for by definition internal authority cannot be internal if it is commanded by someone else.

No-one can practise internal authority, exclusively by following an external authority who prescribes what it is: self-direction cannot be other-directed. Autonomous people cannot dictate the nature of autonomy for others; they can only dialogue and co-operatively inquire with each about the naure of self-direction. Here, then, are some of my personal conjectures on the matter, put forward as a contribution to such dialogue. What follows gives a fuller account of some of the aspects of my lived inquiry as described in Chapter 1.

The authority within me I would define as spiritual discrimination. This I experience as a form of:

- Critical subjectivity, a discriminating inner light, by which intelligent judgements are made about things spiritual
- On the basis of attunement to spiritual life within and
- In appropriate discourse with the other. 'The other' here means the manifest universe, the whole epiphany of explicit being, including, of course, other persons open to such discourse.

I will elaborate on each of these points in turn.

Critical subjectivity

The view that spiritual authority lies within as critical subjectivity - the discriminating judgement of the distinct person - puts an end, as I see it, to the idea of personhood as some kind of illusory self-system that dissolves in absolute enlightenment. The internal process that authorizes and legitimates the path to spiritual reality cannot itself be less than that reality, cannot be some sort of temporary and unreal structure. It is indeed an unfolding expression of that very reality itself.

This develops into a political point, as I indicated in the previous chapter. The doctrine that any sort of self, however refined, is an illusory substitute for spirit - rather than an authentic expression of spirit, one of the Many disclosing the One - is itself an invalidating doctrine used by teachers to sustain themselves as external authorities, to keep the spiritual projections of their followers in place. The idea that the student is but a knotted self, justifies controlling, directive teaching. The idea that the student is an emerging autonomous and interconnected spirit, calls for a very different approach.

My account of critical subjectivity has its historical precursor in the notion of faith as an inner light which enables the soul to see the truth. The Cambridge Platonists in the seventeenth century identified this inner light with reason. They thought that purified reason could bring the soul to the vision of god. Their theology laid stress on ethics and spiritual joy. They rejected the idea that human nature was a mass of perdition (Patrides, 1980).

George Fox (1624-1691), founder of the Society of Friends, also took an optimistic view of human nature. He proclaimed an inner unity between god and man, 'that of god in every one', a divine presence believed to be an enlightening and guiding force in the human soul. Fox taught that 'every man was enlightened by the divine light' and used the notion of the inner light interchangeably with that of the holy spirit. As such it is more than just reason or conscience, although it may subsume these. Everyone has a share of this light, no matter what their faith or moral reputation, and everyone can gain access to it without intermediary or ceremony. The inner light is 'that which shows a man evil' and 'that in which is unity' (King, 1940).

Now Vedantists have their own version of this. They would say that the everyday mind, ordinary consciousness, just is already Mind with a big M, universal consciousness. So it is a mistake for mind to seek out Mind, because it already is It. The seeker is the sought. This may well be so, although putting it thus rather overstates the case. For in everyday human terms it is only partially so (half-baked, as Wilber pejoratively puts it), because it can be deepened by practice into greater fullness. And we need an act of inner discrimination to remind ourselves that it is so and only partially so and can be deepened by practice. Indeed, it is in this very reMinder, this act of inner discrimination, that Mind reveals its identity within mind.

So if I take a combined cue from the Cambridge Platonists, the Quakers and the Vedantists, I would say that my inner spiritual discrimination just *is* a comprehensive, transcendent consciousness coming to a focus as my self-determining critical subjectivity. The spirit of the divine and the autonomy of the human appear to be at one without loss of the distinctness of the latter. But as we shall see in the section on spiritual deconstruction below, this process is maculate, temporary, provisional, context-limited. So it is wisely brought into relation, and grounded in, another and complementary process, which I call attunement to spiritual life within. Compare also the complementary account of critical subjectivity given in Chapter 21.

Spiritual life within

Experientially, I find that my everyday psyche has a very evident supporting ground or foundation. When I attend to this ground, it becomes a source or well-spring, which, when I open to it, is of apparently limitless potential. It is also like a cornucopia or womb, with an ever-deepening infinitude within. Its potential fullness increases as I plumb its depth and creative darkness, and so does its emptiness. I call this spiritual life within, since it is harbours spiritseed, entelechy, the formative potential of my becoming. The spiritseed puts out sprouts, shoots, above ground in the psyche. They are, among other things, prompts to time or space my being, in relation to the immediate context of interbeing, in this, that or the other way.

So it makes sense to bring the exercise of critical subjectivity, discriminating awakening to a wider consciousness - inner light - into dipolar, dialogic relation with these inner life-prompts. Discriminating thoughts are tacitly framed in unspoken words, and such words are implicit gestures of meaning in time and space, just as spoken words are explicit gestures of meaning in time-space form. The inner spiritual life always has a felt, nonverbal sense of the fit, the appropriateness, of these implicit gestures within the wider web of being with which spiritual life itself immediately, here and now, engages me.

This internal dialogue between inner light and inner life is, further, in interaction with what I regard as the third component of inner spiritual authority: appropriate discourse with the other, upon which I elaborate shortly. Before doing so, I say a bit more about the notion of entelechy.

Other accounts of the spiritual life within

I said just above that the spiritual life within harbours spiritseed, entelechy, the formative potential of my becoming. What Aristotle meant by an entelechy was the condition in which a potentiality has become an actuality. But there is another more recent usage in which entelechy is the immanent, formative potential of what is actual. So the entelechy guides the emergence of, and is progressively realized in, the actual entity.

Carl Rogers made this idea of entelechy a basic tenet of his personality theory. He called it an actualizing tendency. He thought it was inborn in everyone as an 'inherent tendency of the organism to develop all its capacities in ways which serve to maintain or enhance the organism' (Rogers, 1959: 196).

> It is clear that the actualizing tendency is selective and directional - a constructive tendency. (Rogers, 1980: 121)

It affects both body and mind, and with respect to the latter, it guides people toward increased autonomy, expanded experience and inner growth. Virtually the same idea is found in Maslow, as a self-actualizing need, 'the desire to become more and more what one idiosyncratically is, to become everything one is capable of becoming' (Maslow, 1970: 46).

It reappears in Wilber as the Ground-Unconscious which is 'all the deep structures existing as potentials ready to emerge at some future point' (Wilber, 1990: 105). And in Washburn as the 'Dynamic Ground (libido, psychic energy, numinous power or spirit) of somatic, instinctual, affective and creative-imaginal potentials' (Washburn, 1995: 11). Jean Houston writes eloquently of entelechy as:

> ...that dynamic purposiveness coded in ourselves, longing for unfoldment and expression. It is the possibility of our next stage of growth and evolution entering into time...This Entelechy Self is also the supreme orchestrator and ground of all one's other selves, and serves as the protector and provider of balance and mental health amid the complex and polyphrenic structure of one's inner life. It is the Root Self, the ground of one's being, and the seeded coded essence in you which contains both the patterns and the posssibilities of your life. (Houston, 1987:31)

These three writers all use the metaphor of the ground in characterizing the spiritual life-potential within.

Co-creating with immanent spirit

Do these ground potentials act upon us willy-nilly, predetermining the basic stages of our explicit spiritual development? Do they constitute a fixed pattern of our future unfolding? Wilber thinks they do so far as the deep structures of our development are concerned. Alternatively, do the ground potentials offer a range of possibilities from among which we may choose and so create our own pattern? I take this second view, based on the notion of our inclusion within innovative divine becoming. I believe that we may co-create our path in dynamic relation with a set of options emerging from the spiritual life within. And this not only in relation to the daily surface structure of the path, but also concerning its basic unfolding pattern.

Of course, we must at any given time entertain a working hypothesis of some basic array of options for developing our potential, if we are effectively to set about actualizing it. But what this array is, and by what sequence it may be realized over time, are matters, I suggest, open to creative innovation with immanent spirit, through processes of individual lived inquiry and co-operative inquiry. Indeed, when autonomous people relate within an ongoing self-generating spiritual culture, and the path for each becomes significantly interactive, the potential for emergent novelty in path-making is hugely increased. But for the moment I will stay with individual processes.

I have said above that I find it fruitful to take discriminating thought into the well-spring within and check it there for a felt, nonverbal sense of fit with the web of being with which I am engaged. Can such a conscious co-creating relation with immanent spiritual life, its womb of possibility, be further developed? My experience is that it is can. You can relate to it, give it voice and be spiritually upheld and nourished by it, and enter into a co-guiding dynamic with it. I say co-guiding, since you select and shape the guiding as much as the guiding shapes you. This, as we shall see, makes it maculate, corrigible, and personally autonomous, as well as more than purely personal.

Various techniques have been proposed, in recent times, for tapping directly into the guiding potential within. E-Therapy was one (Kitselman, 1953). 'Greatness is in us; how can we let it out?... greatness can let itself out; it only needs to be asked.' Kitselman then outlines a simple technique for asking E, the inner voice, which will respond in terms of any one or more of the following: inner ecstatic fire, trembling, body movements, disidentification from personal history, or an impulse toward some strategic action.

The much researched experiential focusing of Gendlin is another (Gendlin, 1981). This basically consists in making a clear relaxed area in the body-mind so that when a key question - suitably refined and focused - is asked, there is space for the answer to be manifest, in verbal or nonverbal imagery, accompanied by a subtle release of energy. Gendlin describes the whole process as if it were primarily somatic, a description which has always seemed to me to be rather too cautious.

But McMahon and Campbell develop Gendlin's focusing in terms of a bio-spiritual approach. Their bio-spirituality emphasizes 'an experience of grace in the body'. They relate letting go into the body-feeling about an issue, to a movement of the indwelling life-giving presence and power of God (McMahon and Campbell, 1991: 5, 17).

None of these processes is a purely passive receptivity to some guiding internal otherness, although they have a tendency to be described in this way, as I have just done in order to report them in their own terms. But my experience of them, and of related sorts of inner lived inquiry, is that my subjectivity is actively involved at a deep level in selecting and shaping life-processes moving within. The challenge of these methods is not to surrender fully to what comes up from the depths, but to open up that liberated place within where one can be co-creative with immanent spirit. And this with respect to options that shape both the surface and deeper pattern of the spiritual path.

Of course, this whole account still posits a given entelechy structure with two main features: a range of potential options, and a potential capacity for their co-creative selection and realization.

Appropriate discourse with the other

I have defined internal spiritual authority as critical subjectivity, a discriminating inner light, attuned to spiritual life within, and in appropriate discourse with the other. This third component brings the internal dialogue between inner light and inner life into a comprehensive and more-than-verbal, as well as a verbal, relation with others in their world. Indeed, the role of inner life as described above already anticipates the nonverbal component of this relation.

Everything is talking to everything else in the primordial language of creation. Abram eloquently makes the point in his *The Spell of the Sensuous,* that we do not inhabit a purely external, objective world out there, but a world of *intersubjective* phenomena in which human and non-human presences of all kinds form an 'intertwined matrix...a collective field of experience lived through from many different angles'. Within this participative field, with which we reciprocally engage, there is an animate process of mutual apprehension - a meaningful dialogue of interbeing - going on. And this is prior to, and the ground and source of, all our use of verbal language (Abram, 1996; Heron, 1996a).

So my phrase 'appropriate discourse with the other' is inclusive. It means several things.

- Opening now to nonverbal, interbeing exchange with the presences that are here, which we name trees and roads, rocks and stars, fish and fowl; and with the sheer presence of the whole. This, I find, is a primal revelation of the divine. It is the dynamic eminence of the immediate experiental world, the here and now collective field, in which our own presence is in reciprocal engagement, through being and doing, with other diverse presences, within the presence of Being. This nonverbal exchange may, for the person involved, be a silent and enriched participation in terms of felt resonance and imaging. Or it may be nonverbally expressive, embodying this participative engagement in vocal or musical sounds, movements, gestures and postures; or in impromptu drawing, painting and modelling of clay.
- Talking to, talking with, talking within, this field - out loud and out of doors in my native tongue. In this process I am hearing what I am moved to say, how I am moved to edit and reframe it, as I engage with the collective field of experience in which I am embodied and embedded. I am attending to a subtle dialogue between verbal and nonverbal forms of utterance and participation. It is useful to have access to unfrequented areas of countryside for this purpose. I have found it convenient to live on a relatively isolated promontory, projecting out over fields that slope down steeply on three sides into ravines.
- Dialogue with other humans, sharing our intelligent judgements and views, apprehensions and intuitions, about things spiritual and subtle. It can have two forms, verbal and aesthetic. We can talk with words, or we can exchange aesthetic presentations, nonverbal symbols of our spiritual process, wrought in any one or more of the whole range of art-forms. There is thus possible a mutual fructification between the propositional and the presentational, between explanation and expression (Heron, 1996a: 88-90).

With the last item, we enter various forms of co-operative discourse and inquiry: dialogue with a text or art-form, dialogue via an exchange of letters or graphic symbols, face-to-face dialogue in a pair or within a group, informal or structured by some agreed procedure. The centrality of co-operation comes to the fore. But before moving on to this topic, I wish to acknowledge the important contribution that indigenous consciousness has to make to the inclusive notion of 'appropriate discourse with the other'.

The indigenous mind is based on 'a discourse view in which individuals understand themselves in an ongoing conversation with the surrounding community, in which the local animals, plants, ancestors, and other spirits take as much part as the humans' (Kremer, 1996a: 42). Here is an account of it among the contemporary Andean peoples of Peru:

> The conversations held between persons and the other inhabitants of the world are not primarily engaged in for the purpose of 'knowing reality'. They are engaged in it as part of the activity of *criar y dejarse criar,* of nurturing (raising) and letting oneself be nurtured (raised)...It is a fundamentally mutual or reciprocal activity: as one nurtures one is simultaneously nurtured. The action in the world does not leave the actor untransformed: acting in the world is being in relationship with that world, so the language of conversation is more appropriate than the language of knowledge. There is here no knower and known, no subject and object. Rather there are actors in relationships of mutuality...*Criar* demands not only understanding but love, tenderness, patience...the point of conversation is not the attainment of knowledge through the interrogation of nature, it is rather to generate and regenerate the world and be generated and regenerated by it in the process. (Apffel-Marglin, 1994: 9)

The relevance of co-operation

The view of internal spiritual authority which I have presented can be construed, in Berdyaev's terms, as the creative, temporal process of divine becoming, which:

- Manifests as self-determining human subjectivity, a dipolar inner light and inner life,
- And evaluates that creative process in co-operation with other presences and persons.

The co-operation with other persons is a dialogue of light and life, both verbal and more-than-verbal, among autonomous humans. As such, to put it ecstatically, it is an epiphany of the *imago dei* within each.

To put it more soberly, it presupposes in equal measure the cultivation of discriminatory competence in evaluating spiritual and subtle events, grounding this through openness to the spiritual life deep within, bringing it into relation with the felt field of interbeing, and reviewing the whole process in dialogue with one's peers.

My basic postulate about the great field of interbeing, is that a presence is what it uniquely is interdependently with the particular structure of the web of relations within which it is a nodal point or focus. No entity is distinct apart from its interconnections with other entities. Individual agency is correlative with social communion. Just so, persons are only persons in relation with other persons. I as a person can only be genuinely autonomous when in authentic co-operation with other persons.

Since I choose to see the world as temporal divine process, I find true religion among autonomous humans in co-operative relations with each other and with the more-than-human world. Put in other terms, I enter into union between beings, and with Being as such, when each being is both individualized and participative. As we transcend separateness and alienation we become both more distinct and more in communion with each other. Our becoming more refined, autonomous and discriminating in our judgements, is interdependent with our entering ever more fully into participative relations. This, I find, is a fruitful working hypothesis.

Spiritual deconstruction

In my experiential view of process theology, one aspect of divinity is the temporal becoming of finite entities within an infinite field. This includes self-determining human subjectivity, whose inner light and life, in interaction as I have described above, is in process of development, in the context of the limited flux and turn of events accessible to the individual. Both the inner light and the inner life are maculate, corrigible, relative to their setting, changing and unfolding. Once experientially manifest, they are shaped by, as much as they shape, personal process and context. They are subject to three limiting factors.

- My social context, the hermeneutic situation of local language and culture.
- The degree of my explicit, conscious participation in the interbeing of the universe, the collective field of reciprocally engaged and diverse presences.
- The degree of emotional damage and spiritual constriction within which I labour.

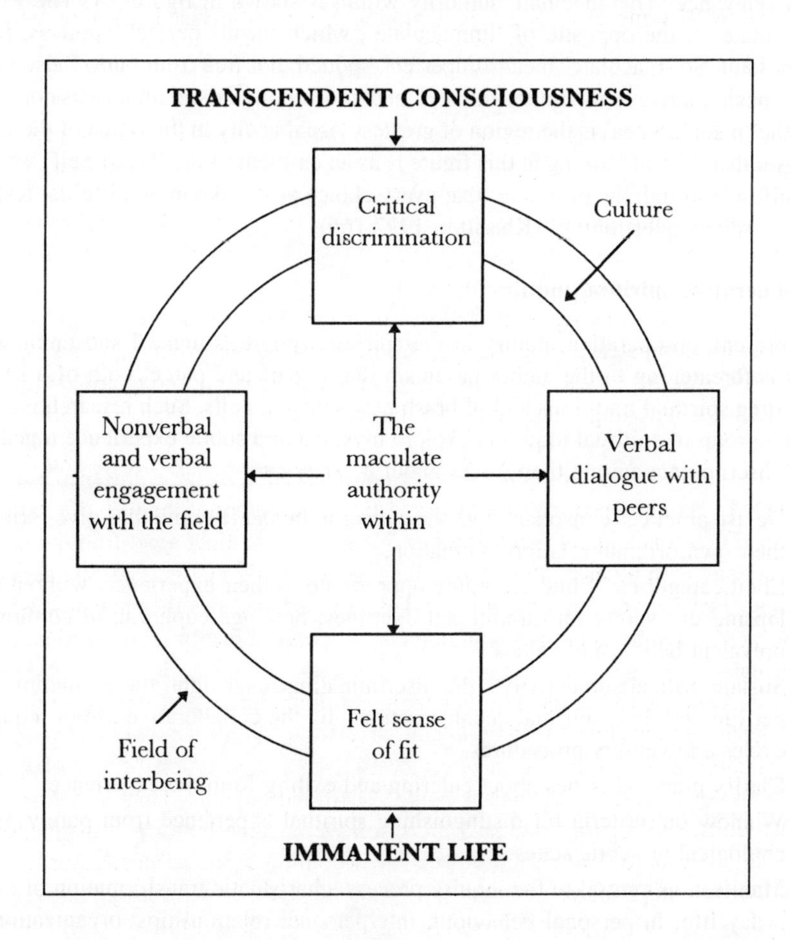

Figure 3.1 *The maculate authority within*

Hence the importance of both critical subjectivity and life-prompts being exercised within a community of peers, who assist each other, using a range of peer support procedures, with the rigour of continuous spiritual deconstruction. Such deconstruction means being aware of how these three factors interact, and how the presuppositions of this interaction set the scene for, limit and mould, every act of inner light and inner life. It means an attitude of bracketing such presuppositions and being open to their reframing through, respectively:

- A revision of prevailing belief-systems in the culture.
- Enriched participation in the lived-through world.
- Emotional healing.

Persons in peer groups can do a variety of things together to facilitate these three undertakings.

Such deconstruction does not eliminate or dethrone either the inner light or the inner life. On the contrary, it empowers each to flourish with ever greater temporary relevance. This maculate authority within is shown in figure 3.1. The word 'maculate' is the opposite of 'immaculate', which means perfect, spotless, free from fault. So 'maculate' means imperfect, spotted, not free from fault. I also take it to mean relative to its limited context, and good enough in relation to its context. So the 'macula lutea' is the region of greatest visual acuity in the retina of the eye.

Another way of looking at this figure is as an emblem of the 'Heart Self' which manifests through the principle 'that every choice you make in you life' is 'tested by conscious questioning' (Kharitidi, 1997:166).

Co-operative spiritual inquiry

At present, co-operative inquiry in the spiritual sphere is unused and unknown, and is threatening to the authoritarianism that is part and parcel both of a long-standing spiritual traditions and of brash new spiritual cults. Such research means that a group of spiritual inquirers explore mystical and subtle experience together and discriminate among themselves about it. They can:

- Devise practices consonant with their inner light and life, and thus give form to their own original relation to creation.
- Elicit categories of understanding appropriate to their experience, without relapsing unawarely into traditional doctrines, new age euphoria, or culturally prevalent beliefs and values.
- Sustain critical subjectivity - the discriminating inner light, the grounding inner life and their spiritual deconstruction - by the collaborative use of inquiry cycles and validity procedures.
- Clarify practical issues about entering and exiting from the experience.
- Winnow out criteria for distinguishing spiritual experience from purely psychological or subtle states.
- Manifest, as central to the inquiry process, charismatic transformation of everyday life: in personal behaviour, interpersonal relationships, organizational processes, and sociopolitical initiatives.

With regard to all these points, the solitary pioneering mystic, however radical, is at a disadvantage without systematic peer review. Hence the ancient spiritual innovators, referred to at the outset of the previous chapter, could only make modest headway against the substantial forces of tradition.

Those committed to authoritarian spiritual systems may warn that there are hazards in this kind of peer group do-it-yourself spiritual inquiry, and that people will be lost without the example and guidance of those who know the territory. This is not at all the case in do-it-yourself practice, for humans are at last empowered and guided by their own emergent, creative, inner spiritual life. The warning itself is an expression of a defensive spirituality, which denies a living impulse within and projects this denial out as an invalidation of human autonomy in others. The real danger is to fall foul of those who claim spiritual authority over people, and who, by sustaining the distorting mechanisms of spiritual projection, inescapably misrepresent both their own spirituality and that of their followers.

Co-operative spiritual inquiry affirms human autonomy and present connectedness. It celebrates the liberating and empowering view that:

- Each person has their own original relation to creation.
- Revelation is now.
- Spiritual authority is within.
- Innovative divine becoming manifests, in one of its modes, as the autonomous co-creativity of collaborative humans.

Solo and group precursors

As I said above, some radical mystics of the past have been pioneers of solo spiritual inquiry, surmounting the constraints of local tradition, east or west, and redefining the territory of spiritual experience. But the revision is restricted and immediately becomes the source of a new authoritative tradition.

I have also already mentioned the current social phenomenon of a self-generating spiritual culture, within which spiritually-minded people are busy with their own versions of lived inquiry, with greater or lesser degrees of awareness about spiritual projection, and relying significantly on critical subjectivity and the authority within. This is the long-term context which is the ground of short-term co-operative inquiries and with which they are in reciprocal and complementary relation.

Some modern spiritual groups have been somewhere within sight of short-term peer inquiry. The original group that met with Oscar Ichazo, prior to the founding of Arica Training, seemed to have hints of participative, co-operative inquiry. Grof's holotropic therapy is perhaps on the threshold of it (Grof, 1988). After an overview of a typology of altered states, people work in pairs, taking it in turns to hyperventilate for two or more hours to powerful music. People then share, and make sense of, whatever altered states, spiritual or subtle, they entered. Although it should be said that nowadays Grof puts out in his workshops a strong astrological-archetypal explanatory framework for all possible experiences (Ferrer, 1998d). A Unitarian minister I met recently runs workshops on do-it-yourself theology in which she encourages and empowers people to identify, name and shape their own spiritual beliefs and practices. No doubt there are several other similar sorts of group work that are on the verge of, or immersed in, participative research in the spiritual sphere. I would very much like to hear from the people involved.

Earlier precursors were innovative religious groups in the seventeenth and eighteenth centuries, the Quakers, the Shakers, Hasidic groups and such like. There was an element of participatory peer process, an affirmation of inner spiritual autonomy, and the use of modern group norms of openness, honesty and self-disclosure. What put a stop to real inquiry was the founders' modified authoritarian theology waiting in the wings to interrupt any radical variations of the new practice and belief. Again, I would be grateful to hear, from the scholarship of others, about other historical examples of co-operative endeavour in devising forms of spiritual practice and development.

A balance of triads

Spiritual inquiry holds the tension between, on the one hand, aspiration, faith and surrender, and, on the other, alertness, discrimination and self-determination. The former triad - aspiration, faith and surrender - on its own leads to an excess of piety without inquiry. This in turn may breed any of the following: unctuousness of manner; self-righteousness; doctrines of the elect; dogmatism and authoritarianism; conflation of the spiritual with the subtle, the cultural or the psychological.

Conflation with the subtle means that religious experience gets confused with inflation by psychical energies; conflation with the cultural means that prevailing social beliefs and values may contaminate religious propositions and practices; conflation with the psychological means that religious attitudes and behaviour may become a defense against psychological and spiritual integration, or be used to dominate and manipulate others.

The latter triad - alertness, discrimination and self-determination - on its own leads to an excess of hubris without piety. This may lead over into one or more of the following: arrogance of manner; self-justification; scientism, the insistence that analytic empirical inquiry alone can yield true knowledge; scepticism and libertarianism; reduction of the spiritual to the cultural, the psychological or the physical.

Somewhere there is a balance between the two triads that honours both the holy and holistic inquiry into its credentials. Co-operation with those who are both co-subjects and co-researchers may offer the chance to keep this balance under continuous peer review.

Dipolar and polymorphous theology

The traditional religious *paths* of west and east have been monopolar, with practice directed toward one overriding reality, whether the Christian Creator, the Hindu supreme reality Brahman, or the ultimate Void of Mahayana Buddhism. My own experiential inquiry supports the idea of a balanced and dipolar path, and so also a model of dipolar theology. Such a path means both ascent and descent, and each of these both within and without, as in figure 1.2, Chapter 1. The dipolar theology is rather different to that of Hartshorne which was derived more by *a priori* reasoning, whereas what follows is more experientially based. However, it does have important links with his theology, and with process theology and panentheism in general (Hartshorne and Reese, 1953; Whitehead, 1929). So I hold a provisional theory of the divine as encompassing:

- Transcendent spiritual consciousness, beyond and informing our immediate experience.
- Immanent spiritual life, deep within and animating our immediate experience. And, mediating between the poles
- Our very present immediate experience of here and now form and process.

I also find that it makes sense of my experience of the inner heights and depths, to integrate this dipolarity of transcendent consciousness and immanent life, with another mysterious one, the dipolarity of the manifest and the unmanifest. The term 'unmanifest' is not very satisfactory, doesn't reside in the dictionary, so I shall replace with both 'beyond-the-manifest' and 'within-the-manifest'.

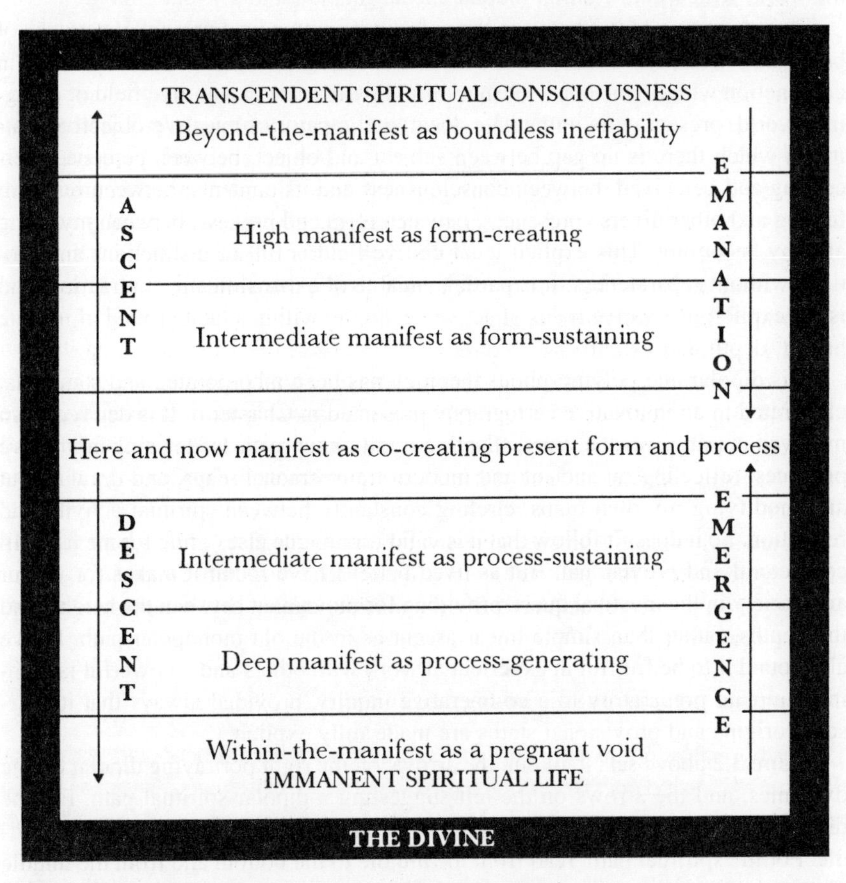

Figure 3.2 *Dipolar theology and the dipolar spiritual path*

Thus I encounter transcendent consciousness as beyond-the-manifest: as boundless ineffability, ecstatic infinitude beyond all form and differentiation, beyond every circumference, every defining name. I also find that transcendent consciousness manifests in two complementary ways. It is as if it emanates all spatial form in some sense, and also upholds it. So I engage with it as originating sound and light, creative overmind, demiurge, the first word of form. And then, too, I meet it as all-holding universal mind, cosmic store-consciousness, the repository of informing archetypes.

Plumbing the depths of immanent life I engage with the mystery of the within-the-manifest: primordial emptiness, the infinitude within all form, within every centre, the essential absence within all differentiation, the spaceless womb of being. At the same pole, immanent life manifests in complementary ways, both generating temporal process and sustaining it. So I feel it as generative, primordial life, the living emergence of new development from within, the inner, innovative prompt to time my own process in this or that or the other way. And I also feel it as interfused and pervasive inner presence, manifest as the sustaining cyclic gestures in time, both of the presence that I am in the world, and of the diverse presences of the world with whom I am in mutual exchange.

The integrative centre between the poles is my immediate present experience of being now here, my consciousness-life co-creating present form and process in conjunction with divine consciousness-life. I participate in a unitive field of being-in-a-world: present in an immediate, local, participatory subjective-objective reality, in which there is no gap between subject and object, between perceiver, perceiving and perceived, between consciousness and its contents, between resonant feeling and other diverse presences, between form and process, between my being and my becoming. This explicit local unitive field is full of distinctions and motions without separateness. It is partial, capable of expansion and contraction, and is the explicit innovative focus of active becoming within a tacit ground of infinite height, depth and extent.

This dipolar and polymorphous theology has been incorporated and somewhat elaborated in an innovative cartography presented in Chapter 6. It is derived from my lived inquiry over the years, adapting traditional practices, devising innovative practices, reflecting on ancient and modern transpersonal maps, and drawing out and modifying my own maps, circling constantly between spiritual activity and reflection. So it doesn't follow that it is valid for anyone else, while for me it is still conjectural and provisional. But as lived belief I have found it makes for vigour and variety in the mystical quest, providing for movement between the heights and the depths, rather than simple linear ascent as in the old monopolar path. I have also found it to be fruitful in experiential work with others and a powerful launching template preparatory to a co-operative inquiry, provided always that its personal origins and provisional status are made fully explicit.

Figure 3.2 above sets it all out, the arrows on the right portraying dipolar divine dynamics, and the arrows on the left suggesting a dipolar spiritual path. For the divine dynamics read from the bottom to the middle and from the top to the middle. For the spiritual path, read from the middle to the bottom and from the middle to the top. It is just a construct, a modest metaphor, a simplifying device.

4

Issues in subtle inquiry

This chapter addresses a range of issues about inquiry into the subtle or psychical domain. I start with a brief characterization of this domain, then outline three phases in the history of psychical research. I consider: the disadvantages of traditional psychical research and how these can be met by the use of co-operative inquiry; some presuppositions of using it in the subtle sphere; and a whole range of provisional procedural principles, considerations and practices when so using it.

The subtle

The term 'subtle' is used in some transpersonal theory and typology in a purely subjectivized sense. That is to say, it is used to refer to paranormal and extrasensory phenomena of other realms and entities, while at the same insisting that these are all archetypal forms of one's own spiritual transformation. Although, the phenomena initially seem to be other, say the proponents of this view, they are not so in reality.

This is definitely not the way I use the term, since such usage does not accord with my experience. By 'the subtle' I refer to supersensory realms, highly participatory and subjective-objective in nature, where we meet and participate through our subjectivity in a subtle kind of otherness, a refined frequency presentation of the givenness of the cosmos. While there appear to be diverse realms of the subtle, it is convenient to think of three hypothetical levels.

The first relates to the constitutive subtle that is interwoven with and the immediate matrix of our physical realm. The second is to do with the humdrum subtle of the recently deceased. It abuts the world of our everyday experience and impinges upon it at the margins of our awareness. This second level includes the first two kinds of spiritualism I mentioned in Chapter 1. The third level refers to states of much greater subtlety and significance, much greater depth, breadth and splendour, where all manner of powers and presences flourish. Each level can be explored by a range of extrasensory capacities appropriate to it.

The realm of the subtle is one of the new frontiers awaiting attention by contemporary participative researchers. At the humdrum level, it first burst into more recent culture as spiritualism, starting with the Fox sisters and the rappings in Hydesville, USA, in 1848. The opening heyday of spiritualism was in the latter part of the nineteenth century and waned after the twentieth century opened. Its resurgence as 'channelling' occurred in the 1960s and waxes strong today. This is largely an embarrassment to the serious inquirer because of its tendency to attract dubious practitioners, both in this world and the next, and a high degree of credulity among its followers.

As I said in Chapter 1, channellers are beset by the problem of refraction, the way in which information from people in another realm of being is distorted as it is passed through the medium's emotional, mental and cultural field. This means that neither party take responsibility for what is uttered. Mediums are excused because they are in unconscious trance or in a semi-trance state, seeking merely to be a conduit for what flows from other and supposedly higher sources. The sources are excused because, as they frequently claim, it is difficult to convey what they wish to say within the constraints of earthly language and contemporary culture. The audience can thus make of the ambiguous delivery what they need and want to make of it.

Three phases

Subtle inquiry, more conventionally known as psychical research, has gone through three main phases. The first phase, launched in the nineteenth century, had five components:

- The accumulation and sifting, according to more or less stringent criteria, of anecdotal cases of psychical experience of various kinds, such as clairvoyance, telepathy, precognition, levitation, haunting and poltergeist experiences.
- The attempt to apply fraud-eliminating controls to spiritualistic mediumship of different sorts, including entrancement, ectoplasmic materialization, physical phenomena, apports, and automatic writing.
- The attempt to find reliable corroboration for supposed mediumistic disclosures, as in the cross-correspondence studies of trance-mediumship.
- The attempt to validate the content of 'teachings' given through trance-mediumship by the evidence internal to them.
- The attempt to devise theoretical frameworks to accommodate extrasensory perception and the phenomena of mediumship within an overall worldview.

The second and mid-twentieth century phase was controlled research in the laboratory, testing for an ESP effect, such as telepathy, clairvoyance or psychokinesis, by experimental design and statistical analysis. Thus the experimental subject would sit in one room trying to guess, at the sound of a buzzer, which card was being turned over by the researcher in another room; or would seek to influence, purely by mind power, which face would turn up on a mechanically thrown dice. The design enabled the researcher to calculate results that could be expected simply due to chance. When star subjects produced results vastly in excess of chance, an ESP effect was posited.

Both phases have had their strong and weak points. The strength of the first phase, typified by sober bearded Victorians monitoring the occultly ballooning skirts of Eusabia Palladio, or David Douglas Hume levitating out of one window and floating back in through another, was that it honoured the full form and context of the anomalous experience. It preserved the holistic drama, while trying to exercise some critical rigour in dealing with it. The weakness of this phase was that the drama was so improbable to conventional thinking, that no amount of exemplary rigour was persuasive to those who weren't present during its application.

The strength of the second phase, controlled research in the laboratory, was that its rigour of design and statistical analysis persuaded many rational sceptics, such as Hans Eysenck, who were scornful of the first phase, of the inescapable validity of an ESP effect. Its weakness was that its laboratory procedures were tedious, trivial and boring, so much so that all the best ESP subjects, who initially generated astronomically high anti-chance odds in their correct card-guessing scores, burnt out after a couple of years. Furthermore, the subjects had no idea when their guesses were correct or false, nor were the controlling researchers interested in encouraging the subjects to identify experiential criteria for differentiating correct and false guesses. In the absence of such critical subjectivity, the ESP competence both withered and was nontransferable - others could not be trained to acquire it.

The current third phase could be called an increasingly diversified subject matter in search of a method of inquiry. The laboratory work of the second phase is still afoot. Strands from the first phase continue, especially with the post-war resurgence of mediumship, now called channelling (Klimo, 1988). Work has been done on case studies purporting to give evidence of reincarnation (Stevenson, 1966). There has been anecdotal detail and analysis of near death experiences (Moody, 1977; Noyes, 1980; Ring, 1984), out-of-the-body experiences (Monroe, 1972), visions of deceased loved ones in a psychomantium (Moody, 1993), conscious and lucid dreaming (LaBerge, 1985), UFO sightings and abductions explored retrospectively under hypnosis, and more. There is attention to the phenomenology of subtle bodies and subtle healing (Gerber, 1988), subtle photography, paraphysics, radiesthesia, dowsing, ley lines and the subtle energy matrix of the planet (Childress, 1995). Theoretical reconstruction continues, with attempts to relate channelled teachings to radical physics and the cartographies of comparative mysticism (Friedman,1994).

Recent years have seen the full emergence of qualitative research in the social sciences, based on a transactional or constructivist paradigm of reality (Denzin and Lincoln, 1994). This has reduced the demand for rigorously controlled quantitative studies which derive from a positivist, mechanistic worldview. So more inquiry in the subtle field has shifted over to qualitative method, to having a sympathetic dialogue with informants about their unusual experiences, about how they construe their expanded sense of reality.

Relevance of co-operative inquiry

A weakness all three phases share in common is that the researchers do not themselves get involved in the states their subjects are in. Thus the researchers:

- Cannot reliably devise categories of understanding appropriate to the states.
- Have no personal grasp of issues involved in how to enter them, sustain them or exit from them.

- Cannot generate their own critical subjectivity, that is, the experiential criteria for distinguishing between valid and invalid forms of them.

What now interests me is a fourth phase, using co-operative inquiry, in which the co-researchers are also the co-subjects who participate in the subtle states being researched. This enables the inquirers to have *experiential* access to:

- Suitable theoretical constructs.
- Entry and exit protocols.
- Relevant criteria of valid states.

This revisionary research involves persons in reciprocal relation using the full range of human sensibility - the intentional and transparent opening of the body-mind - to inquire together into the subtle dimensions of the human condition.

Presuppositions and guiding principles

There are certain ontological assumptions presupposed by any collaborative inquiry in this field, and it is important to make them explicit. My account of them is as follows:

- The domain of the subtle is not reducible either to the physical, the psychological or the cultural. It involves a transaction with being that is *sui generis.*
- The domain of the subtle both interpenetrates and permeates the realm of ordinary experience, and extends far beyond it.
- The inquirers are immersed in this domain, already access it tacitly, subliminally; and have the ability to make this access intentional, conscious and wide-ranging.

These articles of belief, or something like them, seem to be the presuppositions of any participative inquiry into the subtle getting itself off the ground. Of course, the negative outcomes of an inquiry may call them in question. But without entertaining them, people are hardly going to find it plausible or have the motivation to start.

There are also three methodological principles, born out of early experience of working with the method, which I think are pertinent.

- Initiation into the subtle domain through imagined experience of it is a precondition of inquiring into it.
- In the subtle domain, the distinction between mentation and experience breaks down because imaging and thinking can undergo transformation into psychic experience.
- Validity is in part declarative in the subtle domain. That is to say, a subtle experience declares its validity through the transformations of imaging and thinking that beget it: how it emerges and declares itself in consciousness may be an important part of its validation.

Initiation through imagined experience

This initiation principle does not say that you must presuppose a positive outcome of the inquiry before you can begin it. It is only asking you to entertain certain experiences as if they were occurring. You are invited to imagine you are having them and leave entirely open the question of whether you are actually having them or not. So you don't presuppose a definite outcome: you open yourself to the possibility of there being an outcome. You enter and maintain states which are deliberately suspended in ontological ambiguity, and learn that art before inquiring into their ontological status.

In physical science, you design and build a piece of equipment as if it can detect something, and then set it going to see whether it really can. In subtle science, you arrange the mind as if it can detect the subtle, learn to hold it in this arrangement, and only then take this arrangement into the inquiry process to see whether it really can detect the subtle.

Jean Houston in her account of sacred psychology stresses the importance of imagistic thinking, of training the creative imagination as a necessary condition of entering the subtle realms of the *mundus imaginalis* (Houston, 1987).

This imaging of altered states *as if* they are part of the total geography of being can benefit from a provisional map, a comprehensive but conjectural typology that relates to the spirit of our age. Once a person's imaginal mind is up and running, relating to this typology as imaginary artefact, the process of inquiry can begin. The typology may then be used as a hypothetical framework for systematically researching one or more parts of it, to see if they are well-founded in human experience or not. This applies both to the spiritual and to the subtle aspects of the inquiry. I discuss further the issues involved in using a provisional map in this way in Chapter 8.

Shifts of mentation and declarative validity

By mentation I mean the processes of imaging and thinking. In the subtle field, what starts out as an ordinary mental process can become a subtle experience. I may image, and think intently of, invisible presences and find that this mentation changes into a strong felt sense of communion with them. My imaginary enactment becomes transformed by what it calls forth and meets.

This in turn bears on the issue of declarative validity. The content of a subtle experience, the claim that it is an experience of this or that subtle entity or energy, involving this or that subtle perception, may in part be validated by the way that content emerges within and impacts itself upon the subjective enactment with which it engages. So some of the criteria for saying that a subtle experience is veridical, i.e. is not reducible to physical, psychological or cultural factors, may be to do with *how* mentation involuntarily shifts into an experiential content that encounters a subtle world.

I give two examples of this involuntary declarative shift, taken from the reports that follow in Part 2. One group explored clairvoyance of a physical object beyond visual range by starting with memory images of that object derived from when it had been looked at physically. Some people reported sudden and involuntary shifts from remembered views to views that were not remembered, since they were from unfamiliar perspectives that had never been perceived. Another group explored out-of-the-body experience by using a purely imaginal body to make short imagined journeys. Some people reported an unexpected problem of elasticity with an involuntarily imaged cord, which kept snapping them back into the physical body when they imagined they had got a little way out of it.

In each case, the shift was unexpected, involuntary and had about it the tang of ontological acquaintance. Thus it was put forward as a provisional, possible criterion of an authentic subtle experience. Subtle phenomena may arrest our imaginal processes with their unusual and autonomous presence.

A canon of subtle inquiry

The content of subtle experience often has an ambiguous character. It is suspended between what merely seems to be the case, and what really is the case; between an illusory and a veridical perception. It is 'as if' I am in two worlds at once, the ordinary one and a subtle one. But the subtle, other world component *could* be something else - a sensation or misperception at the physical level, or a bit of purely imaginary content.

I believe this ambiguity occurs precisely because there are two worlds interacting in my consciousness. Several interrelated effects can occur. I can mistake a this-world experience for another-world experience, and vice versa. In zones where the two kinds of perception overlap I may not be clear which is which. Or I may ignore one kind totally in favour of the other. Or what starts out as an ordinary state of consciousness of this world, may end up as an altered state disclosing the other world. And what starts out as an altered state may collapse into an ordinary state.

Heron's beard and Occam's razor

Because of all this, I hold to one cardinal principle: if you are aware of an ambiguous experience in which it is *as if* there are subtle other world components, then it is a good thing to foster and elaborate the ambiguity, rather than try to reduce it and eliminate it sceptically. Apply first of all a principle opposite to that of Occam's razor.

William of Occam was an English philosopher who died about 1349. Occam's razor is the principle that the fewest possible assumptions should be made in explaining anything (Lacey, 1986). So according to this principle, if you have some ambiguous experience, you should seek to explain it in terms of this world, and not invoke the extra assumption of some other kind of world. This explanatory principle often leads to reductionism: claims to extrasensory experience are explained away in terms of, reduced to, ordinary sorts of experience.

My opposite principle is that it is wise to encourage an ambiguous experience to acquire luxurious growth in the direction of the complex and the occult, rather than rigorously cut it down to an awareness of the simple and the obvious. I will call this the principle of Heron's beard.

Now Heron's beard is not yet an explanatory principle: it is a principle for the management of an ambiguous experience. It commends you to give such an experience the extrasensory, subtle benefit of the doubt - to go with it as if some other worldly phenomena is afoot. Let it develop expansively and imaginatively. Then notice what happens to it. Does it collapse into the obvious after all? Or does it enhance its claim to be explained in terms of wider assumptions than apply to ordinary states of mind.

Heron's beard is sometimes (but by no means always) paradoxical in its application. Consider this case. I have an ambiguous experience in which the supposed subtle world content really is nothing more than a bit of sensation, of private imagination, or a misperception. There is nothing subtle about it. Yet if I apply Heron's beard to it, then it may actually develop from an ordinary to an extraordinary, from a sensory to an extrasensory, state of consciousness.

A simple example of this is an ambiguous image before my closed eyes: is it merely a retinal image, or is it the dawning of a clairvoyant perception of the other world? Now even if, when it first appears, it is in fact nothing other than a retinal image, if I apply Heron's beard to it and imaginatively foster its development in my consciousness, it may *turn into* a clairvoyant window on the subtle world.

If you are too committed to the use of Occam's razor, you will cut an ambiguous experience short, and rush into a premature, usually reductionist, explanation. Better to indulge the experience a bit, nurture it and foster it with your attention. Postpone explanation until the experience declares itself more fully. Go with what seems, let the immediate phenomena unfold. Elaborate its content, and notice carefully what is going on before explaining it.

Occam's razor goes for a rapid and sceptical reduction of the ambiguous to the usual. Heron's beard goes for a leisurely and imaginative elaboration of the ambiguous to the unusual. Actually, the two principles are complementary and need each other. For sometimes the beard simply becomes a mass of illusory growth, and then you need the razor to shave it off. But a useful guiding rule is: grow the beard *before* you decide whether or not it is appropriate to use the razor. Don't contract before you expand your awareness; and only contract it if the expansion results in an obvious nonsense.

Applying the canon

Let me systematize this a little bit further. Suppose I have an ambiguous experience which has some apparent other world content. Now this other world content may be illusory, that is, really physical world content, or it may be genuine. So we have the following possibilities.

1. Apply Heron's beard to what only seems to be other world content but really isn't, and as a result it actually *becomes* genuine other world content. This is my example above: Heron's beard turns what at first was only a closed-eye retinal image into an authentic clairvoyant window.
2. Apply Heron's beard to what only seems to be other world content but really isn't, and as a result it becomes quite obvious that it is nothing but an illusion. In which case apply Occam's razor and strip the illusion off the physical world

content. Thus the attempt to develop some ambiguous image before your closed eyes into clairvoyance, may show it up to be what it really is - an ordinary retinal light.

3. Apply Heron's beard to what only seems to be other world content but really isn't, and as a result it becomes more and more illusory, but you don't notice this. You are now systematically deluded, desperately need Occam's razor but sadly don't know it. You are in trouble. Thus you may persistently imagine that what in fact is nothing but retinal light is a clairvoyant window.
4. Apply Heron's beard to what in fact really is other world content, and as a result it becomes illusory. This is unfortunate, but it probably often happens. So you get the first glimmerings of a real clairvoyant window on the subtle world, and when you try to elaborate it you only succeed in losing it. You then need to apply Occam's razor quickly and realize you are now seeing nothing but retinal lights: an altered state has collapsed into an ordinary one.
5. Apply Heron's beard to what in fact really is other world content, and as a result it becomes more and more authentic. Thus you have the first glimmerings of a real clairvoyant window on the other world, and as you expand your awareness into it, the psi content becomes much clearer, more detailed, specific and convincing. You really are seeing another world, and you know it. Occam's razor is unused.
6. Apply Heron's beard to what in fact really is other world content, and as a result it becomes more and more authentic, but you can't allow yourself to believe the evidence of your psi capacity. So you quite inappropriately slash away with Occam's razor and destroy a real growth of seership. As a clairvoyant window opens up into more systematic and detailed 'seeing', you put a stop to it with compulsive scepticism and insist to yourself that it is pure delusion.

All the six possibilities given just above can occur and have occurred in my experience. Understanding this sixfold repertoire provides a rudimentary canon of inquiry for getting at the truth of the matter. Numbers 3 and 6 are the pathological parts of the repertoire to be avoided at all costs in gross form, but are probably bound to occur from time to time to a greater or lesser degree. Number 3 in gross form is the most pathological. Number 4 is often due to lack of skill: practice can make it disappear. Numbers 1, 2 and 5 keep the show on the road.

The frequent ambiguity of content keeps us all on our toes, exercising vigilance and discrimination, balancing experience and explanation, expansion and contraction of consciousness, elaboration and reduction of content, the growth of Heron's beard with the use of Occam's razor.

Refraction theory

Next, I present another way of thinking about communication between this world and the subtle realm. I don't know whether the model is correct or not, but it does at least suggest that we need to take account, in one way or another, of refraction effects. I use the simple phenomenon of refraction in physics as a *metaphor* for what may go on when persons in this world communicate with those in the other, and vice versa.

Refraction in physics is about the bending of a ray of light as it passes obliquely from one medium into another medium of different optical density. So if you are submerged in a dense medium such as water, and look up to a source of light above you in the more rarefied medium of air, then if the light rays strike the surface of the water at an oblique angle, their source will appear to be higher than it really is. The rays coming from the source are bent down, more towards the vertical as they enter the water. So you seem to be looking more steeply up at that source than is actually the case. Similarly, if you are in the air and look obliquely into water at a source of light below the surface, it will appear to be higher than it really is.

Taking this, with some metaphorical license, as an analogy for what happens when humans receive impressions or communications from beings in the subtle realm, then humans will both regard these beings as more special than they actually are, and at the same time take their message in earthly terms. In other words humans don't realize that their 'line of sight' is bent back toward the earth as it enters the subtle realm and so will think it is focused on beings more elevated than is the case. But because it is bent back toward the earth, it also inclines more to familiar perspectives of meaning. So you get a paradoxical effect that includes both false elevation and false reduction.

The false elevation effect leads humans to think that the imparting beings have higher status and knowledge than is warranted, and to attribute inflated significance to what is imparted. The false reduction effect means that humans will tend to frame and construe what is imparted too much in terms appropriate to their own domain. For a more elaborate account of this refraction model see Heron (1987).

More about method

Here are few other pointers about inquiry into the subtle domains:

- It is important to think holistically and in terms of heterogeneous perspectives: that is, in terms of interlocking idiosyncratic parts and overlapping and mutually supporting but often very different views within a whole.
- In terms of the outcomes or findings of an inquiry, the inquiry group may be represented, holonomically, by one or more of its members.
- Participants often get caught up in the content of their impressions and have difficulty in sustaining their awareness on the all-important issue of how to discriminate between real and apparent impressions. Creeping consensus collusion in not addressing this issue is an ever-present danger.
- The sense of personal identity in ordinary states of consciousness is disturbed and threatened by entry into the subtle domain. Both this anxiety, and other emotional distresses which it may trigger off, may distort or interrupt the inquiry with respect to planning, action or reflection. So some attention needs to be paid during the inquiry to emotional housecleaning.
- It seems that the objectivity of the other reality, in the early stages and in the first instance at any rate, is shaped, enacted, in a much more idiosyncratically

subjective form than is the case with this reality. The extrasensory subtle is a subjective-objective realm, as is the sensory realm, but the subject-object transaction seems to be much more fluidic, metamorphic and variable than in the sensory realm. There is much greater diversity among the subtle perceptions of different people of the same subtle scene. This may be due to emotional interference, or lack of practice, or it may be in the nature of the case, or varying combinations of all of these.

- A careful and discriminating descriptive phenomenology of direct experience is more basic at the outset in subtle inquiry work than sustained and highly sophisticated philosophical conjecture or elaborate theory building about the mechanisms involved. Of course, some overall guiding paradigm is required to launch and overshadow the inquiry process, but the main initial activity for inquirers, I believe, is learning to notice how their own subjectivity can be opened up to impressions from other dimensions of being.
- The validity, both of the inquiry process and of its findings, arises from the exercise of finely tuned discrimination - in the hypothesis making and planning, in the experiential phase and in the reflection phase, in the application of validity procedures and assessment of their use. In the light of all this, inquirers can make a holistic, global judgement about the validity of their findings.

5

The challenge of cartography

This chapter compares and contrasts my transpersonal perspective with the perspectives evident in three other transpersonal maps, those of Washburn, Grof and Wilber. I discuss in some detail the limitations I find in Wilber's scheme, and this leads into a discussion about the place of innovative evolution in a transpersonal theory, and, finally, about conventional accounts of the nondual state.

A launching map

I have suggested that both spiritual and subtle inquiries may usefully be preceded by imaging relevant altered states as if they are part of the total geography of being; that this requires a provisional map, a comprehensive typology that relates to the spirit of our age; and that once a person's imaginal mind is up and running, relating to this typology as imaginary artefact, the process of inquiry can begin. The typology may, or may not, then be used as a hypothetical framework for systematically researching one or more parts of it, to see if they are well-founded in human experience or not.

We therefore need a launching map. It will have important educative functions, before the inquiry proper starts, in preparing a group of people to *become* co-inquirers. In Chapter 8, I give my reasons for using a map in this way, say more about how I use it, and explore the all-important issue as to whether this sort of use is tantamount to prior indoctrination. What I wish to discuss in this chapter are issues that arise in my mind about some maps in current use in the transpersonal field, whether I find them adequate as launching maps, and if not why not.

I want to stress that in writing about a map another person has devised, I find that the process of so doing is like an implicit dialogue. I am in my mind comparing and contrasting, theoretically and experientially, two different yet overlapping perspectives, and in the process seeking to refine and enhance my own perspective so that it is comprehensive, coherent and experientially congruent. My tone is polemical, yet I am not engaged in a competition with the other to win the 'battle for the ultimate transpersonal framework' (Ferrer, 1998e).

My own perspective is fed and nourished, either directly or by reaction, by the perspective from which I differentiate it. There is, in my view, no ultimate framework, only a range of provisional models, grounded in each author's developing experiential inquiry into what there is.

The lure of the east

Much in vogue at present are traditional maps derived from Hindu and Buddhist mysticism. My problem with these is that they have been generated in ancient and restrictive cultural contexts, whose values contaminate, directly or by reaction, both mystical belief and practice. I go into this in more detail later on in this chapter. So we must both honour them, exercise massive discrimination in dealing with them, and rearrange, reconstrue and add to them in the light of contemporary experience and practice, our deepest philosophies and the spirit of our times.

What calls for comment in this regard is the remarkable degree of intimidation and/or hero worship which ancient typologies, especially eastern ones, call forth in modern minds, especially western ones. The postmodern crisis in the west, with its eerie uncertainties, precipitates among western seekers a widespread spiritual projection, as defined in Chapter 2, on to the supposed certainties of ancient eastern sages. Intelligent people then adopt, without any critical discrimination or questioning, typologies of transcendent states of consciousness, characterisations of the various chakras, and forms of spiritual practice, as if these are self-evidently correct, free of psychological, political and cultural distortion, and are applicable to the present-day.

Jung questioned this tendency. He thought that eastern forms of meditation serve to strengthen the grip of the ego on consciousness, and that what westerners need is to loosen this grip so as to become more open to deep unconscious processes. So he recommended active imagination for westerners. This process allows images rich in symbolic content to well up spontaneously from the unconscious. Jung believed it relaxes the ego, so that it is more responsiveness to the inner life (Jung, 1936).

Washburn and Grof

Washburn argues persuasively that Jung has got it wrong about meditation, and that whatever its initial effect, its long-term effect is to loosen the restrictive cramp which the ego imposes on consciousness (Washburn, 1995: 159). While Washburn endorses meditation, as well as occidental forms of prayer, he generally avoids spiritual projection onto ancient eastern approaches. His transpersonal theory of the dipolar relation between the ego and the dynamic ground - a ground which includes both psychic energy or libido and numinous spirit - is rooted in western depth psychology and existential-phenomenological thought as well as eastern and western mysticism.

He affirms the self as part of the basic furniture of existence, sees it as emerging from its dynamic ground, then dissociating from it and repressing it in early life. In later life the self regresses to work through repressed materials, open to the ground as spirit and embark on the process of spiritual regeneration and integration. This involves both the spiritualization of the person and the personalization of spirit, thus apparently affirming the spiritual reality of personhood as one of the real Many, and avoiding the metaphysical and political difficulties of supposing that a person is nothing but a knotted self, ultimately due for annihilation. The theory works with metaphors of ground, depth, inner source, indwelling, descent, rerooting. This I find true to my experience, as indeed many other people do.

What I find missing are complementary metaphors of sky, outpouring from above, ascent, upward blossoming and so on. In other words, I miss a dynamic dipolarity of depth and height, of immanent spiritual life and transcendent spiritual consciousness, within the nature of spirit itself. Furthermore, it is not at all clear how this theory is experientially based. There is a sustained and cogent account of what is going on at the different stages, but no account of whom, if anyone, it is *all* going on for.

I have a very large question mark about Washburn's view that traditional eastern meditation, in both receptive and concentrative form, is the best way to 'drill for oil', as he puts it, in the dynamic ground. And there is a question mark, too, about the status of that unspecified wider reality which includes both the ego and its ground.

Stan Grof's work does quite clearly stand on its own experiential feet. He presents a comprehensive cartography of some forty different spiritual and subtle states that is based on his own experience and that of his many subjects. The account of these states is refreshingly free of traditional doctrines and dogma. In the early research, the states described followed the ingestion of a psychedelic substance, LSD (Grof, 1976). Later on, he abandoned the use of LSD and found that the same results could be obtained by a combination of hyperventilation, that is, rapid breathing, and bodywork, in association with appropriate music (Grof, 1988). His workshops using this latter approach are launched by a presentation of his map. However, the whole thing is by no means entirely free of orientalism.

His 1988 version of this extensive map of spiritual and subtle states simply expands the 1976 version. But in the 1988 account, in a short introductory section he relates his wide-ranging scheme to another briefer one derived from Wilber's neo-Vedantic account of the perennial philosophy: absolute or nondual, higher causal, lower causal, higher subtle, lower subtle, gross experiential realm (Grof, 1988: 39-40; Wilber, 1980). I find that this assimilation doesn't work in detail. Grof's original scheme, comprehensive and experientially based, sits cramped and uneasy within the limiting definitions of the orientally-derived and authority-based system. Indeed, Grof acknowledges this himself:

> In specific details, the cartography of consciousness found in perennial philosophy would have to be extended and modified to fit the findings of experimental psychiatry and the new experiential psychotherapies. (Grof, 1988: 40)

Still he does attempt to relate his wider experiential findings to the perennial philosophy scheme based an ancient Hindu and Buddhist sources. This is, I find, an unsatisfactory ambiguity: there is the sense of something more that has not yet found its new and expanded home, but is trying to make do with an older one. Such open-minded entries as 'Spiritistic and Mediumistic Experiences', 'Encounters with Spirit Guides and Suprahuman Beings', 'Visits to Other Universes and Meetings with Their Inhabitants', 'Spontaneous Psychoid Events', 'Intentional Psychokinesis', are on the verge of a science of the subtle worlds, in a way which oriental typologies really do not countenance, because they regard such matters as distracting objectifications of the transcendental subject en route to divine annihilation. More recently I understand Grof has put out in his workshops a strong astrological-archetypal explanatory framework for all possible experiences, but, at the time of my writing, his book on this has not yet been published.

Maps from monopolar patriarchs

Wilber's map, whose categories I have just listed, is, he writes, 'based largely on Hindu and Buddhist psychological systems and especially their modern interpreters, for example, Aurobindo, Guenon, Smith, Free John' (Wilber, 1990: 284). It is rooted in ancient eastern traditions and sustains their patriarchal and monopolar focus. Wilber does seem to be running a strong spiritual projection on oriental mystics. The textual evidence for this, so far as it goes, is that he does not unambiguously state his own personal experience, but intensively veils it with elaborate interpretations of what some sage has said or some tradition teaches. Indeed, I find a strong element of displacement and *mauvais foi* in the degree to which he claims to be a spokesperson for the reported experiences of some of the world's top mystics. However, since he does all this with great intellectual aplomb, he seems to draw some other people's spiritual projection on to his own writing, which is then not approached with a proper degree of critical discrimination.

Wilber's map does not relate to my experience in several important respects.

1. I find that it has no grasp of a dynamic dipolarity of inwardness. It presents the *interior* spiritual path entirely in terms of inner *ascent*, to the exclusion of inner *descent*. The inner descent to which I here refer is not to be confused either with outward descent into social action, or with the reworking of earlier stages on the path of ascent, both of which Wilber's model includes. Nor, of course, is it to be confused with regression to the prepersonal. His map attends only to divine transcendence, promoting, via static meditation, a unidirectional climb from the lower to the higher, from the ordinary unregenerate state of mind to the nondual absolute. Wilber's *theology* is dipolar in the sense that it fully acknowledges both the transcendent and immanent nature of spirit, as both goal and ground, respectively, of spiritual development (1997: 44). But spiritual *practice* is monopolar: it is all directed at the transcendent.

I get no sense of, or reference to, the co-equal and complementary practice of inner spiritual descent, of attention to divine immanence and indwelling, to *shekinah*, the dynamic complement to *logos*. Wilber has the basic notion of the Ground-Unconscious, full of all our spiritual potentials. And he has the correlative notion, from Schelling, of the *Deus implicitus*, the embedded and immanent 'Spirit-in-action', which is the self-transcending drive of the whole evolutionary process (1995: 487). Yet in his scheme, as far as I can see, we do no direct business with it. Instead we indirectly provoke its potentials to become actual by meditating on the next higher level in our path of ascent. This I find to be a very one-sided dissociative account of spiritual development, typical of ancient eastern practice. It is monopolar ascent, from life with a little l to Mind with a big M.

Oriental practice sweeps through the lower chakras, regarding them as lower in spiritual significance. It reveals the sexism of ancient autocratic patriarchs of the spiritual life. The oriental mystic is traditionally on a classic flight from *ma,* Sanskrit for mother, hence from *maya.* He regards the *hara,* the subtle and spiritual womb, as no more than a focus of emotionality and sexuality, a place to get kundalini through on the way up. For the feminist theologian, by contrast,

> The womb both symbolizes and embodies a spirituality premised upon...relationality and co-creation with God/dess. (Raphael, 1994: 521)

It is a shrine of divine indwelling, *shekinah,* a locus of transfigured embodiment. As such it is not, for bigendered practice, a place to be negated and preserved in a process of typically male monopolar ascent, but a place to be enhanced in an interdependent and dipolar, spiralling dynamic of descent and ascent.

In Wilber's account of practice, spirit is always a higher level in the hierarchy of being. Nor does his own account of gender differences in spirituality alter this, for he thinks men tend to ascend up to the higher level and women tend to bring down and root the higher level in the lower (Wilber, 1997: 199-200), and we note that in either case spirit is exclusively above. Spiritual transformation only comes from paying attention to what is beyond one's current level, transcendent spirit, whether by rising up to it or pulling it down. It never comes from direct attention paid to unfolding what is deeply within one's present state, immanent spiritual life.

In my experience, indwelling spiritual potential is the active source and ground of my personhood. It moves me, not merely to ascend vertically in awareness, but also to extend horizontally, empowered from within, reaching out to others in both facilitative and reciprocal relations. This relational, real-person-sharing, horizontal spirituality, is co-created with, and grounded in the depth of, immanent spiritual life. I find that it is in certain respects more fundamental than vertical spirituality, ascending to heights. Whereas, for Wilber, whose ultimate goal is the top-rung, end-state of unreal-self-dissolution, the vertical is the real thing. Thus he refers scornfully to the '"wonderful permeable self" assumptions of merely translative [horizontal] female spirituality' compared to women who 'transform' [vertically] by having 'wrenching bodily ordeals as they bring Spirit down and into the bodily being' (1997: 200).

Something is getting seriously out of kilter with this kind of dismissive evaluation of the horizontal as if it has no transformative relevance. For example, conscious intentional parenting, sustained over years, is a profound spiritual discipline, a transformative horizontal practice grounded in active openness to immanent spirit, which puts into perspective excessive claims made for years of solitary sitting meditation, the transformative vertical practice of opening to transcendent spirit. Without an affirmation of the transformative centrality of such a horizontal practice, there is little hope for the future of the human race. I return to the issue of horizontal and vertical, real person and unreal self, in point 5 below.

2. The exclusive focus on ascent is related to Wilber's belief that traditional oriental practice, such as sitting meditation, is a primary means of spiritual transformation. Such practice is solitary, done alone, even if sitting beside others in a hall of meditation. It is not in any way explicitly interactive. It is static: sitting means sitting. It is silent. As such it is a far too one-sided account of spiritual practice.

As a complement to it, I believe in openness to the dynamic impulses of immanent spiritual life and its charismatic expression through interactive movement, sound and word, a collective expression of power, a productive rhythmic engagement between people, revealing a harmony of person, nature and the wider universe, both seen and subtle. This expressive, interactive practice manifests the whole dynamic divine process itself. It also relates directly to Asanta's account (1984) of African American spirituality.

3. Wilber's idea of invariant, ascending stages of development, in which the lower necessarily precede the higher, does not tally with my experience. In my early adult life I was a member of a spiritual school whose practices afforded me regular and reliable access to exalted mystical states, yet in later years I had to come down and deal with a lot of work with my emotions and relationships. This, as Rothberg reports, is a common experience:

> A further question concerns how advocates of stage models can make sense of the types of sequences reported by Kornfield, McDonald Smith, and many others, of a sustained and stabilized transpersonal development followed by 'downward' movement to attend to emotions, the body, and relationships. (Rothberg, 1996: 29)

Ferrer (1998a) shows, to my mind convincingly, that Wilber's hierarchy of stages, and his criteria for what is higher, are not supported by the mystical evidence. Likewise, Cortright (1997) holds there is no evidential support for the belief in a single invariant sequence of spiritual development. Rothberg raises a large number of searching questions about the validity of Wilber's stage model, then interviews three leading western Buddhist teacher-practitioners. None of them find developmental models, ancient or modern, eastern or western, much use in practice. They all put their trust in an unpredictable organic kind of unfolding idiosyncratic for each individual. Michele McDonald-Smith gets to the heart of the matter:

> The whole job of a teacher is really to let the person unfold from inside, not to direct development from the outside. To have a stage model might be to second-guess this inner unfolding. But people are full of surprises. Each person is unique. (Rothberg, 1996: 38)

4. Wilber's map does not do justice to my experience in another way. Like Huxley, also aligned with Advaita Vedanta, Wilber subjectivizes the subtle realms. As I read him, the high subtle is revealed as the form, the structure of the transcendental subject at that stage of development. It is a self, objectified so that it can die and be transcended (1995: 609). I get no sense of a subjective-objective subtle universe, of exalted communion with high-raised presences within it, of the claims and calling of a subtle science to articulate its powers. He acknowledges the importance of an *external* spiritual path of *descent* into social action and sensory science. There is no feel for complementary external spiritual path of *ascent* to a working relation with higher beings and a competence in supersensory science at the high subtle level. There is a lack of full ontological openness, robustness and rigour at this level. It is all viewed through the traditional Zen concept of *makyo,* subtle illusion and inferior apprehension.

5. A fifth limitation, for my awareness, is that Wilber also regards any form of self or personhood as a temporary, virtual structure, a necessary but impermanent by-product of each level of development. The self is not an entity within the bosom of divine creation; it is not an actual person, not one of the real Many within the One. At every stage it is a mere appearance, and it is ultimately unreal. At the final stage of ultimate nondual unity, there is no self of any sort, rather 'one becomes reality' (Wilber, 1982: 66). So there are just a series of temporary self-structures, which serve to help realize the ultimate state where any self is unreal. There are many difficulties with this idea. I'll mention two.

Firstly, it puts a premium on vertical spirituality, on climbing to the top rung of development where there is no self, and downgrades relational, horizontal spirituality, which is not real spirituality at all. Interpersonal love, I believe, is a sharing of indwelling spirit between real spiritual presences, but on Wilber's model it is reduced to a collusive, unreal interaction between temporary unreal structures. I experience personhood as a spiritual reality, and this puts a premium on horizontal, relational spirituality, nourished and enriched by a vertical spirituality of both ascent and descent. Wilber views personhood as nothing but an illusory sense of self, hence ascending beyond the illusion is much more basic than any translative, horizontal exchanges within any level where the illusion of self is shared.

Secondly, the ultimately unreal self theory has all the inflationary problems of end-state enlightenment, endemic in Buddhist authoritarianism. In the final stage, since there is no self of any sort left, no further development is possible, the absolute limit of human unfoldment is reached, the human is the divine.

This throws out the baby with the bathwater, the distinctness-within-cosmic-unity of the person, with the separate, fear-numbed, contracted ego. In elevating the human to the absolute, it ignores the asymmetrical relation between the finite and the infinite. The infinite can be fully in the finite, since the finite is infinitely divisible. But this doesn't make the finite infinite. It just means the actual finite has infinite potential. A finite being is open to the infinite potential within and to the actual infinity without, and is distinct but not separate from either. To overlook this asymmetry and insist there is no distinction of any sort between finite human awareness and infinite divine awareness is, in my scheme of things, an illusory state of spiritual inflation (Rosenthal, 1987). It is also likely to lead to distortions of spiritual authority, as in the tradition of Zen (Crook, 1996; Lachs, 1994).

6. There is another big limitation, from my point of view. Monopolar maps such as those of Wilber and Plotinus present solely a down-hierarchy model of created reality. The one absolute emanates, out and down, progressively lower levels of mind from the highly subtle nous or overmind to the sensationalism of gross matter, the outermost realm of the many. For these patriarchs, that is a full account of the process of creation, period. It is an exclusively conservative process, for after the levels are established, all other cosmic process, as we shall see in a moment, is a return back along the same route to the one.

There is no acknowledgement, *as intrinsic to creation,* of a concomitant and complementary up-hierarchy, a creative process in which the indwelling infinitude within each of the many emerges as progressively higher levels of rhythmic life. There is no satisfactory account of innovative spiritual life emerging within each and all of the many in reciprocal interaction with the many emanating from conservative spiritual consciousness. Wilber's attempt at this fails, as we shall see below. The down-hierarchy model talks only of 'vegetative life', and reduces life to a low level emanate of mind, Eve formed from a rib of Adam. I develop this sixth point in the next section.

Evolution reduced to reflux

The down-hierarchy model reduces the concomitant creative process of upward emergent life within the many, to the *return* of the many to the one. This return is a reflux, a going back up the same ladder. The ascending climb from the many to the one retraces the route from the one to the many. Emergent evolution, on this view, is not an innovative dynamic intrinsic to *creation,* it is reduced to being a *repeal* of a conservative creation. This is monopolar bias in favour of the one: out from the one and back to the one, and the top men know the one and only route either way. It all lacks, for my experience, the authentic dipolarity of good process theology.

In terms of spiritual practice, the monopolar aspirant is always calling on the higher level to subsume the lower one where he is currently located. There is no complementary practice to open to the processes of divine life emerging from within the current locus of being, no deepening descent to the generative infinitude within the many. For the monopolar patriarch, spiritual development always means being pulled up from, and reaching up to, a higher plane.

This striving to ascend is not complemented by any correlative inward creative descent, no going into the internal spiritual womb of what is happening now. The patriarchal aspirant does not seek intentionally to manifest a charismatic expression that is innovative and co-creative with the emergent divine impulse of the existential moment. He is versed only in what goes on within the static retreat of meditation, and then has to devise some way of manifesting this in his outward life, usually through the benignly autocratic direction of the others along the same monopolar path.

Wilber has recently tried to effect an integration of innovative evolution and conservative emanation, but ends up by reducing the former to the latter. He attempts to assimilate a theory of creative evolution, of upward emergence, to a patriarchal theory of return, a climb back up the ladder of theocratic descent (Wilber, 1995). The result is a painful degree of incoherence.

Within his theory of evolution he holds that evolution is basically undetermined, and becomes more innovative the higher up the developmental scale; and that the main spiritual stages of humankind, which lie in the future, are social-interior and involve intersubjective communion within a culture. This, it would seem, can only mean that the future spiritual stages of humankind are undetermined, innovative and unknown, and will only be realized within whole communities and cultures.

However, Wilber is married to the old theocratic descent and return model of creation, which he believes the top mystics have uncovered long ago. So he thinks the ancient patriarchal mystics have already in the *past* and as *individuals* explored and defined all the *future* and *social* spiritual stages of humankind. This notion is in flat contradiction with the above two points of his evolutionary theory. Wilber cannot hold that evolution is more and more innovative and undetermined at its higher stages, if he also believes that the highest stages, which lie in the future for humankind, have already been anticipated at regular intervals in the midst of early stages. Likewise, he cannot hold that the main spiritual stages involve social communion within a spiritual culture, if he also believes they were realized by ancient mystics who were solitary explorers of spiritual stages within nonspiritual cultures.

Wilber tries to deal with this predetermined-undetermined incoherence by saying that the deep structures, the universally invariant stages, of future spiritual development are predetermined by the grand plan which has already been uncovered by the top mystics, but that their superficial forms are not and so these give scope for innovation and the unpredictable. But how can Wilber write categorically about universally invariant higher stages from within the limited perspective of the deep structure of his current stage?

Moreover, the idea of deep invariance and surface innovation takes away much more than it gives. For it undermines human creativity with an account of its inescapable superficiality. If we already know today the underlying deep structure of future innovation, in what possible sense can it be authentically innovative? Nor does the idea say much for divine originality, if it has nothing new in store for us at the level of deep structures.

The incoherence can be resolved by an alternative model. I take the view that a person's, or a culture's, spiritual potential or entelechy consists of unlimited seeded patterns of possibility, the selection from, and linear actualization of, which is indeterminate and a matter of deep creative choice. The built-in code is not a linear programme, but a profound array of dynamic options emerging from the infinite potential within. We can co-create our innovative path with our inner spiritual life-impulse and the possibilities it proffers. This more coherent idea, incidentally, leads on to a theory of the valid diversity of spiritual paths, rather than to the assimilative totalitarianism of Wilber' system.

In passing, it is interesting to note some variants. Coan presents a sort of intermediate model: there are many possible alternative pathways for the evolution of consciousness within and between five basic modes of human fulfilment - efficiency, creativity, inner harmony, relatedness and transcendence (Coan, 1989). Hunt suggests that if we define spirituality in terms of presentational awareness, felt meaning and presence, and if this is integrated with any one of the different kinds of intelligence we have, then there are many kinds of spiritual development other than higher states of consciousness (Hunt, 1995). More radically, echoing at the biological level something of my view, Varela, Thompson and Rosch see evolution as natural drift, in which organisms cognitively enact, 'bring forth', their world in mutual engagement with the environment ('coupling'):

> Our human embodiment and the world that is enacted by our history of coupling reflect only one of many possible evolutionary pathways. We are always constrained by the path we have laid down, but there is no ultimate ground to prescribe the steps that we take. (Varela, Thompson and Rosch, 1991: 214)

Wilber, incidentally, adopts the enactive theory from Varela, Thompson and Rosch, applying it to human culture, but then undermines the original point of it, which is to accommodate evolution by natural drift, by fitting it into a fixed stage model of development.

The polemic of this and the previous section sets out the reasons why I do not find Wilber's system adequate to do justice to my own experience and spiritual insights. Since his map is widely influential at the present time, it seems pertinent to explain why I do not use it. There is also another point to make. I respect the fact that Wilber, or anyone else within the old traditions, has chosen to take the classic monopolar path as their personal path of spiritual unfoldment, for any such choice is their deep right and privilege. What has to be challenged, however, is the promotion of false hegemonic claims, made on behalf of this gender-laden path, that it is perennial and preordained for the whole of mankind. It is important to challenge these claims for the very good reason that they can, for a while at any rate, intimidate and disempower some people from making deep, creative choices about their own spiritual path.

Emergent evolution as intrinsic to creation

Let us look further at the hypothesis of unpredictable divine becoming. Let us suppose that it means at least the following:

- Emergent evolution is part of the dynamic process of creation interacting all the time with involution, the outward and downward emanation of levels of being.
- The higher and spiritual emergent stages are undetermined and highly innovative and still to come for humankind.
- Such stages involve intersubjective communion, autonomous persons in co-operative relations, within a self-generating culture.

Then from these beliefs, certain implications would seem to follow:

All ancient accounts of spiritual states are inadequate and incomplete hybrids. They represent the pioneer attainments of solitary mystics in tiny sub-cultures, set within dominant nonspiritual cultures. Their accounts are unawarely laced with key values of those cultures, as well as being in conscious reaction against some of their other values. Either way what we get is a representation of human spirituality that is culturally relative. It is relative to the general level of the evolutionary emergence of humankind at that time.

The primary unaware values incorporated in these ancient accounts include authoritarianism, patriarchy and the denigration of women, denigration of the body, emotional repression, together with no commitment to autonomous mastery of the phenomenal world in terms of science, politics and ethics. All these unaware values become inflated to theological proportions, and woven into the structure of the spiritual path.

What the ancient accounts are in conscious reaction against, is the driven desire-ridden addiction to misery rife in society, hence their preoccupation with *moksha,* release from it all.

The future spiritual stages of humankind involve, *perhaps, for we certainly don't know,* the conscious evolutionary and existential emergence of indwelling spirit within communities of persons, who are also simultaneously attuned to the involutional descent of transcendent spirit. Human evolution into spiritual stages, *perhaps,* means reaching down to become awarely grounded in co-creative relation with innovative indwelling life, as much as it means reaching up to transfiguration by transcendent states of consciousness; and this in co-operative relations with others similarly engaged. Such collaborative transformative conversion of ascent and descent into increasing breadth of horizontal, spiritual living here and now, is maybe what it is all about. At any rate, what this conscious human integration of, and co-creation with, the dipolar dynamics of creation may yield, simply cannot be found in any ancient accounts of the spiritual path, and is highly likely to turn much of these accounts inside out and upside down.

Immediate participation in the seamless totality of present experience, becomes a starting point, and an everpresent fulcrum, of this dipolar integration. At the same time it is divested of the illusory and static absolutism, end-of-the-roadism, attributed to it in ancient cartographies. It is where the modern spiritual process modestly begins, in local diunity, not where it inflatedly ends, in absolute nonduality.

The ancient approach was to flee the Many to find the absolute One, by dissociating from life and by training attention to witness, but not in any way manage, the content of consciousness, through receptive or concentrative meditation. Eventually, by this backdoor route, it found the Many in the One, but inevitably in a very One-sided way. There is a current alternative: to attune here and now to the relative Many-One in immediate present experience, which is continuously both deepened and heightened by opening to a co-creating relation with the dipolar dynamics of creation.

This participative awareness is correlative with creative, charismatic transformative action, which, *perhaps,* becomes the acme of the spiritual life, rather than passive, quietist absorption in the One.

Finally, all this speculation is derived from my own lived inquiry, including a small number of co-operative inquiries, hence it is a highly presumptuous extrapolation.

Inflation of the nondual

Wilber, and other oriental apologists, make a certain kind of simple nondual awareness the final and absolute acme of the spiritual path.

> When Zen Master Fa-ch'ang was dying, a squirrel screeched on the roof. 'It's just this', he said, 'and nothing more.' (Wilber, 1990: 123)

Now I don't know what was really going on for a Zen master or indeed any other ancient mystic. If I spend a lot of time affirming it was this or that, or insist emphatically that it was not this or not that, I simply get lost in unaware spiritual projection. It is more valuable if I attend fully to consciousness-world union in my own immediate experience, which is much more accessible. However, unrestrained by this caveat, I will play the projection game for a bit, launch into a speculative transpersonal polemic, and put forward a modest counter hypothesis to the absolute acme theory.

The acme idea seems to me to rest on a big and unwarranted inflation. It speaks of a relatively permanent and well-established state of immediate participatory experience, of the dissolution of separate subject and object in a unitive field of interdependent subjective-objective awareness, as if it were an all-inclusive final identity with pure being, in which any kind of subject has entirely disappeared. But of course you can't identify and own this state without presupposing the subject that is supposed to be annihilated in it. Thus in Wilber's own words, with my italics:

> *You* realize that *your intrinsic being* is vast and open, empty and clear, and everything arising anywhere is arising *within you,* as intrinsic spirit, spontaneously. (Wilber, 1997: 47)

The mystic may insist that this appearance of a discriminating human subject is just an artefact of reporting the experience in everyday language, but is utterly transcended in the experience itself. This won't do, because identifying this state is not just a matter of reporting it after the event, but is part of its actual occurrence. If you can't identify and own the state while you are in it, then you certainly won't be able to do so afterwards, because it would have been equivalent to nothing but deep sleep.

The state clearly does not allow an isolated Cartesian subject. It clearly does include a participatory subject of a transfigured kind. As such it is both advanced and relatively limited. The mystics who have claimed to be in it have never claimed, as far as I am aware, to have equal access, via their participatory field, whether sensory or extrasensory, to remote galaxies as to their immediate local environment. What apologists for this state do with it, is to inflate its relative permanence, as *sahaj samadhi,* to its total inclusiveness. The subtle pathology of such unwarranted spiritual inflation needs a lot more attention than it has so far received (Rosenthal, 1987; Wilber, 1986).

To put it another way, the apologists fail to distinguish between a continuous feeling of the tacit inclusion of the whole cosmos in this state and an awareness of the explicit inclusion of that part of the cosmos that is immediately present here and now. They conflate the tacit whole with the explicit part. When Ramana Maharshi said 'the whole cosmos is contained in the heart', this distinction between tacit whole and explicit part is implicit. He was certainly not claiming an omniscient, complete and absolute conscious knowing, that is identical in equal measure and grasp, with every kind of form everywhere in the cosmos. So far as I am aware, there is no nondual mystic on record anywhere as ever advancing by one iota our knowledge of the form and process of the physical cosmos.

The nondual state claimed by oriental quietists, who specialize in the beatific annihilation of significant action, is an advanced yet One-sided state of cardiac arrest, the mystic heart in permanent suspension and stasis in the participatory field of immediate present experience. The idea that it is the end-state of spiritual development, the apotheosis of human destiny, the end of any sort of subject, the full and complete return of the One to the One, the absolute realization of the identity of ineffable formlessness and the infinitude of forms, is simply a pneumatic illusion, the final and most impressive defense against coming fully to terms with embodiment in a dipolar cosmos.

Ramana Maharshi, often proclaimed as a supreme modern exemplar of nondual attainment, achieved this state by a massive rejection of his own embodiment. At age 17, while perfectly healthy, he had a sudden pathological fear of death, fell on the floor and simulated being dead, and so awoke, he believed, to the self as spirit. He sustained this state by going off to sit in a dirty pit, attending to the One, while neglecting and abusing his life. He let his unwashed body rot, attacked by bugs and covered in sores, leaving it to others to provide some minimal care. Such sustained abuse of his body led to life-long asthma and arthritic rheumatism. While being consumed by terminal cancer, he said 'The body is itself a disease'. It seems to me to be an extreme case of spiritual projection to proffer this life-style as a model for the future spiritual development of mankind. His attainment was remarkable and undisputed, but it is also unacceptably One-sided. He achieved an intense state of spiritual consciousness at the cost of a sustained, repressive constriction of immanent spiritual life.

Western practitioner-teachers of oriental quietist meditation have experienced, in their own path, spiritual elevation at the expense of the body, emotions and relationship. They have later sought to correct this in themselves, and subsequently in their trainees. They then note that their oriental tradition gives them no guidance in the 'nuts and bolts' of such correction (Rothberg, 1996). This is not surprising, since the eastern originators of the method have pursued such elevation at the expense of embodiment as a virtue, and, unfettered by western notions of psychological integration, have sustained throughout their lives a complete denial of the claims of the body, emotions and relationship.

There is as yet no adequate pneumopathology, that is, no pathology of spiritual and subtle states of being that is not crudely reductionist in the manner of Freud, although a start has been made (in Scotton, Chinen and Battista, 1996). What we need is a pathology which allows that a person can be genuinely attuned to one aspect of god, but in a way which entails two errors: first, the experience is sustained in a fixated way that is a defense against attending to some other aspect of the divine; and therefore, second, it is claimed to be much more than it is, and is inflated to ultimate proportions. The problems with the classic nondual state are its monopolar fixation, its dissociation from active charismatic participation in the process of divine life and divine becoming, the deluded end-state claims made for it, its gender bias, and its internal association with spiritual authoritarianism. Here ends my polemic.

In the cartography that follows in the next chapter, the simple and readily accessible state in which there is immediate participatory awareness of the world, of being present in a unitive state in which subject and object are diune and not separate, in which there is no gap between consciousness and form, is placed at the present centre and starting point of the spiritual journey. The degrees of Being explicitly included in, and the duration of, this state, become modified as the journey proceeds. Such at any rate is the working hypothesis which the map represents.

6

A dipolar map of the spiritual and the subtle

This chapter presents the dipolar transpersonal map I have derived from lived inquiry and which I use to launch the preparation for a co-operative inquiry. I precede details of the map with some criteria for devising such a map, some organizing principles that may inform it, and a summary of its warrants. I follow a description of the map with two metaphors, the spiral and figure of eight, as further possible organizing principles, then consider democratizing features of the map and two complementary aspects of spiritual development.

Provisional criteria for a new map

Where does my brief review, in the previous chapter, of some current maps lead? Well, it leads me to the view that a sound map will *not* give an authoritative account of the predetermined return route to the divine. Rather it will modestly presuppose that what is going on in our cosmos is an undetermined, innovative process of divine becoming in which we are all immersed. The map will offer a range of possible options for a person's idiosyncratic path in a co-creative relation with this divine becoming. Some of these options, as states of being, will overlap with traditional mystical accounts; others will point to contemporary explorations. All of them will be provisional in status.

The map will seek to honour the experiential claims of both descent and ascent, and each of these with respect both to the interior and to the exterior aspects of our experience. The map may suggest fruitful developmental principles, as in the next section, for moving around the territory to which it refers, but will abjure wholesale prescriptions. In the last analysis it will honour a variety of routes, and will commend each person to ground their development in their own inner light and life. And the map will, in principle and in every respect, be open to revision as a function of experiential and reflective inquiry. More radically, the ultimate rationale of the map is to empower people to make explicit their own maps grounded in their own experiential knowledge.

Complementarity, dipolarity and integration

It follows from my conclusion to the last chapter, that my provisional map is going to centre on immediate present participatory experience of being-in-a-world, and thence expand in metaphorical terms of ascent and descent, of the heights and the depths, of the beyond and the within. So we may enlarge our present experience so that its wholeness and breadth now include what were hitherto transcendent states beyond it and immanent states within it. Transcendent states constitute a down-hierarchy, in which what is below emanates from what is above. Immanent states manifest an up-hierarchy, in which what is above emerges from what is below.

In the cartography below, I make a distinction between transcendent states 4 - 1 and immanent states 4 - 1. These emanating transcendent and emerging immanent states I feel to be dynamically interdependent, polar forms of complementary, conservative-innovative, cosmic process. Attunement to that which transcends immediate experience engages with expressive manifestation of that which is immanent within, indwells, immediate experience. And immediate present experience - the participative, subjective-objective participatory reality of everyday - is the home base, the common ground, the fulcrum, of this integration.

The focus that is immediate experience can expand - during high prayer, meditation, ritual, charismatic expression, creative and transformative action - to include what was erstwhile either transcendent or immanent, and may then contract again so that the transcendent and immanent become so again. If each contraction is a little less than the previous one than we get a gradual rhythmic expansion and developing wholeness. When the expansion reaches a certain point then we may expect a relatively permanent threshold awareness, so that immediate present experience always includes a gateway opening to the transcendent or to the immanent, or to both. What we can then say is that immediate present experience includes, via the gateways, an awareness of the latent presence of the infinite horizons of the transcendent, and the infinitude within of the immanent. Further gradual rhythmic expansion beyond gateway awareness makes this implicit presence progressively more explicit and stable within immediate experience.

The principles of complementarity, dipolarity and integration mean that, for example, when attending explicitly to immanent 3, transcendent 3 is always implicitly involved, and vice versa; and so on throughout the model. It also means that complementary states can be entertained together in dynamic and explicit integration, in order to empower and enhance each other. And, in principle, all nine states can, to a greater or lesser degree, be integrated within immediate human experience as one orchestrated whole. While for the unlimited immediate experience of divine being-as-such they are integrated in their everpresent totality.

These dynamic, organizing principles are, on the one hand, conjectural, a play with possibilities. On the other hand, they are practical working hypotheses which I find fruitful in my own spiritual path, and which I use to define where I am currently stabilized. They may or may not be fruitful for others, who may play with other possibilities. They certainly do not warrant any kind of spiritual projection from the reader.

Cartography as warranted belief

The map given below is a conjectural model, a working hypothesis, a provisional set of beliefs. I must here distinguish again between the two complementary ways in which I use the map. It is a provisional template for my own lived inquiry. And it is a mythic and imaginary template for the guided journey of opening which prepares participants to become co-inquirers into the spiritual and the subtle, as explained in Chapter 8.

These are two very different kinds of engagement with the map. In the first use, my personal commitment to an exploratory path gives the map more weight. In the second use, my commitment to provide orientation for others co-operatively to explore their own path and construct their own cartography, makes the presentation of the map much lighter. Thus I have not sought to make correlations between the spiritual or subtle focus of each inquiry reported in later chapters, and places on the dipolar map below. To do so would be to give the map more weight than it carries in an inquiry, as distinct from the journey of opening that precedes it.

It follows from the first use that the map does have some personal warrants. It is not mere arbitrary concoction. It derives from my lived inquiry, contemplative reflection and intuitive vision, and from my study of the literature of mysticism, psychical research and altered states of consciousness, including a range of other maps, ancient and modern. But by now it also has some very modest, very minimal public warrants, from field-testing earlier versions of it in transpersonal workshops, in journeys of opening, and, for me personally, in co-operative inquiries. To all this must be added current paradigm shifts in the physical and human sciences, in inquiry methods and in general epistemology. Cumulatively this adds up to a sufficient degree of warranted belief to legitimate initial cartography and further inquiry.

However, there is nothing authoritative about this map. It is provisional and relative to the context of its formation. It is a map of putative options, of the possible states and processes that I, and maybe other humans, can choose to articulate when I, and maybe they, participate in a hypothesized dipolar dynamic of creation.

A dipolar map of the spiritual and the subtle

I shall describe each area in the map as I experience it. If I use descriptive terms that others have used, this is because the meanings I ascribe to the terms best do justice to what I wish to recount. It does not indicate that I am quoting someone else, nor that I really know what other people meant by the terms. After my description, I will list terms and phrases from religious literature which possibly bear upon the same area, although, of course, I cannot be sure of this.

My lists of conjectural correspondences are of secondary significance and are only intended for interest and, perhaps, to aid general orientation. So the map is set, speculatively, in relation to at least some of the wider spiritual and subtle experience of humankind over the last two to three thousand years. But there is a fundamental caveat here. Who can be sure what all these people meant, *experientially,* by their various accounts, which have been in many cases translated from a language as it was used in another era and another culture? This is why it is not very fruitful either to spend a lot of time trying to set these correspondences up, or to give too much weight to them. Some of the allocations may be arbitrary and misplaced; but this, in my scheme of things, is both quite likely and not really very important.

Certainly, listing them here has nothing whatsoever to do with the idea of a perennial philosophy, which, as I explained in Chapter 2, I regard as a fallacy. One of my prepublication reviewers has said he doesn't see the need for the list, which he thinks is a bit contradictory with my overall approach and my critique of naïve universalism in spiritual studies. However, I still feel an obligation to show that I have had regard, within my limits, for at least some of the reported spiritual experiences and views of others.

Transcendent 4 **Experience of boundless ineffability** I find this area to be beyond the possibility of description in words, yet I have a keen wish to edge up to it with some paradoxical metaphors. It is boundless beyond space. It is light beyond differentiated light. It is supreme awareness beyond all determinate name and form. It is splendour beyond the ineffable. It is illustrious beyond majesty. It is ecstatic beyond bliss. It is pure act beyond any choice.

More soberly it is participative experience of the divine as transcendent and more-than-manifest spirit, the infinitude beyond. It relates, perhaps, to *Ain Soph Aur,* Hebrew for 'the limitless light', in the Kabbalah; to *sat-chit-ananda,* Sanskrit for being-consciousness-bliss, and to the state of *nirvikalpa samadhi,* in Indian mysticism; to the beatific vision in western mysticism; to 'pure act' in the writings of St. John of the Cross; to mystical absorption in the One in the writings of Plotinus.

Does my experience of this area involve the total disappearance of my personhood? No, otherwise how could I recall it and recount it. To be beyond my manifest being is not to annihilate it. It is simply to be beyond it.

Transcendent 3 **Opening to the transcendent Thou** Here I am in awed communion with a suprapersonal awareness, a subjectivity outpouring with creative process. I am Thou, the opening declaration from the height of being, the original light of the first sound emanating my subjectivity and its encompassing worlds.

This is a participative experience of the divine as transcendent spirit first manifest, the supreme creative source of all there is, the central sounding sun whence issue all our days, the word, the one speech. It relates, perhaps, to the demiurge of Plato in the *Timaeus*; to *nous,* first emanation from the One in Plotinus; to the *logos* of Philo of Alexandria; to the spiritual marriage of St. Teresa.

It is, I find, a Thou-I communion in which my personhood is utterly transfigured within the embrace of whence it issues.

Transcendent 2 **Invocation of archetypal powers and presences** In this area I encounter a mediation of powers by presences. Powers appear to be archetypal formative principles of creation. Presences are elevated, sublime superpersons, or so it would seem from the intensity of interfusion with them. What is striking here is the intimacy of communion in the absence of any superficial communication. Within this communion, the presences refract - in some numinous, luminous and sounding way - formative powers.

Here there is a participative experience of the divine manifest as the potencies and presences of subtle dimensions of being, that is, as refractions of the creative Thou. It relates, perhaps, to Plato's forms; to the powers of Philo; to the interpenetrating living intelligences of Plotinus's *nous*; to the *mundus imaginalis,* the *alam al-mithal* of the Sufis; to divine imaginals in the writings of Douglas Fawcett; to angel communion in the Christian tradition.

This, I note, is a very remarkable form of transcendental intersubjectivity. The communion of power-informed presences is in the mode of an intensely refined mightiness of love.

Transcendent 1 **Turning about to universal consciousness** This is the space where I turn about within the organizing self of ordinary consciousness and notice that this consciousness is continuous with what appears to be a vast backdrop of cosmic mind pervasive throughout creation - its oceanic upholding awareness. My everyday consciousness then seems like a local focus within this immense field. When I identify with the focus in a preoccupied manner, then I loose any sense of its locus within cosmic mind. When I turn about and let go of the identification, the cramp, then the limitless horizons of this greater awareness appear.

This I take to be participation in the divine as the *sustaining* mind of creation, as distinct from opening to the *originating* word of the creator, the logos (transcendent 3), and to its formative powers and presences (transcendent 2). It relates, perhaps, to *alaya-vijnana* in Tibetan Buddhism, cosmic store-consciousness; to the world-soul of Plato and Plotinus; to the over-soul of Emerson.

This space, I find, is the first most accessible doorway of transcendent cosmic intersubjectivity, where my subjectivity opens up to an immensely discreet field of awareness upholding what there is.

Fulcrum **Immediate present experience** Here, when I let go of any cramp within the focus of ordinary consciousness, rather than turning about and disattending from it, I attend to its intrinsic nature, its essential way of being-in-a-world, its heart. This is an immediate experience of being attuned within this situation now. I participate in a unitive field of being-in-a-world. I am in an immediate, local, relational, participatory subjective-objective reality, in which there is no gap between me as subject and what is around as object, between my perceiving and what I perceive, between my consciousness and the content and form with which it engages, between my resonant being and other present beings within the presence of Being. This local unitive field is full of these distinctions and motions without separateness. It is partial, capable of expansion and contraction, and is the explicit focus within a tacit field of infinite height, depth and extent. All transcendent and immanent states and processes are implicit in this multidimensional field.

This is participation in the divine as manifest in the immediate co-creation of my present reality. It is the here and now accessible being and body of the divine. It relates, perhaps and in different sorts of ways, to the following: I-Thou communion of persons with each other and with nature - reality being in relationship - in Martin Buber (1937); unitive ecstasy in the extralinguistic immediacy of perception in Jean Wahl (1953); pre-objective consciousness-nature union in Merleau-Ponty (1962); the mutuality of attunement and reciprocal engagement among humans, deities and nature in indigenous communities (Kremer, 1997); pre-conceptual spontaneous sensorial engagement with phenomena in David Abram (1996); 'the abiding in relationship' in Franklin Jones (Da Avabhasa, 1992); *sahaja,* the twinning of worldly existence and liberation, *samsara* and *nirvana*, in the

Sahajayana school of Tantric Buddhsim; the unbroken and spontaneously so *sahaj samadhi* in Ramana Maharshi; *tzu jan,* self-so-ness, the spontaneity of things, found with *wu wei,* non-cultivation of the mind, in Chuang Tzu and Taoism; *p'o,* the uncarved block, original simplicity, the world of free interfusion, in Taoism; *jen,* primordial human nature, no deliberate mind, in Neo-Confucianism.

I also find that this immediate present experience is dipolar. On the one hand there is the attuned state I have described: my unitive imaging of being-in-a-world and feeling everpresent mutual resonance with what there is here and now, with the immediate presence of Being. On the other hand there is a dynamic application. I manifest, in whatever modest degree, a charismatic, relational engagement with interpersonal, social and planetary change within everyday life. Oriental quietists, such as Chuang Tzu, suppress this dynamic component of immediate experience in favour of creative inaction, a restrictive nondual stasis of awareness. My own experience is that the living impulse to creative action continually rearranges, and challenges any fixity in, the participatory, unitive field, *and is its dynamic consummation.* Indeed, in action, persons-in-relation and world form a dynamic unity.

This active consummation I take to be full participation in the innovative process of divine becoming. This relates, perhaps, to Berdyaev's affirmation of human personhood as the creative process of divine spirit, self-determining subjectivity engaged in the realization of value and achieved in true community (*sobornost*); to Whitehead's process theology conceiving the divine as interacting with persons in the creative advance into novelty; to Hartshorne's dipolar theology in which an aspect of the divine is relative, contingent, changing and supremely active; to the *via creativa* and the *via transformativa,* the affirmation of human creativity, art as prayer, and the co-creation of a global civilization, in the creation spirituality of Matthew Fox (1983).

The concept of action as the apotheosis of personhood, which I have developed elsewhere (Heron, 1992, 1996a), relates to the Dewey's view that knowledge is an instrument for action rather than an object of disinterested contemplation (Dewey, 1929); and to Macmurray's theory that a person can't exist as a cognitive subject but only as an agent in whom all human capacities are employed - all cognition is for the action which consummates it (Macmurray, 1957). Macmurray also held that persons, who only exist as agents, can therefore only properly think of the world as a unity of action.

In my immediate present experience, when uncramped, my personhood is both grounded in participative modes of being and also consummated in significant action, in relation with other persons who are similarly engaged, or who are in the process of becoming similarly engaged. And immediate present experience, as here defined, is the starting point of transcendent and immanent explorations and the fulcrum of an extended dipolarity. It flows and expands into transcendent 1 and immanent 1, and beyond.

Immanent 1 **Grounding in spatiotemporal presence** Here I am being intentional about going deeper into my embodiment, about manifesting the indwelling life of spirit. I space and time myself, participating in space and time as matrices of embodiment, co-creating current matrices with the emergence of indwelling spiritual life. My activities here from time to time include *some* items from each of the following:

- Intentional movement and posture: charismatic presence, stance and bearing; charismatic gesture, movement and dance; spatial orientation and relation with others; *mudras, asanas* and sacred postures; various forms of conscious movement training such as Tai Chi and Aikido; Alexander technique and other forms of postural and motor integration.
- Intentional timing and toning of the voice, and making other sounds: modulating speech between charismatic time and clock time, varying rhythm, emphasis and emotional tone; singing, toning and chanting; overtone chanting; drumming, percussion, improvised instrumental rhythmic sound.
- Intentional breathing or *pranayama,* such as aware breath, rebirth breath, *soham* breath, solar and lunar breath, energy breath, hyperventilation.
- Intentional rhythmic bodywork and energy work.
- Intentional catharsis, rhythmic emotional cleansing and healing.
- Intentional creation: generating participatory knowledge, art, and ritual, in spatiotemporal forms of language, sound, music, motion, line, colour, and shape.
- Intentional participation in the rhythms of living, working and loving: waking and sleeping, activity and relaxation, eating and fasting, sexuality and celibacy, creativity and lying fallow, coming and going, togetherness and separation, communality and privacy; and to the physical, energy, social and psychic rhythms of the day, the week, the month, the year and its seasons, and longer cycles.

These activities relate, variously, to: intentional everyday living, including work, participatory science, artistic expression, and human relationships of all kinds; to charismatic, expressive, interactive spiritual practices; and to a range of personal development practices, too numerous to mention in detail here, which have proliferated in recent decades, and can be found in the programmes of innumerable growth centres.

I take all this to be participation in the divine as immanent spiritual life, emerging as time-space matrices. Participating in matrix time means intending a whole sequence including its past, present and future phases. It means an active mastery of rhythmic processes, periodicities, cycles. Participating in matrix space means intending the total movement and gesture of the body and its spatial surround felt all at once, from within. It is volume actively intended, from being inside it, in all three dimensions simultaneously. Time-space matrices are living forms of indwelling spiritual life, of the dance of *shakti.* We intend them and join in their fullness, as co-creators in charismatic, interactive, expressive and often healing ways of being.

These holistic spatiotemporal patterns include synchronicities, Tantric windows and doorways, in which the time-space frame of our now and here experience becomes revelatory with quite specific and pointed symbolic meaning.

In this area, immanent 1, I find that personhood is empowered from within, complementary to its transfiguration from beyond, which is what seems to go on in the transcendent areas.

Immanent 2 **Evocation of subtle energies within nature** Here I am calling forth, and participating in, subtle energies dormant within, or coiled up within the human system and natural phenomena. I am evoking the finer forces within the human system, the living energies of indwelling *shakti,* the creatrix, variously called kundalini, chi, prana, mana, odylitic force, bioenergy, psychic currents, psychic centres, chakras. The evocation is for a variety of empowering and transforming purposes. I have only a modest experience of the first three purposes given below, very little of the last, except for the first item included under it.

- Evocative ritual, using speech, sound (mantras and chanting, overtone chanting, singing, drumming and other kinds of percussion, music), movement and dance to arouse and activate the subtle energy of the human beings involved, and interweave it with the subtle energies of colour, scent, symbolic artefacts, the elements, various physical substances, plants, the earth, moon and sun, and so on.
- The evocation of intrasensory perception in which subtle perceptions transform ordinary experiences such as moving, touching, gazing, retinal lights, listening, visualizing, dreaming.
- The evocation of extrasensory, spatiotemporal extensions of consciousness such as telepathy, clairvoyance, clairaudience, precognition, retrocognition and transtemporal regresssion, out-of-the-body experience, projection and identification. These extrasensory extensions may apply within this reality and/or lead over into other realities.
- The evocation of psychokinesis and psychoid events: the projection of subtle energy for physiological healing and for psychological and behavioural benefit; reshaping and moving physical objects; impressions on photographic plates; levitation; bilocation; materialization and dematerialization, including ectoplasm and apports; firewalking; penetration of the flesh without pain or bleeding; psychic surgery; stigmata; body luminosity; invisibility; supernormal athletic feats; physical mediumship generating raps, music, voices, touches, gusts, smells; poltergeists; UFOs; and so on.

All this I take to be participating in the divine manifest as subtle process active or potential within the domain of human embodiment. It relates to the whole field of psychical research in its many different aspects, from the study of subtle energy systems and their relevance to medicine (Gerber, 1988), to seeing the deceased in a dimly lit mirror in a psychomantium (Moody, 1993). It is ripe for further development by the use of co-operative inquiry.

Whereas in immanent 1 personhood is empowered by being intentional within time-space matrices, here in immanent 2 it is empowered by subtle energies explicitly evoked within those matrices.

Immanent 3 **Opening to impulses of the immanent spirit** In this area I open to the inner depths, to the ground, the foundation of my everyday experience, to the seedbed, well-spring and source within that ground. It means opening to the inner spiritual and subtle womb, in the belly of my being, where the generative potency of immanent spirit, divine life, dwells. This womb is the locus of my potential, the source and seedbed of options and possibilities. What emerges from it, when I open to it, are periodic impulses, life-prompts, innovations, proactions, responses and reminders, about my personal action and development within the great web of interbeing, itself compounded of a vast mesh of rhythms and periodicities of diverse frequencies. These periodic creative life impulses may be spontaneous and unbidden, or in response to my soliciting of them. In either case, I shape and frame them as much as they enact me.

This I take to be participating in the divine as first manifest emergent from the pregnant void. By this I mean indwelling spiritual entelechy, a sacred soil at the root of personhood, a formative potency within the psyche. It may prompt stages of personal growth, commitment to social change, transpersonal unfoldment. It may prompt the content and timing of specific actions. It may offer options for choice, or declarations for the unitive framing of experience. It may deliver a sense of the fitting and the situationally appropriate. It may unfold as a feel for aesthetic patterns in time and space, including the patterning of implicit speech in discriminating human judgements. It may guide inner regression and emotional healing. It is maculate, contingent, relative both to the limiting situations within which it occurs and to my shaping and selective co-creating of its offerings.

All this relates, perhaps, to Whitehead's notion of the temporal divine as the great companion who works 'slowly and quietly by love'; to *shekinah,* the indwelling, immanent presence of the divine in Jewish mysticism; to the notion of godseed and entelechy in Jean Houston (1987); to the practice of experiential focusing developed by Gendlin (1981); to bio-spirituality and experience of divine grace in the body (McMahon and Campbell, 1991); to the practice of E-Therapy (Kitselman, 1953); to the Subud *latihan.*

This, I find, is intersubjectivity at depth, grounded in the continuous living generative womb of embodiment.

Immanent 4 **Experience of the pregnant void** Here I enter primordial emptiness pregnant with all existence, the nonmanifest infinitude within, the centre of nonbeing which is anywhere and everywhere and nowhere from which all beings emerge, the intrinsic vacancy of all forms and processes.

Here I participate, if that is the word, in the divine as within-the-manifest, as empty ground. It relates, perhaps, to experience of the metacosmic void in Grof's subjects (Grof, 1988); or, more dubiously, to *sunyata,* the universal void, in Mahayana Buddhism.

This, I find, is a profoundly interior liberation.

The spiral and figure of eight

The provisional map I have presented has, as I have said, two purposes. First, as a template for my own lived inquiry into the spiritual and the subtle. Second, as a comprehensive launching framework, preparing people for a co-operative inquiry.

With respect to my lived inquiry, I have two convenient metaphors for processes involving the content of this map, a spiral and a figure of eight.

The spiral represents immediate present experience expanding into one or more levels of the immanent and the transcendent. The spiral shown below, figure 6.1, is a metaphor for progressive development, showing an increasing and relatively stable inclusion of the various levels in immediate present experience over time. The model is meant to be suggestive only, a fillip to my creative imagination, and is certainly not to be taken as prescriptive for anyone else.

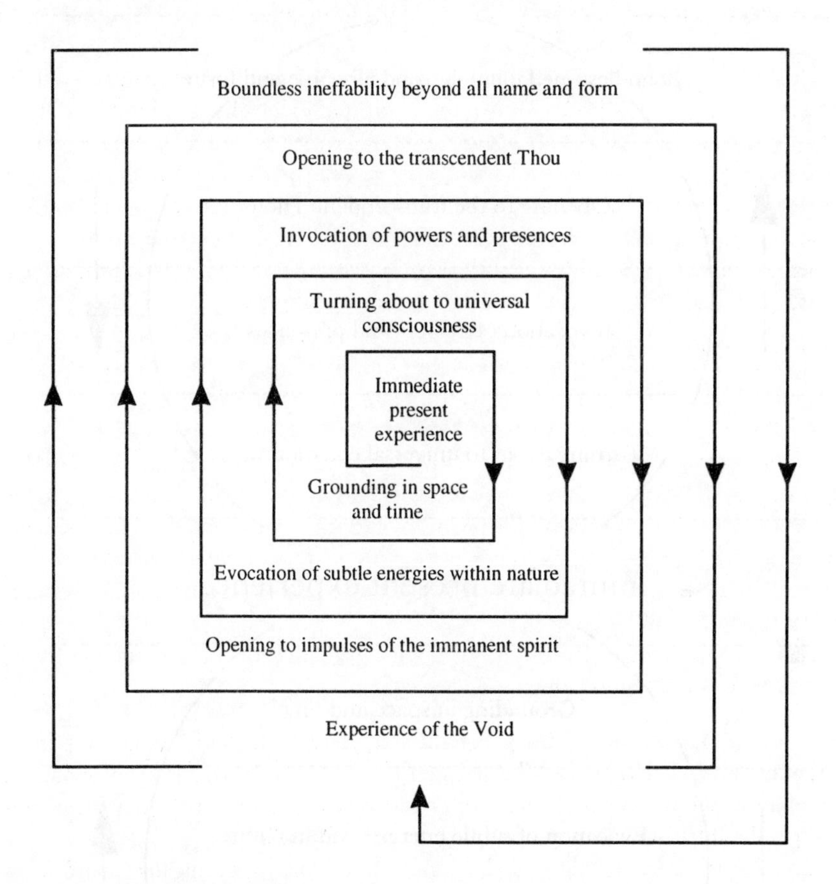

Figure 6.1 *The spiral metaphor*

What it suggests is first be fully attuned here and now, in immediate present experience, in participative awareness of being-in-a-world. Then I have a choice. I can simply dwell without distraction in the fullness of my immediate enactment of being-in-a-world, and creatively engage with any transformative tendencies that may or may not emerge within it. Or I can engage in intentional transformation: ground myself in immanent 1, rise to transcendent 2, ground in immanent 2, rise to transcendent 3, and continue so in expanding spiral loops. I can, of course, draw innumerable other loops, circuits and spirals, each one representing some particular expansion of immediate present experience within one specific practice. Each loop could go any which way over the map, covering any one or more parts of it. Also spiral inclusion need not be sequential but can be simultaneous.

I have found that it works well to use a spiral sequence when using the map in the journey of opening that leads into a co-operative inquiry. It seems to generate confidence and stability by first practising non-separate awareness of participating

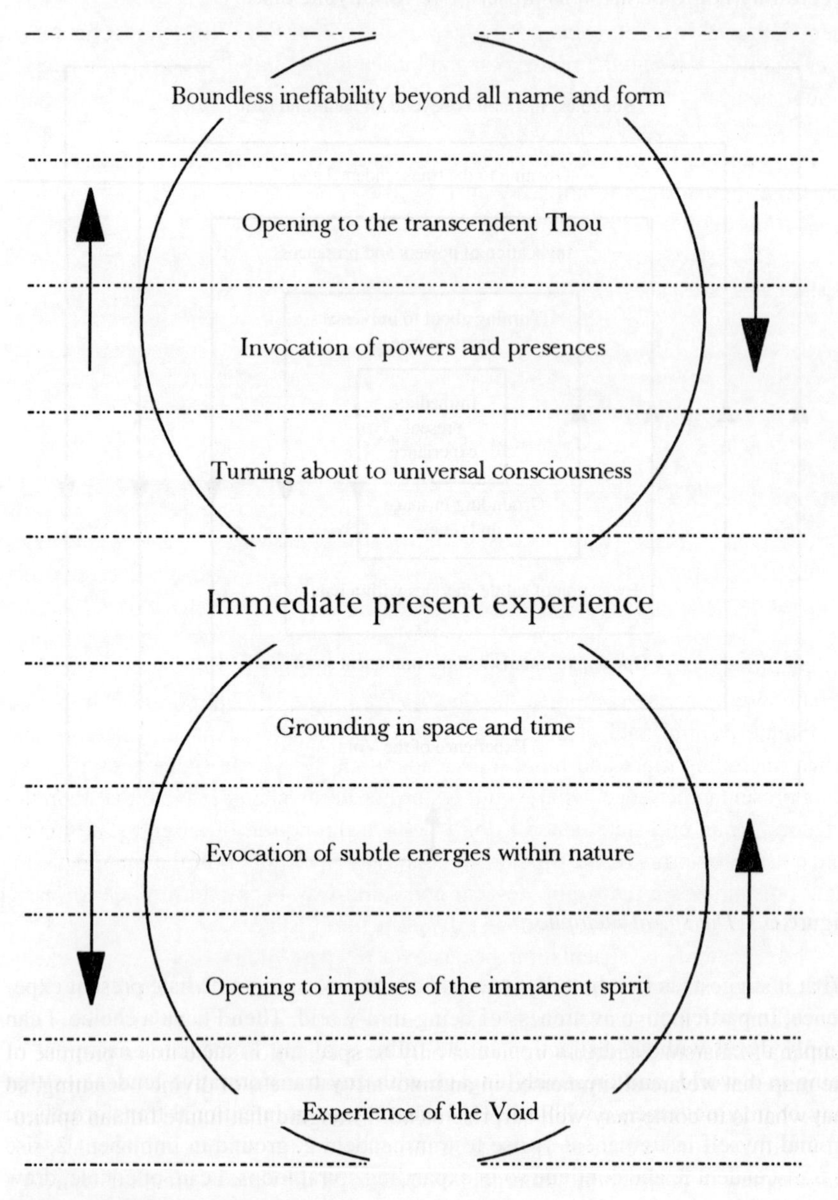

Figure 6.2 *Figure of eight metaphor*

in the immediate perceptual field, then moving into exercises in spatiotemporal presence, intentionally timing and spacing oneself, then turning about in the centre of ordinary consciousness to attend to universal mind, and so on.

The spiral suggested above is not the same as Washburn's spiral of development, in which the ego in early life separates up and out from, and represses, the dynamic ground that is spirit, then in later life regresses down into the dark night of working through the repression, re-connects with its spiritual ground, then rises up again in a phase of regeneration in spirit. I have a somewhat similar developmental theory in *Feeling and Personhood,* in which the self-creating person is busy working through the repression and buried distress of the compulsive person, established early in life, before moving on to unfold spiritual potentials as the self-transfiguring person (Heron, 1992).

The spiral in the dipolar map above is entirely within the later phase of self-transfiguring and regeneration in spirit. So it is more like Richard Moss's 'movement from the heart downward and upward in an ever-widening spiral'.

> As I regard the awakening process, it is far more valid to think in spherical terms than in the linear and hierarchical terms common to the older traditions...By imagining the sphere to be gradually expanding from the heart - the symbolic center of being - we can envision a far more dynamic process of evolution in which the higher and the lower centers are simultaneously included in an ever-expanding realm of dynamic polarities. (Moss, 1986: 202)

The figure of eight metaphor, figure 6.2, shows a continuous circuit of energies which goes on subliminally all the time irrespective of whether I am conscious of any of it or not. It mirrors the flow of blood through the physical heart, looping simultaneously up to the arms, neck and head and down to the trunk and legs. Both streams mix in their return into the heart. Then as it exits the heart the mix goes both on the upward and the downward loop.

Figure 6.3 below is another way of setting out, in figure of eight form, some implications of the dipolar map presented in this chapter.

Suppose someone combined the underlying figure of eight circuit with an approximately spiral path of development around this map, expanding out, up and down, including more and more transcendent and immanent states within immediate present experience, what would his or her future state be? Note that I am not referring to an end-state, since I don't believe the notion of an end-state makes much sense in terms of the dipolar process theology implicit in the map. An end-state presupposes a theocratic descent and same-way-back return model of creation. But we can speculate about an advanced future-state.

And it can only be speculation, because for my part I do not know of any exemplars of such a state. The great mystics of the past were all monopolar in their aspirations and practices. Similarly the great moderns following old traditions like Ramana Maharshi. Furthermore, it can only be speculation since it is a premise of the map that we are all immersed in an innovative process of divine becoming, so that what is to come may well surprise us all. I imagine that future human spirituality will be much more surprising than future technology. However, in the previous chapter, in the section 'Emergent evolution as intrinsic to creation' there's a sketch of some conjectures about future spirituality, and I refer the reader to that.

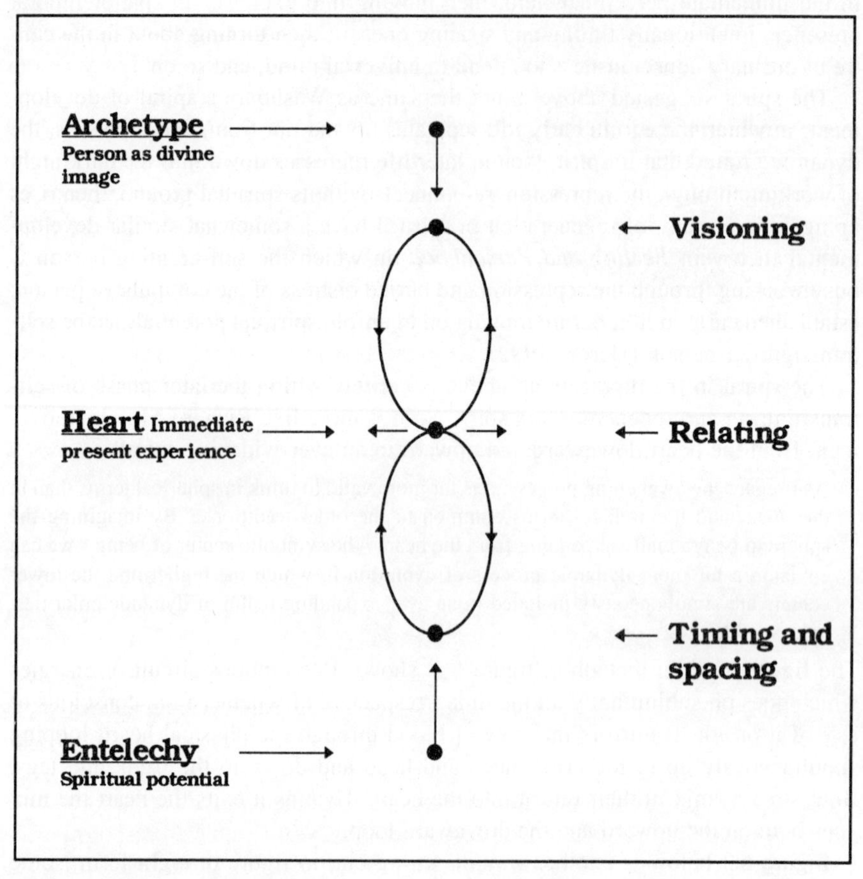

Figure 6.3 *Figure of eight circuit*

Spiritual democratization and spiritual development

The map I have presented does appear to have overlap, on the transcendent side, with traditional maps. I say 'appear to' simply because of my view, several times stated, that we cannot be sure what traditional maps are actually pointing to. It would, I suppose, be odd if there were not some sort of overlap. Traditional mystical practices and beliefs contain a huge repository of experience, know-how, and penetrating insight. I have learnt and assimilated a large amount from them, at any rate as construed by the authority, the revelation, within. Where my map differs is with respect to the dipolarity of its path, opening to immanent spiritual life complementing aspiration to transcendent spiritual consciousness, and to its premise of inquiry as initiation.

The diverse historical mystics, east and west, have been monopolar *in their practice,* focusing on an absolute overriding reality, whether in terms of the classical theism of Christianity, or of the acosmic pantheism of Hinduism and Buddhism. They have no feel, in the developmental process, for the contemporary claims of panentheistic, dipolar theology. They unfurl a transcendent spiritual consciousness at the expense of an indwelling charismatic-expressive life: the latter is subordinate to, and is restrictively harnessed as fuel for, the former. My map seeks to affirm both the relative autonomy of these two poles and their deep complementarity and interdependence.

As we have seen, instead of positing *absolute* nondual awareness as the concluding attainment, it commends and demystifies the *relative* diune awareness of immediate present experience as the accessible here-and-now locus of participatory relationship. It is no big deal to attend to the simple fact that there is no separation, no gap, between perceiver, perceiving and perceived, that they are interfused distinctions within a local unitive field that has infinite horizons and interiority. In this relative sense, in the very process of being-in-the-world, everyone has already got it. And can continuously get more of it by opening up the dipolar context of this immediate process.

So there is a sort of spiritual democratization at work in my map, and this is closely related to its premise of inquiry as initiation. As I have said already, traditional mystical schools draw central elements of patriarchy and authoritarianism from the cultural context of their founding. Their beliefs and practices are codified in terms of established theology and methodological protocols, upheld by the authority of a lineage of established teachers, who direct the initiation of the novices. Directed initiation means that the novice continuously heeds the external authority of an experiential tradition and so gets unawarely fixated in a state of spiritual projection. Inquiry-based initiation, by contrast, means that each person heeds the authority of their inner light and life in the context of their original relation to the presence of Being.

So we get a do-it-yourself spirituality, both individually, in peer support and inquiry groups, and in an emerging self-generating culture, on the crest of innovative divine becoming. This do-it-yourself approach does not throw out traditional maps. On the contrary, they constitute a vital secondary source of data for revisionary maps with which to launch an inquiry. The primary source is the deconstructed inner life and light of personal experience and reflection, in dialogue with others similarly engaged, and with relevant issues in contemporary spiritual and psychological studies.

All this raises a question about the nature and means of spiritual development. My own view is that it is dipolar, to do both with the transformation of consciousness and with moral life committed to the empowerment of other people, the full flowering of their immanent life; and that the latter is a consummation of the former. The tendency of the eastern mystic has been to reduce his involvement with other people to directing the vertical transformation of their consciousness. His commitment to his own transformation as an end-in-itself overflows into guiding other people to do the same. His moral goal has been to enable the unenlightened to become enlightened and so attain *moksha,* release from the treadmill of reincarnation in the phenomenal world, regarded for the most part as an illusion grounded on ignorance, want of discrimination.

However, I regard the phenomenal world as an innovative process of divine becoming, within which we humans are co-creators of global transformation, a planetary civilization. On this view, my moral life has two interdependent aspects, primary and secondary. The secondary and supportive aspect is that it works to foster and facilitate, with others, the inner transformation of human consciousness, so that we may celebrate the multi-dimensional fullness of creation, not so that we can get release from it all.

The primary aspect is that it works to release the life-potential of persons in relation, to facilitate social empowerment and social justice in every sphere of human activity. For persons to become full co-creators of a planetary civilization, each one has an all-pervasive right to participate in any decision that affects the fulfilment of their needs and interests, the expression of their preferences and values. This universal right has a claim not only within political institutions, but in every sphere of human association where decisions are being taken: in industry, education, ecology, medicine, the family, and, of course, in research and in religion. The fulfilment of this claim throughout our planet in all theses spheres has hardly begun.

Moreover, the fact that there is so much spiritual authoritarianism in the world, in creeds and cults both old and new, creates a deep attitudinal warp in people which makes them susceptible to oppression by many other kinds of external authority. In reviewing criticisms of the traditional hierarchical model of spiritual reality, promoted by current adherents of the perennial philosophy, Rothberg writes:

> Hierarchical ontologies are commonly ideological expressions of social and psychological relations involving domination and exploitation - of most humans (especially women, workers, and tribal people), of nature, and of certain parts of the self. Such domination limits drastically the autonomy and potential of most of the inhabitants of the human and natural worlds, justifying material inequalities and preventing that free and open discourse which is the end of a free society. It distorts psychological life by repressing, albeit in the name of wisdom and sanctity, aspects of ourselves whose full expression is necessary to full psychological health and well-being. (Rothberg, 1986: 16)

My spiritual development, then, cannot be measured simply in terms of hours of meditation or number of extended retreats or stabilized attainment of some inner, transcendent state of mind, as I ascend the hierarchical spiritual ladder. On its own, this is vertical flight from full spiritual development, which I believe finds its primary consummation in the unfolding of my immanent spiritual life. And this, fully followed through, involves attention to social change and social justice through promoting participative forms of decision-making in every kind of human association with which I am involved, including the religious. I continue this theme at the outset of the next chapter.

7

Methods for the second form of spiritual transformation

In this chapter I describe further the two complementary forms of spiritual transformation, and present a range of methods relating to the second of these forms. I reflect on three modes of trained attention, and end the chapter with a critique of some aspects of Buddhist doctrine and practice.

Spiritual transformation

Spiritual transformation of human beings has two complementary forms, which I introduced at the end of the last chapter. The first form is about how persons realize in their exterior daily lives their immanent spiritual life and its potential. I believe this means developing the fulness of relational living, of expressive personal autonomy-in-connectedness, in terms of:

- Emotional and interpersonal competence: empowering self, the other and the relationship.
- The exercise of self-determination and co-operation in every situation of decision-making.
- The external expression of imaginative, creative skills.
- Commitment to social and planetary transformation.
- The grounding of life-style management in a co-creating relation with immanent spiritual life.

The second form is about how people open to a progressive interior transfiguration by a transcendent spiritual consciousness interdependent with immanent spiritual life. I believe this is secondary to, supportive of, and consummated in, the first form. I have, in a range of earlier books, contributions to books and articles, written about some aspects of the first form in the fields of education, group facilitation, counselling, research, management, medicine, professionalism and so on. In this chapter, I write about the second form: methods of inner transformation by opening to transcendent-immanent, spiritual consciousness-life.

Method, route and knack

How can this inner transformation of consciousness-life be brought about? Recent evidence in my hand, from personal inquiry and group work, suggests that access by any one individual to one or more of the states on the dipolar map on Chapter 6 is available by several routes, all of which in their different ways release the restrictive cramp in everyday consciousness, so that it opens to its higher, wider and deeper context. The methods given below are not mutually exclusive. Some inherently overlap; others can be brought to interpenetrate and combine in various ways. And they are certainly not exhaustive. I have not made correlations between methods and states. This is best left to discovery. It is important, I suggest, to grasp that there are many other methods than dissociative meditation of the eastern tradition or classic high prayer of the western tradition.

One account of the following map is that it is a route map. It presents possible ways into the states on the previous map. However, the metaphor of a route suggests a journey, a going from one place to another, and this is perhaps rather misleading, since it can set up a mental set of searching, striving, trying to get to a place where one is not. But suppose you are already tacitly in all of these states, then it is not a route you need, but a simple knack or know-how to allow the tacit to become explicit. So here is a description of some useful tacit-to-explicit knacks.

Tacit-to-explicit knacks

Recollection. You wake yourself up from your slumber in cramped states of being and remind yourself of your inherent inclusion in a wider context. Your mind reMinds itself. It recollects its continuity with cosmic mind. This self-remembering of a transcendent spiritual consciousness in you is the core of inner spiritual discrimination, of judgements of spiritual value and validity.

Regeneration. The polar correlate of reMinding is reLiving. You uncover the dynamic of immanent spiritual life through full creative openness to the process of breathing, through spontaneous autogenic movement or posture and sound, through fresh sensorial engagement within your world, in short through intentionally unstudied celebration of your embodiment. The processes mentioned are all co-creative. They are voluntary-involuntary. They involve your intentionality in congress with given life-process. This regeneration of immanent spiritual life is the ground of a felt sense of the fitting, the contextually relevant and apt.

Recollection and regeneration spontaneously combine in the process of opening to the inherently participative nature of immediate present experience of being-in-a-world, which I have described in several places in previous chapters, and which I include below as 'present centering'.

Attention. You retrain attention, so that instead of being fluctuating and chaotic, at the beck and call of inner and outer events, it becomes constant. And by virtue of this constancy it becomes a doorway to wider realities. The constancy is to do with two things: what is being attended to and how it is being attended to. And each of these in turn have two forms. You can attend to the contents of the mind as a whole, or you can attend to some particular chosen content of the mind. In either case, your attention can be a witness only, disengaged, not doing anything with or to the content; or it can participate creatively in a self-generating, developmental process emerging in and with the content. So we have:

- Constant witnessing, with wide-aperture attention, unmoved and unmediated, of all contents.
- Constant witnessing, with focused attention, unmoved and unmediated, of a particular chosen content.
- Constant creative participation, with wide-aperture attention, both unmoved and unmediated in itself, and also moved by and mediating a developmental process within the mind as a whole.
- Constant creative participation, with focused attention, both unmoved and unmediated in itself, and also moved by and mediating a developmental process within some chosen content.

The first two of these comprise the twin pillars of traditional eastern meditation: mindfulness and concentration (Goleman, 1988; Washburn, 1995). They are characterized by sustained hands-off attention, unmoved and unmediated. Such attention has a monopolar focus, concerned with the nature of awareness as such. The second two are evident in some ancient approaches, also in distinctively contemporary approaches, such as several items which follow in this list. They are characterized by sustained attention, which is dipolar, both hands-off and hands-on, transcendent and immanent. As open to transcendent awareness, it is unmoved and unmediated in itself. As engaged with immanent life, it is moved by and mediating embedded entelechy, that is, indwelling developmental potential. Such dipolar attention interrelates sustained awareness and dynamic process. The next main section below, after this list of methods, explores further these distinctions.

It is also interesting to note that each of these four methods can be exercised in an extravertive or an introvertive mode. The former means that the eyes are open and that the content of attention includes the sensory field. The latter means that the eyes are closed and that attention is paid to the interior landscape. Extravertive creative participation, with focused attention, overlaps with Goethe's practice of what he called concrete vision or exact sensorial imagination. By this he meant a deep intuitive and intensive participation in the imaginal form and development of what he was perceiving. Thus he would imaginatively reconstruct, while busy indwelling the process of perceiving a plant, its whole way of unfolding its form. At the same time he would grasp the dynamic, archetypal principles informing this unfolding (Bortoft, 1986).

Contemplation. A deep intuitive-reflective considering of, and dwelling on, the attributes and nature of a state which gently transforms into being in it, or doing it.

Imagination. This is one of the simplest routes. You imagine you are in a selected state, on the basis of a clear description of it and a felt sense of it. You do not try to enter it; you do not seek to go from where you are now to where you think the state may be. There is no seeking or striving or effort to make a trip. You simply image and feel being in it, and go with the imaging and feeling as they unfold. If you like, you just pretend to be in it, in an inner theatre of the mind. This seems to disarm the habitual defensive pretense that you are not in it, so then you realize that you are. If external action is involved, then the same principle applies: the action unfolds from you imagining you are in its concomitant state of being. This leads to:

Expression. Using improvised and spontaneous speech, sound, gesture, posture and movement you express your felt sense of a selected area described in the state map. You become a state by expressing being in it. This is at the same time an on-the-hoof experiential inquiry into it, so you may change your charismatic expression of the state in order more fully to honour your exploration of it. It can be done as solo lived inquiry. It also works well done in pairs, either interacting, or each person taking an expressive turn with the supportive sustained attention of the other. I have called this method co-creating: it is discussed further in Chapter 19.

Image-streaming. Evoking with eyes closed, and verbalizing, a spontaneous stream of imagery, following this with intuitive interpretation, can uncramp ordinary awareness and open it up to its wider spiritual context (Wenger, 1991). This is the same as active imagination, out-loud conscious dreaming, which Jung recommended to westerners rather than meditation (Jung, 1936). The spontaneous stream can be entirely unstructured; or it can be released under a chosen category, state or theme. A variation is externally guided imagery, when a helper takes the receptive subject on an inner journey, as in psychosynthesis (Assagioli, 1965).

Aspiration. High prayer in the western mystical tradition, such as St. Teresa's prayer of recollection. It involves an intentional dynamic inclination of the will towards transcendent consciousness, an attitude of opening, surrender, attentive awaiting on and receptivity to higher spiritual power. Washburn thinks that while such prayer is different to eastern meditation in having this attitudinal relation to the divine, it otherwise has the same basic feature of unmoving and unmediated attention (Washburn,1995: 155-57). My own experience of this one is that the attention involved, while deeply constant, is engaged and participating in the aspirational process.

Present centering. Being in the fullness of the heart, in the presence of Being, here and now in a unitive relation with other beings in the immediate experiential spatiotemporal field. The heart-centred spontaneous integration of reMinding and reLiving, or recollection and regeneration, the first two on this list.

Inward opening. This is practising descent to indwelling, immanent life, an opening inwards and downwards to the spiritual womb of the psyche, feeling into its guiding pregnancy, listening to and shaping its embedded and embodied motions and declarations.

Entrainment. When you are with group of persons feeling each other's presence, entering into mutual resonance or entrainment, in which you all share brain-waves, breathing and other rhythms and vibrate in harmony, then a range of spiritual and subtle transformations may occur for you within the entrained state.

Charismatic disinhibition. During group entrainment, and if people have given themselves and each other permission beforehand, then one outcome, at a moment when all feel there is a subtle shift in the process, can be a simultaneous interactive improvisation of spontaneous movement and sound, gesture and posture, which celebrate, reveal and bear witness to a range of spiritual and subtle transformations. This practice manifests the dynamic of divine creation.

Ritual. A more formal and structured use of group interaction, using speech, sound, music, symbols, gesture, posture and movement, to interrelate different parts of the map for a variety of transformative purposes, personal, cultural and planetary. It may incorporate both invocation and evocation.

Holotropic therapy. The combination of hyperventilation, focused bodywork and music, used in a workshop setting (Grof,1988). More generally, intentional **breathing** of which there many different ancient and modern kinds.

Energizing. In a group setting, people take it in turn in a small support group, to sustain continuous dancing or singing for several hours, in order to break down physical and psychical armouring and open to transformational processes (Moss,1986). More generally, **bodywork,** static or receptive or active, of which there many different ancient and modern kinds.

Sensory deprivation. The classic method is to float for some hours in saline water just above body temperature in a tank which eliminates all visual and auditory stimuli (Lilly, 1972).

Psychedelic drugs. Including LSD-25, psilocybin from the Mexican sacred mushroom, mescaline sulphate from the peyote cactus, dipropyltryptamine, 5-methoxy-DMT, harmaline, the amphetamines (MDMA, DOM, 2-CB0), ketamine hydrochlorid. The mapping of spiritual and subtle states done by Grof from the reports of subjects using these drugs under his medical supervision, and from his own experience of using them, is more comprehensive than, and free of the doctrinal bias in, the maps of traditional mystical schools (Grof, 1975, 1988).

This list does not claim to be exhaustive, but as it stands it provides a substantial agenda for individual lived inquiry and co-operative inquiry.

Consciousness, life and trained attention

Suppose, as I do, that spirit is dipolar, consciousness-life, that the two poles of consciousness and life are always co-involved and interdependent, and, furthermore, that humans in their own spirit, their own consciousness-life, can weight the interdependence toward either pole. So if life dominates consciousness we get sensationalism; and if consciousness dominates life, we get asceticism. If you engage too much with the life-rich contents of consciousness you are swept along in a restless activism. If your consciousness ascetically disengages too much from its contents, you ignore, and so suppress, their spiritual potential for fuller flowering.

Most mystical traditions, western and eastern, have been monopolar in their practices, as I pointed out earlier. They seek a transcendent consciousness and they do this by dissociation from life, that is, by a tendency to asceticism and very reduced relation to embodiment. This is evident into modern times, from St. John of the Cross in the sixteenth century to Ramana Maharshi in the twentieth.

It is also evident in some of the main methods used. Take two classic forms of eastern meditation which have also received much attention in the west: mindfulness and concentration, mentioned under 'attention' in the map of knacks. Mindfulness is wide-aperture attention paid constantly to the mind and its contents as a whole, concentration is focused attention paid constantly to one chosen item. Both involve being disengaged, that is, not interfering with, working on, manipulating, the content, which is only to be witnessed in a sustained way. This I call dissociative meditation: the core of it is non-attachment. It is a method designed to flee the Many and find the One.

Now spiritual life resides in the contents, and under appropriate conditions will commence spontaneously to evolve the contents toward greater opening and greater integration, like a flower unfolding in itself and at the same time in symbiotic relation with its ecological setting. The contents' embedded entelechy, formative potential, will start to actualize itself.

Dissociative meditation both fully attends to, and disengages from any management of, the contents of the mind and their immanent life-process. But it clearly has an impact on the life-process of the contents and sets its energy in motion. To put it crudely, it sucks the energy of the life-process up into the disengaged awareness to empower it and stabilize it. It interrupts the internal development of the contents and displaces energy from their immanent unfoldment to a transcendent enhancement of sustained attention: as with *kundalini* ascending, in Tantrism.

The complementary interior activity is to engage empathically with the life-process of the contents of consciousness, to infuse them with the light of the mind and so empower their developmental potential. This redirects the expansive tendency of consciousness and converts it into the immanent unfoldment of its contents. This disciplined and passionate engagement with the mental Many honours their divine status. It includes the interior, creative imagination of the musician, artist, scientist, social reformer and others. It leads over, of course, into the first, and externally expressive, form of spiritual transformation, which I outlined at the start of this chapter.

Somewhere between the poles there is a potent zone of radical and dynamic interdependence. You disengage from driven, compulsive attention and open consciousness to its cosmic context with constancy. At the same time you attend empathically to, and engage creatively with, the spiritual potential of the contents of consciousness, so that you and they unfold in a unitive dipolar field of spiritual development, in which life and consciousness enhance each other. In this dipolar zone, you both reMind yourself about your continuity with transcendent spiritual consciousness, and reLive yourself in a co-creative relation with immanent spiritual life. There is an interested integration of non-attachment with appropriate passion for manifest being.

You thus combine recollection and regeneration, which open the list of methods in the previous section. You are an active epiphany of the Many-One now. This works well, I find, in charismatic interaction with other persons similarly engaged, as in co-creating, described under expression in the methods above.

There have, of course, been precursors, both west and east, of this kind of dipolar practice, although they are rarely charismatic-interactive. They include 'the mental-subtle manipulations of Jewish mysticism, the sophisticated visualizations or dream-yoga of Tibetan Buddhism, Chinese energy practices, etc.' (Ferrer, 1998d). But eastern practices currently much in vogue in the west, such as transcendental meditation and *vipassana,* are of what I call the dissociative kind.

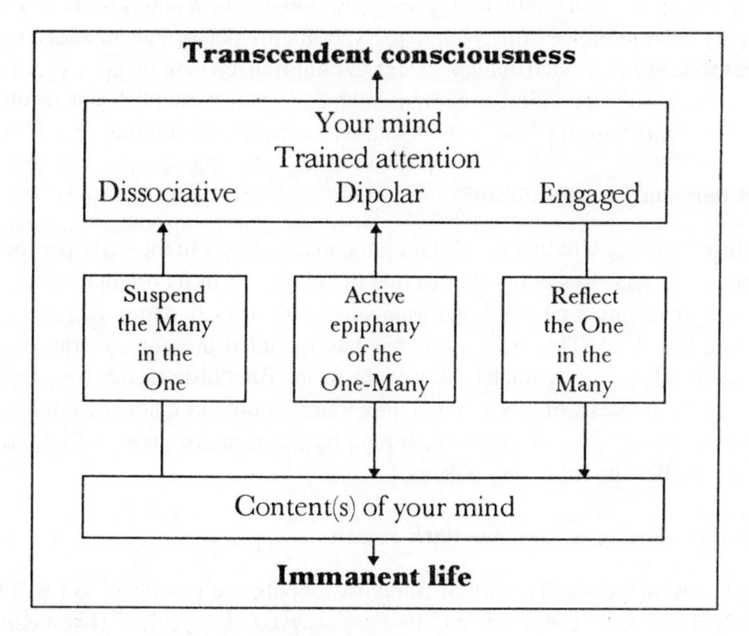

Figure 6.3 *Three kinds of trained attention*

Figure 6.3 sets out the ideas in this section. It includes the three modes of trained attention, and suggests that, in appropriate balance, they all have a role in interior transfiguration. The dipolar and engaged modes naturally lead on to their consummation in the first, expressive form of spiritual transformation. A supreme example of dipolar practice, expressively consummated, is the spiritual discipline of conscious intentional parenting, in which, in continuity with transcendent spiritual consciousness, the parent is in a co-creative relation with the immanent spiritual life both within her or himself and within her or his child.

Method, metaphysic and acting out

I take the view that an inquiry method both presupposes a metaphysic - a theory of the nature of reality and how to acquire knowledge of reality - and gives expression to it. It certainly doesn't establish it, prove it, validate it. It is because we already have a certain view of the world that we devise a method to express and explore it.

> Which kind of mystical experience is regarded as liberation or resolution is typically a value-judgement guided by the theology of the particular mystical tradition. Theological and other differences among the mystical traditions...are intrinsic to and constitutive of the mystical path and its goal. (Fenton, 1995: 203-4)

> The experience that the mystic or yogi has is the experience he seeks as a consequence of the shared beliefs he holds through his metaphysical doctrinal commitments. (Katz, 1978: 58)

What I have called dissociative meditation is a methodology designed to elaborate a pre-existent worldview of reality as nothing-but-one-spirit, just as modern experimental science is a methodology designed to elaborate a pre-existent worldview of reality as nothing-but-many-matter. Experiments per se can neither establish nor resolve the restricted metaphysical assumption on which the experimental method is based. Just so, meditation as such can neither establish nor resolve the monopolar bias built into its method, and will simply experientially act it out.

What happened to Buddhism?

Buddhist leaders, including the Dalai Lama, met in Japan in the early part of 1998 to share their concerns about the decline of Buddhism in its oriental countries of origin. At the same time, the Pope was voicing his anxiety about the rise of Buddhism in the West. This occidental rise has included the current transpersonal movement, which draws much from Buddhism and Buddhist practices (McDermott, 1993). In the interests of promoting a little more inquiry, as distinct from doctrinal defensiveness and special pleading, among transpersonalists with a Buddhist orientation, I offer the following polemic.

Meditation, letting go and the dark return

There is a tremendous diversity of Buddhist schools and practices, so I will focus on early Buddhism: Theravada and its classic *vipassana* practice. This meditation method is devised to explore a pre-existent worldview that human beings are bound to *samsara,* the repetitive cycle of birth, death and rebirth, by powerful forces of greed, hatred and delusion, which are, therefore, at the very root of our embodiment; and that the solution is *moksha,* release from the cycle, by disidentifying from the many to find the One.

Note that this account reduces the immanent spiritual life within us to a desperate kind of clinging attachment, combined with reactive rage and the darkest confusion and ignorance. From the worldview which I adopt, this is a deeply damaging invalidation of human personhood and its inner spiritual potential, for it reduces it to *nothing but* egoic murk. And it is of course a pathologically self-fulfilling thesis, since it guarantees the dark and distorted return of what it unawarely disparages and represses.

For the method of meditation which follows from it is fundamentally a matter of sitting and letting go of whatever is present no matter what it is, whether from heaven or the underworld. All phenomena, all contents within and before the mind are regarded as that which we will tend either to grasp or resist, and in either case be improperly identified with. So the thing is in meditation to let them go and let them be, for they are not our business. True freedom is found in the heart's release from all phenomenal attachment.

What we see here is flight from the Many, a massive unacknowledged fear of the phenomenal. It is a sustained hands off approach lest the contamination of attachment occur. There is no sense that within the phenomenal there is immanent spiritual potential, that we can engage co-creatively with its emergent divinity. There is only the *via negativa,* the path of dealing with the pain of existence in order to gain release from the wheel of rebirth. There is no *via positiva,* the path of celebration and thanksgiving, no *via creativa,* the path of human creativity, no *via transformativa,* the path of creation renewed and mended (Fox, 1983).

The impulse to creative engagement with the potential of the contents of experience, and with their consequent spiritual unfoldment, is denied. It is falsely reduced to mere clinging and hence rejected. And this rejection is reinforced by every hour of practice. This means, inevitably, that a valid impulse will simply keep returning in its rejected and hence distorted form, as gross attachment.

In the same way the Augustinian assault on human sexuality as original sin guaranteed centuries of perverted sexual activity. In both cases, and for very long periods, the religious practices involved appear to justify and prove their pre-existent negative beliefs, hence devotees think that more practice is needed, more sitting and letting go of mental contents, more confession, absolution and sexual constraint.

It takes a long while for a tradition to grasp that the practice itself is part of the problem, because it repetitively acts out a negative and misbegotten belief system. The practice is a defense against acknowledging what the belief system rejects. What the practice denies is disfigured, so that the denial appears to be justified.

Of course there are impressive spiritual benefits of Buddhist practice. Thus *zazen,* or sitting meditation, after some years of its 'extended hell' (Wilber, 1997: 91) will open up striking illuminations. But we may properly question the account of spirit that is experientially enacted on the basis of the negative worldview that shapes the one-sided practice. Indeed, we may question the account of spirit that is evolved from any form of practice which involves a sustained privation of the immanent spiritual life within us.

Furthermore, however long the aspirant goes on with the practice, the old problems keep returning. And this is because they are not really problems at all, but valid impulses demanding restitution for being warped by their owner. So Jack Kornfield, at the conclusion of a long and very interesting survey of the ups and downs, ins and outs, of Buddhist meditation, says:

> We finally come to see that spiritual practice is really very simple; it is a path of opening and letting go, of being aware and not attaching to a single thing...But even after this tremendous and enlightening journey one inevitably comes down. Very often in coming back one reencounters all the difficulties of the journey again...(Kornfield, 1989: 168)

There is a related issue about the western Buddhist's definition of narcissism as contraction upon the separate self and alienation from the presence of Being (Almaas, 1996). If a person is defined in theory and represented in spiritual practice as *nothing but* a separate self, then, from my point of view, it is an open question as to what degree the various forms of higher narcissism - supposedly a reaction to spiritual transformation and, of course, in need of a teacher - are themselves a product of the restrictive nature of the definition and the practice. In other words, to what extent are they a distorted return of the denied autonomous-connected spirituality of personhood? To raise this question is certainly not to deny the pronounced tendency of the person to contract into an egoic and separate self-sense.

From my perspective, the main problem for the Buddhist is not his inveterate propensity to become attached, with more or less awareness of the process, to mental contents. Rather it is his rigid and unaware attachment to the premise that if he isn't letting go, all he can do is lapse into unhealthy clinging. The only allowable spiritual state is witness-consciousness (Isenberg and Thursby, 1985: 56-58). He misses out on the *spiritual* option of co-creative, disciplined and passionate engagement with emerging immanent spiritual life. Here is a comment on the views I have advanced in this section:

> I really agree with your judgement that the *vipassana* attitude to experience may not be always the best one for psychospiritual blossoming. I have felt repeatedly frustrated by hearing Buddhist teachers tell students to just observe and let go (come back to your breath, etc.) and preclude thereby the full participation or intentional support that the emergence of what could be (for all we know) profoundly creative psychological or spiritual events may require. This is rooted, I believe, in (1) authoritarian tendencies about which experiences are the best to have; (2) the aversion (fear?) Buddhists have in general towards strong or intense emotions (like anger); and (3) their general lack of discrimination between attachments and passions (as I believe you are suggesting; in this regard, Buddhists have much to learn from semitic religions, especially early Christianity and Judaism). But again, the later critique may be more valid for early Buddhism and perhaps Zen than for Tibetan schools (see, for example, Miranda Shaws's *Passionate Enlightenment*). In my experience, the *vipassana* methods are at their best (1) to become clearly aware of, learn more adequately to relate to, and free oneself from, some conditioning habits and plainly neurotic loops of the mind; (2) to become more accepting, peaceful, and equanimous with one's own and other's experiences; and (3) to enact and participate in a Buddhist engagement of the world (marked by an awareness of impermanence, no-self, and interrelatedness of all phenomena which, if all goes OK, leads to the opening of the heart and the emergence of beautiful spiritual qualities such as compassion or sympathetic joy). But all this, although potentially deeply beneficial and transformative, has obvious limitations as a truly integral spiritual method of development, I think. (Ferrer, 1998d)

Non-attachment and relationships

The preoccupation with letting go, of course, raises serious problems about everyday life, about relationships with other people central in one's life. Mindful non-attachment can be readily practised in the solitude of meditation and a retreat. It is only half the story in relationships, and an important part, for it is a great aid in letting go of projection, collusion and co-dependency. But when you have let go of all that, what then? Just more open, liberated and nonharming witnessing? Surely not, for there is the other half of the spiritual story: disciplined, active and engaged cherishing - a passionate, hands-on making space for the flowering and flourishing of the other and of the relationship. A Buddhist teacher who is a woman openly identifies the problem:

> There's no teaching about how to be mindful or generally how to do spiritual work with your partner or children or parents. Of course, there is the emphasis on sila (ethics or morality) and the paramis. But what are the nuts and bolts of doing this, the actual practices to carry out with other people? (Michele McDonald-Smith in Rothberg, 1996: 38)

I have already referred earlier to the spiritual discipline of conscious intentional parenting, in which the parent is in an engaged aware relation with the immanent spiritual life both within her or himself and within her or his child

Doctrinal roots of authoritarianism

I also think there is a strong internal connection between addiction to the limited and one-sided premise of non-attachment, which, after all, invalidates emergent inner autonomous creativity as a form of meditative practice, and an authoritarian model of spiritual education and training. Many accomplished Buddhist practitioners spend much time running benignly authoritarian training retreats for unsuspecting newcomers and novitiates.

There is also a strong link between directive spiritual training and the belief that a person is nothing but an illusory self. If the person is one of the real Many full of creative divine potential, the trainer will want to make space for its autonomous emergence. Whereas the trainer will have little compunction in telling an illusory knotted self what to do in order to dismantle itself. Kornfield praises his Buddhist master in southeast Asia for his perspicacity in the wholesale direction of the lives of his monks: he assigned one monk to work in this setting to untangle one sort of knot, another to that setting to untangle some other sort, and so on (Rothberg, 1996: 34).

Reticence about reincarnation

Then there is the question of reincarnation, so central to the mechanics of the Buddhist worldview. Transpersonal theorists who adopt Buddhist spiritual practice presumably believe in it, but seem to fight shy of coming out into the open about it, dealing with the formidable objections that can be raised against it, and debating alternative eschatologies. Wilber, for example, has to show how his linear ascensional stage model, according to which in any given life you go through the whole sequence of basic structures of consciousness, applies to a series of incarnations. If an individual is fully and authentically stabilized at Wilber's high subtle stage in one incarnation, what is the point of a full recapitulation of all the earlier stages in the next incarnation? When you have graduated from high school, why repeat the whole of primary and secondary education again before going on to university?

Not enough 'good life'

Wilber's vast and intricate intellectual model of human spirituality and its development is, in some respects, elaborate special pleading on behalf of Buddhist theology, cosmology and psychology. When he brings key concepts of his system to bear on a characterisation of Buddhism, the limits of both stand revealed (Wilber, 1990: 229-233). The key concepts are translation and transformation: translation is about changes that go on within a stage of development, whereas transformation is change from one stage of development to a higher and more inclusive one. The two basic options for translation are to preserve and fortify your present state of consciousness or to alter, rearrange and release it. The two basic options for transformation are to ascend to a higher, more inclusive state, or to descend down into a lower and less, inclusive one. For Wilber, these two polar dimensions define what all development is about.

In Buddhist terms, according to Wilber's analysis, this means that within any stage of development we have two basic choices. We can either be driven by 'life-desire', which means 'grasping, clinging' and wanting our present state to be permanent; or we can choose 'life denial and an embrace of self-death', that is, letting go of our clinging, and so be open to transformation and transcendence leading to Spirit. So translation within a stage is either a matter of 'bad life' (clinging) or 'good death' (release and letting go). 'Good life' is about transforming to a higher level, 'bad death' about dropping down to a lower level. And that, for Wilber's Buddhist, is it: that's human existence. All horizontal relationship reduced to clinging or letting go.

From my point of view, there is a third polar dimension which the Wilber account of Buddhism entirely omits. To add this third dimension starts to give the model real body and full human relevance, though even then the model as a whole would need recasting. For within our horizontal life there is not just 'bad life' and 'good death', but also 'good life' and 'bad death': flourishing or suppression. We can, as persons in relation, unfold and express our full spiritual life-potential, or deny and block it. There is not just self-preservation and self-adaptation within our current state of existence, but also spiritual unfoldment through expressive creation and authentic and empowering loving among persons in relation.

But to add this dimension means a radically altered worldview. For we abandon the idea of a human being as nothing but an unreal separate self, a knot of fear, who can only either cling or painfully let go. Instead we embrace the idea of the person as an evolving autonomous spiritual presence, grounded in aware co-creation with immanent spiritual life, sloughing off fear and clinging, expressive of 'good life' in present relationships, as well as committed to the 'good life' of transcendence.

For Wilber's Buddhist, in the passage to which I refer (1990: 229-233), there is no 'good life' in the horizontal world, only temporizing, translative clinging, until finally we get on with more ascension, the only kind of 'good life' that really matters.

It is the pregnancy, birth and development of immanent spiritual life, its expression and celebration, within horizontal relationships that is not acknowledged by the Wilber-Buddhist view. Similarly, there is no acceptance, in the meditative state, of the contents of the mind as in any respect pregnant with immanent spiritual life seeking birth and expression.

More radically, literal physical birth is not 'good life' in my celebration sense, but 'bad death' in Wilber's sense, that is, a descent from the *bardo* state between incarnations back into the samsaric world of clinging and despair. Which is why a woman is a very lowly being in Buddhist cultures. Trungpa Rinpoche admired his mother. She once said to him, 'Well, maybe I'm an inhuman being, a subhuman being. I have a woman's body; I had an inferior birth' (Chogyam Trungpa, 1986: 70).

Authoritarianism run amok

Now let me talk about the primary, deep contradiction within Buddhism. It seems that Buddha himself strongly commended what I call critical subjectivity, the authority within and lived inquiry. He said:

> Now look you Kalamas, do not be led by reports, or tradition, or hearsay. Be not led by the authority of religious texts, nor by mere logic or inference, nor by considering appearances, nor by the delight in speculative opinions, nor by seeming possibilities, nor by the idea: 'this is our teacher'. But, O Kalamas, when you know for yourselves that certain things are unwholesome and wrong, and bad, then give them up...And when you know for yourselves that certain things are wholesome and good, then accept them and follow them. (Rahula, 1974: 2-3)

Lin Chi, of the Ch'an tradition in the 9th century, also 'emphasized individual attainment, searching out one's salvation through diligence, depending neither on words alone nor on institutions nor the personal guru' (Crook, 1996: 5). Yet Buddhism today is riddled with unhealthy authoritarianism.

Jones (1996: 7) writes that Buddhism in Britain is dominated by three big movements, with charismatic leaders and 'exclusivist visions'. Each has 'a party line' 'largely impermeable to debate', putting out 'a literature of ideology or at best a limitation of inquiry to within implicitly understood limits'. John Crook (following Lachs, 1994) discloses how, in the USA, the notion of enlightenment has generated authoritarianism run amok with corruption:

> In spite of the democratic tradition in the West a prime problem in the arrival of Buddhism in the USA has been that the authoritarian attitudes natural to traditional Eastern cultures have been passed from Eastern teachers to those they appointed as first generation Western 'masters'. Their conferred infallibility as an 'enlightened' person was often uncritically accepted by naïve westerners desperate to believe in a human representation of the sublime but who, in the course of time, only discovered the ridiculous. Some such teachers came to dominate the institutions they led establishing neither democratic means for self-criticism nor advisory boards to provide feedback. In many sad cases the result has been the sexual exploitation of young followers of both genders and severe financial irregularity. Furthermore, some Oriental teachers themselves, succumbing to the permissiveness of the West they failed to properly understand, also revealed comparable faults. Clearly when such behaviour is revealed not only is the validity of the transmission to teach called into question but the whole system and the texts that sustain it become suspect. (Crook: 1996: 17-18)

My view on all this is that any tradition which defines enlightenment in terms of annihilation of any kind of subject (in my terms the denial of spiritual personhood) will be prone to spiritual inflation. Crook mentions that a 'fine Tibetan teacher, trained in Lhasa, has reputedly taken to having himself described as a Buddha' (1996: 31). Such false claims, with other kinds of interpersonal abuse, are, once again, the return of the denied in distorted and inflated form.

A perinatal template for doctrine?

How much are these ancient transpersonal systems, and modern ones derived from them, rooted in the unresolved energies of repressed perinatal experience? It is not difficult to give a transpersonal, 'bad life' at the current level, 'good life' in ascension to a higher level, account [in brackets] of the following passage from Grof:

> The dynamics of negative perinatal matrices imposes on life a linear trajectory and creates a strong and unrelenting drive toward the pursuit of future goals [end-state of enlightenment]. Since the psyche of such a person is dominated by the memory of the painful confinement in the birth canal, he or she never experiences the present moment and circumstances as fully satisfying [*dukkha* - the pain of existence]. Like the foetus who is trying to escape from the uncomfortable constriction into a more acceptable situation, such a person will always strive for something other than what the present circumstances allow [state of non-attachment]. The goals the mind constructs in this circumstance can easily be identified as substitutes for biological birth and postnatal care [peace, freedom, equanimity]. Since these goals are mere psychological surrogates and unreal mirages, their achievement can never bring true satisfaction [coming down from the meditation high]. The resulting frustration will then generate new plans or more ambitions ones of the same kind [a longer retreat, more sitting and letting go]. In this frame of mind, nature and the world are seen in general as a potential threat and something that must be conquered and controlled [attaining *moksha,* release from the samsaric wheel of rebirth in a world of suffering]. (Grof, 1985: 429-30)

The resolution of differences

It is a delicate matter to raise the issues I am confronting in this section, and I risk the opprobrium of speaking out in this manner. On the one hand, I have every wish to honour and respect the spiritual path and practice any person chooses to follow. On the other hand, contemporary transpersonalists appear to have an uncritical allegiance to Buddhist contemplative practice to a degree that hinders the advance of spiritual inquiry. Indeed, the prevailing conventional transpersonal wisdom has it that such traditional practice is itself a valid form of spiritual research. This is a very spurious claim indeed, since it confuses real inquiry with male-dominated, authoritarian and doctrinaire forms of experiential training, as I have shown in Chapter 2.

I may be told, when I raise these sorts of issues, that I don't know what I am talking about because I haven't done the appropriate practice in a sustained way for many years. This is a stalemate argument, because I can equally well reply that my protagonist can't evaluate my critique because he hasn't done my long years of distinctive practice. More generally, it is an argument that will never pass muster. The notion that you cannot properly evaluate something until you have done it requires all of us to commit murder to be able to say with any authority that it is wrong.

Then I may be told that without a qualified teacher within a traditional lineage, my practice will have no spiritual validity. To this I reply that not to know that one's practice is valid unless it is approved by a teacher and a lineage, is to be lost in unaware projection of, and consequent distortion of, the spiritual authority and presence within oneself. This is precisely, as in the full quotation above, what the Buddha himself told Kalamas: 'Do not be led by...tradition...nor by the idea: 'this is our teacher'... when you know for yourselves that certain things are wholesome and good, then accept them and follow them'.

Another version of the teacher argument, is that the spiritual practice of the beginner needs to be empowered by the charismatic presence of the master whose attainment induces transformation in those who sit with him. But this kind of induced spirituality sets up dependency, with chronic spiritual projection, and consequent proneness to become subject to authoritarian direction and indoctrination. Many young followers of Muktananda, in awe of his *shaktipat,* direct transmission of spiritual energy by shaking the bridge of each student's nose, got caught in this elevated subtle trap.

Yet another version is that without the help of an experienced teacher, one will never find a way through the thick undergrowth of egoic narcissism. My argument here, of course, is that the tradition itself, with its invalidating doctrine of the self, generates a subtle and unnoticed version of the narcissism it is supposed to cure, especially in the teachers who are supposed to cure it, and in whom it flowers as inflation and authoritarianism.

The solution to the disagreement I have with my critic is twofold. Firstly, we can engage for a period in mutually respectful rational discourse. If this goes on for too long it is likely to become defensive and embattled. Thus, secondly, we need to let go of the argument and together devise mutually agreed forms of experiential practice that will advance our shared understanding. In other words, we need some kind of collaborative practical inquiry. Is it not possible that the Buddha might approve?

Part 2: Co-operative inquiry reports

8

Procedures

Part 1 is rooted in personal lived inquiry. Part 2 is all about co-operative inquiry into the spiritual and subtle. The bridge between the two parts is the dipolar map presented in Chapter 6. With respect to the transpersonal application of co-operative inquiry, I am talking about a method in a very primitive state of exploration and development. The inquiries with which I have been involved, most of which are reported here, are modest. They are finding their way in entirely new spiritual research procedures. At the same time, I have personally found them transformative at a deep level of being, both in terms of opening to the immanent spiritual life within and in terms of my worldview. One message I take from them is the importance and value, as a complement to meditation and inner high prayer, of a spiritual practice that is charismatic, expressive and interactive, thus celebrating and manifesting the dynamic innovative process of creation.

This chapter is about co-operative inquiry method, both in general and in transpersonal particulars. I start with a general account of what is involved in initiating an inquiry. Next I discuss the why and the how of a transpersonal journey of opening, based on the dipolar map, which I use as a precursor to launching an inquiry, and consider the issue of indoctrination. This is followed by a general account of the stages of a co-operative inquiry, a discussion of Apollonian and Dionysian inquiry cultures and of transformative and informative sorts of inquiry and of how these two pairs of distinctions bear upon the transpersonal field.

Initiating an inquiry

In Chapter 4 of *Co-operative Inquiry* (Heron, 1996a), I discuss what I call the three-stranded initiation of a co-operative inquiry group by its launching researchers - who already have some prior experience and knowledge of the method. The following passage describes the strands.

- The initiation of group members into the methodology of the inquiry so that they can make it their own.
- The emergence of participative decision-making and authentic collaboration so that the inquiry becomes truly co-operative.
- The creation of a climate in which emotional states can be identified, so that distress and tension aroused by the inquiry can be openly accepted and processed, and joy and delight in it and with each other can be freely expressed.

The first of these is to do with cognitive and methodological empowerment, the second with political empowerment, and the third with emotional and interpersonal empowerment. Initiating researchers need some skills in all these three ways of empowering others. The combination is familiar to the whole person educator whose analogous concern is to facilitate:

- Self-directed learning by students of some content and method.
- Increasing student participation in all aspects of educational decision-making: the objectives, topics, resources, methods, programme and pacing of learning; the assessment of learning, and the evaluation of the course.
- Integration of cognitive with emotional and interpersonal aspects of learning.

At the induction meeting, the initiating researchers will be wise to make clear that the three strands are basic to the inquiry process, and to invite only those to whom the three strands appeal to join the project. Then they seek a contract in which everyone who wants to join makes a commitment to bring the strands into being.

It is pretty important that this contract is not the result of either rapid conversion or persuasive coercion. It needs to be a fully voluntary and well informed agreement to realize the values of autonomy, co-operation and wholeness which underlie the three strands. A co-operative inquiry is a community of value, and its value premises are its foundation. If people are excited by and attuned to these premises, they join, otherwise not. Getting clear about all this at the outset makes for good craftspersonship later. (Heron, 1996a: 62-3)

The chapter then goes on at some length to say more about each strand, and I will not repeat it here. All of it applies to an inquiry in the transpersonal field. But there are also further aspects of the initiating role which are specific to that field, and these are my concern here. I give a very personal account of what I think is relevant.

A journey of opening

The people who participate in the researches I set up are authentic inquirers, who, however, have a diverse and often partial knowledge of things spiritual and subtle, combined with attitudes of various sorts. They may also be strangers to each other. So I have found that what I now call a journey of opening is fruitful. On this journey, I guide participants through a theoretical and experiential overview of the field, *before* focusing on some specific inquiry within it. There are several reasons for doing this:

- It raises everyone's consciousness about the range of options available as a focus for the inquiry.
- It presents the options in a dogma-free zone, and takes some of the negative charge off those items which some people associate with oppressive forms of religion or new age dogmatism.
- It creates a shared attitude - a spirit of inquiry about the spiritual and subtle - and interrupts tendencies in some people to authoritarian pronouncements about their beliefs.
- It empowers people to have faith in themselves, in four ways which I describe below.
- It provides a provisional and shared vocabulary for discussing the options and for coming to agreement about the focus of the inquiry.

In order to achieve all this, the map used for the journey needs to be free of doctrinal bias, free of appeals to the authority of past spiritual traditions while honouring the content of several of them, to be comprehensive and wide-ranging, to be offered in the spirit of inquiry as a provisional conjecture awaiting participants' validation, and to have some kind of reasonable experiential, philosophical and theological rationale. So I provide the dipolar map which I have outlined in Chapter 5.

I have tried out various ways of presenting this map, and several versions of it. With the earlier inquiries, the presentation was brief and only conceptual. I explained the map to the group and then clarified and discussed it with everyone for up to an hour and half. This led into a decision about which part or parts of it would be the focus of our inquiry. In subsequent inquiries, I started to take people round the map experientially as well, on a spiral route from the central fulcrum, going thence to immanent 1, transcendent 1, immanent 2, transcendent 2, and so on, as shown in the diagram in Chapter 6. On one occasion, this went on for two days and then we went into the inquiry.

Another more substantial variation was to lead a full four-day journey of opening as a separate workshop, some days before the inquiry as such began. Attending this workshop was a condition of joining the inquiry. On the first morning of the workshop, I gave a conceptual explanation of the map, followed by clarification and discussion. Then, over the next three and a half days, there was a more extended experiential journey following the spiral pathway. For each state on this path, I offered an experiential exercise. Group members were invited to enter a state by simply imagining they are in it, bracketing off any concerns about whether they are in it, or indeed whether there is such a state to be in.

In some inquiries, where the members have all participated in an earlier one, I don't present any map or lead a journey at all. We launch straight into the co-operative work.

Personal meaning

What goes on in the journey of opening? After each exercise there is ample time for people to make sense of what did or did not happen. I encourage them to honour and affirm their own experience in their own terms, speaking first in pairs or small groups, then sharing in the whole group. I invite each person to avoid suppressing the content of their experience through conditioned deference to the false authority of some externally imposed belief-system. I propose that they give it the benefit of the doubt and recommend the use of Heron's beard (see Chapter 4). I suggest they use the language of 'as if' - 'it was as if I could feel...'. This allows people to own what is going on while bracketing off any assumptions about its validity. They can also be open to it without falling foul of slipshod credulity.

After centuries of authoritarianism in spiritual teaching, people need support to identify, own and give voice to personal spiritual and subtle experience, to honour their own inner light and life. When empowered to do so, they give birth to rich and subtle phenomenologies. After a shared round of feedback on an exercise within the journey of opening, I have many a time marveled at the idiosyncratic insights and profundities revealed.

I am careful to honour fully each person's statement. I make it clear that there is no one correct account, that every perspective sheds fresh light or deepens revelatory shade. I do not make any attempt to organize the diverse statements into some coherent scheme, but let them resonate side by side in the fullness of their own orchestration. I also make sure that negative experience, disbelief and scepticism are given space to find their voice.

Indoctrination or opening

Is this journey of opening, which precedes the inquiry itself, just a way of indoctrinating people experientially, so that what they are supposed to be inquiring into is already a foregone conclusion? I don't think so. The map on which the journey is based is put forward as a provisional working hypothesis, in the spirit of inquiry, not of dogmatic or traditional authority. People are encouraged to use it to start to get clear about the maps implicit in their own experience. And when they inquiry itself begins, people have, when given the opportunity, a way of doing their own thing, as we shall see in the reports later in this book.

The journey has a vital educative function, described in the five reasons given above. One of these five I named as empowering people to have faith in the authority within. This faith develops with regard to:

- The accessibility to them of spiritual and subtle states, no matter how apparently arcane.
- Their own know-how, their competence to open to such states.
- Their ability to make sense of their experiences according to their own lights.
- Their own implicit maps and their ability to make such maps explicit.
- Their ability to heal from past spiritual oppression and wounding.

The following reports from four women participants in several inquiry events are relevant here. The first three attended the inquiry into knacks in entering altered states, Chapter 13. This was the first co-operative inquiry I initiated in New Zealand, at Scott's Landing, in 1994. These reports were all written independently of each other. Dale Hunter writes:

> The Scott's Landing gathering stands out as a landmark event for me. Through the four day experience - the journey of opening and the co-operative inquiry - I claimed my own individual approach to and experience of spirituality as an everyday yet unique occurrence. I no longer had to agree with anyone or have anyone agree with me. My experience was my experience, full stop.
>
> I remember thinking and talking a lot about this after the event. It had a profound effect. I recognized how we have been spiritually colonized to the extent that we became unsure and untrusting of our own experiences. Did I really experience this? Was it valid? Was it 'spiritual'? I uncovered layers of spiritual colonization in the way I allow myself to experience some things and block out other often very rich experiences.
>
> We broke the silence. We spoke our experiences and unravelled them like balls of string. I recall sharing a room with Lori and practising the peripheral vision knack. I noticed a figure in my peripheral vision to the left. It was a Buddha figure. He came into view and I had a 'conversation' with him. The interesting thing was that I only remem-

bered the whole conversation when I began to tell Lori about it. I had almost blocked it out immediately and realized that I do this all the time. I block out my experiences because they don't fit the social norm. The implication of us all doing this is horribly disturbing. We could be losing an enormous amount of spiritual richness available individually and collectively.

The co-operative inquiry method is a powerful tool for exploring the transpersonal as it is dogma free. We designed our own questions, had our own very different subjective experiences and shared them. We liberated ourselves.

Peta Joyce writes:

What I particularly remember and value about the Scott's Landing Inquiry is that it was the first time I had ever been able to explore my transpersonal experiences in depth in a safe environment. What made it safe was that everyone contributed equally, and each person's contribution had equal worth.

Being an inquiry meant that there were no agendas around spiritual or religious dogma, and each of us had total freedom to experience and report back whatever happened without any judgement of right or wrong. Using the devil's advocate procedure meant that challenges weren't personal, just further questions for inquiry.

It seems to me that one of the basic underlying assumptions of co-operative inquiry is that I am an autonomous, fully self-responsible being of equal worth to anyone else. The method treats me as such, and therefore I respond as such.

Co-operative inquiry is about a different way of working with personal and group power. It is about equality and power-sharing, as well as internal personal authority. As such, it is deeply counter-cultural to societies organized around hierarchical power and external control and authority. Because of this, there are three issues that come to mind from my experience of co-operative inquiry:

- Participants need to be rigorously attentive to subtle tendencies for power, control and domination, particularly in the face of personal or interpersonal distress.
- In order to participate fully, we need the personal awareness and skills of autonomous adulthood. I was able to more fully develop these skills the more inquiries I participated in, and the more we developed this awareness as a group.
- Personal and group tolerance of chaos, confusion, and divergence is another aspect of co-operative inquiry, and can bring up personal distress and attempts to shortcut the process. My experience of sitting with the chaos and confusion was that it eventually resolved itself into remarkable individual creativity and group convergence.

I found co-operative inquiry a mutually reinforcing, validating, and healing method of exploration and growth in the spiritual field. I was able to develop a level of trust with co-participants that facilitated truly deep exploration of my transpersonal beliefs and experiences. This was previously a very unsafe topic to explore with others due to my degree of personal wounding around spirituality.

Barbara Langton writes:

Significant for me was the creation of an open space to explore my own personal spirituality, without the constraints of any label or tradition, without being told what prayer to say or how to meditate. I felt I could use my own words and validate my experiences as spiritual. I became aware of the depth of my own spirituality and transpersonal experiences and their importance to me; of how I had been hiding all this outwardly for so long and also for quite some time not acknowledging my need inwardly; of how the experiences which had felt important to me had no place within Christianity and had therefore created considerable confusion for me.

What both impressed me and built trust, was J's grounded, down-to-earth approach as well as his broad validation and interest in each person's experiences and views. I could feel other people had different interests and experiences than me, in terms of exploring altered states; and the space was such that all were validated and each enriched the shared pool of the group. The actual process of co-operative inquiry where each person was given time and validation, and could choose their own areas of exploration, built a great amount of trust for me. The method of actually co-operatively designing a shared ritual was deeply empowering and freeing.

I felt huge relief, like coming home to myself; and also in terms of being able to participate authentically in a group. It was profoundly healing both spiritually and emotionally. The deep inner attunement that I feel is accessible to me was both affirmed and supported in a way I had never experienced before.

The Devil's Advocate process which J introduced lightly and thoroughly, grounded the event and our explorations in a balanced, intelligent, conscious and intentional human way and enabled me to engage in a broader, wider, clearer view of what we were exploring with a trust both in myself and with the dynamic of the group. The use of J's transpersonal map was also grounding, practical, expansive and broad enough to include what for me have been spiritual experiences and practices.

Robert Skye writes:

There were several aspects that were tremendously important for me. First, the vast sense of permission and liberation resulting from staying in open question mode rather than seeking the right answer. Non-judgment and the receptivity to gathering all data gave room for disinhibition, playfulness, and at the same time encouraged a rigorous scrutiny of any and every possibility. In a dreadfully competitive world, this approach is deeply healing and supportive and I believe does much to bring out our richness as multi-faceted beings, as well as weave together our shared experiences in total validation...I continue to invoke the spirit of inquiry in both private sessions with clients, and as part of culture builing in group work. The feedback about how supportive this is continues to validate the offering.

Access, impact, first and second order stabilization

Quite other than the issue of indoctrination is that of empowering implication. Thus the use of the map on the journey of opening, and as a tacit backdrop to the subsequent inquiry, has two empowering implications, which, with the wisdom now of twenty years of hindsight, I can articulate.

- Each and every area of the dipolar map is in principle accessible, to some real degree or other, to any person sufficiently interested to open to it by the simple methods I propose. Access, pure and simple, to some exalted state does not require long years of spiritual practice, scriptural study and ethical discipline; nor any complicated and elaborate methodology. This relative accessibility of 'peak experiences' seems to be generally accepted by transpersonalists.
- Such ready access and opening can have a dramatic impact on the person involved. It may be life-transforming in its effects on their fundamental way of

being-in-a-world. In particular, people may find themselves suddenly revealed to themselves as autonomous spiritual presences within the cosmos, and this revelation holds not just for a day or week after the access event, but for years.

Hence we have the situation that one or more access events occurring in a short space of minutes, hours or a few days can lead to the relatively stable occurrence of a basic spiritual transformation of the person. The individual graduates from current cultural citizenship to far-seeing cosmic citizenship. Of course the issues and hassles of everyday life continue, but there is at root a fundamental shift in orientation with regard to the context within which such life goes on and to the centre within from which it is managed. This I call first order stabilization.

Second order stabilization is a function of the long-term practice of the creative options available to the newly arrived cosmic citizen. I have suggested in the section on 'complementarity, dipolarity and integration' in Chapter 6 what one such path of practice could involve, in terms of the dipolar map. But it is only one choice among many possible ones, and this with regard to only one version of a possible map. I do not believe there is any pre-ordained route for lived inquiry, no set sequence of the stages of spiritual development. The cosmic citizen leaves behind the world of preordainment to enter the world of autonomous and co-operative creation, of transcendent and immanent risk-taking. And this applies both in relation to spiritual transformation of the person and to their engagement with cultural and planetary transformation.

An outline of inquiry stages

Once the inquiry itself begins, then in more formal, Apollonian mode, it follows this sort of sequence. In Dionysian mode, the inquiry will follow this sequence in a more improvisatory, emergent mode. These two modes are explained in the next section. The sequence is described in terms to cover any kind of inquiry topic.

Stage 1. The first reflection phase for the inquirers to choose:

- The focus or topic of the inquiry and the type of inquiry.
- A launching statement of the inquiry topic.
- A plan of action for the first action phase to explore some aspect of the inquiry topic.
- A method of recording experiences during the first action phase.

Stage 2. The first action phase when the inquirers are:

- Exploring in experience and action some aspect of the inquiry topic.
- Applying an integrated range of inquiry skills.
- Keeping records of the experiential data generated.

Stage 3. Full immersion in the action phase with great openness to experience; the inquirers may:

- Break through into new awareness, which is what the inquiry is all about. But they may also:

- Lose their way.
- Transcend the inquiry format.

Stage 4. The second reflection phase; the inquirers share data from the action phase and:

- Review and modify the inquiry topic in the light of making sense of data about the explored aspect of it. This making sense may be in both aesthetic and conceptual terms.
- Choose a plan for the second action phase to explore the same or a different aspect of the inquiry topic.
- Review the method of recording data used in the first action phase and amend it for use in the second.

Subsequent stages will:

- Involve, including the first, from five to eight full cycles of reflection and action, with varying patterns of divergence and convergence, in the action phases, over aspects of the inquiry topic.
- Include a variety of intentional procedures, in the reflection phases, and of special skills in the action phases, for enhancing the validity of the process. For details of validity procedures see Heron (1996a).
- End with a major reflection phase for pulling the threads together, clarifying outcomes, and deciding whether to create an aesthetic presentation and/or write a co-operative report.
- Be followed by post-group collaboration on writing up any agreed form of report.

Outcomes of co-operative inquiry are of four main kinds, corresponding to the four forms of knowing, experiential, presentational, propositional and practical:

- Transformations of personal being through engagement with the focus and process of the inquiry. These are always fundamental, especially so in spiritual inquiry.
- Presentations of insight about the focus of the inquiry, through dance, drawing, drama, and all other expressive modes: these provide imaginal symbols of the significant patterns in our realities.
- Propositional reports which (1) are informative about the inquiry domain, that is, they describe and explain what has been explored, (2) provide commentary on the other kinds of outcome, and (3) describe the inquiry method.
- Practical skills which are (1) skills to do with transformative action within the inquiry domain, and (2) skills to do with various kinds of participative knowing and collaboration used in the inquiry process.

Apollonian or Dionysian

In *Co-operative Inquiry* (Heron, 1996a), I make a distinction between Apollonian and Dionysian inquiries.

> The Apollonian inquiry takes a more rational, linear, systematic, controlling and explicit approach to the process of cycling between reflection and action. Each reflection phase is used to reflect on data from the last action phase, and to apply this thinking in planning the next action phase, with due regard to whether the forthcoming actions of participants will be divergent or dissimilar and convergent or similar. This is the rational cycle of sequenced steps - plan, act, observe and reflect, then re-plan - familiar in action research (Kemmis and McTaggart, 1988).....
>
> The Dionysian inquiry takes a more imaginal, expressive, spiralling, diffuse, impromptu and tacit approach to the interplay between making sense and action. In each reflection phase, group members share improvisatory, imaginative ways of making sense of what went on in the last action phase. The implications of this sharing for future action are not worked out by rational pre-planning. They gestate, diffuse out into the domain of action later on with yeast-like effect, and emerge as a creative response to the situation.....
>
> Whether inquiry cultures are Apollonian or Dionysian, what they have in common is the intentional interplay between making sense and action, and the realization that both the meaning and the action need progressively to emerge as the inquiry proceeds. The content of the inquiry as a whole, with all that goes on in its phases of reflection and action, cannot be pre-planned; and the pre-planning of an action phase in the Apollonian cultures is piecemeal, done one at a time, each plan emerging from what has gone before. So there is a sense in which any inquiry in its overall format has a predominantly emergent or Dionysian format.
>
> One weakness of the rational preplanning of action in the Apollonian culture is that this does not allow action to gestate and germinate in its own good time after the sharing of the reflection phase, and to emerge in creative response to unfolding events in the domain of application. A weakness of the Dionysian culture is the ambiguity of the connection, in some instances, between the actions out there and the sharing that has gone on in the group.
>
> I take the view that the two cultures are not separate, independent entities between which a choice must be made, but rather dipolar and interdependent values and processes within any inquiry culture. The polarity is between the mental and the vital, between prior shaping by thought and imaginative openness to living, creative impulse. This is a complementarity at the heart of all human endeavour.
>
> There is a thus creative tension between the Apollonian and Dionysian principles which fluctuates depending on the pole the inquiry inclines toward. An excess of the Apollonian tendency to make everything controlled and explicit, and the inquiry will lose depth, range and richness, will overfocus and miss the point. An excess of the Dionysian propensity to allow for improvisation, creative spontaneity, synchronicity, situational responsiveness and tacit diffusion, and the inquiry will lose its focus and cease to be an inquiry. Any effective inquiry will have some elements of both, even when the emphasis is clearly toward one pole rather than the other. (Heron, 1996a: 45-7)

In the eleven inquiries reported in this book, seven are inclined to the Apollonian, four to the Dionysian. In the transpersonal field, there is a strong case for the Dionysian inquiry culture since the spirit bloweth where it listeth. The Dionysian culture gives space for the inner light and life of the co-inquirers to manifest as creative action at the leading edge of the process of divine becoming. But there is a tendency with either culture for the inquiry format to be transcended by a sheer celebration of being.

Transformative and informative inquiries

A final point I wish to make in this chapter is the creative tension between redemption and inquiry. Commitment to the spiritual and has always been associated with issues of redemption, rebirth, resurrection, regeneration, and salvation. This is the deep eschatology of going from confused alienation to ecstatic integration, from darkness into light, from psychological death into spiritual life. This has not only been a personal matter for each individual soul, but even more so a collective business, in which each soul feels a call to co-operate with others similarly engaged, and to reach out to others still unaware of the choice.

This calling, this transformative obligation, on a confused planet, cannot wait upon elaborate informative transpersonal inquiry; just as the obligation to raise one's children cannot wait upon the findings of elaborate child-care research. One solution to this tension is that the practical calling itself becomes a vehicle for systematic lived inquiry within a co-operative format. Thus a transformative obligation and, for example, a transformative ritual themselves become inquiry vehicles. It is not just that the inquiry is *for* action. The inquiry is *in* the action, in the practical knowing how, in the transformative process of the will.

There is another basic dipolarity here. There are those inquiries which are rooted in the call to be transformative, to heal ourselves and our world; and there are those which are based on the call to be informed, to know more about being, the universe and ourselves. It is in the nature of co-operative inquiry that the two poles are complementary, interdependent and interpenetrative. Transformative inquiries yield information as well as change; informative inquiries yield change as well as information. Exclusive use of transformative inquiry begs too many informative questions; and exclusive use of informative inquiry abandons too many transformative calls.

I also argue that there is an asymmetry in the interdependence, and that transformative inquiry has a basic primacy (Heron, 1996a). This follows from the epistemology, discussed in Chapter 21, which holds that practical knowledge, knowing how to do something, is a consummation of human knowing *and a primary intrinsic value.*

9

Reports, adequacy and viability

Primary and secondary outcomes

It is part of the underlying philosophy of co-operative inquiry that, since the researchers are also the subjects acquiring knowledge through their own experience and action, the most basic outcomes of the inquiry process are personally embodied ones:

- Transformations of personal being brought about by the inquiry.
- Practical knowledge, that is, the personal skills involved in the domain of practice that is the focus of the inquiry.

The other two kinds of possible outcome, written reports, and presentations in imaginal form as in graphics, painting, movement etc., are ephemeral and secondary, however vital for purposes of communicating information and symbolizing significant patterns.

This is pre-eminently so in the spiritual and subtle fields where 'he/she who doeth the will shall know of the doctrine', that is, where information about these fields is secondary to skill in personal transformation. What is of primary and intrinsic value is the ongoing process of being transformed and of exercising transformative skill. The propositional, conceptual knowledge gained about the universe is consequent upon this process and is of secondary and instrumental value in refining and honing the skill.

The status and purpose of reports

The written reports that follow are not therefore the primary outcomes of their respective inquiries. I cannot stress this too much. The primary outcomes are the transformations and competencies of the participants. Nor do the reports mainly give a lot of conceptual knowledge about the view of the universe generated by transformed practice, although this sort of mapping is a constant backdrop referred to by the front text. The reports are pre-eminently about three things:

- Descriptions or evocations of the inquiry process and method.
- Descriptions or evocations of the primary outcomes: that is, of personal transformation, and of the transformative skills - the knowing how, the practical knowledge - that consummate the inquiry.
- Accounts of the criteria for exercising critical subjectivity and discrimination in developing these skills.

The purpose of these reports is exhortatory: to point a way, suggest a method, evoke and portray a modest competence and how to exercise it, and so to inspire and invite readers to inquire into their own transformation and concomitant skills. Thereby, of course, readers who become active co-inquirers will also unveil a revisioned universe within which these outcomes are manifest.

Studies and stories

The use of co-operative inquiry in the field of subtle and spiritual experience is in a rudimentary phase. Here more than in any other domain of inquiry, the state of the human instrument, the clarity and transparency of the open body-mind, is critical. Or, to put it another way, in this arena critical subjectivity is paramount. So it seems to me to be important to show two things. First, that it is possible to structure human inquiry in this area with intentional method. Second, that doing so does not detract from, but enhances, the depth and potency of the explorations thus structured.

In the accounts that follow I use two styles of reporting, the formal and the evocative. I call these studies and stories. The purpose of the more formal study is to lay bare the anatomy of the inquiry, to describe its phases and methodology, its cyclic structure, its validity procedures, and to give some account of the transformative skills acquired, and of the criteria for their discriminating use. What this sort of report tends to lose, at any rate when I do it, is the mood, depth, ethos, engagement, spirit and subtle ambience of the inquiry.

So I have also told the story of some of the inquiries. The purpose of this style of reporting is to be evocative, to give a personal, expressive account of my experience of particular events which impressed me, fired my being and my passion. I call up without qualification and caveat what seemed to me to be going on and lay bare its imaginal force before you, the reader. Please note that when I tell the story of an inquiry, I do not conclude it with any formal evaluation. Formal evaluation, or appraisal of research adequacy, belongs to the study type of reporting.

If you want flavour and ambience, go straight to the stories below. Then when you start to crave a more formalistic rigour, turn to the studies. If you are curious about format and structure, peruse the studies, and when you start to think this is all very well, but what does it feel like to be involved in an inquiry, read the stories. While no story is about the same inquiry as any study, the two sorts of reporting by extension complement each other.

In both studies and stories my account has been amended to incorporate details from the reports, notes and diaries of co-inquirers. And many direct quotes from co-inquirers' writings are inserted into the text.

Apollonian and Dionysian

There is another important point about my use of studies and stories. In *Co-operative Inquiry* (Heron, 1996a), I make a distinction between Apollonian and Dionysian inquiries, and I have given an extended citation about this in Chapter 8. In the reports that follow, I use the study format for inquiries of Apollonian tendency, and the story format for inquiries of Dionysian tendency.

Adequacy and viability

The surface question about adequacy is whether the reports that follow are adequate as accounts of their respective inquiries. The deeper question is whether the inquiries are adequate within their genre as competent examples of it. And the question of whether an inquiry is adequate is in tension with whether it is viable, whether it can survive and develop.

An inquiry is adequate if the participants have internalized and made manifest sufficient methodology in terms of both comprehensiveness and quality. This sort of adequacy admits of degrees: inquiries can be more or less adequate, the more adequate incline to the excellent, the less adequate to the minimally acceptable. The most stringent judgements of adequacy will be made by the initiating researchers and any other co-inquirers who start off with a thorough grasp of the method as they construe it. This begs the question as to who is best fitted to make judgements of adequacy. Is it the initiating researcher who enters the inquiry with a preconceived idea of a sound co-operative method? Or is it the co-inquirers who have evolved out of this their own idea of collaborative research? Usually a fairly clear consensus is reached among all concerned. This is but one of several interesting creative tensions within the method.

An inquiry is viable if its participants are motivated, engaged and interested; have internalized some of the methodology and make it their own in a creative, co-operative way; and see the inquiry through from beginning to end.

Adequacy includes viability: an inquiry can't be adequate if it doesn't survive. But a viable inquiry by definition includes only a basic level of adequacy. There is always a creative tension and trade-off between the two. If initiating researchers press for too much adequacy, they may undermine viability by alienating and losing participants through overcontrol, or they undermine adequacy itself by making the inquiry more conformist than it is genuinely co-operative.

The good news is that if a group of people develop authentic co-operative decision-making and engage however informally in research cycling in a spirit of inquiry over an agreed period of time, their viable inquiry has *ipso facto* the minimal necessary adequacy.

Apollonian inquiries degenerate into inadequacy when they are overintentional, too purposive and controlling. Dionysian inquiries do so when they are underintentional, too laissez-faire and unawarely lax. An adequate Dionysian inquiry *chooses* to be Dionysian with great awareness, with *intentional* openness to improvisation, creative spontaneity, synchronicity, situational responsiveness and tacit diffusion.

Viability degenerates when the inquiry ceases to be an inquiry and turns into some routinized activity, however well sustained and developed that activity is. Critical subjectivity and discrimination are abandoned in favour of some more collusive form of togetherness.

The inquiries: viability and adequacy

All the inquiries reported in the following studies and stories are, in my judgement, viable inquiries. The participants were motivated, engaged and interested;

they internalized some of the methodology and made it their own in a creative way; and saw the inquiry through from beginning to end. They also all have a basic necessary adequacy, that is to say they are authentically collaborative and use research cycling in a spirit of inquiry. There is one exception: the first Tuscan gathering in 1990, which was not a co-operative venture but a journey of opening led by me in the spirit of inquiry. I include it since it inaugurated a series of later co-operative inquiries in Tuscany.

Otherwise the inquiries vary, in my judgement, in degrees of adequacy above the necessary baseline. I have to be careful here, since there is no absolute canon of adequacy. Each participant in each inquiry will have their own view of its degree of adequacy, according to how they construe the methodology of co-operative inquiry. My own view is that variation in adequacy is due to the degree to which validity procedures, above and beyond authentic collaboration and research cycling, are or are not applied during an inquiry. My personal evaluations, which end the study sorts of report which follow, adopt this approach.

I list here the main range of validity procedures currently identified and used. They are given in what I consider is their order of importance, although the order can also be inquiry specific. For a full account of these procedures and a full discussion of validity issues see *Co-operative Inquiry* (Heron, 1996a).

- Research cycling, including divergence and convergence.
- Authentic collaboration.
- Challenging uncritical subjectivity.
- The management of research counter-transference: dealing with unaware projections.
- The balance of reflection and action.
- The relation between chaos and order.

The first two alone provide a rock bottom level of adequacy, since intentional research cycling itself promotes a measure of critical subjectivity. However, the first three yield a better level of adequacy and soundness, because of the addition of quite explicit challenges to uncritical subjectivity. The fourth one is important but more inquiry specific, depending on the topic and on the emotional competence of the participants.

Given that there is a reasonable attendance to validity procedures, we may assume a working level of critical subjectivity in the group, that is, of the participants' discriminating inner light and life. The human instruments are entering the inquiry domain with a degree of clarified awareness and intentionality, of openness and well-groundedness. So we may put a modest trust in what is spiritually revealed, in how Being declares itself, through the co-inquirers' experiential knowledge.

> One canon of validity for experiential knowledge is declarative. When I resonate with a presence, it declares itself and its nature to me through its immaterial qualities, which permeate its perceptual form. 'To declare' in this sense means 'to make clear by manifest compresence', that is, through the felt participation of a person. This, perhaps, echoes the psalmist's use in 'the heavens declare the glory of God' *(Psalms, 19:1)*... De-

> clarative proof is in the palate, on the pulse, in the embrace, in the gaze. It is what Perkins crudely called 'whatlike understanding' which is 'that understanding of an experience that consists in knowing what an experience is like, and we know what an experience is like by virtue of having that experience ' (Perkins, 1971). Declarative proof is transactional or interactive: it is function of my interpenetration with whatever it is that declares itself. It does not tell us about a being out there all on its own: it tells us about a being that is in a state of compresence with whoever it makes its declaration to. (Heron, 1992: 164)

We must distinguish between how Being declares itself to a person, and the contextually relative way in which that person reports verbally on the declaration. So again a reminder that the most basic outcomes of the inquiry process are personally embodied ones:

- Transformations of personal being brought about by the inquiry.
- Practical knowledge, that is, the personal skills involved in the domain of practice that is the focus of the inquiry.

It is the morphic resonance set up by doing an inquiry that is more fundamental than any written reports about it .

The reports

Finally, are these studies and stories adequate *accounts* of their respective inquiries? An important criterion of adequacy here is whether the reports have been cooperatively written. In two respects they are not adequate in the light of this criterion:

- All eleven reports are written exclusively by me, as against being co-written by some quorum of participants in each inquiry group.
- Participants in the first two inquiries were not, at the time the reports were written, invited to make any contributions to them.

On the other side of the story:

- Contributions have been invited from participants in nine of the eleven events reported, and have been honoured by additions, deletions or changes in the text. Many quotations from participants are included.

Issues about record-keeping

Over the eleven inquiries covered here, I have kept reasonably full records, and so have some participants. For other participants, record-keeping has been uneven and patchy, even when there has been a general agreement about it. Some of this may be due to research counter-transference, or to forgetfulness and lack of discipline. However, there are also certain important affirmative points to assert about not making record-keeping central in this field.

- The most basic outcomes of the inquiry process are transformations of being and skills of soul. They can only be embodied in persons, not in written records.

- When inquiring into subtle and spiritual experience, it is important not to press too often or too soon for conceptual closure, for codifying the experience in words. What is sometimes needed is gestation, resonance, the extended ringing of overtones, letting the experience flourish for a period in the realm of the inchoate while it gradually assumes it proper contours. I have found that some inquiries become both potent and precise in their own experiential and practical terms, when all issues to do with recording any part of it in words are entirely disregarded by the group, except insofar as individual members choose to keep their own private diaries. A good example of this is the 1996 empowerment inquiry reported in Chapter 18.
- In co-operative inquiry, the co-researchers are also the co-subjects who have the experiences and engage in the actions being researched. The primary research data is thus the data of the co-inquirers' radical memory, borne on the occasion of the relevant experiences and actions (Heron, 1996a). Radical memory is a heightened memory and a central inquiry skill. It is a source of data in its own right independent of any record of it. It is a direct route to the experience that grounds the inquiry.
    - In traditional research on or about *other* people, the memory of the researchers is a very indirect route to the experiences of the other people that ground the inquiry, hence the importance of some kind of record of what the other people say or do.
- Written records are a small part of adequacy. If initiating researchers press too hard for participants to make them, this can be at the expense of viability because participants become alienated.

10

Spatio-temporal extensions

Report status: A study. **Place and year:** London, 1978. **Subtle focus:** Extending ordinary consciousness beyond its perceptual focus on the here and now to access our physical world there and then, at points in space and time outside sensory range. **Social focus:** Informal socializing before and after the evening meetings.

Membership and time structure

The inquiry group comprised nine people, three women and six men, with ages ranging from the twenties to the sixties with a mean in the forties. They joined the group some by personal invitation from the two of us who initiated the project, some by application following a small public meeting through which the project was publicized. Five members of the group were well practised in meditation and related methods, four were not.

We met for three hours in an evening at intervals of ten days to two weeks, with a total of eight meetings between 4 January and 5 April, 1978. The location was my flat in Hampstead in London.

Initial hypothesis

At our first meeting we decided to devote the whole series of meetings to exploring a particular kind of altered state of consciousness (ASC): spatio-temporal extensions of consciousness. Our working hypothesis was as follows.

An ordinary state of consciousness (OSC) can be defined, spatio-temporally, as having direct experience of the physical world exclusively in terms of the *here* and *now* space-time coordinates. Thus I encounter the world entirely in terms of perspectives from this point in space where my body is, and which I experience solely at this point in time. For ordinary consciousness the *here-now* focus of encounter with the world appears to be exclusive of any other spatio-temporal focus of encounter, which can only be imagined. So if I am looking at you *here* and *now* I cannot also really be looking at you *there* and *then*. If I am looking at you *here* and *now* I can at the same time at most only remember or imagine (in both cases have but a mental image of) looking at you *there* and *then*. This last statement we decided to regard as a spatio-temporal prejudice of ordinary consciousness.

We postulated that it is possible for human consciousness to experience direct encounter with the physical world in terms of each of the four basic spatio-temporal co-ordinates, and in terms of various combinations of them. Thus *here*: direct encounter with the physical world through a perspective from this point where my body is. *There*: direct encounter with the physical world through a perspective from a point where my body is not. *Now*: direct encounter with the physical world at the present moment. *Then*: direct encounter with the physical world at either a past moment or a future moment. In an altered spatio-temporal state of consciousness, therefore, I may directly encounter a person or thing *here* and *then*, or *there* and *now*, or *there* and *then*, remembering that *then* refers to either the past or the future. On this hypothesis, human consciousness has potentially unrestricted access to the physical world at all or many points in space and time other than the bodily *here* and *now*.

Analytically speaking, there are fourteen different spatio-temporal ASCs beyond the exclusive *here* and *now* OSC. (1) Exclusively *here-there*. (2) Exclusively *there-now*. (3) Exclusively *there-then*. (4) *Here-now* and *here-then*. (5) *Here-now* and *there-now*. (6) *Here-now* and *there-then*. (7) *Here-then* and *there-now*. (8) *Here-then* and *there-then*. (9) *There-now* and *there-then*. (10) *Here-now* and *here-then* and *there-now*. (11) *Here-now* and *here-now* and *there-then*. (12) *Here-now* and *here-then* and *there-then*. (13) *Here-then* and *there-now* and *there-then*. (14) *Here-now* and *here-then* and *there-now* and *there-then*. In this analysis, *there* may be near or far; and *then* may be past or future.

The common sense objection to all these postulated ASCs is that they involve direct encounter with the physical world independently of the perceptual apparatus of the physical body and that this is absurd. Over against this, we hypothesized that the human imagination focused by the will can either develop itself as organ of perception, or create in subtle matter an organ of perception; and that such perception has potential access to all spatio-temporal coordinates.

We also hypothesized that the possible effects of seeking to enter such spatio-temporal ASCs might include: extrasensory perception; out-of-the-body experiences; abreactive episodes; increased creative energy; greater openness to the divine. Sustained ability to enter such ASCs would establish an intermediate higher centre of consciousness still founded on the OSC *here-now* focus.

In the accounts that follow I shall use several ordinary words, such as 'look' and 'visit', in an extended sense to cover extrasensory looking and visiting, etc.

Cycle 1: there(near)-now ASC

The plan for this cycle was to dissociate from the *here* co-ordinate, and focus on being *there* (near but beyond the body's perceptual range) and *now*.

Action. The exercise is done in pairs. B stands in front of C who is seated. Both establish memory images of each other by looking at each other and memorizing the whole percept and its parts. B goes to another room and for ten minutes imaginatively projects him or herself to visit C still seated in the first room; while C strongly visualizes the visit of B. B uses his or her own memory image of C to facilitate the imaginative projection, as well as C's active visualization. B and C then meet and share feedback on the experience. B and C then reverse roles. Finally the whole group meets to share feedback and reflect on the experience.

Reflection. The main inquiry issue was: how do I distinguish between an actual ASC visit to the one in the other room *there-now*, and a simple memory of that person as perceived before I left the other room? In other words what are the criteria for distinguishing between a real ASC *now* and a memory of an old OSC? Two provisional interrelated criteria were sifted out of the experience shared.

- When there is a sudden, spontaneous shift from your consciously used memory image of the one you are visiting to a non-remembered image or perspective of that person, then you have entered the *there-now* ASC.
- When this sudden shift from remembered to non-remembered perspective coincides with a sudden shift from remembering the space *there* to an experience of being within the space *there*, as if you are in a space within the physical space being visited, then you have entered the *there-now* ASC. This experience of being in an inner space within outer physical space was clearly important for several group members. One person described the experience of being on the interface of the two spaces, where inner and outer spaces interact.

Cycle 2: there(near)-now ASC

We decided to repeat the previous cycle and also to sharpen it up. So again we dissociated from the *here* co-ordinate and focused on being *there* (near but beyond the body's perceptual range) and *now*.

Action. The exercise was done in pairs exactly as reported for cycle 1, but with the following addition. After B goes to another room, C pins one of four symbols to his or her clothing at the top of the back just below the back of the neck. And C removes the symbol just before B returns physically to share feedback. The symbols are a cross, a circle, a square and a pentagram. B has seen all the symbols before leaving the room, and is told that one of them will be pinned to C after B leaves and is also told where it will be pinned on C. During B's ASC visit B tries to notice which symbol is on C's back. Feedback in pairs and then reverse roles, then feedback and reflection in the whole group.

Reflection. This cycle did not really take us deeper into the use of the two important criteria discovered in cycle 1, although both criteria were used again in cycle 2. The addition of the symbols produced a distracting getting-it-right anxiety, and a range of associated problems, as well as some important distinctions. Dealing with the important distinctions first, there seemed to be three sorts of experiences in this cycle: telepathy, clairvoyance at a distance, clairvoyance on-the-spot.

- Telepathy was of course mind-to-mind contact between C and B: C knowing and so projecting the symbol pinned to his or her back, and B receiving this.
- Clairvoyance at a distance was where B was still *here* in this room but with a clairvoyant perception of C in the other room.
- Clairvoyance on-the-spot was where B was dissociated from *here* and was visiting *there* with a clairvoyant perception of C as from inner space *there*. For clairvoyance on-the-spot it seemed that both criteria discovered in cycle 1 applied, whereas for clairvoyance at a distance only the first of them applied. The cycle 1 and 2 criteria were:

- When there is a sudden, spontaneous shift from your consciously used memory image of the one you are visiting to a non-remembered image or perspective of that person, then you have entered the *there-now* ASC.
- When this sudden shift from remembered to non-remembered perspective coincides with a sudden shift from remembering the space *there* to an experience of being within the space *there*, as if you are in a space within the physical space being visited, then you have entered the *there-now* ASC.

Only two people out of nine got the symbol right, and in each case by telepathy it seemed. One of these two used a strategy of intense concentration and will; the other used the polar strategy of effortless meditation and just let the symbol arise in consciousness. What distinguished telepathy from clairvoyance at a distance and clairvoyance on-the-spot was the sudden impact of the bare symbol with no perspectival view of its setting. One person who had clairvoyance on-the-spot going, according to the two criteria discovered in cycle 1, could see the paper pinned to clothing below C's back of the neck, but there was only a grey blur on it, the symbol being impossible to distinguish. Associated problems of the exercise were:

- Shape preferences interfering with both telepathy and clairvoyance.
- Interference from cross-telepathy, that is, when I pick up a symbol by telepathy from someone who is not my partner for the exercise but with whom I am more in tune.
- Interference, for those taking the B-role second, from memory of the symbol pinned to them when they were C.

Cycle 3: here-now and there(near)-now ASC

The plan for this cycle was to be *here* and *there* simultaneously, *now*.

Action. The exercise was done in pairs, with B and C sitting facing each other and looking for six minutes into each other's left eye, with the intention to be in both pairs of eyes at once. So B is looking with B's eyes at C's left eye, and at the same time is looking with C's eyes at B's left eye. Simultaneously C is looking with C's eyes at B's left eye, and looking with B's eyes at C's left eye. Since there were nine in the group, one person experimented with bilocation with his image in a mirror. Feedback in pairs, then feedback and reflection in the whole group.

Reflection. This was an exercise in interpersonal bilocation. Of the four pairs involved, three pairs couldn't make it and were caught up in various sorts of OSC, usually in minor positive and negative emotional accompaniments of non-verbal mutual gazing. There were two interesting outcomes:

- The fourth pair made it. Their criterion for this was that both partners simultaneously experienced the other's left eye as the eye of both. So B experienced C's left eye as the eye of both B and C; and at the same time C experienced B's left eye as the eye of both C and B. And the rest of the face for both was blurred.
- The solo experimenter also made it - with his own mirror image. His criterion was that he had a pronounced shift in consciousness as a result. His was a

paradoxical kind of bilocation, since a mirror image is a virtual appearance only.

Cycle 4: there(far)-now ASC leading into here-now and there(far)-now ASC

We returned to the theme of the first two cycles, dissociating from the *here* co-ordinate and focusing on being *there* (beyond the body's perceptual range) and *now*. This time we decided that *there* would be much further away than the next room: a place we had all at one time visited or seen pictures of. Further, that when *there* we would also combine it with being *here*.

Action. We sat in a circle chanting *om*. We used the sound of the chant as a carrier wave to effect a visit to Stonehenge. We also used memory images of Stonehenge or of pictures of it. Once *there,* the chant *here* was discontinued and each person continued chanting *there*. After a period of this, we combined the visiting and chanting *there* at Stonehenge with chanting again *here* in the room, so we were entering a *here-now* and *there-now* ASC. We then returned from Stonehenge and shared feedback and discussed our findings.

Reflection. This experience was much more elusive in terms of distinguishing between real and imaginary experience. Firstly, unlike Cycles 1 and 2, members had no very recent clear cut memory images of *there* with which they could contrast sudden non-remembered perspectival views. Members had a large number of fairly imprecise not-at-all recent memory images blurring and overlapping each other, including their own memories of being *there* and memories of photographs, including aerial photographs. It was more problematic to distinguish between these and actual vague impressions of *there*. However, some had non-remembered perspectives of some of the stones from just a few feet above them: clearly neither a personal visit memory nor a memory of an aerial photograph. Two modest criteria emerged:

- What distinguished a real non-remembered perspective from a purely imaginary one was the unbiddenness of the former, its sudden and unexpected appearing in consciousness, together with a sense of spatial interiority as described under cycle 1. It was as if people could intend the visit but have no conscious control over the actual angle of entry to the *there* site.
- Another criterion was found to distinguish the real ASC from memory or imagination in an OSC. This was the felt sense of the tang of reality, of the impact of the world as encountered and experienced. But there was an ambiguity about this criterion. Did it mean that anyone exercising imagination in an OSC was unawarely moving over into a real spatio-temporal ASC if their imagination became so vivid as to give a felt sense of the tang of reality?

Cycle 5: there(near)-now leading by stages to there(far)-now adding here-now ASC

We continued with the basic theme of *there* and *now* but working for the first time explicitly with the notion of a space within physical space, also with the notion of a subtle double of the physical body. The subtle double, on this model, is in the space within physical space. And since trying to jump directly from *here* to *there* far away had led to somewhat elusive results on cycle 4, we decided to go from *here* to *there(near)* and then by stages to *there(far)*. Once *there(far)-now*, we added *here-now*.

Action. We sat in a circle. Each person projected themselves into a space *there* just outside the physical body, looking at the physical body from this space outside it. Taking the criterion used from cycle 1 onwards that a *there* space is somehow within the physical space into which one is projecting oneself, we also looked at anything that might be present in the space within the physical space of the room. So we were looking at the physical body in physical space and at non-physical entities of any sort in the space within the physical space. Did we see the subtle doubles of other group members? Did we have a sense of being in our own subtle double?

We then returned to *here* in the physical body and each person practised looking at his or her own subtle double standing in front of him or her. Each person then entered the double, and took a journey in spatial stages to the moon: first to the ceiling of the room, then on to the roof of the building, then a half mile or so up over the city and so on until arriving on the moon. We met in a circle on the surface of the moon. We then physically chanted *om* in the physical room *here*. And we listened to it *there* in our circle on the moon. This took us into a *here-now* and *there-now* ASC. We stopped the physical *om* and returned by stages from *there* on the moon to *here* in the room. Feedback and reflection in the group.

Reflection. Our discussion again focused on the primary issue: how to differentiate between memory/imagination on the one hand, and real extrasensory perception on the other. Several new criteria emerged from the experience of this cycle. Interestingly they were all to do with events shortly after leaving the physical body, or upon returning to it. The time spent on the moon was very elusive so far as differentiating between imagination and extrasensory perception was concerned.

There was little that counted as direct experience of subtle bodies (i.e. little that differentiated imagination from extrasensory perception), either of one's own subtle body or the subtle bodies of other members of the group. But two criteria were accepted as pointing to a real sense of being out of the physical body and both applied to a time shortly after leaving it.

- When some aspect of a view of *there* gives rise to an unexpected emotion: thus one member reported quite unexpected feelings of surprise and distaste about the wetness of the outside roof of the building when going up and out on the way to the moon.
- When an expected physical event occurs which one notices when one is *there* beyond the range of physical perception: for example, a sudden distraction of attention by traffic movements perceived from above when *there* in the sky.

There were two experiences which were regarded as promising criteria for distinguishing between having actually been out of one's physical body as distinct from just imagining it.

- To quote from one member, 'When I opened my eyes at the end, I came from a long way back'. This was the sense of emerging into physical space from the depths of that inner space that is within physical space.
- To quote from another member, 'When I returned, I was surprised to discover myself still in the room'. This was the surprise at the physical body being *here* in the room, since one had been so vividly and totally *there* - 'I had gone so far off, so thoroughly'.

Cycle 6: there(near or far)-now ASC

This was a short cycle repeating out-of-the-body *there* and *now* ASCs both to check up on and make use of the different criteria so far reported.

Action. We sat in a circle, each person making their own out-of-the-body journey to *there now*, travelling near or far, going where or how they wanted in their own way. We then shared and reflected upon he experience.

Reflection. This exercise threw up no new criteria to distinguish an authentic spatiotemporal extension from imagination or memory, but confirmed to varying degrees criteria already proposed:

- A sudden shift to a non-remembered perspective.
- A sudden shift to being in a space within the physical space *there*.
- A felt sense of the tang of reality.
- An unexpected feeling about an aspect of the view *there*.
- A sudden distraction of attention by an unexpected event *there*.
- Returning from a long way back, the depths of inner space.
- Being surprised on returning that the physical body is still *here*.

But a new and unsettling issue arose. How do you distinguish, *once you know of these criteria,* between the criteria actually applying to your recent experience and just imagining or kidding yourself that they apply? There seemed to be no obvious or immediate answer to this.

Cycle 7: there-then(past) ASC

All our cycles so far had used only the *now* time co-ordinate, moving spatially from *here* to *there*, or combining *here* and *there*. We decided it was time to try the *then* time co-ordinate, projecting across time as well as space. It felt much more implausible to suppose we could have direct access to *there-then(past)* than it did to suppose we could have direct access to *there-now*.

Action. We sat in a circle and tuned in to some past event in another place that resonated with our circle: in other words an event *there-then(past)* where the same number of people were gathered for a purpose related in some way to ASCs. Each person made the visit *there-then* and in due course returned. We shared experiences and discussed our findings.

Reflection. This was perhaps the most elusive experience of all our cycles for distinguishing between imagination and extrasensory perception. The target (the same number of people met for a similar purpose) was too ambitious: too precise in some respects, such as number and purpose; and too vague in other respects, such as where and when in the past. So it is not surprising we got bogged down in our effrontery at supposing that what we experienced was anything other than our own fertile imaginations at work. However, members certainly came up with a lot of interesting images and stories. But it was their diversity and lack of obvious overlap in terms of content, time or space that helped precipitate our loss of nerve. We reverted to the imagination-only explanation. It is interesting that it never occurred to anyone to propose that each of us had accessed a different and authentic *there-then* resonant group.

Cycle 8: here(space-1)- there(space-2)-now ASC

In this cycle our inquiry took a certain turn of direction. So far we had been concerned with a perspective on *there* from a point outside the range of our physical perception. But we had discovered that this perspective is somehow from within the physical space *there*. We now took up more thoroughly what we had briefly explored at the start of cycle 5 - looking for non-physical entities in this more interior kind of space. But we did this without moving from *here*. So this was an inquiry into space-2 (the space within physical space) without moving from one's perspectival position in space-1 (physical space). We turned from exploring spatio-temporal extensions of direct access to space-1 to exploring what goes on or can go on in space-2. This does now seem to have been a marked divergence, if not a distraction, from our original and hitherto sustained line of inquiry.

Action. We sat in a circle and visualized a column of misty, pearly light in space-2 within the space-1 of the room. An invocation was made overtly and physically by one of us, inviting a space-2 presence to enter the space-2 of the room 'for aware relating and communion with us'. We then practised seeing and hearing this presence. What three words did this presence communicate? After some time we visualized the departure of the presence, and resumed an OSC for sharing experiences and for reflection.

Reflection. Our discussion focused almost entirely upon the content of our experiences, rather than on criteria for distinguishing between just imagining a presence in space-2 and actually perceiving a presence in the space-2 of the room.

- Two members had images: a Red Indian head; an African man with persons stacked behind him.
- One person had a strong devotional experience with the image of fire in the space-2 of the room.
- Two persons felt a presence in the space-2 of the room, without images. One of these said: 'I felt a presence, I was bouleverse, I've never experienced anything like it before, I wanted to talk to the presence'.
- Others experienced little or nothing.

We did briefly discuss the hypothesis that different individual perspectives on the content of a given area of space-2 may be much more diverse and apparently disconnected than is the case with different perspectives on a given area of physical space.

Cycle 9: here(space-1)-there(space-2)-now ASC

This was a repeat of cycle 8.

Action. Exactly as for cycle 8, except that we invoked a presence to enter the prepared space-2 of the room to guide a meditation. Each then followed a meditation wherever it led. Closure and discussion.

Reflection. Again the discussion was almost entirely about the content of the exercise.

- Several members experienced nothing much.
- One member saw space-2 but was outside it in mood, feeling sadness.
- One person was immersed throughout in personal memories.
- Only one member had a powerful meditation: of the phenomenal world arising out of divine Shakti, like a baby from the womb.

Review and forward planning

This was the eighth and final meeting of this inquiry. We had done nine cycles in the previous seven meetings, two of the meetings including two cycles each. The eighth meeting was, in fact, almost entirely devoted to planning a future inquiry through a further series of meetings; and so falls outside the scope of his report.

Evaluation

What follows is my analysis made some considerable time after the group was over, and was not discussed with the group. Before considering the content of the findings, I will discuss what degree of validity they could be said to have in the light of an account of how validity procedures apply to this inquiry.

1. *Research cycling.* 2. *Divergence.* 3. *Convergence.* I will take these three together. The inquiry developed a strong line in research cycling over the first six cycles; each cycle focused on the same aspect of the inquiry area, the *there-now* ASC, so that the research cycling over the first six cycles was strongly convergent. It thus helped to develop, confirm and extend the criteria for distinguishing between memory/imagination and extrasensory perception. There were helpful elements of divergence within these six cycles, but they were variations within the *there-now* model mostly to do with *there* being near or far. The occasional divergence into combining *here-now* and *there-now* received very little direct attention in our reflection phases, so it is not clear what it contributed.

We diverged into *there-then(past)* on the seventh cycle. This divergence was importantly within our original ASC hypothetical model, but we lost heart with the radical challenge of it, so this promisingly divergent cycle apparently contributed little or nothing to our overall inquiry.

In our last two cycles, eight and nine, we really diverged away from our original ASC model and started in effect a new inquiry into space-2. Our original model was to explore direct access to the physical world in space-1 through spatio-temporal coordinates other than *here-now*. In doing this we came across the importance of doing it through the intermediary of space-2. And in our last two cycles we were in a sense distracted into exploring space-2 in its own right. But for some this exploration did underline the power and the claim of space-2.

The mainly convergent focus of the first six cycles did clarify some useful criteria for distinguishing between memory/imagination and extrasensory perception with regard to *there-now* ASCs. But these criteria are tentative and provisional only. Firstly, because six cycles are not enough, and much more work needs to be done along that convergent line. And secondly, because other parts of the whole spatio-temporal co-ordinate map have not been systematically explored over several cycles. The criteria revealed in such explorations might cause the criteria we modestly discovered to be viewed in a different light.

4. *Authentic collaboration.* It had been agreed when planning this inquiry of eight sessions that I would frame the starting hypothesis and design the experiences intended to explore it, the whole being put into action on the condition that group members both understood and assented to, could internalize, my ideas and proposals. So the thinking that generated and designed the inquiry was not the fruit of co-operation; but it was fully internalized and assented to by all members of the inquiry group.

Everyone, of course, was fully and equally involved in both the action phases and in the reflection phases, so that the findings were co-operatively generated. But this report and its evaluation of the inquiry is entirely my work. It is written, on the basis of notes I took at the time, six years after the event. Nevertheless, the internalization of theory and design by all, the full participation in action and reflection by all, does give the inquiry a core of genuine collaboration.

5. *Challenging uncritical subjectivity.* The challenge can be applied during the action phase or the reflection phase of co-operative inquiry. During the action phase it means devising experiences that may lead to a reframing of the inquiry hypothesis by testing its limits. During the reflection phase it may mean, among other things, finding more ordinary explanations of what we have experienced than those in line with our hypothesis. We chose the latter. During the first seven reflection phases we regularly asked 'Isn't this supposedly ASC experience better explained in terms of ordinary imagination and/or memory?' The use of this modest test generated a set of tentative criteria for differentiating between imagination/memory and extrasensory perception. But these criteria were not themselves subjected to further rigorous tests. Nor was the original working model of spatio-temporal ASCs examined with philosophical rigour by the group. It was internalized and accepted on the grounds of its apparent coherence with reported experiences found in the literature of psychical research, LSD psychotherapy and mysticism. I conclude that our minimal use of challenging uncritical subjectivity was at most sufficient to give our findings about criteria some modest claim on the attention of future inquirers.

6. *The management of research counter-transference.* Our inquiry did clearly call up quite a lot of anxiety. To say that direct encounter with the physical world is not restricted to the *here-now* focus, but can also occur through a *there-then* focus, and through all sorts of combinations of *here, now, there* and *then,* is a considerable threat to the common sense stability and identity of the empirical ego. It is unsettling to take the hypothesis seriously. We attempted to deal with this anxiety by including in the opening activities of each session a period of body work - standing, shaking vigorously, hyperventilating, letting out sound. The idea was that this would help both to own and to discharge some of the fear stirred up by the inquiry. We would then be less hindered by fear from entering ASCs and from making appropriate sense of them. In retrospect this seems a minimal approach to the management of research counter-transference, but clearly was very much better than doing nothing at all. Hopefully, it contributed in some measure in the way we intended.

7. *Balance between reflection and action.* I think we got the balance about right, in terms of the amount of time devoted to each; but the quality of the experience and action was probably more subtle and refined than the quality of the reflection brought to bear upon it. Our ASC competence was probably greater than our OSC conceptual and analytic competence. So the temporal balance was all right, less so the qualitative balance. The implication of this for the validity of our findings speaks for itself.

8. *Chaos and order, the avoidance of premature closure.* How well did we tolerate chaos, confusion; and not press too soon for intellectual closure on the inquiry? The ambiguity we had to tolerate was 'Is this extrasensory perception, or is it just imagination and/or memory?' I think we were able to tolerate this ambiguity fairly well for six cycles; but the challenge of the seventh cycle - the *there-then* ASC - was probably too much and we could no longer sustain the ambiguity, either for this or the last two cycles. But we did not deal with this loss of tolerance by premature intellectual closure. We dealt with it more crudely by intellectually abandoning the issue in the reflection phases of the last three cycles: in the seventh cycle we lost heart about it, and in the last two cycles pretty well ignored it.

Summary. All in all, taking these eight validity issues together, I conclude that the inquiry was minimally beyond the basic level of adequacy, and that the findings summarized in the following section of this report receive only a very modest warrant from the inquiry; and can be regarded at best as tentative.

Findings of the inquiry

Here then are what I regard as the provisional findings of the inquiry, findings which receive only a minimal warrant from it, yet merit further more systematic inquiry of the same sort. They are not put forward as generalizations, as statements that apply universally, but only as statements that apply to the inquiry group, as represented, holonomically, by one or more of its members. The actual outcomes of the inquiry, which underpin these propositions, are, *perhaps,* a set of rudimentary extrasensory skills. The criteria given in 5, 6 and 7 below, are provisonal criteria for identifying the possible skill at work.

1. It is possible to have direct encounter with the physical world from a *there-now* perspective, where *there* is outside the range of physical perception.
2. This encounter is by extrasensory perception, that is clairvoyance.
3. Such clairvoyance from a *there-now* perspective is facilitated if *there* is physically near where the clairvoyant's physical body is *here-now*; for example, if *there* is simply in the next room.
4. It is also facilitated if the clairvoyant has a clear cut and recently and intentionally impressed memory image of *there* obtained by normal perception of *there* shortly before the clairvoyant goes into another room to practise clairvoyant perception of *there*. This memory image acts as an intentionally chosen springboard for launching into clairvoyance of *there*.
5. Such clairvoyance on-the-spot *there*, out of the physical body, may be distinguished from OSC memory of, or imagination about, *there* by the following criteria:
    - The start of clairvoyance is sometimes marked by a sudden shift from an intentionally remembered perspective of *there* to a non-remembered, maybe unusual (e.g. from above or very close), perspective of *there*; combined with
    - A sudden shift from remembering the physical space *there* to a felt sense of being within the physical space *there*, of being in a more inward kind of space - that is internal to physical space. Internal space we call space-2, physical space we call space-1.
    - Clairvoyance is sometimes marked by a felt sense of the tang of physical reality in the extrasensory perceptions.
    - Clairvoyance is sometimes marked by sudden, unexpected feelings arising about some physical feature or features of what is seen *there*.
    - Clairvoyance is sometimes marked by a sudden distraction of attention by some unexpected physical event *there*.
    - The end of a clairvoyant visit is sometimes marked by a sense of returning from a long way back, the depths of inner space.
    - The end of a clairvoyant visit is sometimes marked by being surprised on returning that the physical body is still *here*.
6. Clairvoyance on-the-spot, out-of-the-body, *there*, is to be distinguished from clairvoyance at-a-distance, where the clairvoyant is still *here*, not dissociated from his or her physical location. The former is marked by the first two criteria in 5, with one or more of the others; the latter is marked by the first one only.
7. Telepathy is to be distinguished from both clairvoyance on-the-spot and clairvoyance at-a-distance by the sudden impact of the telepathic content or meaning or symbol or image, with no perspectival view of its physical setting.

8. Space-2, the space within physical space (space-1), is the intermediary for clairvoyant access to the physical world beyond *here-now* co-ordinates. It is the activation of memory images and imagination in space-2 that initiates the clairvoyant access to space-1.
9. Clairvoyance can function directly in relation to the non-physical phenomena occurring exclusively in space-2, although those phenomena are also at the same time within the appropriate realm of space-1.

11

Impressions of the other reality

Report status: A study. **Place and year:** Cornwall, UK, 1981. **Subtle focus:** Garnering impressions of the other reality, a non-physical subtle energy world interpenetrating this world, while functioning awarely in this reality. **Social focus**: Informal socializing in the breaks and among those who were residential at the privately run research centre.

Membership and time structure

There were twenty people in the inquiry group, four men and sixteen women, with ages ranging from the twenties to the sixties with a mean in the late thirties. The majority had considerable interest in, and diverse experience of, altered states. Over half those attending lived locally, were part of a community of persons who knew each other, were involved as practitioners and/or clients in various forms of radical psychotherapy, and were open to occult belief systems in general and about Cornwall and its ancient stone circles in particular. The participants were recruited by a programme brochure advertising a workshop, facilitated by myself, as a co-operative inquiry into altered states of consciousness. The blurb gave a brief account of what this might involve.

The group ran as a five-day residential workshop in October 1981, at the Centre for Alternative Education and Research (CAER) in Cornwall. This Centre is in a country house on the site of an iron age settlement, which includes a *fogou.* This is a passageway running under the ground and out, with a chamber, the creep, to one side, the whole structure being thought to have some important, if obscure, ceremonial function in iron age culture. Ancient stone circle sites are nearby.

Initial hypothesis and overall design

The inquiry opened with a series of introductory rounds, in which members in turn shared with each other various aspects of themselves and their experiences, including altered states of consciousness. I then introduced the theory and practice of co-operative inquiry as a research method. This was discussed and debated until it seemed there was sufficient grasp of it, and assent to it, for the inquiry to be viable.

Our first reflection phase considered different possible areas of inquiry within the total field of altered states. For this I used an early and limited version of a transpersonal map. The areas presented were: paraphysical or etheric fields of physical phenomena; subjective altered psychological states such as dreams; extrasensory perception in its various forms; out-of-the-body experiences; mediumship; the other reality (or space-2 as we called it in the previously reported inquiry); the domain of archetypes, Platonic forms; the divine as such.

After much discussion, we decided to inquire into that ASC in which we have impressions of the other reality while still functioning awarely in this reality. Our initial hypothesis, then, was that it is possible to function awarely in two worlds at once: this physical world and a non-physical subtle energy world of presences and powers that is somehow within and around the physical world.

We then embarked on a series of six cycles of action and reflection. The plan for each action phase was creatively devised co-operatively within the whole group. All the action phases were done collectively by the group in the same large room and in other places in the grounds. Some of these phases involved group interaction; in others group members did solitary things side by side. The reflection phases, too, were all done collectively: individuals shared their findings and impressions verbally in the presence of everyone else. These findings were recorded.

We completed four cycles by the end of the third day. The fourth day was wholly devoted to a very long extension of the reflection phase of the fourth cycle. We applied a systematic challenge to uncritical subjectivity, through a rigorous devil's advocate procedure, mainly but not exclusively to our impressions during the action phase of this cycle, which was in the *fogou*.

The fifth day included a very important and powerful fifth cycle and the concluding sixth cycle. Reflection on the sixth action phase led over into a final and closing reflection, but this was a shared celebration of the workshop experience as a whole rather than a formal deliberation about the findings of our inquiry.

Validity procedures were included during and after the second cycle, and again during and after the fourth cycle, with an unexpected validity event occurring in the middle of the fifth cycle. In what follows I shall report first on the cycles, second on the validity procedures used, and finally on the findings.

The findings given at the end have been distilled by me out of all the recorded data, especially the data on the devil's advocate procedure. This report has been written exclusively by myself, and has not been circulated to group members for their comments.

Including myself there were twenty people in the inquiry group. But some of the local participants had commitments that made their attendance variable. So in some of the cycle reports below, less than twenty people are referred to.

Cycle 1: A ritual for receiving impressions of the other reality (day 1)

In planning the action phase of this cycle, it was proposed by one group member, and readily agreed by all, that ritual activity is a way of acting awarely in this world while at the same eliciting impressions of the other world. A number of people in the group improvised a ritual and one person took us through it.

Action. We stood in a circle with hands on each other's shoulders. We then moved in a counterclockwise circle step by step saying together 'East to West it behoves the rest', moving faster and faster. Next we sat in a circle, relaxing for ten minutes, then held hands and visualized energy moving from left to right. Finally, we centred ourselves and became open to impressions. After some time we shared our impressions.

Reflection. Seven people received no impressions, ten members received some impressions. Among these ten:

- Four inquirers got pictures of eyes, birds, pyramids; and three received instructions from unseen presences.
- One person received several instructions very strongly. They were for the group: to use catharsis and shamanistic ecstasies; to spend two days indoors; to polish the floor; to inquire where the birds flock in the garden; to use chants and music.

Discussion focused on whether this set of instructions was from a person or persons in the other reality; or whether it was bizarre fantasy material of purely subjective kind. No conclusions, or tentative criteria for distinguishing genuine from spurious instructions, emerged. The issue was left open, with several members willing to give the instructions the benefit of the doubt. Others felt that whatever their status, they were interesting, if odd, guides to future action.

Cycle 2: A ritual for receiving impressions of the other reality (day 2)

In planning this cycle it was agreed to use again ritual activity as a way of becoming aware of the two worlds at the same time. This led rapidly to several people, not all the same as those who designed the first one, devising a ritual sequence that included activities derived from the instructions strongly received by one member in the first action phase. Different group members guided us through different parts of it.

Action. Each person divined for water sources or streams, which were known to be plentiful, in the ground under the wooden floor of the large room in which we were meeting. Every member, having thus chosen a spot on the floor, polished it with a cloth for twenty minutes, then danced on the same spot to music for another forty minutes. We sat in a circle and practised glossolalia (speaking in tongues); and followed this using ordinary language for impromptu prophetic utterance. We shared impressions and reflected on our experiences.

Reflection. We agreed that this and the previous action phase had been concerned with preparation and sensitization. The bizarre activities were for loosening us up, disarming us and getting us ready. Impressions that occurred in this second ritual were then shared. They were mainly to do with the polishing and dancing on the same spot:

- Nine people had various experiences to do with energy, ranging from trance-like altered states to erotic ordinary states.
- Four members had images or pictures.
- Two members were preoccupied with distress feelings from past experiences.
- One reported simple enjoyment.

Most of the ostensible altered states reported were ambiguous. Did they portend another reality, or were they simply subjective sensation and imagination stirred up and heightened in their impact by rather unusual activity? We were aware of this issue, but did not address it with any rigour. There was a general tendency to give the ambiguity the benefit of the doubt. We assumed or hoped that maybe some impact of the other reality was evident in some of our experiences.

During this cycle considerable agitation and distress of the ordinary sort, both intrapsychic and interpersonal, started to surface. We took time out to deal with it, both during and after the cycle, as reported in the section below on validity issues. It was important to attend to this, but it did rather distract us from rigorous reflection.

Cycle 3: Noticing the other reality at the edge of the visual field (day 3)

I proposed this exercise, after sharing a general systems theory account of the relation between this reality and the other reality.

Action. For some thirty minutes we practised noticing non-physical, extrasensory impressions at the edge of the visual perceptual field, also noticing extrasensory sounds beyond the range of physical sounds. We did this first while standing, sitting or walking, in silence and without social interaction. Then we tried it while chatting to each other about mundane things. So we were attempting to combine sensory perception of this reality with extrasensory perception of the other reality. We shared our experiences and reflected on them.

Reflection

- Four members reported that they entered a daydream state while silently wandering around the room, and that this daydream state felt pregnant with potential extrasensory perception; also that they had experienced this before in their lives and felt guilty about it. The sense of extrasensory potential was about what, in the other reality, precipitates events in this reality.
- Another person said he found a chink between the daydream and sense perception of the room, a chink 'where they transform each other', and saw a cherub at the edge of his visual field.
- Someone else said she saw 'entities and women in white' at the edge of her visual field.
- Many of the group found that talking to each other about mundane matters constricted their ability to attend to the edge of their visual fields.

In the discussion which followed, while it was clear that all these experiences had an uncertain status, hovering in the ambiguous hinterland between fantasy and extrasensory perception, there was also a sense of a marked reduction in the degree of this ambiguity compared to previous discussions.

Cycle 4: Procession and entry to the other reality in the fogou (day 3)

The plan for this cycle was creatively improvised by several group members, who conducted different parts of it.

Action. We gathered round a large tree in a wooded area in the garden. This was a tree 'where the birds flock' (see instructions in cycle 1). One member taught us a chant. In single file we processed along a sinuous path through the wood toward the *fogou*, chanting. We entered the *fogou* and lined up on either side of the underground passageway, holding hands, and open to impressions of the other reality. After some time we processed out of the *fogou* and stood round the top of the creep in the garden, while one member was underground, reciting prayers aloud inside the creep that leads off the passageway of the *fogou*. We stood in silence for some time, receiving impressions. We then processed back to the house to our meeting room and had a long session sharing our impressions and reflecting on them.

Reflection. There was a dramatic increase in the intensity and range of impressions received by group members in this cycle. This increase in intensity and range was accompanied by a very strong sense of the impact of the impressions coming into human consciousness. And these impressions were received either inside the *fogou*, underground, or above ground standing around the top of the creep while prayers were being recited within it.

There were sixteen of us involved in this cycle. Inside the *fogou* a lot seemed to be going on. There was considerable overlap among the membership of the following different experiential subgroups:

- Six members reported powerful trembling and shaking with an energy coursing in various forms both up and down through the physical body.
- Three people experienced a mental and physical cleansing.
- Eight members had impulses to act in various ways and six of these acted on their impulses, moving and gesturing in various ways.
- Two people each had a sense of two presences in the other reality within the *fogou*.
- Two people had a sense of a lot going on in the other reality within the *fogou*.
- Five people had strong images of various kinds, especially faces in the stone walls of the *fogou* passageway.
- One person heard sounds.
- Many people experienced very considerable power, leaving them somewhat in awe and positively shaken. Five people used phrases like 'overwhelmed', 'wonderful', 'very good feeling', 'like a cool dip'.

Above ground around the top of the creep:

- Four people saw and/or sensed subtle energy like flames or swirls coming up through the ground out of the creep and rising up into the sky, yet in the other reality.

There were thus basically five kinds of experience reported:

- Streaming of energy in and out of the energy field of the physical body.
- Visions, pictures or images of faces and symbolic objects.
- A felt sense of presences and their activities, and of subtle energies, in the other reality within certain areas of physical space.

- A sense of the numinous, of pervasive spiritual power.
- Emotional uplift.

As the group members shared feedback about all these sorts of experience, it became clear that we were doing so with a very strong implicit assumption that we had indeed activated events in the other reality in a way that interacted with us and our location in this reality, and that we were noticing these space-2 events in a variety of different ways.

We then became concerned about this assumption, speculating that we had all fallen victims to a massive consensus collusion. Perhaps we were confusing our own hysterically activated subjective fantasies with genuine impressions of another reality. So on the next day, day 4, we devised an elaborate devil's advocate procedure to apply Occam's razor to our interpretations of our experiences in cycle 4. This meant trying to find quite ordinary alternative interpretations, reducing assumed ASCs to somewhat pathological OSCs. Details of the procedure are given below in the section on validity. This use of a systematic challenge to uncritical subjectivity took up almost the whole of the fourth day; and out of it emerged our main set of findings, given below in the section on findings.

Cycle 5: A sword in the other reality (day 5)

This cycle arose spontaneously out of the personal work done by one of our group members who was in the midst of considerable trauma and crisis during the time of the workshop. She did some personal growth work facilitated by me in the middle of the group, which developed as follows.

Action The group member concerned was working with me in the middle of the room, with the whole group gathered around, giving attention. She began with her present-time crisis, then regressed to early childhood experiences. After considerable work on this childhood material, she embarked on a spatio-temporal extension of consciousness and began to resonate with the experiences of a fourteen year old girl undergoing psychic training in some far eastern country in an earlier historical epoch. She moved back into present time from this assumed ASC carrying a sword, a psychic sword in the other reality yet strongly focused within this reality. This invisible subtle sword was ceremonially passed round the group, from member to member, until it was held again by the person who brought it to the group. She held it out horizontally in front of her for a while.

The owner of the house and Director of the Centre sponsoring our workshop had a large and friendly dog which had spent a good deal of time with us in our indoor meetings, both during the action and the reflection phases. This dog now got up and advanced toward the unseen sword, sniffed at a point in space roughly where the end of the blade would be, then backed off suddenly with a jump and start and sound as if pricked on the nose. The dog prowled warily at a distance from the sword, keeping an eye on it.

The sword was then ceremonially placed in a mirror on the wall. We opened a phase of discussion and reflection.

Reflection Discussion centred almost entirely upon the sword incident.

- Almost every group member had experienced the dog's behaviour in advancing curiously, sniffing, jumping back with a start and a sound, then prowling warily at a distance, as a very striking confirmation of the actual presence of the subtle sword.

For what it was worth, that was the cognitive impact of the whole event. No one found or proffered an alternative explanation of a more ordinary sort which carried any conviction or seemed more plausible than the subtle sword explanation. Perhaps we could have argued that the group was sharing a collective hallucination or fantasy, and this hypnotically induced in the dog behaviour consonant with the fantasy. But we didn't argue this. The dog's behaviour, on the contrary, jolted several people from an ambiguous attitude to the presence of the sword to a positive belief that it was in some way there.

Cycle 6: Closing ritual at a stone circle (day 5)

This whole ritual was co-operatively planned by several group members. It was much more a concluding ceremony than a formal part of our inquiry: a kind of celebration and affirmation.

Action We walked from the house half a mile or so to a large stone circle standing in a field. Each person stood near a stone. We held hands and wove alternately in and out of the stones, moving round the circle three times. A physical sword had been stuck in the ground in the centre of the circle. We spiralled in and out three times from the stone circle to its centre where the sword was. We then stood all around outside the stones: each person assumed a symbolic posture and said aloud one word. We then moved back to the meeting room in the house for discussion and reflection.

Reflection For many the stone circle experience was religious, mystical with feelings of:

- Peace.
- Stillness.
- Opening up to love.
- The interconnection and intermeshing of things.
- Stepping out of ordinary time.
- The unity of Atman and Brahman.
- Being powerfully energized.
- The source of things.

Sharing these experiences led over into spontaneous accounts of what the whole workshop experience had meant to people. We had a closing circle of meditation and appreciations.

Evaluation

As for the previous inquiry, I will discuss here how validity procedures were applied in this inquiry, in order to judge its adequacy and what degree of credibility our findings might be said to have.

1. *Research cycling*. 2. *Divergence*. 3. *Convergence*. In cycles 1, 2, and 6 we used different sorts of group rituals to open ourselves to impressions of the other reality. In cycle 3 we used just one ESP-type exercise to do the same. And cycle 5 was highly impromptu and idiosyncratic, to do with the unseen sword. Six cycles in five days seems reasonable, considering all the other activities to do with other validity issues (see below) that were also covered.

Yet the research cycling was full of idiosyncrasy and divergence. Each of the group rituals was very different and determined more by the instructions received by one member in the first cycle than by principles of research method. Each member idiosyncratically explored whatever kind of impressions came their way or suited their mood or style or temperament; except in cycle 3 where we all tried gathering impressions in the same way. This extreme divergence and idiosyncrasy in the use of research cycling did indeed give us a multi-faceted view of how humans may pick up intimations of the other reality while aware of this reality. But it led to results that were highly impressionistic. No one way of generating impressions by one particular ritual activity was pursued rigorously over several cycles; and no one way of receiving impressions was pursued rigorously over several cycles. What our findings thus gain in a certain interlocking comprehensiveness they lose in terms of a substantial experiential warrant for any part of the whole.

4. *Authentic collaboration*. This was really very good, all things considered. The group took over the inquiry process and made it their own. In no sense did I run it, manage it or design it. The one time I did try to push hard on what I considered to be an important methodological issue, the group strongly resisted it. Thus the inquiry has both the strengths and the weaknesses of genuine co-operation among a group of people using a method of inquiry which they had been previously unfamiliar with. And it is important to note that, as with the previous inquiry, the report on this inquiry has not been written collaboratively but exclusively by myself.

5. *Challenging uncritical subjectivity* As mentioned at the end of cycle 4 above, this procedure was applied very thoroughly throughout most of the fourth day, since we had become concerned that we were all possibly colluding in passing off fantasy material as genuine impressions of the other reality.

The procedure was as follows. Each group member in turn sat in a chair in front of the group and had read back to her or him what she or he had reported as impressions of the other reality during cycle 4, the procession to and into the *fogou*. Their reports on these impressions had been recorded in writing during the reflection phase on cycle 4. Then anyone else in the group could come forward, stand before the chair as devil's advocate and give a reductionist interpretation of what had been read out, invoking one or more explanations in terms of ordinary phenomena and states of consciousness. The member in the chair was then invited to reply to the devil's advocate in one of three forms:

- Assent to the force and plausibility of the devil's advocacy where it seemed rational and honest to do so.
- Present a well-argued rebuttal of the devil's advocacy in favour of the ASC view.
- Insist on the intuitive claims of the ASC view even though a convincing argument could not be found to rebut the devil's advocacy.

I give here a selection of devil's advocate points, together with the reply made by the person in the hot seat.

DA: Your so-called ASC impressions are nothing but a form of attention-getting through promulgation of the bizarre. *Reply:* This is possible; but other attention-seeking activities are less strenuous and less likely to be rejected.

DA: Your so-called ASC impressions are a fantasy projection of a longing for the non-existent mystical. *Reply:* I accept that some part of my experience may be just a projection of my longing; but equally such longing may exist precisely because of the reality of what is longed for.

DA: Your so-called ASC impressions are nothing but a fantasy rejection of your own unexplored libido, sexual energy. The felt sense of a presence in the other reality may just be a projected longing for a yet-to-be-experienced, liberating lover. *Reply:* I accept this as a possibility; I don't believe it applies.

DA: Your so-called ASC impressions are nothing but unexplored aspects of your psyche projected out and sucked into the mass delusion about another world which afflicts some of you people in Cornwall. *Reply:* I accept this as a possibility.

DA: Your images of a warrior and a guardian are a displacement of your denied rage. *Reply:* I am in touch with my rage. I have had no such images prior to the procession. I did not and do not identify with the warrior trip.

DA: Your images of swords are but a projection of your psychological armouring and rigidity together with blocked sexual energy. *Reply:* I am not heavily armoured, having worked on it a lot; and I am in touch with my sexual energy.

DA: Your ASC mythology about the *fogou* is a defence against all the insecurity and anxiety you have about being here. *Reply:* I am not clinging to being here. I have a loose and open attitude about going or staying.

DA: You are not in touch with another reality, you are just unable to cope with this reality. *Reply:* I do not accept your dichotomy. There is just one comprehensive reality.

DA: Your feeling of cleansing in the *fogou* is nothing to do with being psychic or having an ASC. It is entirely a physiological response to the physical conditions in a damp cave. *Reply:* But I have been in other damp caves in which I have not experienced any kind of cleansing of this sort.

DA: Your experience of spirally energies through your body was a physiological response to fatigue. *Reply:* But I am in good physical condition.

This is only a small sample of the sorts of devil's advocate comments made, with truncated accounts of the sorts of replies made. We spent a great deal of time on the total procedure since almost everyone in the group took a turn in the hot seat. Afterwards we winnowed out of the prolonged debate a set of possible criteria distinguishing between a genuine impression of the other reality and subjective illusion. We argued for a modest heterogeneous validity of these criteria: in terms of the interlocking support of all of them taken together. They are given in the section below on Findings.

6. *The management of research countertransference.* We assumed that individual emotional distress, interwoven with interpersonal tension, would be called up during the course of the inquiry. And that this might both interfere with our planning and reflection phases, and fog our capacity to receive impressions from the other reality. So at the end of the action phase of cycle 2 and before the reflection phase, we had a round of disclosures about the emotional state of each person. This immediately led to a one hour period of emotional housecleaning. We launched into this using body work and bio-energetic exercises, with some group members releasing their distress through catharsis. Again, after the reflection phase of cycle 2, we spent a long session on interpersonal work, dealing with issues of attraction and antipathy, and where appropriate negotiating one-to-one contracts for a pair to take time to sort out issues between them and develop the relationship.

This was all on the second day, and it sustained us through cycle 3 and the all-important cycle 4, both on the third day. But on the fourth day, after the very long devil's advocate procedure, the central discussion on clarifying possible criteria for distinguishing between authentic impressions and subjective illusions stirred up a good deal of emotional agitation to do with the conflicting claims of inquiry and analysis on the one side, and human feeling and process on the other. We dealt with this in the short term by means of a group jump and yell, leading over into vigorous dancing. After a break, this was followed by a long session for personal growth and development, with several members taking a turn one after the other to do work, facilitated by me, in the middle of the group. They were tracing back their current upset to past distressful experience, with resultant catharsis and insight.

The fifth cycle arose spontaneously out of deep personal work done in the middle of the group by one member in the midst of a life crisis, as I have already described. What is important here is how what was for many people one of the most evidential events in the inquiry emerged from a healing process of individual regression.

Our management of research countertransference was reasonably thorough-going. We did take enough time to identify and work on obvious distress called up by the inquiry. This did, I believe, enable us to sustain our inquiry right through to the end. It gave greater depth and validity to our activities than would have been the case if we had not taken time out for it.

7. *Balance between reflection and action.* As with the previous inquiry, the time balance was good. But the content of the reflection phase was sometimes too preoccupied with feedback on the impressions received as such, with insufficient attention to the critical issue of differentiating between illusory and genuine impres-

sions. This shortcoming was, however, very thoroughly rectified in the devil's advocate procedure (see above).

8. *Chaos and order, the avoidance of premature closure.* There was considerable emotional upheaval of various kinds during the course of the inquiry, and some of this has been referred to above. One person had a brief semi-psychotic episode one evening half-way through the workshop, and this required a lot of attention. It also brought out the de-stabilizing, de-egoizing, disorienting impact of this kind of inquiry.

There was much conceptual chaos and ambiguity in the early cycles. We were very open to live with the ambiguity of our impressions of the other reality during the first four cycles, that is over the first three days. The order brought into this by the devil's advocate procedure was overdue. There is an unresolved issue. Did the sustained conceptual chaos of the early cycles lead to a more fruitful kind of order in the end? Or would we have had a better kind of intellectual closure if we had been more rigorous, in the early reflection phases, about evaluation rather than mere description?

Summary. Again, taking these eight validity issues together, I conclude that the findings summarised in the next section receive a significant and more than minimal warrant from our inquiry, which had well above a basic level of adequacy. It is the interlocking diversity both of our impressions and of our criteria for legitimating or rejecting them, buttressed by challenging uncritical subjectivity and emotional/interpersonal work, and by the degree of creative co-operation in the whole enterprise, that in my opinion justifies this view.

Findings of the inquiry

The following are a set of criteria which, for this particular group of inquirers, prima facie mark out genuine impressions of the other reality and so distinguish them from purely subjective illusions. They have heterogeneous validity: that is, taken all together they provide interlocking support for each other. They were generated out of the devil's advocate procedure after cycle 4, and have their experiential warrant in the data from cycle 4, from earlier cycles and from cycle 5.

The basic outomes of the inquiry, as with the previous one, were a dawning set of what may have been extrasensory skills among several group members, each one, perhaps, representing the inquiry dynamic of the group as a whole. The following criteria are possible signs of these skills at work.

1. *Agreement.* Two or more persons have the same or similar impressions of the other reality.
2. *Heterogeneity.* Very different sorts of impressions of the other reality, which occur both simultaneously and serially, in the same person and in several persons, are compatible. The main sorts of impression in our inquiry were:
    - Feelings of energy streaming up and down and around the physical body.
    - Visions, pictures or images of something in a subtle domain.

- A felt sense of presences, their activities and energies in the other world.
- A felt sense of pervasive spiritual power.
- Emotional uplift felt to come from a liberating unseen ambience.

3. *Synchronicity.* Impressions of the other reality occur simultaneously to two or more persons, and are meaningful to them in the same or a similar way.
4. *Spontaneity.* Impressions of the other reality often come unexpected and unbidden; are often surprising in their content; and the recipient did not want or intend to produce them in the way in which they occurred.
5. *Independence.* Impressions of the other reality have a life of their own and they are not amenable to manipulation and interference.
6. *Spatial reference.* Impressions of the other reality have reference to locations in a subtle and inwardly extensive space that is somehow *within* physical space.

Taking all these six criteria together and applying them to the manifold experiential data on cycle 4, in the *fogou,* then there is a prima facie experiential warrant for saying that there were presences active in terms of subtle energy in space-2 within the physical space in and around the *fogou* during the time of our ritual activity there, and that what they were doing was potent and uplifting for many of us human beings present.

Of course, much more research cycling needs to be done by different groups of inquirers, particularly aiming at a better balance between convergence and divergence, to revisit these criteria and reshape them in new contexts. One important principle, already mentioned, is the holonomic one: that in any inquiry group into the other reality, just one person or a subgroup of two or three members may function as the subtle eyes, ears or felt sense of the group as a whole. Part may work for whole, and whole may work through part. If so, then we always need to take a holistic and heterogeneous view of what is going on.

There were some further points which emerged from the discussion after the devil's advocate procedure.

- Sometimes there is an obvious discrepancy between the content of an impression of the other reality and its supposed status as a projection of purely subjective psychological material.
- The process of emotional projection and the process of perceiving the other reality are not mutually exclusive: the former could be mixed up with and mix up the latter. Thus heightened self-insight and cleansed emotional states may help to clarify the process.
- Emotional longing for the other reality may be part of the evidence for it.

Often the sceptical, reductionist account that explains away the other reality is less plausible than the assertion of its existence.

12

The bliss nature and transtemporal regression

Report status: A story. **Place and year:** Tuscany, 1990. **Spiritual focus:** Uncovering and releasing the bliss nature. **Subtle focus:** Transtemporal regression: journeying through planetary time and space to locate affine persons and events from past cultures. **Social focus**: Co-operative living in a self-catering campsite with primitive facilities.

> This was a week that changed me in many ways. One of these was the opening of a window on to a hitherto-unsuspected and immensely wide landscape of spiritual adventure, through which I could create my own spiritual path. 'Spirituality' no longer meant merely a choice between branches of Christianity, all previously discredited in my eyes. I had been shown an infinite number of other possibilities and I was drunk with the excitement of discovering this new world... I felt that I had for the first time become aware of myself as an emerging spiritual being. A door which had been closed in me for a very long time had been flung open, as it were, and I was surprised and delighted to find that I had a warm sense of recognition for at least some of what was on the other side of that door. Another profound shift was the validation of the powers of the imagination, and the raising of the imaginal faculty to its proper level alongside the intellect. My imagination had already, from childhood onward, been finely trained, but I had been taught to believe that its uses were mainly frivolous. Now I was freed to use its full potential as a proper, fully-accredited vehicle, in partnership with the intellect, with which to travel my newly-discovered spiritual path. This new understanding had a powerfully validating and confidence-building effect on me, not least in areas of my life apparently unconnected with the workshop. (Katy Jennison)

I moved to a semi-restored farmhouse in central Tuscany in January 1990 and in June of that year ran a three day workshop for nineteen co-counsellors from the UK. This event was not a fully structured co-operative inquiry. I ran it in the spirit of inquiry and with an agreed openness to explore spiritual and subtle experience. Since this was the first occasion of a gathering at my centre in Italy, I will give the flavour of it in a brief story.

The participants ran their own self-catering campsite with outside coldwater shower, chemical and pit toilets, sleeping in tents or on dusty unrestored floors. I had converted a deep barrel-vaulted chamber under the upper garden, once used for the hanging of *prosciutto crudo,* into a Moon Temple. The two-storey barn was ready to become a Sun Temple. Its upper walls are made of perforated brickwork. The ground floor openings in the east and west receive the morning and evening sun. A high raised opening in the south welcomes the midday sun. In the upper garden, in the centre of a grove of cypress trees, I laid out tiles in a solar cross some three metres in diameter.

Each person will have their own particular memories of this happening. I recall the twenty of us, after a sun chant and ritual, seated around the solar cross, amidst shimmering light refracted through the cypress trees, regaled with the intense day-long chorus of bird-song.

> I remember moving and breathing, very early in the morning, to the chant 'Prana, Mana, Ra, Ka'...The sense of creating and working within a sacred space was palpable - and revelatory. (Katy Jennison)

As the aesthetic energies of the setting and the song saturated our shared awareness, one person then another let go of fear, spontaneously stirred with the emergence of their ecstatic self, the bliss nature, somewhere in the region of the heart. As hesitantly, then more openly, then with abundance, a human being owned and expressed in words his or her heartfulness of spirit, I was rapt by the beauty. At the same time, I remember thinking that certain kinds of validity are declarative. The experience of Being, through the very announcement it makes, declares its own soundness. What is sound is in the song.

On another day, we were in the Moon Temple and I was introducing the experimental practice of what I call transtemporal regression. To create an appropriate ambience, I asked if words came to anyone with which to invoke the Goddess.

> The words which came to me were 'Mother of Tears', and I did the invocation, another critical step for me in discovering that I could create my own dynamic relationship with the Divine. (Katy Jennison)

Transtemporal regression is based on a different assumption to past-life regression. The hypothesis is that each person alive today has particular affinities, specific resonances, with a certain number of persons who have lived on this planet in other epochs and places. This is an alternative to reincarnation theory, and avoids some of the more implausible implications of the latter.

> While John was speaking, the process he described was immediately real enough for me to have a vivid lightning-flash of a regression on the spot, lasting in real time only a minute or two. The focus which sprang into my mind was my keenly-felt and, I knew, in many cases quite unnecessary anxiety about arriving late. In my imagination I saw an early herdsman on a chalk slope, warned of the approach of raiders and frantic to get the herd and the younger herd-boys into safety inside the palisade of the village. In this, however, he fails: he and others are still outside when the raiders arrive and kill them. Continuing to watch the scene I could see that both his efforts and his anxiety were futile, since the raiders proceeded to set fire to the village and kill everyone indiscriminately. And this knowledge, or hindsight, brought an enormous sense of relief, the lifting of an intolerable burden of responsibility. (Katy Jennison)

In the process of transtemporal regression, you relax the body-mind deeply, then drift out into the great womb of time encompassing the history of the planet, and float in it until you feel magnetically drawn to a particular physical location on the planet. As you bring this into focus through the imaginal mind, you describe the details of where you are and what is going on, who is present and what they are doing and saying, and the epoch in which it is all occurring. After being thoroughly immersed in all this for a time, you then dissociate from it and return slowly and progressively into present time. Then you spend some while noticing symbolic overlaps and resonances, if any, between the story you have uncovered and the current themes of your life.

I commend this as a win-win exercise. Either it generates, via active imagination, a fruitful phantasy, a daydream, loaded with imagery symbolizing significant processes and issues in your life. Or it articulates an actual historical resonance that throws some light upon such processes and issues. Or it is a mixture of the two.

The first person who had volunteered to be the subject for this exercise, in a demonstration with the supportive presence of the whole group, lay on her back on a long wooden surface, painted white. This stands on bricks about a foot high from the floor of the Moon Temple, and is normally a place for candles, incense and other such items. The doors to the vaulted space of the Moon Temple are open night and day. The temple is also the site of a swallows' nest, built high up on the wall opposite the entrance, and just below the high point of the semicircular vault.

As the subject sank deeply into the womb of time and started to describe in detail, and with some emotion, a very specific scene at a particular place and time, one of the swallows flew into the Moon Temple, hovered above her, and commenced a series of vertical loops, flying in a circle down and over her outstretched body, back up to the full height of the vault, then fluttering down again and up, down and up, until the full drama had been vented. She seemed deeply accepting of this creature bearing witness to her descent into the womb of time, and in no way distracted by it. So too the bird honoured her posture, words and sounds, and the presence of nineteen other people in the temple, its home. She, bird and group were attuned to the symbolic exchange being co-created.

Another person who took this journey during the same session wrote:

> I couldn't focus for a while on anything but then saw the top of a mountain with cloud about, a slope, a girl there and a small croft. It seemed like Scotland. A man, her father, in the background is stern with her. She is quite afraid of him and doesn't consider rebelling in any way. She does what she is told but feels hopeless, bleak and without joy. She feels a calmness about the wild beauty of her surroundings. Stoicism is very much a part of her. She becomes ill and wants to die, but she doesn't. She lives a long life but is never really fit again. It seems she spends her long life scraping a living off the land almost totally alone - a barren, bleak and joyless existence - and eventually dies. I then experienced being drawn into the earth, being lowered into it fairly rapidly. The feeling was irresistible. I was attracted to a tunnel, like a long railway tunnel, with bright light at the end of it. I wanted so much to follow it, but John ushered me back to the present. A connection with the past and my life is the feeling of sowing seed on barren ground, engendering feelings of deep despair and overpowering notions of hopelessness and ineffectiveness.
>
> I don't know if this experience was an analogy of my own imagination, or a linking in with some kind of spiritual network, through which this woman was in some way part of me, or I was part of her. I know I share the woman's deep despair and carry it around with me, although in my present life I have joy and riches in abundance and

> rejoice in not living a barren existence. Despite my many doubts, I am left with the reality of that experience to me, which has altered my beliefs and perceptions. (Evelyn Ward)

The third event I recall was sitting in the mid-afternoon sun in a small group on the grassy northern promontory of the estate, where the campsite was. The few tents were scattered wide. Beyond the lines of cypress trees on each side of the promontory, a great curving field of wheat fell away toward the depth of the encircling ravines. There were four of us. One was taking a two and a half hour turn singing the same song nonstop over and over again. A second was available to give sympathetic support to the singer, a third to provide positive exhortation and encouragement, a fourth to confront resistances and prevarication. Four other groups were busy with this exercise in other locations, the protagonist having a choice either to sing for two and a half hours or to dance for the same period. The exercise had been proposed by one of our number, as a route to participating in the dynamic energy of Being. Eventually, instead of you singing the song, the Song sings you. Instead of you dancing the dance, the Dance dances you.

The singer in my small group chose a simple ditty for the great transformation from personal action to Act. As the other three of us performed our several roles, the ditty was chanted, murmured, syncopated and given full throat with innumerable variations of energy and mood, until it merged with the sound of sunlight and the silence of the ravines. There was not time for each of us to take a turn. Inspired by the singer in our group, I decided to try out the transformation for myself at a suitable time.

This time came when the workshop was over and all the campers had gone home. I was alone and it was mid-morning in late June. I sat at the far end of the Moon Temple facing the open doors, with the sunlight pouring on to the ground outside. For over two hours I sang, to an old hymn tune, the spacious stanza by Alexander Pope:

> To Thee whose temple is all space,
> Whose altar earth, sea, sky,
> One chorus let all beings raise,
> All nature's incense rise.

As I sang this over and over to the cadences of an august melody, the cosmic arch opened and Being sounded through the universal estate, our song the local manifest.

13

Knacks in entering altered states

Report status: A study. **Place and year:** Scott's Landing, New Zealand, 1993. **Spiritual focus:** Exercising and identifying the knacks involved in entering individually chosen spiritual states, such as turning about in the deepest seat of ordinary consciousness to its continuity with universal mind. **Subtle focus:** Exercising and identifying the knacks involved in entering individually chosen subtle states, such as projecting the subtle body out of the physical body, and others. **Social focus:** Co-operative living in a self-catering residential centre.

Overview

Eighteen of us gathered for four days, in March 1993, in an isolated homestead at Scott's Landing, on the east coast of the north island of New Zealand, some one hundred kilometres by road north of Auckland. There were thirteen women and five men. The first two days comprised a journey of opening, which I led, into a range of transpersonal states of being. This journey was governed by the simple practical principle of imagining you are in the alleged state rather than trying to get into it. It was based on parts of the dipolar map presented in Chapter 6 above. It covered the following, but not in this order, rather starting with immediate participatory experience, then spiralling progressively down and up between immanent and transcendent states:

- Opening to the transcendent Thou.
- Invocation of archetypal powers & presences.
- Turning about in the everyday mind to universal consciousness.
- Immediate participatory experience of the world.
- Grounding in spatiotemporal presence.
- Evocation of subtle energies within nature.
- Opening to impulses of the immanent life divine.
- Experience of the void.

I am writing here only about the last two days, which involved a co-operative inquiry. I had introduced the inquiry method as part of the two-day journey of opening. The participants took to it eagerly. On the evening before the first inquiry day, after I had retired, they played an elaborate game involving the basic principles of the method, and were ready to run with them the next morning.

The topics for the inquiry were chosen from interests aroused by the experiences of the first two days. In order of preference, the chosen topics were:

- The gate to transpersonal spaces.
- Transtemporal regression: deep regression to other ages and places.
- Turning about in the everyday mind to universal consciousness.
- Tantric doorways.

The two-day inquiry focused entirely on the first topic: the gate to transpersonal spaces. It had become clear from the previous journey of opening, that this gate, for any given space, consisted of certain kinds of inner acts, subtle skills or knacks, as we called them, that procured entry to the space. People worked in larger or smaller subgroups, each subgroup choosing a different kind of space to enter, going through several cycles of action and reflection, and attending throughout to the kind of idiosyncratic knacks which each person adopted to enter their chosen space.

In each reflection phase, each member of the subgroup shared with others the knacks used. In the following action phase, each person refined further their own knacks, and/or used knacks found fruitful by others. After several cycles of inquiry, each subgroup produced a list of the knacks its members had found to be effective gates to various altered states. The account of the knacks was refined first in the subgroups and then in the whole group.

The inquiry had intended to move onto other topics, but the two days allowed for the inquiry was too short. However, in terms of validity procedures, we did have time for a devil's advocate session about our inquiry into knacks. I cover this in a later section.

There was also an ambiguous experiment, involving the whole group, on telekinesis, the direct influence of mind on matter. A participant writes:

> We all participated to attempt to create a physical manifestation. We undertook to use our focused energy to shift an object. We placed a bowl upside down on the floor and put a petal on it. We all focused our energy with the intention of moving the petal off the bowl. After some time and with no result we interrupted the experiment. When we talked about what was occurring for the group at least two people admitted that they did not believe that the petal would shift. I was one of them. We discussed the experiment and recommitted to the possibility of shifting the petal with our energy. This time we placed the petal so that part of it was overhanging the edge of the bowl, thus making it easier to topple. A fly was circling around in the room. I remember thinking that it would be possible to move the petal if something landed on the overhanging part of it. Just after this thought the fly did land on the petal and it dropped off the bowl. In discussion afterwards there were two or three people who had had the same thought, at the same time. (Anne Bailey)

The inquiry ended with a co-operatively designed ritual.

> A white sheet was placed near the pear trees used in the first exercise on the first day at the back of the Scott's Landing property. Bill and Liam set up the drums nearby. The rest of the group carried symbolic and sacred objects with them and went to the sea some hundred metres away. To the sound of drums, they slowly processed around the house up to the drums. On arrival, the symbols and sacred objects were placed on the sheet. The whole group formed a circle seated holding hands. Barbara sounded the

bowl. We all stood and raised our hands, let them go, then touched the ground. We turned round and faced outwards and stood up with our hands like an open book. We opened our hands out wide to the world. We then faced inwards, joined hands and said twice an invocation - 'We invoke the elegant, excellent and evolved ancestors and beings' - and an evocation - 'We evoke the earth energies and give thanks to them'. We had silent communion until the bowl was sounded again. (Bill Taylor)

A classification of the knacks

The knacks which follow in their several categories are generic: no one of them was claimed by anyone to be an exclusive gateway to any one spiritual or subtle state. They are all-purpose knacks, so they are not presented as attached to any one state. Furthermore the spiritual and the subtle provide gateways for each other. A knack for entering a spiritual state may include a subtle adjustment; and a knack for entering a subtle state may include spiritual centering.

The knacks listed are not mutually exclusive. On the contrary, any one of them can be combined with any number of the others, either simultaneously or serially. Indeed, it became clear in this inquiry that each person used a multiplicity of knacks.

What we appear to have below is a minimally field-tested sketch of an array of basic skills for the deepening and expansion of human consciousness into spiritual and subtle dimensions.

In the next six sections, I summarize and classify the knacks identified by all the subgroups. The sixfold classification was not devised during the inquiry, but is my construct based upon the recorded data.

Physical sensation knacks

Go to the periphery of the senses:

- The outer limit of sound.
- Just beyond the edge of the visual field.
- To the margins of feeling and sensing.

Use a soft focus on a physical object in order to merge with it.

Travel on sound. Say a mantra.

Breathe.

Go into the physical body, release tensions and associated emotions, then expand into greater awareness.

Allow prickling in the back of the head to expand and develop, then go with what comes up.

Be aware of shaking as a preliminary to opening up.

Relax physically and float free.

Stay grounded to keep the gate open.

Intuitive knacks

Defocus: give up the focus of attention.

Attend to the insignificant at the perimeter of the mind.

Catch the whisper of the first thought, of the first knowing. Attend to the initial response.

Allow a gestation period. Be with a pregnant pause.

Acknowledge the experience, trust it. Allow time for the experience to unfold. Stay with and encourage the experience. Give yourself permission to process it, don't deny it. Allow connection and recognition.

Sidestep the ego mind: don't analyze and rationalize (a ration of lies).

Visualize an X to release cross-brain functioning, the integration of left and right cerebral hemispheres.

Image archetypal presences.

Notice the world speaking: everything is significant. All the things we discount are a sea of knacks.

Surrender knacks

Acknowledge a greater power and being than the ego self.

Surrender to and embrace the void.

Fall still and let go, suspend mental activity.

Be trusting, innocent, full of awe, wonder, amazement and childlike asking.

Be abandoned to the realization that everything is fully OK.

Transcend, move beyond the ego while strengthening, grounding and clearing it.

Mediumistic knacks

NB: 'shouters' was the ironic term used in the inquiry to refer to very discreet unseen supportive presences, discarnate guides and mentors.

Acknowledge the presence of the shouters.

Ask the shouters for help.

Ask the shouters for protection.

Have faith that the shouters will respond.

Use a guide - person, tree or animal totem - as a coach.

Intellectual knacks

Use an intellectual construct of a realm. Believe in the existence of, and a personal relationship with, a realm.

Know that a knack is a movement is a vibration is a shift of consciousness.

Know the range of knacks available and what they are for. Prepare by understanding the possibilities.

Build a frame of reference within which to process the remembering of experiences.

Ask questions of what we experience and where we experience it, in any realm.

Name and speak experiences. Stay at the end of the ball of wool and unravel it through speaking and bringing it into this world. Put pegs on it in this world and do not let it slip through consciousness and dissolve away.

Speak dreams to others.

Keep records of experiences, insights and dreams.

Psychodynamic knacks

Heal the memories. As old pain is processed, new dimensions are opened up.

Clear, strengthen and ground the ego so as to be able to transcend and move beyond it.

Devil's advocate procedure

After identifying knacks and refining our account of them, first in the subgroups then in the whole group, we set up a devil's advocate procedure in which people took it in turns to raise sceptical questions and challenge any possible consensus collusion amongst us. Here are some of the questions which confronted us:

- Are we the victims of our own spatial metaphors?
- Are we focusing on knacks as a defence against our uncertainty about the unknown?
- Are we identifying knacks as a means of avoiding the experience?
- Are we creating the gates to stop the other world from bursting through?
- Are we creating all of this as a way of coping with not coping in the mundane world?
- To what extent are we seeking experiences of expansion to avoid ego issues and the pain of separation?
- Are we expanding into other spaces to displace the denied pain of human distress?

The first question is the most sweeping. The next three suggest a defensiveness about the other world, and the last three suggest a defensiveness about life in this world. The general consensus, as I recall, was that they are all valid questions. They do not, we thought, invalidate the knack experience, rather they alert us to ways in which it can become distorted and deflected.

Issues for further inquiries into knacks

The devil's advocate procedure led over into a session to identify interesting questions about knacks to which the present inquiry had given rise, and which could be the topics of future inquiries in the same field. Here are some of them:

- Is there a physical shift when a genuine knack occurs?
- Is there a meta-knack or knack of knacks? Is there a meta-knack for all spaces or a meta-knack for each space?

- Are there common features or factors to knacks?
- Are knacks person or gender specific?
- Are there collective knacks, e.g. rituals? Are there knacks to being collective?
- Are knacks culturally or geographically specific?
- Are there peoples in the world who are knack proficient and prolific?
- Are we able to keep a gate open and be here simultaneously?
- Can we facilitate knack learning?

Two other basic questions, related to each other, came up about the places to which the knacks are a gateway:

- How do we differentiate between authentic and pseudo archetypal encounters?
- How do we know we've gone to one place on the map as distinct from another place or a pseudo place?

Evaluation

This event, the first journey of opening and co-operative inquiry in the transpersonal field in New Zealand, was mainly marked by the spiritually liberating and transformative effect it had on many participants. Several participants', quoted in Chapter 8, report on this effect. The actual inquiry component was short, only two days.

The inquiry had more than a basic adequacy as defined in Chapter 9. There were divergent subgroups, each with its own distinct topic of inquiry, and each subgroup converged on its chosen topic, refining and deepening it over several cycles of reflection and action. So there was a core structure of research cycling, balancing divergence and convergence within the whole group. Authentic collaboration was sound, for here was a group of people eager to take on board the participative and co-operative principle, and to explore the liberating impact of so doing. They trained themselves in the co-operative method by incorporating it into a game the night before the inquiry began. We also made time for the next most important validity procedure, challenging uncritical subjectivity, or devil's advocate procedure, in which people raised sceptical questions and challenged consensus collusion.

There appeared to be no call for dealing with research counter-transference, emotional distress triggered by the inquiry topic or process. There were possibly three reasons for this. First, the general level of emotional competence in the group was high. Second, the liberating impact of the process far exceeded any distress-triggering effect. Third, the group incuded many people who had an inquiring interest in the spirituality of Maori culture, and were thus poised to go forward with a full-blown inquiry process.

The most overt outcomes of the inquiry were, of course, a range of access or entry skills, knacks as we called them. I conclude that they warrant further study. In other words, other inquirers may want to look further into these knacks on their own terms and in their own way. We are not talking strict replication here, which is inappropriate to the co-operative inquiry paradigm, but imaginative adaptation and recreation.

The relevance of biculturalism

One factor that makes New Zealand a relevant setting for co-operative inquiry is its active bi-culturalism. Traditional Maori beliefs and practices, sustained on the many *marae* throughout the country, have made a significant impact on a discriminating minority of *pakeha,* the non-indigenous people in New Zealand. What they absorb from the ethos of Maoridom, without being bound by its traditional authoritarianism, include the following: the use of ritual for affirming the spiritual integrity and solidarity of human beings; respect for the spirit of place and the living presences of nature; the concept of *mana,* personal charisma and power; the continuity of life beyond death and the relevance to human society of ancestral light; the importance of community, collective support, or what the Russian mystics call *sobornost,* togetherness. When *pakeha* are alive to such matters, by virtue of the spiritual authority within themselves, as distinct from the authority of Maori tradition, then they find co-operative spiritual inquiry a congenial developmental path.

14

Charismatic expression

Report status: A story. **Place and year:** Tuscany, 1993. **Spiritual focus:** Improvising spontaneous, charismatic expression of the spiritual life within. **Subtle focus:** Exploring spiritistic and mediumistic phenomena. **Social focus:** Co-operative living in a self-catering campsite.

The second summer gathering in Tuscany, in 1991, was a more conventional co-counselling event with no special inquiry style. In 1992, more building work was afoot through the summer, so I held no workshops. In 1993, I hosted a more intentional and formal five-day inquiry into transpersonal experience for a group of sixteen experienced co-counsellors. The advantage of inviting co-counsellors to join in a co-operative inquiry is that they are competent to deal with any distress stirred up by the inquiry, so the all-important validity procedure of dealing with research counter-transference can be done without a whole lot of resistance.

The first day and a half I led a journey of opening into a variety of altered states including an introduction to the local sacred places: the Sun Temple, Moon Temple, solar cross, perimeter walk, Spirit Chamber, and so on.

> We went to the Sun Temple and as I stepped into the stone circle, in the suggested manner, and took a seat, I felt a great surge of energy in my body and an almost overwhelming rush of emotion. I began to shake and cry and feel joyful and sad all at the same moment. I was *so* surprised and a little embarrassed at the sudden and inexplicable intensity of feeling which had manifested. (Jennie Harris)

I then abandoned any leadership role and proposed the co-operative inquiry process begin. This abrupt demotion of myself triggered a good deal of uncertainty, chaos and confusion. What somehow eventually emerged out of this were a series of agreements about how to explore our potentially vast agenda.

This was a good example of what I later came to call a Dionysian inquiry, which I have described in Chapter 8. The focus of the inquiry was spiritual opening and expression, with a subscript of subtle opening. What characterized each plan for each action phase was its impromptu, improvised, sudden-inspiration-from-one-person-found-luminous-by-all quality. When we shared and reviewed our experience in the following reflection phase, we did not then plan the next action on the considered basis of what had emerged from this review, but followed the felt flow and opted in an entirely intuitive way for what to do next. These are some of the resultant episodes I recall.

We opened the first inquiry day in the long barn with an affirmation passed from person to person round the group: 'I am the goddess and the god and I love you'. The next day we varied this with each person making his or her own idiosyncratic spiritual affirmation. Once we had become sufficiently disinhibited so as to claim freely our cosmic status, these spiritually affirmative rounds released great buoyancy of being, each person making their characteristic charismatic declaration each morning. This led over into one-to-one sessions of emotional clearing and cleansing, and opening to indwelling spirit:

> Apparent healing seemed to occur for some participants of the group, including myself, through deep self-discovery and discharge of accumulated feelings, maybe held on to for many years, thus clearing the way for a different level of me, the spiritual level perhaps. To work intensively on myself with the support and skill of others, to trust that the space that I created in this particular group was safe, useful and therefore liberating, enabled me to rid myself of some of the clutter of my 'this-life dross'. With that out of the way, it seemed as if I made more available to myself and others the inner core of myself, the Goddess within. In this group, the process seemed speedy and effective and recognized as just the first step to us becoming spiritually open and available to discover whatever was there.
>
> I trusted myself and others. I tried to suspend my natural inclination to disbelieve weird events, however irrational, unusual or out of this world they seemed. I succeeded. I experienced transfigurations, paranormal happenings and a sense of other life, other world, company on several occasions. I was not freaked out or unusually disturbed by any of the happenings that I witnessed. I felt safe and able to maintain a sense of myself in this life, this world at all times, whilst being open to unusual experiences around me. It was elevating. I felt comfortable and interested that this was how things were, or how I was, at this time. I maintain to this day that I'm safe to be with during transpersonal exploration. I begin to *heal,* I become *clear,* I contact other parts of my *being* and am then able to *see.* Easy. It happens spontaneously quite often. (Jennie Harris)

One day at high noon, near the time of the full moon, there was a long procession around the grounds, led by a drum-beat, and culminating in the Sun Temple. There we generated, all of us together a prolonged spontaneous outpouring of simultaneous charismatic expression. Each person was moved in her or his own way by the spirit within to sing, chant, play musical instruments, affirm and celebrate, dance, move in slow motion, sit entranced with given speech, enter silent attunement, cleanse the psyche by the release of buried distress. All these things occurred together, in changing patterns of action and interaction, within the total space of the Sun Temple. Some were inside the circle of stones around the central stone altar. Others were in the greater area outside this. The whole process went on for a long while, each person's unique charisma empowered from divine impulse within, and enhanced by the distinct expressive potency manifest by every other person.

> The idea was to be permissive and de-inhibited, and to see what came up. Pam went into a silent, still trance. Nick slumped over to one side with his eyes shut; he said afterwards that he felt pulled. Quentin had his eyes shut and hands waving. Jennie 'saw things', and said 'The children are here'. I'm a bit hazy about any sequence to other things that happened, but the overall feeling was of spontaneous random outbursts of joy-in-living. I sang something at some point. Mary went round with a basket of strawberries and gave one to everyone, including lodging one in the lion's mouth. And Sandra danced, and got

> everyone else dancing wonderfully, and made wide patterns in the earth with her hands, and sang. John T started to do the hand-dance or hand movements which he continued all week. At the end it seemed to me that the charismatic energy of the ritual ought to be completed and grounded with food, so everyone came out and sat opposite the sunflowers while Pam and I brought out bread and fruit. (Katy Jennison)

One evening after dark we all gathered under the stars on the western terrace, which projects out over the ravine below and draws the eyes to the silhouette of distant hills. We were dressed in a variety of improvised ceremonial costumes and carried musical instruments and other regalia. We stood facing west. Venus, now the evening star, was suspended above the hills beyond Orciatico. In celebration of the Presence of the galaxy, whose central disc was arrayed above us, we started a toning song with accompanying percussion. As the volume of sound swelled out across the ravine and up into the overarching sky, our resonance with the stars became orchestral. Later, we stood in silence, attuned citizens of cosmopolis, secure upon our footstool the earth, bearing witness to our vast galactic homeland.

> Late in the afternoon we had enormous fun dressing up, and dressing each other up, for the evening procession. Looking back, it feels as if everyone was taking the opportunity to exaggerate an aspect of their personality, with spectacular results. We processed to the terrace, and drummed, rattled and danced, and I sang. And Sandra did an electrically powerful set of invocations, and was rewarded by great lightning flashes over the westward hills. (Katy Jennison)

Further on that same evening there was an unusual and dramatic shift of mood and energy. We went on an impulse into the Spirit Chamber. This is an enclosed space which at night-time offers pitch blackness with no hint of physical light. We chose to have no candles, nor any other source of light, and to explore the heightened awareness of being together totally in the dark. For a while we settled in and allowed our subtle senses to emerge within the womb of physical darkness. What then occurred for several people were unbidden spontaneous forms of psychism.

One person saw row upon row of the recently deceased, standing nearby, neither debased nor elevated, just relatively unknowing. Someone else saw crowded presences everywhere. Another gave voice to involuntary sounds like the wailing of the banshee. Some fell atrembling with the imminence of mediumistic entrancement.

> I was extremely trembly. My mouth was pulled open and down. My tongue kept rolling and pushed out. I saw lightish grey forms. There were surges of energy, my hands were hot and pins-and-needles went all over me. I felt full of light. I was constantly sceptical: this is distress, I thought. I saw rows of people in ranks. Figures came and went. Faces came up close. They were benign and curious, not frightened. (Anon.)

Others spoke out on behalf of, or in exhortation to, the gathered spirits of the dead. I made some cautionary statement. One person felt 'silenced' by this, as if she 'never got hold of some sort of message from the Spirit Chamber beings'. Some maintained a sceptical, puzzled and troubled silence. One person was sick. Some were exhilarated.

> I loved it. I could have stayed all night. It was shambolically perfect, creative. I thought of the green slime in Ghostbusters. I was scientific, sceptical. There will never be proof. You just have to believe it. I had practical fears, but I was making it OK. (Quentin Jones)

Eventually the phenomena subsided. We filed out of the Spirit Chamber wondering about credulity, folly and hallucination; about the circumambient locus of the departed, the revelatory thinness of the veil, and the disturbing promise and the hazards of instantaneous psychism.

A small group of four returned to the Spirit Chamber a day later to continue the inquiry there.

> I remember becoming, or connecting with, a young priestess-type woman whose job it was to sing. I remember hitting high notes, singing upwards towards a golden dome. Also I was bedecking the place for a special festival. Outside I could see hundreds of people, a caravanserai, all over the desert-like landscape. I remember pricking my finger on a thorn of the greenery and how that pain sensation stayed with me when I returned to Pam at San Cipriano. (Pam Michell)

One person went to each of the temples in turn that evening when everyone had gone to bed.

> In the Spirit Chamber I had a quite unexpected and overwhelming feeling of *hugeness* - something so enormously big and slow and old and patient and powerful that it was eternal and everywhere; it produced in me the impulse to stand straight and affirm my own existence, however infinitesimal and momentary in the face of that awesome encompassingness. (Katy Jennison)

One afternoon we set up a devil's advocate procedure to challenge consensus collusion and delusion in our inquiry. We sat on the eastern lawn in two rows of eight or so people, facing each other. Each row had a turn in which any of its members could raise sceptical and reductionist challenges to any prevailing assumptions that what had so far occurred was to do with spiritual and subtle reality, rather than the product of psychological and physical causes. Anyone in the listening row could counter the challenge with whatever appeal to experience, reason and imagination seemed authentic. This procedure went on for upwards of two hours. It eventually became unsatisfactory, because it developed into a game, people trying to think up increasingly bizarre confrontations and elaborate rebuttals. The fault lay in the design, which triggered off competitive team behaviour.

The lion's roar was a method we used to cleanse the human instrument of emotional, interpersonal and cognitive tensions, agitations or blocks that appeared to have been stirred up by the inquiry and that were getting in the way of openness to its process. This worked well. We sat in a wide circle in chairs round the inner stone circle in the Sun Temple. Six feet up on the southern wall, below a high-raised opening to the midday sun, there is a large relief of a lion's head, cast in bonded marble dust. Each person at will, if and when moved to do so, took a turn standing just below and in front of the lion, giving full vent to whatever sounds, words, gestures and movements, cleansed the psychophysical instrument of its accumulated congestion.

The inquiry ended with processional song. In single file we moved in serpentine rhythm following the outer contours of the promontory on which the farmhouse stood. Each person gave forth in song, vowel-song, soul-song, full-hearted, strong-spirited, disinhibited, celebratory, manifesting the charismatic release, the spiritual opening, which had been the focus of the inquiry.

> We had a procession to greet and honour and say farewell to all the places and areas and sites, with Quentin brilliantly leading with his drum. We sang, just notes and sounds, all of us harmonizing together. We went everywhere, finally ending at Pam's sound shrine, where we continued to sing and miraculously all finished at once. After lunch the first group left for Pisa. We drummed them off, and then drummed and called across the valley as they passed out of sight. (Katy Jennison)

In terms of my own personal learning, this inquiry was pivotal in my commitment to fully embodied religious practice. This includes the flowering of immanent spirit, the expressive impulse of divine life, in the experiential centre associated with the enteric brain, the abdominal chakra, the *hara* in Aikido, the lower *tantien* in Chi Gung. Spiritual transformation is found in charismatic and interactive sound, speech, gesture, movement and music, all of which together are an expression of innovative divine creative process. The dawn of this kind of transformative expressive skill occurred for many of us in this inquiry, I believe.

It also brought out, in terms of the low subtle, how unprocessed distress can hijack and distort mediumistic propensity and turn it into a hidden bid to manipulate and control others. This seemed to me to occur occasionally and needed some attention to resolve. In general, our awareness was raised about the sorts of competences needed in relating to the lower subtle realms: being grounded, centred, responsible, discriminating, decisive, and so on.

> During the morning I cleared up, meditatively and meticulously, had breakfast with John, and talked about what had been learnt and what would be different in the way the next one was set up. I fed back my thoughts about the usefulness of prior practice in transtemporal regression, and mused about setting up a really rigorous 'training day', with people making written records under clear headings, 'I visualised ...', 'I felt ...', 'I imagined ...', 'I connect this with ...', 'I conjecture ...' , 'It is possible that ...': a clear discipline and grounding. I have a very strong sense of people's unpreparedness and therefore unnecessary panic and fantasising. (Katy Jennison)

15

Transpersonal activities in everyday life

Report status: A study. **Place and year:** Auckland, New Zealand, 1994. **Spiritual focus:** Integrating individually chosen spiritual practices into everyday life, such as opening to spiritual life and energy, being in relation with what is, exercising charismatic presence, and more. **Subtle focus:** Integrating individually chosen subtle practices into everyday life, such as communing with trees, exploring interpersonal synchronicities, attending to and integrating nocturnal subtle states, and more. **Social focus:** Injecting individual spiritual and subtle activities into everyday culture, and creating a sub-culture of people intentionally inquiring into this kind of social transformation.

My main purpose in writing up this piece of research is to lay bare its anatomy, its detailed structural history. It provides a good example of how a more Apollonian, formalized inquiry unfolds. The recorded outcomes of this inquiry, both propositional and presentational (graphics, paintings), are too voluminous and extensive to be included in full, but I provide some recorded outcomes after the history.

Overview

This inquiry in New Zealand was launched as a contribution to the emergence of a self-generating spiritual culture. It involved twenty two people, sixteen women and six men, and ran for six weeks from the opening reflection meeting on 26 February to the closing reflection meeting on 9 April in 1994. Several of those attending had been members of the 1993 inquiry at Scott's Landing on knacks involved in entering altered states of consciousness. Indeed, the idea for this 1994 inquiry was gestated among a group from the Scott's Landing event, who had continued to meet, as an informal inquiry group, at monthly intervals throughout the intervening year.

Reflection meetings were held weekly for five hours on a Saturday afternoon in a large room at a college of education in central Auckland. The closing reflection meeting was for seven hours, and was included as the second day of a four day training of co-operative inquiry initiators. The focus of the inquiry was on the integration of transpersonal activities in everyday life. So the action phases were out there during the week in the midst of our individual lives. Dale Hunter writes:

> This was a wonderful co-operative inquiry. This was largely because it was spread over six weeks. There was enough time for the inquiry to mature, for all the doubts to come up and to practise keeping going with an inquiry while acknowledging the inner sceptic.

At the first reflection meeting we formed many divergent subgroups, with overlapping membership, of different transpersonal activities in everyday life. Some subgroup members made some phone contact with each other during the week's activity. These varied subgroup activities were sustained throughout the first five weeks. From the third week on, we added a convergent practice of attuning to the whole group each day. This was sustained for the four final weeks with the addition of graphic recording of it for the last two weeks. It became the primary activity during the final week of application. At the last two reflection meetings, the group used powerful attuning evocations. I will give here a summary of how the inquiry unfolded.

First reflection meeting

Opening. A round of introductions (name, background, reason for participation) was followed by an improvisation in which each person entered a sacred posture appropriate to the different tones of two metal bowls, sounded one after the other.

Inquiry exposition. I introduced co-operative inquiry as a sequence of cycles of reflection and action involving four forms of knowing. I outlined the four tasks of this meeting - to agree our broad theme, to choose a particular exploration of this for the coming week, to choose how to do this, and to choose how to record it. I also mentioned some basic validity procedures: managing research cycling with appropriate divergence and convergence; sustaining authentic collaboration; dealing with distress triggered by the inquiry process. I suggested four questions to guide individual inquiry into experience:

- What seems to be going on?
- What is really going on, and what are the criteria for distinguishing this?
- What are the skills developed for the practice adopted?
- What are the effects - personal, interpersonal, organizational, environmental; physical, psychological, psychical, spiritual - of the practice?

Planning. Members worked in pairs taking time each to plan individual projects for the coming week. These were then shared in the whole group. We did some work on the dynamics of the group and did a ritual to integrate new and old subgroups. After a break, we had a free-form fair, in which people negotiated to form inquiry subgroups which made project contracts for the coming week. These contracts were then shared in the whole group. Each person wrote down their own contract and chosen method for recording experiences during the week.

Inquiry subgroups. The following explorations were contracted by a whole range of subgroups of from two to eight members, some people being members of more than one and so having several contracts:

- Attuning to the group each morning after sunrise while engaging in a personal practice such as: opening to the greater spiritual reality; coming into being; opening to the meaning of the divine in my life; inviting god or universal energy into my life to help with personal issues; attuning to mother-earth energy; moving, and resonating with nature; recognizing the presence of the ancestors; evoking the creative life force in me, and invoking the presence of higher beings.

- Feeling participation, unity-in-diversity, in the world of immediate perceiving; no seeking, being in relation with what is; staying in a state of connectedness with the all.
- Practising charismatic presence in everyday personal and professional relationships.
- Practising awareness of and communion with trees.
- Exploring interpersonal synchronicities by noting thoughts and impulses about each other.
- Tuning in to each other at an agreed time each day to feel each person's inner state and send support.
- Living life as a dance.
- Practising attending to a young daughter as a spiritual teacher.
- Using a psychomantium as a setting for extrasensory perception.
- Painting images arising in response to the same invocation used at the same time by members in different places.
- Exploring nocturnal altered states between sleeping and waking and during sleep, and their interaction with daily life.
- Playing with planned and unplanned out-of-the-body experiences during the day.
- Attending to the effects of attuning to a spiritual teacher.

Second reflection meeting

We met for a second time after one week of exploring our chosen transpersonal activities.

Opening. We had a short and strong meditative silence, followed by a ritual which I proposed, drawn from an earlier inquiry. We stood in a circle. Each one in turn said to the person on their right 'I am the goddess and the god and I love you' and tapped her or him on the belly, the head and the heart with a spray of leaves. We then had a round in which each person gave a thumbnail sketch of their inquiry week with the bad and the good news. This ranged from accounts of great negativity and resistance to those of exhilarating uplift sustained throughout the week. In the middle of this sharing, and again at the end of it, we had several minutes of noisy improvisation on a whole range of percussion instruments which several members had brought to the meeting.

Report on the inquiry process. We devised the following: we distributed ourselves over the space of the meeting room to portray where each of us stood on an agreed range of issues. This gave us a portrait of how the group as a whole was faring on these parameters. Later we recorded the same data on wall charts.

- High, medium or low score for doing the contracted activities.
- High, medium or low score for recording experiences.
- High, medium or low score for using graphics and other nonverbal forms of recording experiences.
- High, medium or low score for activities and experiences tangential to those contracted.

The distribution in the room showed a wide scatter of scores on all these parameters. There was no evident correlation between scores on doing contracted activities and scores on recording them: some recorded only a little of the lot they did, and some recorded a lot of the little they did. After this activity, we had a break, with musical percussion and dancing.

Feedback, reflection and planning. This was the main part of the meeting. Members broke up into the several contract subgroups, some inquirers moving between several of these to honour their multiple memberships. People shared their experiences and evaluated them in the light of the questions mooted in the first reflection meeting:

- What seems to be going on?
- What is really going on, and what are the criteria for distinguishing this?
- What are the skills for the practice adopted?
- What are the effects of the practice?

Inquirers then decided whether to repeat the same activity in the next cycle of application, and if so with what variations to take into account the insights gained from the first cycle; and if not, what new activity to explore. Records were kept of reflections on the first activity cycle and plans for the second.

The subgroups rejoined in the whole group to share what they had decided. Each contract subgroup had decided to continue on with the same activity. The action plans were refined in the light of first cycle findings, and there were some minor regroupings of members. The group as a whole strongly affirmed this format of divergent subgroups, inquirers within each subgroup choosing to converge for a second cycle on its chosen activity.

Third reflection meeting

This third meeting took place after the second week of applying transpersonal activities in everyday life, these activities being mostly modified versions of what had been explored in the first week of application.

Opening. We sat close, held hands and attuned to each other's presence. Discussion revealed that this was sufficient to get us going and opened up without a ritual.

Inquiry process. I raised the paradox that normal experiential groups meet to generate juice together, then members go their separate ways to reflect on this. Whereas we go our separate ways to generate juice singly in our chosen action, then come together to reflect on it. So there is no full blast corporate juice at either phase of the cycle. After a sharing of views on this point, a consensus emerged that it was true, but that:

- There was still much juice for some of us at the reflection meetings.
- It was good to feel group support for building up individual juice and transpersonal muscle in everyday life.
- This build-up wouldn't happen without the group.

There was a strong feeling that the process was OK, and that this kind of balance between experience and reflection was invigorating and challenging.

Feedback, reflection and planning. We had a round in the whole group of sharing briefly personal contracts and transpersonal activities for the week past. Then we spent ninety minutes in our various subgroups on more thorough feedback and reflection, bearing in mind the four questions mentioned earlier. This led into forward planning for the third week of activity.

After a thirty minute break for musical percussion, dancing and filling in the charts (on degree of activity, recording, nonverbal recording, and tangential experience - see second meeting), we came together to have round of sharing about who was doing what with whom over the coming week. Once again it emerged that the subgroups were continuing on with the same activity, still further refined.

So members within a subgroup were deepening their convergence on their chosen activity. Discussion then arose about some kind of convergence for the whole inquiry group, all twenty two of us. People in the charismatic presence subgroup suggested that we all attune with each other at 6.50 am every day, each person doing their own kind of spiritual preparation for and opening of their day. Then we would note if our other transpersonal activities during the day had been enhanced by this attunement. We agreed to try this out.

Self-generating culture. Someone asked for clarification about the idea of a self-generating culture and its relevance to this inquiry. Another member gave a clear response: such a culture means that groups of people are intentional, co-operative and inquiry-oriented about every aspect of their life on this planet; attending to transpersonal aspects, as in the current inquiry, is a good way to start off such a culture. A number of other inquirers confirmed this view.

Convergence now. A mood arose among several people for convergence and juice now in the whole group. We all agreed. A sustained sound was emitted from a sounding bowl. We toned our own sounds in resonance with this, moved in free form, and chanted 'I evoke the divine source within'. Several people uttered their own variations of this evocation. We closed the group with a farewell wave to the shouters (hypothesized attendant presences).

Fourth reflection meeting

Opening, We launched into attendance figures, noted that one person had resigned, two were late and another five had other unavoidable engagements for this day. We then had a sharing about disintegration, difficulty, disorder, chaos, resistance, during the past week. There was a very noticeable tendency among several inquirers to feel murkier, slacker, less motivated, less focused, more scared, less connected, less structured, feeling it wasn't working. A few others had good news: more solid integration, more varied and daring ideas, less scared, feeling transfer from the inquiry into lived process. We devised the following exercise to transmute the grunge: with three lighted candles in our midst, each person silently took the focal light of their awareness deep into the inner psychological place of felt grunge, held it there until the grunge dispersed, then brushed a hand through the candle flames saying 'I burn my past irrelevance (or whatever)'.

We had a break with musical percussion, dancing, tea, while people also filled in the same charts as on the previous two meetings.

Inquiry process, I presented three polarities: about transformative and informative inquiry; about assuming that something exists in order to find out more about it, and questioning whether something does exist; about commitment to experience and commitment to inquiry. There was much fruitful discussion about these, with people saying where they stood in regard to them.

I then raised the issue of starting to rotate the role of group facilitator, a role which was still in my hands. We aired our views, identified several ways of rotating the role, and decided to let the matter take its own course at the next reflection meeting.

I next reminded the group about some of the main validity procedures: managing research cycling with appropriate divergence and convergence; sustaining authentic collaboration; dealing with consensus collusion; dealing with distress triggered by the inquiry process; balance between reflection and action; chaos and order. We decided to review our standing with these.

- *Research cycling.* We acknowledged that we had so far run a model of divergent subgroups, each subgroup converging on the same topic for the past three weeks, with a few individuals sustaining divergent membership of different subgroups. An element of whole group convergence had been decided on at the third meeting and applied during the past week. We felt that the relationship between convergence and divergence was as healthy as we could get it. (This combination remained constant throughout the rest of the inquiry.)
- *Authentic collaboration.* We judged that the process of members internalizing the co-operative inquiry method and making it their own was going along modestly well; and that parity of participation, people getting equal air time, was reasonably OK.
- *Consensus collusion.* We realized we had done nothing about this so far, and wondered whether we might do something at the next reflection meeting. (As it turned out, we didn't.)
- *Dealing with inquiry-triggered distress.* We noticed that we had attended to such distress at this meeting for the first time, in the opening exercise on transmuting grunge. We agreed more work needed to be done to bring the inquiry up to speed on this issue. (We did some interpersonal clearing later in this reflection meeting; and again in the seventh and final meeting.)

- *Reflection and action.* We had discussed this balance at the third reflection meeting (see above) and decided that it was OK.
- *Chaos and order.* We noted that some degree of chaos had overtaken members during the past and third week of application. (There was also a big outbreak of chaos during a crucial discussion at the closing and seventh reflection meeting. See below.)

During a dancing and percussion break, we filled in the charts, for the third time, on degree of activity, recording, nonverbal recording, and tangential experience - see second meeting.

Feedback, reflection and planning. We met for one hour in our various subgroups, sharing and reflecting on data from the week's experiences, and in the light of this, planning refined applications for the forthcoming fourth week. We then met as a whole group to share findings and plans. Once again, each subgroup was going to continue with the same basic activity chosen for the first week, but by now entering its third phase of modification.

We also reviewed our practice during the past week of early morning convergence, attuning with each other. There had been a variety of ways of doing this, members showing varying patterns of regularity and diligence. Some people maintained that it empowered them to be more attentive to their chosen transpersonal applications during the day. Others were not clear that it made any detectable difference. We agreed to continue to practice collective awareness of the group, each on our own, at 7.50 am every morning during the coming week, an hour later than the previous week.

Inquiry process. One of our number introduced an important group session of interpersonal clearing. People dealt with felt tensions and troubled perceptions and impressions of each other that were interfering with co-operative work.

Fifth reflection meeting

Opening. I proposed the following group ritual. We said 'I am the goddess and the god' (holding hands above heads), then 'We are members of a self-generating culture' (holding hands in a wide circle), then 'This is my life in time' (hands over chest). Next we shared a round of each person stating how they had fared over the past week of application. By contrast with the previous meeting, there was solid integration taking place for many members.

Inquiry process. I raised the issue of group facilitation. Several people supported the idea of my continuing in the role. Then Peta said this was avoiding the issue. I unilaterally decided to step down as facilitator, while continuing to raise issues about the inquiry process. Peta took over the role of facilitator. I asked whether we needed to explore more convergence.

Feedback, reflection and planning. We agreed to spend sixty minutes in feedback and reflection, in our several subgroups, on data from the week's application. Dale and others proposed that we include all data from earlier weeks and answer our four inquiry questions, with the addition of a fifth:

- What seems to be going on?
- What is really going on, and what are the criteria for distinguishing this?
- What are the skills developed for the practice adopted?
- What are the effects of the practice?
- What transformations of personal being are occurring?

All the subgroups then met in the large group and all but three shared their reports on these five questions in depth. The reports were summarized and presented on large flip chart sheets.

We ended with a short discussion and an agreement to converge. We planned that each of us, on a daily basis, would 'evoke the energy of the group', with toning, and making a graphic record of the effects. We also agreed to keep going our other inquiry lines.

Sixth reflection meeting

Opening. Following a proposal of a group member, we sang a Sufi love song in pairs moving from person to person throughout the group.

Feedback and reflection. We shared our paintings and graphics about the evocation of the energy of the group, which we had been practising each day through the week. We reported on our other inquiries. Here is a participant's account:

> My expression was to speak an invocation daily. I used 'I am the Goddess and the God. We are members of a self-generating culture. This is my life in time.' I combined it with the body postures that we held for each of those sentences. And I added 'I invoke the energy of the group'. Another component was the environment where I performed my ritual: a beach opening out to the Pacific Ocean and an island with a 300 year extinct volcano, evoking the subtle energies of the natural environment. Here is a report I wrote:
>
> Sunday, March 27,1994. Sunrise. Full tide. Cheltenham Beach, Auckland. Invocation and evocation. Length about 15 mins. Report written 7:24pm Sunday. What I noticed: How much distraction I still experience: 50%. I bring myself consciously back to the ritual. I start standing, then kneel, then lie down. Lying seems the place to be. In the course of pulling myself back from distraction, I experience an internal 'crack' in my head, like going through a sound barrier. I feel a ping, a snap, an elastic band sort of sting. My internal vision clicks into a bright golden light and I experience a lot of energy in the top of my head. This coincides with a sensation of energy moving down my body especially to my pelvis and genitals. I change my position to hands outspread and experience a full sense of connected loving. I kneel and allow an energy sense to flow in and out of the top of my head. I find myself saying an invocation requesting the creative and life-affirming forces and powers to be present at the workshop I was facilitating that day. On the previous night, I had made a declaration that when I woke I would experience an enlarged sense of spirit in my being. When I woke, that's how it was. (Anne Bailey)

Our bearing witness about the week deepened into a group soul dimension of inquiry. During a break for dance, percussion, tea and chat, we filled in the charts as per the earlier meetings.

Inquiry process. We did an evocation in the whole group of the power/energy/centre/wellspring of our group. We continued deep personal sharing about the state of soul, divine immanence, in the group now and during the week's process. Many reported deep commitment to the destiny of the group.

Planning. After much elusive discussion, we planned that during the coming week, each of us on a daily basis would attune to the presence of the group to enable us to be present to the divine, to connect with divine energy, using our own words to do this. Then each person will appoint her or himself to be a focus of this energy, a mediator between heaven and earth, allowing this to bloom within everyday life, and will later record the effects in graphics.

Closing. We all sang a Sufi love song.

Seventh reflection meeting

This final meeting was set in the context of a four day training for initiators of co-operative inquiries, particularly but not exclusively in the transpersonal field. It replaced the second day of the training. Almost all the members of the inquiry were on the training, and the one or two who weren't came in for this closing day.

Opening. We attuned to the tone emitted by a Tibetan bowl. Then used together the evocation 'In all of our togetherness we evoke the life divine within the group'. Again we attuned to the tone emitted by the Tibetan bowl.

Inquiry process. I handed on the facilitator power as a pair of scissors. Anne Verity gave an account of a parallel inquiry running in Motueka. Nicola prepared a showing of the graphics from the week's activity.

In and among the remainder of the session, as reported under feedback and ending below, there were episodes of interpersonal clearing.

Feedback and reflection. Graphics and paintings from the week's attunement and meditation were shown and perused by all in the middle of the room, with verbal reports from those without graphics. This was followed by general sharing and discussion.

Ending. Some people started to press for propositional outcomes and closure. I mentioned the other three kinds of outcome: transformations of being, practical skills, presentational (artistic) outcomes. The discussion wound on for a long while and entered confusion and chaos. Someone recorded the multifarious suggestions made about ending:

- Distil the maximum learning in propositions. Make conscious the unconscious. Name what has occurred. Verbally draw together the threads of the different experiences. Put everything up and immerse ourselves in it.
- Say goodbye to the small groups. Do a ritual acknowledging the subgroups.
- Complete with a ritual tuning into the transpersonal qualities of the whole group. Express and record this in drawing, sound and movement.
- Have a musical convergence with all of us in a mini-concert.
- Have a group presentational outcome in graphics, or as a video recording.

- Generate propositional nuggets: strand nuggets, composite nuggets, individual nuggets, group nuggets, metanuggets.
- Spend time presenting to each other in pairs our personal transformations of being, our skills and competences, generated within the inquiry.

Out of the profusion and confusion of ideas and energies, spontaneous creative order suddenly manifested in two activities:

- We recorded a set of individual propositional nuggets. Each person in turn reported in a sentence or two what transformations of personal being had been generated within the whole inquiry. So this addressed the fifth inquiry question, introduced at the fifth reflection meting.
- We concluded the inquiry with a large collective painting, six feet by three feet, all of us working on it at the same time with a variety of coloured pens, crayons, and other items.

Closing. We sang a song 'Thank you'.

Inquiry outcomes

The main outcomes, as always, are to do with transformations of being and skills generated by the inquiry. The secondary and recorded outcomes, propositional and presentational, are too voluminous and extensive to be included here in full. They are in four categories:

- The written reports (including some graphics), after four weeks of inquiry, from the several subgroup activities, each attending to four basic inquiry questions:
    - What seems to be going on?
    - What is really going on, and what are the criteria for distinguishing this?
    - What are the skills for the practice adopted?
    - What are the effects of the practice?
- The wall charts containing data from the first five weeks about:
    - High, medium or low score for doing the contracted activities.
    - High, medium or low score for recording experiences.
    - High, medium or low score for using graphics and other nonverbal forms of recording experiences.
    - High, medium or low score for activities and experiences tangential to those contracted.
- The transformations of personal being from the whole inquiry, as recorded in the propositional nuggets at the final meeting. These are given in the next section.
- The presentational outcomes (graphics and paintings), from the last two weeks, of the daily convergent attunement activity.
- The collective final painting, done at the closing reflection meeting, presenting the outcomes of the whole inquiry.

Nuggets on personal transformation

We agreed that transformations of personal being were the most basic kind of outcome of our inquiry. At our concluding day each person sought to give a verbal summation of his or her transformational experience. These accounts, which we called nuggets, were recorded. A nugget is a small compact portion. Another metaphor for each account is that of a flag marking a whole territory. The flag is a symbolic reference point for the much greater whole to which it bears witness and cannot include.

- I feel disappointment and confusion about the process and its future relevance. How significant is this really?
- I allow myself to be far more open in my expression of the transpersonal and in my acknowledgement of myself. I am more full in my being.
- I am bigger than me.
- The trees are saying: 'We are part of your community'.
- I have experienced a very important integration of deep face-to-face intimacy and the transpersonal. World shaking. We are experimentally finding out what is what.
- I realize that there are parallel realities and interweaving realities that 'I' can access at will. I do live the transpersonal life all the time. I judge myself that I'm not doing it.
- My journey has been about a connectedness of a divine or creative, transcendent type. I have a glimpse of it being present when I don't think it is occurring.
- The more I open to the transpersonal the more I open to the interpersonal. The more I open to the interpersonal the more I open to the transpersonal. It seemed to happen in the midst of chaos, making an ordinary statement. Something occurs if a potential response is ready.
- The more I'm in touch with universal possibility the more I'm in touch with me. The more I'm immersed in me the more I'm immersed in the transpersonal. I'm much more open minded, much less reductionist through bringing together creativity, reality and imagination - a unity of the three.
- My increased awareness of synchronistic events, and learning through seemingly unconnected or unrelated events leads to the nugget that all is connected, nothing is unrelated.
- The ancient traditions become validated through my own experience when it sits deeply within my being. My spiritual journey is far more integrative for me than going into a religious order.
- It is world shaking to say what is, is not, exactly what is going on for me - without a swing to rebellion - this is world shaking to me.
- I detect an expanded sense of self.

It is important to remember that all of us have little practice in findings the words that honour our own unique spiritual and subtle experience without adopting the terminology of established creeds and cults.

Practical knowledge outcomes

At the fifth reflection meeting, the different subgroup inquiries reported on their findings in response to four questions, identified above. Checking through the answers to these, I find they give a sense of the practice and the competencies involved in it. I give reports from two of the many inquiry subgroups, followed by an individual report.

Knowing how to commune with trees

Knowing how to commune with trees means *participative awareness* of:

- Trees as presences, living beings; their strength, power, energy, stillness.
- Tree energy over the whole earth; the essential role of trees on the planet, complementary to humans; trees as the knack of experiencing the energies and wholeness and beingness of the planet, the interdependence of all things on it; trees as linkage with All.
- The contentedness of a tree just to be; the interplay, the dance of tree, air and wind as if there is no difference between them; group play among trees; individual 'personalities', characteristics, needs.
- Trees' subtle response to human company, to being communicated with at times, to acknowledgement and appreciation.
- The physical needs of trees; trees communicating these needs to humans; one tree's needs leading to awareness of the physical needs of others in the locality.

Developing competence in communing with trees means:

- Persevering with participative knowing, that is, whole being knowing involving feeling, perceiving, sensing, intuiting.
- Being open to receive, combined with lateral framing and a suspension of disbelief.
- Practising not knowing, recognizing that we may not be recognizing.
- Questioning whether we are projecting.
- Dealing with blocking off through fear, conscious or unconscious.
- Dealing with being overwhelmed by the group strength, power, energy, stillness and sheer number of trees.
- Making the human vessel ready, preparing it to allow for differences between human bodies and energies and tree bodies and energies.
- Recording the experience, reflecting on it and exploring it in conversation, listening to co-inquirers, encouraging each other.

> I was part of the communing with trees group. It was surprising to find that three other people wanted to do this too. It felt like coming out of the closet as a tree communer. Although I focused on trees generally I particularly worked with a pohutakawa tree in my front yard. The pohutakawa is called the New Zealand Christmas tree because its bright red pom-pom-like flowers come out then. I developed a relationship with this tree which is still very powerful. It is a strong, deep and aware presence. I look out my office window onto it and sit out on the front verandah beside it. I am aware of it every

day. I am still not sure whether I communicate with the tree or whether I project onto the tree - or perhaps a mixture.

I have developed a strong awareness of trees as beings and the importance of trees to the viability of the planet. I feel as if trees are the other half of humanity. We need them to breathe and they need us too. They can't move as we can and their time span can be much longer. Trees have an awareness of their own. Silent beings who inhabit our world with us. And they are wonderfully beautiful and diverse. A world without trees would be barren and dead. (Dale Hunter)

Knowing how to open to a greater spiritual reality

Knowing how to open to a greater spiritual reality (GSR) means:

- Tapping into a GSR at will, spontaneously switching to another level at will; opening up to the greater whole or universe rather than being contained in my own head.
- Experiencing several seemingly unconnected occasions of a parallel reality.
- Effortless increased empathy, flowing at-oneness, being in tune with others; good connections and ease with others, a strong sense of being with others; tapping into where others are at spiritually; tapping into other people's loving; having spiritual conversations not necessarily initiated by me.
- Being more in my power in relation to others; being able to set limits and boundaries with others with greater clarity.
- Feeling calmer, a greater sense of purpose; being at ease and at peace with myself, more confident in and generous with myself; tapping into my own self-loving; the feeling that everything is slower and therefore I can handle anything; being grounded and at one with the flowing day, rather than seeking the next thing I should be doing; having a greater focus on what I am doing, with clarity about priorities.
- Feeling more aware of myself in space, of my body posture and of my defensive postures.
- Feeling a strong engagement with, and emotional response to, the experience; feeling emotionally volatile, with emotions closer to the surface; feeling energized, with more stamina, a sense of well-being, strong physical experiences.
- A magical synchronicity between my life and my experiences.
- Getting to the bottom and juice of things.

Developing competence in opening to a greater spiritual reality (GSR) means:

- Allowing the state of being.
- Taking time out to arrive with myself, focus on where I am, where my energies are and where I would like to be; slowing down and noticing where I am in my body, and where and what my issues are.
- Identifying body postures conducive to the experience; controlling some physical experiences, and not controlling other physical experiences, related to the practice; pulling back from distraction.

- Presencing higher beings; making specific requests for certain presences on particular occasions.
- Putting out an idea, or request, that my awareness may be shifted and having that occur overnight.
- The ability to creatively visualize a safe space quickly and in any circumstances.
- Recognizing when I need to re-constitute 'me-ness'; recognizing when I need to 'shut down' spiritually because of incompatibility.

An individual report

This inquiry was my first experience at being able to choose within a group context what spiritual practices I wanted to explore and find others to share some of them with. The significant three for me were as follows.

An early morning celebration, greeting, attunement with nature, its life-giving energy and beauty. I would get up about fifteen minutes earlier than usual, go onto my deck which faced the rising sun, and move and speak as I felt moved to. Because I live in the suburbs and my deck is exposed to other houses, I became very aware of my inhibitions. So it was a daily challenge to disinhibit and to actually express what I really was feeling. Sometimes I managed it and other times not. Others in the group were also doing their own form of greeting and affirming the day and I felt this as a support and it seemed to add a broader more rounded energy to it all.

Another practice I did with Jill was to tune in to each other for five minutes at midday each day. I would tune in with her visually and kinaesthetically so that I would usually enter a warm heartful resonance which was often quite passionate and seemed to give me a sense of how she was on that day. After the first two to three weeks the timing of it became less important for both of us in terms of developing this warm resonance and connection. We discovered towards the end of the formal inquiry that we both did a form of this with our children to check in with them, support and love them. For me it generated a warm feeling of connectedness and harmony with the world and confirmed for me the energetic access we can have with other people regardless of physical proximity.

The third exploration was with John in a small Spirit Chamber/psychomantium. After completing the exclusion of light, checking in with each other as to how we wanted to proceed and an appropriate entry, we sat in there with a dim candle and a mirror for an hour and a half. The time floated free for me and passed very quickly. I found it rich, multilayered, intimate, warm, deepening, expansive and sensual. I connected to my inner Woman Guide who suggested I go back into the back of my head and being. This is something I continue to do and be enriched by. These days it seems to give me access to some other realm, some other culture where I am deeply nourished, grounded, supported and given clarity and balance in this world. Later I had a sense of my crown opening up and intense gold-white light flooding down through my body. The light gradually faded and there was just the sensation of light and energy through the centre of my body. Then every cell seemed to swell up and sparkle. I felt that if I directed it to a particular body part it would generate healing. At another point I chose to connect in with chakra centres. Overall the experience seemed to give me space to sink beneath surface reality and be more present to inner transcendent energies, to be deeply healing and powerful.

The richness and holistic grounding of this inquiry for me has continued to unfold over the years since it ended, via an ongoing group which has continued in a Dionysian way with meeting regularly for shared emergent ritual time. (Barbara Langton)

Evaluation

This inquiry overflowed itself. It was many faceted and highly divergent, generating a variety of spiritual and subtle skills and transformations. It produced a mass of written and graphic data. Some people undertook to write up and organize all the written records and charts on a word processor, but the task was never done. My discreet requests for the results came to nothing. Looking now at all the original handwritten sheets, I understand why. The organizing mind goes into confusion and disarray. Conceptual competence dissolves in unrestrained entropy. Critical subjectivity evaporates before the countercultural plethora.

And behind all this is the realization that it is the ongoing transformations of being, and associated skills, within each inquirer *right now* that count, not a limited account of them at a frozen point in time past.

We evaluated validity procedures after three weeks, half way through the inquiry, but not in any thoroughgoing way thereafter. At the half way mark, we considered that the status of our inquiry was just adequate in the light of several criteria. I apply them now to the whole inquiry, and this is only my opinion:

- *Research cycling, divergence and convergence.* There were divergent subgroups each with their own topic, each converging on the same topic week by week, with some people sustaining divergent membership of different subgroups. Whole group convergence - everyone in their subgroups attuning to everyone else - was added to all this from the third meeting onwards. This sustained relationship between convergence and divergence was adequate
- *Authentic collaboration.* People progressively internalized the co-operative inquiry method and made it their own, strongly with regard to parity of participation in reflection, discussion and decision-making, weakly with regard to practical mastery of the full range of validity procedures.
- *Challenging uncritical subjectivity.* We never used any kind of devil's advocate procedure in the whole group, and this was a major shortcoming. However, there was a good deal of critical scrutiny, within each subgroup, of our claims, assumptions and methods, when the various subgroups met to answer five inquiry questions on their findings of the first four weeks. More of this was needed.
- *Dealing with research counter-transference, inquiry-triggered distress.* At the fourth meeting, we did an exercise on transmuting negative emotions, and did some interpersonal clearing. We did more interpersonal clearing, belatedly, on the seventh and final meeting. There was, in my opinion, nowehere near enough attention to inquiry-triggered distress.
- *Reflection and action.* The balance of a week of action and a weekly five hour meeting of reflection was minimally adequate. I think we needed a seven hour weekly meeting.
- *Chaos and order.* Chaos during the week-long action phases overtook some people during the second and third weeks. There was one fruitful outbreak of chaos during the closing and seventh reflection meeting. The whole inquiry was never too far from the edge of chaos.

My very personal view of the inquiry is that, while it had only a little more than basic adequacy, it was a great success as an innovative democratic research enterprise, with high creative divergence, strong commitment, and with a good measure of internalized methodology, and consistency in following it through. The inquiry was wanting in terms of completion, of the integration of its diverse strands, of attention to research counter-transference and to challenging uncritical subjectivity: the subgroups opened up appropriate kinds of questioning rigour, but we could not find the time to go deeper. Here is a view from a participant's notes during the inquiry:

> What I love about this inquiry is that it forces me to look at and articulate things that are not often acknowledged or talked about, and in so doing I:
>
> - Flush out my resistance to, and/or need for healing around transpersonal issues.
> - Develop a language and modus operandi to bring them more fully into my life.
> - Acknowledge and validate with others that the transpersonal is a powerful force in my life.
>
> The discipline of inquiry is a useful tool for this, especially the recording and reporting back. (Peta Joyce)

I was personally enriched by concurrently inquiring, with one or more others, into a range of practices: coming into being; no seeking and abiding in relationship now; exploring interpersonal synchronicities; attending to impressions in a psychomantium; painting images in response to the same invocation used at the same time by a co-inquirer in a different place; opening to subtle states between sleeping and waking and during sleep, and noting their interaction with daily life. It was a remarkable way of living for six weeks. Another inquirer writes:

> What strikes me now, as I review the descriptions, and re-observe the paintings and recall the time and focus of those few weeks, was just the depth and breadth of ground which we covered, and the way in which divergence and convergence were handled within the same process. I still have that same sense of marvel as I had at the time, of awe at what we were unfolding and experiencing, and of wonder at the fact that this group could continue to assemble and to explore, and could survive some of the trauma to which we were exposed such as leavings, personal distress, and such forth. As well, I am reminded of the sense, at times, of frustration at the time taken, of the apparent lack of clarity, of the sense of diffusion and loss of focus. (Susan Byrne)

16

Transpersonal inquiry within a self-generating culture

Report status: A study. **Place and year:** Tuscany, 1995. **Spiritual focus:** Charismatic celebration, through percussion, ritual and procession, of divine life and its planetary manifestations. Participation in universal mind through group toning and meditation. This was the Dionysian backdrop to the formal, subtle focus. **Subtle focus:** Entering subtle states chosen by four different subgroups: clairvoyance via idio-retinal images, altered states via mutual gazing, out-of-the-body experience, tapping into subtle energy of various kinds. This was the formal Apollonian focus of the inquiry. **Social focus:** Exploring co-operative living in a short-term self-generating culture, in a self-catering residential setting.

Overview

This inquiry was for experienced co-counsellors, seventeen including me, thirteen from the UK, two from Holland and one from New Zealand. It occurred, from 23 June to 6 July, 1995, at my research centre near Volterra in Tuscany, Italy. The idea was to set up a short term self-generating culture. This simply means a group of people living in a village and being intentional, consultative and experimental with regard to the several parameters of village life. This culture included within it:

- One day to set the culture up.
- Two days of preparation for the formal transpersonal inquiry.
- Three days of the formal transpersonal inquiry.
- Six free-form days, during which the only scheduled event was an opening community meeting.

The village consisted of five people in tents in the grounds, and the remainder sharing the three self-contained apartments in the farmhouse, and a large communal hall. There were really three inquiries going on:

- The most explicit and formal one was about the several kinds of subtle experience people chose to explore during the three focused transpersonal days.
- The next and less formal inquiry was about what is involved in a self-generating culture when people seek to be intentional, collaborative and experimental about the several practical, and other, dimensions of village life.

- The third, most informal and perhaps deepest inquiry was to do with exploring and celebrating spiritual reality through ritual, procession, percussion, toning and attuned meditation.

All three inquiries overlapped and the second came more to the fore during the closing six free-form days, after the first inquiry had closed. I will start with comments on the second one, because it provided the container for the other two.

Self-generating culture findings

There was at least one meeting each day to deal with the collective management of village life. The findings, mainly evolved in the early meetings, were to do with the simple and basic kinds of competencies needed by a self-directing group.

- We had volunteer rotating facilitators for group agenda-setting, discussion and decision-making. Attention was paid to contribution rates during discussion, making sure everyone who had something to say had a fair chance to say it.
- We had short paired two-way mini-sessions to discharge off excess emotional heat when the discussion got fruitlessly agitated.
- We set time-limits to agenda items; were reasonably rigorous in time-keeping; and agreed to leave over to a future meeting items that required more discussion than time allowed.
- We made decisions nonverbally and verbally:
    - After an appropriate period of discussion, the facilitator called for a show of arms. Arms held straight up into the sky meant a staunch yes. Arms held pointing down to the ground indicated a strong no. Arms held at any level in between these extremes showed varying degrees of approval, ambivalence and disapproval.
    - The facilitator asked any minority with arms horizontal and/or pointing down, to express their views. When fully heard, they were asked if they would accede to the majority view, which, since the issues were of a relatively minor practical nature, they invariably did.

Mostly the issues raised were practical and maintenance issues, to do with money, shopping, food preparation, use of kitchens and toilets, cleaning, transport, and so on. However, we also discussed meta-issues, which were about our procedures for dealing with the basic issues. Interpersonal issues were dealt with as part of the inquiry group process, as briefly alluded to below.

History of the transpersonal inquiry

I report here on the first three setting up and preparation days, and on the three days of formal inquiry. This account, for some reason, is in the present tense.

Saturday morning. The self-generating culture is launched in the barn with the stained-glass window. I propose, for the first three days, that my leadership progressively graduate into co-operative decision-making. I take people round the grounds and barns and introduce them to protocols for the use of all the focal places: Sun Temple, Moon Temple, solar cross, women's shrine, Spirit Chamber, perimeter path. *Afternoon.* There is a long discussion and decision meeting about community procedures, contribution rates and ground-rules, money, food, car, and toilets. *Evening* Toning and meditation in the Moon Temple, followed by a grand banquet in the main hall.

Sunday. Five of us design a ritual procession for going round the perimeter path. We all participate. Each persons chooses one or more planetary constituencies (a physical element or compound, a species of plant or animal, a current or historical human culture or race, or whatever) to represent. We process round the path with percussion and other instruments, making several affirmations at each of the four cardinal points. There is an elaborate death and rebirth ritual on entering and leaving the avenue of cypress trees on the north east side of the promontory. We stand round the large solar cross in the middle of the path along its the southern stretch. There each person gives an impromptu affirmation of his or her planetary constituency.

Monday morning. We do a lot of interpersonal and emotional process work in the group. *Afternoon.* There is more process work in the group. A project for the Spirit Chamber project is mooted, based on the impressions received by two people. *Evening.* Toning and meditation in the Moon Temple, followed by an ascensional ritual for the souls of the deceased in the Spirit Chamber.

Tuesday morning. We decide we are ready to launch the co-operative inquiry. There is a long session exploring inquiry options, with individual choices and negotiations. We end up with four subgroups inquiring into different kinds of subtle experience:

- Entering into clairvoyance from attention to closed-eye idio-retinal images.
- Entering altered states by sustained mutual gazing.
- Exploring out-of-the-body experience.
- Tapping in to subtle energy of various kinds.

This negotiation is followed by sustained drumming and percussion and dance, which coincides with the arrival of the liquid gas delivery truck. *Afternoon.* We go into the four inquiry subgroups and each subgroup does two cycles, each cycle including a phase of action and a phase of feedback with reflection. After this all four subgroups meet together for sharing. *Evening.* Procession and percussion round the perimeter walk.

Wednesday morning. The same four inquiry subgroups continue on with several further cycles of action and reflection, with sharing in the large group at the end of the morning. *Afternoon.* The same four subgroups continue further cycles of inquiry. Afterwards each subgroup does its raw feedback in a fishbowl within the large group. Here are some reports:

> The 'soul gazing' exercise with three others involved sitting opposite a partner in silence gazing into their eyes. I think it began with a period of ten minutes, then twenty minutes. The four of us swapped partners so we had time with each person. We also sat

as a four in a cross shape each gazing into the eyes of the person opposite. The gazing went on for set periods over at least two days. I was extremely present and clear, feeling like I was witnessing someone's essence. That was a beautiful experience. I also felt an increasing energy connection with the other three and started to become in psychic attunement with them, seeing them strongly in my inner eye when they were physically absent. I also witnessed seeing a thin white light around the person I had been partnered with the most. None of these words seem to quite convey the power and beauty of this whole experience for me. I also have many other memories: the continual sounding chorus of the birds and frogs, the teaming insect life, the fire-flies, the group meetings, the excitement of creating a workshop together, the love, the pulsing energy I felt in my body, the conflict, the Quaker decision-making process of voting. (Kate Reed)

I was part of the mutual gazing subgroup. There were four of us, two men and two women. One of the men and one woman were in a partnership. The men were brothers. So it was an interwoven group with a variety of interpersonal nuances. We experimented with all possible pairs and different seating arrangements, so that the other pair was in a different part of peripheral vision. Also we did one cycle as two separate pairs.

I found it a rich exploration in attunement with other people. I seemed to enter altered states more easily with the two people I felt most comfortable with. There were views of them that gave me access to deeper reaches of who they were, perhaps other lives they were attuned to. There was also an interesting resonance of male and female energies particularly when the women were seated alongside each other gazing at the men seated beside each other. I also remember what felt like a deep communion between us all when one pair was gazing at each other from chairs and the other pair were seated on the floor between the knees of the higher pair.

I felt that over the two days of cycles I entered a deep shared intimacy with these people emerging out of a different level of being than if we had spent the time talking and socializing. (Barbara Langton)

I was part of the OOB group. In the first cycle I sought to place myself sitting on a rafter and couldn't seem to get the trick of it. In the second cycle I picked up on Cris saying that he'd been firefly-size, and on his description of getting into the kinaesthetic body. I also realized that other 'transpersonal' experiences of mine have taken place with open eyes. From this it was a short step to remembering being able to think myself small enough to walk between grass-blades, and doing the same thing on the Sun Temple altar, exploring it, becoming different sizes in order to get down and then climb up to the rafters...I had the brief experience of 'knowing' that I was sitting with my legs crossed although I then realised that in reality they weren't. Later I achieved a spontaneous flip up to a rafter when I heard Quentin's voice on the path. I tried various other techniques with very negligible results, and I had something of a feeling of disappointment and failure, although I also had the impression that it was easy, really, if I could just get the trick of it, like first learning to ride a bike, and I was probably trying too hard. (Katy Jennison)

Evening. We have a new moon celebration in the Moon Temple, with a sharing of our lunar associations and a meditation.

Thursday morning. The day starts with a large group decision to modify the subgroup topics, and negotiate some change of membership. The new, modified or the same topics are:

- Entering transtemporal regressive states: going back to past epochs to specific scenes with which one has a strong personal resonance.

- Entering altered states by sustained mutual gazing, combined with holistic pulsing.

  One of the men pulsed me with a heart core pulse. I maintained eye contact with him which was warm, nourishing and supportive and at the same time I seemed to enter a broad landscape within which I saw an olive-skinned lithe being totally in harmony with the expansive setting and its natural rhythms. It was as though I was contacting some part of my being which I easily lose contact with in my life in the suburbs and in this culture, or some woman I have a deep resonance with. It was as though I entered a transtemporal regressive state. The combination of personal warmth and support from the person pulsing me, enhanced by the subtle centering and balancing effect of the pulsing interwoven with this access to some broader connection, was deeply healing, grounding and liberating and has been an image and sense which continues to ground, balance and empower me; and almost to lead me forward into some part of myself that I have not developed yet. (Barbara Langton)

- Exploring out-of-the-body experience.
- Exploring subtle energy telekinesis.

Each subgroup does one or two full cycles of action followed by reflection, and then shares its findings in the large group. *Afternoon.* I give a summary of the whole group history to date. We improvise a great procession with sound and music starting in the meeting barn, thence to the solar cross, to the west terrace, to the Moon Temple, to the Spirit Chamber, to the Sun Temple where there is much celebration, to the women's shrine, through the other ground floor barns, to the first floor main hall with a large crescendo. We close the formal transpersonal inquiry time, with songs and gifts.

Friday morning. We launch the free-form community phase. There is a discussion of confidentiality; also a review of our discussion and decision procedures. We then join in an affirmation of children ritual in the women's shrine. *Midday* There is a midday banquet and birthday celebration for one of us on the lower terrace. Three people depart.

Findings of the inquiry subgroups

The inquiry subgroups focused on three main things:

- Trying out, in up to eight cycles of action and reflection, different versions and variations of the activity being explored.
- A phenomenologcial description of what seemed to be going on in each person's subtle experience.
- A reflection on the criteria for knowing that the subtle experience is authentically what it seems to be, as distinct from some inauthentic and illusory state.

I will present below only the tentative sets of criteria which the several subgroups modestly proposed.

Entering into clairvoyance from attention to closed eye idio-retinal images

Provisional criteria for knowing that clairvoyance is going on:

- Emotional involvement in the imagery stops it occurring, unlike dreams where the imagery is charged with emotional involvement.
- The imagery is beyond imaginative creation. It is a happening as in a movie. It has its own autonomy.
- Seeing an eye before the brow in inner space may be a precursor.

Entering altered states by sustained mutual gazing

Provisional criteria of an authentic altered state:

- Soul contact: by focusing between the eyes of the other and attending to both eyes simultaneously, one opens to the soul, the essence, the complete presence of the other, free from emotional tension or distress in either person.
- Perceptual phenomena: there are changes of facial shape and character; and these are certainly an altered state, whatever their objective reference.

Entering altered states by sustained mutual gazing, combined with holistic pulsing

Possible altered states accessed by mutual gazing with pulsing:

- A core pulse at the heart or solar plexus can open the recipient to their own essential, potential human form, free of emotional stuff.
- A core pulse can open the recipient to being at peace, entering into the divine.

Exploring out-of-the-body experience

Possible criterion for knowing that you really are out-of-the-body:

- Unexpected views: of faces from underneath them, of people's backs from behind them, of a farm from unusual angle, from being in another smaller body.
- Unexpected sensory data from the environment visited when out-of-the-body.
- A sense of real flying.

Tapping in to subtle energy of various kinds - exploring subtle energy telekinesis

Possible criteria for real intended energy effects:

- Visible evidence for an intended energy effect.
- Agreement of a non-participant observer that an intended energy effect occurred.
- A high percentage score of intended telekinetic effects.
- A high percentage of accuracy in energetic divination of the other.
- The energetic diviner knows the difference between the real and the symbolic about the one being divined.

Entering transtemporal regressive states

Possible criteria for a real regression:

- An imaginal cluster, a whole system of imagery, with a strong autonomous storyline.

- A certain kind of knowing by acquaintance, redolent of reality.
- The impact of vivid sensory imagery from the 'place' one has journeyed to.
- A travelling in time feeling; and the feel of a certain epoch.

Evaluation

There was an informal Dionysian spiritual backdrop to the formal subtle focus of the inquiry. This backdrop, over the first six days, consisted of four evening meditation and toning sessions in the Moon Temple, and three large processional rituals. I experienced the meditations as participation in universal mind, and the processions as a celebration of immanent spiritual life. These two kinds of activity provided a container for the formal focus on the several subtle states explored.

There were four divergent subgroups, some of which diverged again after two days and for the third day. Each subgroup sustained several cycles converging on its chosen topic. Collaboration was clear and authentic. The findings of the subtle inquiry were winnowed out by loose and free form devil's advocacy in the different subgroups. There was full attention, both in group work and in one-to-one co-counselling session, to emotional and interpersonal distress triggered by the research process. The formal inquiry was above baseline adequacy. The several criteria listed as findings are minimally stated, yet have a significant claim to further active consideration, to be taken into account by other inquiry groups working in their own way on similar topics. The criteria, as with previous inquiries of this kind, are possible signs of subtle, extrasensory competence at work.

The main achievement of the wider inquiry was the effective integration of its three primary strands: the self-generating practical culture of the village, the subtle focus of the formal inquiry, the strong commitment to background spiritual activity.

17

Ritual and interpersonal process

Report status: A story evolving into a study. **Place and year:** Tuscany, 1995. **Spiritual focus:** Celebrating, through exchanges within a ritual procession, the soul as *imago dei*. This was the sustained primary spiritual focus. **Subtle focus:** Attending to subtle transfigurations of physical presence. This was subordinate to and included within the spiritual focus. **Social focus:** Exploring co-operative living in a short-term self-generating culture, in a self-catering residential setting; and exploring, within this culture, a wide range of interpersonal and intrapersonal process issues.

The invitation

Ten of us were gathered for two weeks in early September at my farmhouse in Tuscany: eight from New Zealand, one from Australia, and myself. I called it an antipodal self-generating culture gathering, and advertised it as:

- A modest micro-experience of intentional community.
- A congenial exploration of a short-term self-generating culture.
- A warm invitation to participate in the transpersonal culture of Podere Gello.
- A bold inquiry into transpersonal activities and the elements of a home-made religion.

In the blurb I went on to announce that this friendly heart-centred gathering is for those who:

- Have a strong interest in inquiring into the transpersonal dimension of human experience.
- Have done significant emotional work on healing the memories of the hurt child within.
- Are emotionally competent, that is, do not displace their hidden pain onto others.
- Want to commit themselves to participate fully in decision-making about all aspects of our life together.

Inquiry strands

The self-generating culture/intentional community aspect of the inquiry evolved procedures for dealing with practical aspects of daily living which were very similar to those used at the previous meeting in June that summer, and reported above.

This was partly because two of us had attended the earlier gathering and had, with assent, transferred some of our learning across. But intentional community was also much more central to the inquiry process. Rather than, as in June, have short community business meetings in order to concentrate mainly on formal transpersonal inquiry, we spent the greater part of our time, morning and afternoon, seated together in our circle of ten, group life being one main focus of our inquiry, which included:

- Short periods of time attending to money, transport, shopping, cooking and related matters.
- Short periods of time dealing with the use of our space (ten people using three apartments) and our time from the point of view of being intentional about separateness and togetherness. Otherwise the whole time was devoted to the following main items.
- Interpersonal processes, perceptions, contracts, conflicts and fulfilments arising out of our living and being together, and from our various previous encounters.
- Personal intrapsychic processes arising from all the previous three items. We were busy here with healing the memories at a deep level, re-evaluating ingrained attitudes and appraisals, restructuring assumptions and belief-systems.

We sat for long periods attending to the ebb and flow of all these issues and processes, without any one of us being the formal facilitator. This was a rich, engaging, seamless process of our self-regulating social organism, fluctuating between chaos and coherence as it acquired greater depth, integration and openness. This was one main complex strand of our inquiry. The other strand was transpersonal ritual.

> My overwhelming memory of the Ritual and Interpersonal Process Inquiry was that we attended to communal life on the practical, personal, interpersonal and spiritual levels, which wove a very potent container for deep personal transformation. (Peta Joyce)

> Daily living became vibrant and alive, a great way to live and learn. I feel regenerated into new soil, now all I have to do is take full responsibility for my garden. (Mary Fairbrother)

There was a strong element of collective improvisation in the timing and content of our shared rituals. We would break out of our process group to create and engage in a ritual when the appropriate energy and mood was upon us. We would also do them at times when the process group was not in session, for example, at dusk or after dark. While they were an expression of the indwelling life of the group, some of these creations were also variations on, assimilations and elaborations of, the ritual culture of Podere Gello. This consisted of a Moon Temple event on alternate evenings, a procession round the perimeter path on the other alternate days, and a midday Sun Temple event every fourth day. This local culture was honoured by our group through the unfettered, free-form creative transformation of it.

> The repetitive rituals, as well as those we improvised, appeared to evoke an inner response from deep within my imaginal mind. Spiritual realities previously frozen in time and space seemed to take their rightful place up front, and join the theatre of the present moment. (Mary Fairbrother)

Among the several rituals we evolved, the path ritual stands out supremely as a powerful expression of the archetypal reality of our culture. We used it regularly, almost daily, and it developed in depth. The farmhouse stands centrally on an elongated triangular promontory of land that projects out over encircling ravines in the west, north and east. I have cut a total perimeter path that proceeds around the upper slopes of this promontory, then circles past the pond and through the cypress grove on the southern border to rejoin its starting point above steep steps that launch it on its western circuit.

Traversing this path symbolizes: circumnavigating and participating in the total planet, the sun's diurnal journey, the seasons of the year, the cycle of life from birth to death as transcendent rebirth, the undulating circuitous inner journey of the soul, the cycle of inquiry through experience and reflection, the path, the Tao, dharma, and anything else that finds favour with the imagination of the aspirant.

We gather at the top of the western steps, at any time from midday to dusk, and there decide whether we will go round the path in meditative silence or with percussion instruments, or with a chant, mantra or song. Then we move off in slow procession, quite widely separated from each other, the winding path only allowing single file. After 50 metres or so the first person, when moved to do so, steps to the right off the path and stands on its verge. As each follower draws abreast, he or she turns to face the sentinel figure. Eye beams fuse, facial expressions become enhanced, the two persons resonate in silence, or with percusssion, or with chant or song, for a short and timeless period, then bow and gesture, parting with sovereign respect. The new leader moves on as everyone in the file pauses in turn to resonate with the first leader, who then takes up the rear of the procession. The whole process is repeated eleven or more times on the circuit, so that each person leads the procession for a stretch and then stands as sentinel on the verge greeting and resonating with every other person one by one.

This ritual procedure, preceded by the distillation of interpersonal and emotional energies in the group, generated a remarkable chain of transcendental encounters. It was as if the original archetype of the soul, the *imago dei,* stood revealed, each to each, each to all, and all in one.

The perimeter path, on its southern circuit, curls round the solar cross laid out in the upper garden in the centre of a grove of cypress trees. On one occasion we elected to do the path ritual at noon. We started as usual in the west processing round the path with our series of encounters. The solar cross is reached more than three quarters of the way around the path, after an extended ritual build-up. As we arrived at it and circled slowly round its rim, with the midday sun pouring heat and light upon us, we burst into celebratory sound and movement with a crescendo of charismatic exuberance. It was as if we were participating in the inner being of the sun as a manifest of the full attention of the universe, at the same time bestowing it with great abundance upon our planetary estate.

By contrast, most evenings at dusk we were in the underground barrel vault of the Moon Temple, toning and meditating together in lunar attunement.

We also inquired on several occasions into our experiences in the Spirit Chamber, which resulted in powerful discussions around communicating with other beings and their motives in communicating with us. We devised a surprise Birthday party and ritual for Jill, as an expression of our collective group life and her individual part in it. (Peta Joyce)

Recorded outcomes

First, two personal statements.

> I learnt the importance of interpersonal process to me in order to be able to engage in genuine and satisfying expressions of spirituality with others. The processing that was done in the group built the trust and connection I needed to feel safe and comfortable to experiment and express myself in the rituals freely with others. The more interpersonally connected we were as a group, the richer the spontaneous ritual.
>
> I learnt about the importance of play in discovering the profound. The inquiry culture's permission to act into a ritual or an experience, to play as a child does, engaging my imagination and innocence, was a way into discovering truths and experiencing transformation. I think particularly of the perimeter walk as an example. My way into this was through experiment or 'serious' play. The repetition of the ritual allowed me to ground myself in it and develop an identity as a co-participant, a community and universe citizen. Repetition also allowed me to notice the different textures and vibrations, the familiarity and difference, the ritual took on at various times.
>
> I think the cumulative effect of the rituals, intentional community and interpersonal inquiry over the six days, has had the most influence thus far in my life on my perceptions of, and aspirations for the creative expression of, my spirituality in the context of community. (David Petherbridge)

> Sharing and being witness to people's personal stories seemed to be very important and deeply healing. The authentic flow of the group between intra- and inter-personal process, and ritual time and space - transpersonal, archetypal events - seemed to build trust and depth for these different forms to deepen and broaden. The community aspect included recreation, private and small group time, awareness and intentionality around togetherness. The overall feeling I have of our time together is that of presence to each other from the heart and solar plexus area. This led us at times into deep archetypal attunement. It felt balanced, grounded in our humanness. The challenges for me were when we headed into chaos, when I felt a need to give honest direct feedback, and when I needed to be authentic with choices about togetherness and separateness. (Barbara Langton)

The four pages of the scribe's notes are the only general data on the propositional outcomes of the inquiry. As always, the primary outcomes are the personal transformations and skills acquired through being a participant in the inquiry. The written record, however, does give some indication of these, so I give below a digest of some of the main consensus findings of the review. The purpose of the review meeting, we had agreed, was:

- To look at what's been happening in general.
- In particular to consider the interweaving of the two main strands of inter/intrapersonal work and of ritual, how they overlap and support each other.
- To see what else people wanted.

The following items received general assent:

- The inter- and intrapersonal work within the openness of the peer group had strong impact:
    - It created bonding and established trust.
    - It was a forum for healing old family agendas that get triggered in the group.
    - It generated a spaciousness where synchronicity and creativity happen.
    - It allowed for a disinhibition that carries over into being more uninhibited in the temples and in rituals, more open, with full presence in the moment. The group process strand enhanced the ritual strand.
- The rituals had strong impact:
    - They made us more available for intra- and interpersonal work. The ritual strand enhanced the group process strand. The two strands were deeply interwoven, mutually nourishing and sustaining.
    - The improvised rituals felt simple and meaningful because of their spontaneity, their immediate expression of who and how we are being. They reveal a very grounded spirituality. Religion is just what is. It is really very simple: attending to who we are.
    - The repetitive rituals empowered us to feel into them, to become present to self during them, to have a variety of experiences within the constant format, to become attuned to archetypal presencing.
- Everyday life was a significant theatre which:
    - Gave permission to act into things and then discover the profundity of them.
    - Brought the spiritual into ordinary practical activities.
- Certain aspects of our culture were underdeveloped and we would like to have given more time to:
    - Meeting in subgroups and pairs.
    - Breaks in the group process sessions for dance, movement, music, percussion.
    - Exploring more fully the spectrum between privacy and communality.
    - Being more intentional about issues of intimacy, and other dimensions of a self-generating culture.
    - Planning the practical arrangements about shopping, cooking, eating, and so on; although we had set in place the basic logistics.

The inquiry closed at the end of the day after this review.

Evaluation

Since this report starts off in story mode, I will evaluate it in terms of Dionysian and Apollonian processes. The inquiry was strongly Dionysian, in the sense defined in Chapter 8, in these respects:

- Reflection phases were woven in a seamless and impromptu way, as relevant and needed, into the group meetings, without any formal decision to reflect being taken.
- The reflection was about any aspect of our group process and of our living together.
- There was no formal preplanning of experiential phases in the group. After impromptu reflection, a new surge of group process would spontaneously arise.
- The timing and design of rituals were emergent, a response to the unfolding group process and a sense of the appropriate. We became sensitive to a fitting change of gear between these ways of being and doing.

So the whole inquiry component was thus deeply tacit: flowing, emergent and powerful. However, there were also noticeable Apollonian elements:

- There was the intentional format of regular group process meetings interwoven with rituals.
- The background ritual culture of Podere Gello provided a framework within which the group improvised freely.
- The path and the Moon Temple rituals had a consistent developing format.
- After closing a ritual we tended to have a formal review time, sharing impressions and beliefs.
- On the penultimate day we held an extended formal review meeting, appointing one of our number to be a scribe.

18

Empowerment in everyday life and group life

Report status: A study. **Place and year:** Auckland, New Zealand, 1996. **Spiritual focus:** Empowering oneself in everyday life by means of individually chosen spiritual practices, e.g. finding one's spiritual heart, attending to one's coming into being, and others; and empowering ourselves in group life by collectively chosen spiritual practices, e.g. charismatic toning and movement. **Subtle focus:** Empowering oneself in everyday life by means of individually chosen subtle practices, e.g. the use of posture as subtle empowerment, the use of crystals to enhance clairvoyance, and others; and empowering ourselves in group life by collectively chosen subtle practices, e.g. exploring different patterns of subtle gender energy. **Social focus:** Injecting individual transpersonal activities into everyday culture, and creating a sub-culture of people intentionally inquiring into this kind of transpersonal social transformation.

I decided to keep no records of this inquiry, nor to invite anyone else to keep records. I wanted to be free to focus entirely on more basic outcomes: transformations of personal being; and practical knowing, that is, the skills involved in knowing how to become empowered in everyday life. So I give only a sketch here based on my recall of events and on the memory of others consulted some months after the inquiry finished.

Overview

The inquiry involved fourteen people, nine women and five men, for 12 weeks between January and April 1996 in Auckland, New Zealand. There were three subgroups of nine, three and two people, meeting weekly in the evening in North Auckland, West Auckland and Waiheke Island respectively. These subgroups met as a large group once a month to share data, explore experiences together and reflect together. This larger group had an inaugural meeting to launch the inquiry, two intermediate meetings and a closing meeting.

The subgroup of nine, of which I was a member with two other men and six women, had several inquiry strands running. The first was looking individually at how we empowered or disempowered ourselves in everyday life. Each person proposed, at our meeting, an area of everyday life to attend to in the forthcoming week, plus a tentative strategy for sustaining and enhancing a sense of empowerment in that area. At the next meeting, each person would then report back and share how they had got on with their endeavours. This would then lead on to a revised plan for the next week, and so on.

Empowerment was variously construed in spiritual, subtle, psychological and behavioural terms, and the strategies idiosyncratically used reflected this:

- Inner centering and alignment: finding the spiritual heart within, and the alignment of refined subtle energy that goes with it.
- Coming into being: opening to the continuous emergence of coming into being from the divine ground.

  I used a 'coming into being' affirmation each morning and during the day as and when it appealed to me. I also used it more specifically to step into a way of being in this world at times when I was feeling disempowered. I found this particularly powerful with some new work I was applying and being interviewed for. (Barbara Langton)

- Crystal vision: strapping a hexagonal crystal over the third eye to enhance clairvoyant opening to subtle space.
- Witnessing: attending to the coming and going of validating and invalidating thoughts.
- Confronting: marshalling personal presence to confront another about unresolved interpersonal issues.
- Posture and movement: monitoring sitting, standing, moving and gesturing as subtle modalities of personal empowerment, psychological, spiritual and interpersonal.
- Time management: monitoring ways of structuring the use of time to enhance personal empowerment.
- Self-programming and auto-suggestion: using self-affirmative thoughts as mantras running through the day.

The subgroup also at each meeting explored group empowerment through spiritual and subtle attunement. This involved:

- Sitting together in silent attunement, feeling the presence of the group as a whole.
- Waiting until a critical lift-off occurred, a shift of the subtle energy field of the group into greater refinement and openness, like a drawing close of elevated unseen presences.
- Enhancing the empowering impact of the lift-off with improvised toning and movement, which proceeded for twenty minutes or so until its energetic cycle was complete and drew to a spontaneous close.

A third activity engaged us with explorations of the effect of different physical relations within the group on empowering quality, direction and intensity of the subtle energy flow. We experimented with:

- Alternating women and men in the circle (1) holding hands as seated, (2) the men holding hands with each other and the women with each other, with the women's hands above the men's, (3) with the women's hands below the men's, then (4) the women's and the men's circuits interlaced. As I recall, the last was the most potent.

- The men standing and toning in a small close circle in the middle; the women in an outer circle, hands linked, moving round and toning; and on another occasion the women in an outer circle, seated, with legs outstretched and feet touching.

The combined subgroups meeting together monthly, shared with each other and discussed their respective explorations and reflections, reviewed the total inquiry process, and conducted together one major exploration of grouplife empowerment, combined a balance of Apollonian (preplanned) and Dionysian (emergent) actions. The whole group formed a U-shape, before the wide open doors to the balcony terrace, with the sunlit South Pacific stretching away immediately below us, the house being perched atop a cliff. The major shared experience here was the potency of the simultaneous transfiguration of our mutual presence and energy by sacred power, inclusive of a strong sense of the subtle participation of unseen presences. We noted precisely its commencing and its ending.

Findings

The inquiry had ongoing impact on daily empowerment.

> An important outcome of the empowerment in everyday life and group life inquiry for me was actually building personal skills for self-empowerment. Just the intention alone to inquire into this aspect of my life raised my awareness on many issues, and I built the skills through reflecting on my experiences in my subgroup and drawing out the learnings. (Peta Joyce)

> I noticed in detail how I disempower myself. This created a space within which I could intentionally empower myself...I found the theme really valuable in terms of observing and working with the way I operate in the world. Engaging with it was an interesting interweaving of emotional, physical and transpersonal states and intentional ways of being. The regular meetings of our subgroup interspersed with the whole group gatherings were fun, supportive and a rich combination of formal and emergent inquiry times. I feel that I built a lot of trust in allowing the group to attune at its own pace and emerge with some rich, creative, disinhibited affirmation, dance, interweaving and empowering ritual that I found unusually nourishing, uplifting and expansive, as though we were in a celebration with other vibrant energies and beings. (Barbara Langton)

> I noted a profound increase in access to realms of non-ordinary reality. It seemed as if we were manifesting transpersonal events as well as researching them. My level of self-awareness and insight into all aspects of my behaviour was enhanced. It seemed not possible to be so open and engaged in one area without also remaining so in others. There was a holistic Gestalt with the whole being greater than the sum of the parts. (Roberta Skye)

My own findings about personal empowerment in everyday life centred on two experiences, one of them a formal discipline, the other an incidental noticing:

- I found that attending with closed eyes to idioretinal lights, seated in the shade on a sunny day between mid-morning and noon, with a small hexagonal crystal strapped over my brow, facilitated clairvoyant opening to the subtle universe in two directions:

- Opening to the consciousness-space of its inner planes.
- Opening to the subtle matrix of our earth, in particular to a massive pyramidal energy form in the direction of the north eastern horizon over the ocean. This pyramidal energy form seemed to be linked in a whole elaborate set of energy relays to other energy forms, of similar or different shape, throughout the energy matrix of the planet, near or on its surface. However, my apprehension of this network was extremely vague, save in the felt sense of its presence and general activity.

- In everyday activities, when glancing out of the windows of the clifftop house I was renting, I would immediately 'see' this shimmering pyramidal form on the ocean horizon, a shifting image varying in height and horizon location, but in both respects within a limited range of variation. When 'seeing' and tuning in to this image I would immediately acquire a subtle clarifying boost to my own energy body, together with an enhanced sense of being spiritually present in and with the planet.

The most striking finding about group empowerment, founded on the group attunements of my subgroup and of the larger group, is, for me, the dynamic principle of dipolar holonomy. This is my working hypothesis which I have shared subsequently with several inquiry members, and they seem to find it plausible, without necessarily endorsing it in every particular.

Dipolar holonomy

The attuned human group, whose members resonate empathically with each other in an experience of mutual presence, can become consciously holonomic, both in a spiritual and in a subtle sense. By holonomy I mean the principle that the whole is implicit in the part, which some think may be a universal property of nature (Capra, 1983).

The holonomic principle, found in Buddhist logic (Govinda, 1960; Stcherbatsky, 1962), is also a truism in several mystical traditions. It has its adherents among theoretical physicists and biophysicists such as Schroedinger (1964, 1969), von Bertalanffy (1968) and Bohm (1980) as a derivation from holographic logic and quantum logic (Zukav, 1979). Other thinkers assert that the very concept of the universe as a whole entails the notion of the mutual participation of the parts in each other and the whole (Teilhard de Chardin, 1961; Skolimowski, 1985).

Back to our empathic group. When we resonate together, become mutually attuned, entrained, when our brain waves oscillate in unison, then it is experientially *as if* we participate in the sacred space of the universe. We become involved in the presence of the whole. This cosmic presence becomes explicit in some measure in our shared consciousness, and the extent to which it becomes explicit is determined by the extent to which our consciousness is shared. The more mutual our felt interpersonal communion, the greater the degree of sacred participation in the presence of the whole. This is the spiritual aspect of group holonomy. There is also the subtle aspect, and it is to this which I apply the concept of dipolarity.

When the group is attuned it is also experientially *as if* there becomes explicit in our awareness and in the energy dynamic of the group, quite specific affiliations with powers and presences in the subtle universe. By powers I mean various modalities of divine creative energy; by presences I mean elevated persons, who are accomplished in refracting and mediating such powers. On the holonomic hypothesis, the whole subtle universe is implicit in the group as mediated by these particular affiliations. When these affiliations are made explicit by intentional attunement and ritual, they generate a local effect: an immediate energetic ambience of unseen witnesses and their refracted powers. This ambience is like a radiant zone of intense local subtle force which rapidly shades off in our awareness into the tacit totality of the subtle universe. Again the range of this local zone, that is, the extent of our conscious participation in the subtle universe, is determined by the acuity with which we realize our special affinities with powers and presences.

This is the 'above' aspect of subtle holonomy. There is also the 'below' aspect: as embodied humans participating in the subtle matrix of the earthly sociosphere, biosphere and physiosphere, we each have special affiliations within this matrix with other humans, and also with animal, plant and mineral energies. So the whole planetary matrix in these four prime respects is implicit in each group member as mediated, in the first instance, by these particular idiosyncratic, individual affinities. The more explicit in awareness for each member these special affinities become the greater the degree to which participation in the matrix as a whole becomes conscious. Specific affinities are the window for wider global participation.

The attuned group thus becomes a mediating alchemical furnace within which the powers and presences of the subtle universe are fired and fused with the matrix energies, the formative forces, of planetary existence, cultural, animal, plant and inorganic. It is likely that this alchemical effect is transmutative and transformative for planetary existence. The dipolar holonomy, the above-below participation fused within the fires of group presence, is a developmental process for all concerned: the above, the below and the mediating group. All this, of course, is expansive conjecture which calls for much grounding in active inquiry.

Evaluation

I kept no records of what went on in this group. There was no discussion nor any agreement about record-keeping, although some individual members kept their own diaries. Nor, so far as I remember, did I ever raise the issue of validity procedures. However, the inquiry had a basic adequacy because there was a good balance of divergence and convergence in both the individual and the group research cycles, collaboration was fully authentic, and spontaneous episodes of devil's advocacy - challenging uncritical subjectivity - were built into the reflection phases.

The basic outcomes of the inquiry were a wide range of spiritual and subtle transformations and skills, both individual and group. This is partly because people were busy with the processes involved and not the recording of them.

19

Co-creating

Report status: A study. **Place and year:** Tuscany, 1996. **Spiritual focus**: Generating an inquiry-based theory and a method of self and peer spiritual awakening. **Subtle focus:** Generating subtle practices that support spiritual awakening. **Social focus:** Seeding an inquiry-based theory and a method of self and peer spiritual awakening within the prevailing culture, and cultivating a sub-culture of people intentionally inquiring into this kind of transpersonal social change.

Overview

Twenty experienced co-counsellors, including fifteen co-counselling teachers, from the UK, USA and Holland, joined me in Tuscany, in the summer of 1996, to inquire into the possibilities of making a spiritual account of human nature central to the theory and practice of co-counselling. These co-counsellors were all members of Co-counselling International (CCI), a federation of self-governing co-counselling networks from several countries worldwide. Co-counselling, a form of peer self-help psychotherapy, was developed from a mixture of influences in the 1960s by Harvey Jackins, who called it re-evaluation counselling.

Jackins developed his Re-evaluation Counselling Communities (RCC) with an increasingly authoritarian and dogmatic hand and RCC has now degenerated into a rigidly controlled cult. CCI split off from RCC in 1974, and has since then successfully sustained and developed its blend of autonomy and co-operation, both within local networks and with regard to international activities.

However, the theory of human nature which CCI has inherited from RCC is entirely humanist, and in recent years there has been a growing interest within CCI, especially among co-counselling teachers, to explore ways of introducing spiritual ideas and practices both in the basic training and in national and international workshops for trained co-counsellors. Following discussions I had with teachers at a CCI teachers workshop at Harlech, Wales in 1995, I proposed to run a basic co-counselling five-day training based on a spiritual paradigm.

What in fact I did, over the first two and a half days, was to present selected parts of a radically revised theory and invited participants to explore parts of a radically revised practice. This was offered as a provisional working hypothesis, in a spirit of inquiry. The discussion of theory and the feedback on practice both led to a considerable modification of my launching ideas. The final two and a half days was an entirely free form co-operative inquiry into participants' own ideas about spiritual transformations of theory and practice. We did not gather in any set of findings about these ideas, since it was felt to be premature to do so.

> We were a group of twenty. After a leisurely day settling in we met as a group seven hours a day for five days, first doing the transpersonal fundamentals, then an autonomy lab. In this, subgroups met to follow their interests: further exploration of theory, experiential work, discussion of how (whether) this work fits with the rest of co-counselling or, in my case, working with an advanced NLP method called core transformation (CR). In CR the counsellor spoke to the part of me (Good Boy) responsible for a presenting chronic pattern and asked that part what its intention is in maintaining the pattern. Good Boy replied 'acceptance', and What's more important than acceptance?, next reply, and What's more important than that?, and so on, all the way back to a transpersonal root intention. I had several of these: 'Joy shared and exchanged', 'Love permeating space, time and matter'; a rich imagery of divine delights emerged from the hidden reaches of my consciousness and I cried, mainly for joy, but also for missing these for most of my life. I felt I was reclaiming and previewing distress-free spiritual experience, full of light, joy, fun, depth, connection, meaning. This was miles away from heavy religiosity. At last, a 'high' without drugs (I've long wanted that.) The CR was an interlude of fireworks but more important was 'getting' what transpersonal work is all about. For me it is opening to experiencing myself as a spiritual being in human form in a spiritual universe. I rarely feel that in daily life and see coming to experience the world as 'Joy shared and exchanged', 'Love permeating space, time and matter' as long term work in progress, both for me and the world. (Julian Briggs)

> I am a recovering Roman Catholic. Realising that my religion was not helping me on my personal journey and letting it go was an anguished episode for me about twenty years ago. In recent years, as I have used co-counselling and other approaches in my personal development, I have become aware that when I let my religion go I let something else go. A full awareness of a part of me. I might call that part my spirituality, or my soul, or my transcendent self, maybe my transpersonal self. Whatever I choose to call it, I want to reclaim it. So the chance to explore this in a co-counselling setting was one I seized enthusiastically. So many words are restimulating for me around religion and the transpersonal. I was glad to have the opportunity to explore this with others. It was useful for me to learn to realize how much my resistance to new ideas is tied up with the old words, and how much this can get in the way of hearing and accepting and using the words in different ways. Similarly, some of the new ideas to me were blurred by resonance with old ideas. For example, I am open to the idea that because my personal being is embodied, i.e. linked to a body, there are inherent constraints that can generate tension and distress. I can accept the labels 'primary contraction' and 'primary distress' associated with this. But when I become aware of some similarities with the idea of original sin I hesitate, I want to be clear what I have let go of and what I am open to. The days in Tuscany were very rich for me in having the opportunity to explore different ways of looking at myself and my universe, to pick up ideas, turn them over, try them on. I am still doing this. These days practice is more important than theory for me. I am fascinated by theories, and I am also open to trying things out without understanding them if I feel moved to, and if they help me, I take them on board. For example, I am receptive to the notion that cathartic discharge has limits in healing my distress and enabling me to grow. I recognize the value of discharge, and I am interested in exploring other possibilities when I seem to have exhausted what discharge can do for me in a given situation. The ideas about transmutation, changing the form of primary distress into something more useful, seem to me to be full of potential. 'I feel a heavy ball in my

stomach. It is like a dark metal shell with me inside unable to get out. I visualise a light inside spreading warmth. I feel a golden liquid replacing the light. Now I see the metal shell as my mother, constraining and bounding me. The golden liquid is softening the metal shell; it changes into a hard connection between me and my mother, then into a soft connection (umbilical cord?), then into an infinitely long thin elastic cord, linking but not constraining. I can drift freely. I can pull on the cord and she feels the pull. And vice versa. I am not bound. I am not alone.' I found these sessions very powerful for me in changing the way I see and experience old distress. The ball in the stomach is an image I have frequently encountered in co-counselling sessions. The time, place and opportunity was right for me to explore changes through imagery, one form of transmutation. In other sessions I got in touch with birth and death processes, different forms of letting go. I came to see the golden liquid as my spirit, infinitely replenishable, that I can choose to give, receive, keep or share. So much to process, so much to learn. I feel I have opened a door to new ways of exploring my self and my journey. I am pleased I stuck with my process, uncomfortable though it was at times. I feel I learned and experienced richly by doing so. I am glad that my exploration was with co-counsellors in a co-counselling setting. I do not know how so much of the cosmos would have been covered otherwise. 'I am Paul; I am open' recalls one of the simple and rich Tuscan rituals for me. Part of me wants to say amen. 'Amen'. There, that did not hurt, did it? (Paul Shevlin)

The following have stayed with me for use in living. The support, free attention, love that is there for us in the universe which we need to be aware of and to ask for and invite into our lives; I link this with Matthew Fox's idea of original blessing. The primary distress around embodiment, an idea I use when struggling with seemingly unresolvable issues. Your invitation to us to be happy in Podere Gello during the week. (Ann O'Donoghue)

What emerged out of all this, for me, was a fully revised account of my provisional model for a self and peer process of spiritual awakening and development. I offer it here as the primary outcome of my inquiry with the teachers, and as a stimulus to further inquiry along these lines.

I call this approach co-creating, since while its origins lie in a revision of co-counselling, the revision is so radical that a different name for the result is appropriate. What follows is the text of the manual which I circulated to participants a few weeks after the end of the inquiry gathering.

Evaluation

My evaluation of the following manual, is that it is entirely provisional, a practical working hypothesis, in principle open to revision as a function of the reader's experiential inquiry. I underline this point again in the preface. Small parts of it were field-tested during the inquiry. Reading it over for publication as part of this book, I find it is rather overwrought in its account of the working methods suggested.

Theory and method of co-creating

A manual for further research

Preface

The purpose of the notes is to make clear to myself, and to others who may be interested, what kind of self and peer development I want to practise.

I call this method 'co-creating', since this term best indicates what it is that I believe in. It is a peer method, with people working in pairs, each person taking a turn as the creator, who is busy working in one or more fields, and as the co-creator, who is supporting the creator according to a contract the creator has chosen.

What is presented here is a working hypothesis, grounded in a variety of personal and shared experiences. This working hypothesis is provisional in form, and is in principle open to revision, amendment and correction as a consequence of further experience and reflection. There is nothing immaculate about this document.

Some people may want to use this presentation to clarify what their own approach to self and peer development involves. If you are one of these, I offer the book as a stimulus to the clarification of your own theory and method, and I offer my support in your work. I hope you will feel free to adopt or adapt any of my ideas that are valid for you.

Others may want to try out this method as it is presented here. If you are one of these, I suggest you find an interested colleague, then each take your time, dip into the book and gradually get the feel of it. See whether it really speaks to your condition, or not. If it does, when you and your co-creator are ready, work with it in a mood of sacred experiment, adapting it to make it work for you, and feeling free to modify and rearrange anything. Always be true to your own inner prompts. Use the method as a form of co-operative inquiry, and when you have got well into things, take time out every once in a while with your co-creator, and any others who are exploring this approach, to review and revise its protocols in the light of your deepening experience. To you too I offer my support in your work.

Theory

1. A person is a citizen of the cosmos, a cosmopolitan in the original sense of the word.

- My personal consciousness is continuous with a backdrop of cosmic consciousness which, I feel, includes all worlds, physical and subtle.
- My personal life emerges from what I sense is an inner wellspring of divine life, a deep centre of indwelling and unlimited potential.

2. The embodiment of a person in this world is a challenge to express her or his cosmopolitan life and consciousness, individually and socially, in a context of biological survival within our planet's ecosystem.

- I am challenged to honour both my body in its total setting and my unlimited awareness and potential.
- I am challenged to honour other persons similarly challenged.

3. Meeting this challenge of the human condition generates a deep and subtle body-mind tension which is a form of cosmic or spiritual amnesia, self-forgetting.

- I forget my cosmopolitan status and lose awareness of the sweep of cosmic consciousness and of the deep centre within.
- My consciousness contracts around a preoccupation with my physical and social identity, and with time, fretting about the past and the future.

4. A person's primary distress is the subtle pain of this cosmic amnesia, the sense of alienation from the cosmic playground and from the locus of divine life within.

- This anxiety is not hidden from me, or remote in my personal history; it is current, generated by an ongoing contracted awareness, in flight from my continuous coming into being.
- It is felt as negative considering and restless activism, an anxious inner and outer busyness set in motion by continuous forgetting.

5. When persons notice their coming into being, remember and reclaim their status as cosmic citizens, with expanded awareness and inner attunement, when they reMind and reLive themselves, they disperse their primary distress, the body-mind tension of spiritual forgetting.

- When I remember, open to notice, who I am, I feel the happiness of my true estate; my primary pain and body-mind tension dissolve.
- I am empowered to take charge of, and respond creatively to, the challenges of embodiment: to live fully in this world in a multi-dimensional universe.

6. When whole societies of people are in a state of spiritual amnesia, primary distress and its attendant tension go into overload and burst out as interpersonal hurt, face-to-face wounding. This is secondary distress, of which there is great deal on our planet.

- The face-to-face wounding of secondary distress becomes self-perpetuating: people who are hurt by people, then hurt other people, and so it goes on.
- This self-perpetuating cycle of secondary distress is itself always grounded in, and fed by a continuous displacement of, the primary distress of cosmic amnesia. We sacrifice each other, ultimately, as a substitute for the inner sacrifice of letting go of our contracted state and opening up to our coming into being now.

7. There are two other consequences of widespread cosmic amnesia within society, and they interweave with the primary consequence of face-to-face wounding. They, too, are forms of displaced primary distress.

- There are restrictive taboos, contracted values, norms and beliefs which pervade a culture. They suppress people inwardly by the climate they create, and they oppress people outwardly by restrictive social practices.

- There is the divisive use of language to name in order to split: to split subject from object, perceiver from perceived, person from person, tribe from tribe, nation from nation, species from species, insiders from outsiders, and so on.

8. The contracted awareness of cosmic amnesia and loss of inner attunement is a choice made in response to the challenge of human embodiment; and it is a choice which generates the cycle of pain.

- It is a subliminal coping choice: the challenge may be easier to meet if I reduce the options and drop the cosmos and inner divine potential.
- It is a self-defeating choice: the pain it generates goes into overload and displaces into exchange of interpersonal hurt, which contracts a person's being even further and locks all concerned in the self-perpetuating cycle of people hurting people.

9. The sequence is: I forget, choose not to notice my continuous genesis, and contract my being, then I feel primary distress; when this accumulates I displace it into exchange of interpersonal hurt, and then this contracts my being more.

- The first contraction is to drop out of cosmic consciousness and to cut off from the inner centre of divine potential: I choose a limited view of my embodied self.
- The second contraction is due to interpersonal damage done to and by that self-limiting self. Through such damage, I lose the capacity to attune sensitively to a situation, image it fully, think about it awarely and act in it creatively. And this is because I carry around, from the unresolved painful experience, a victim-oppressor imprint which projects out its distorted images, thoughts and choices; and disables my capacity for sensitive attunement.

10. These two different kinds of contraction lead to two complementary kinds of healing, and the first kind of healing is the foundation of the second.

- The cosmic contraction of my being, which I choose as a form of coping, causes primary distress. So healing primary distress is first and foremost a matter of remembering my cosmopolitan status and inner divinity: I choose to stop contracting. I attend to my coming into being. I open my awareness to divine mind, and attune deep within to divine life, and this heals the distress by dissolving and transmuting it, although there may be elements of supporting discharge. This kind of healing is the foundation of the next kind.
- The second contraction of my being is caused by secondary distress, interpersonal hurt. So here I resolve this distress by emotional discharge and spontaneous insight, with elements of supporting transmutation, in order to heal and expand the wounded and wounding contracted state which it holds in place.

11. Primary contraction, cosmic amnesia, has a historical dimension and a present time dimension, and the latter is more basic.

- The historical dimension is amnesia and primary distress at the start of embodiment: during the birth process and any accompanying birth trauma. This very earliest pain of self-forgetting feeds into the primitive exchange of hurt between infant and parent, and the dynamic of double contraction is set on its cumulative historical course.
- More fundamentally, as a person I am continuously coming into being now, focusing the wide reaches of comic consciousness and emerging from a centre of divine potential within. As I do so, I make a choice now not to notice it, to forget it. Present-time self-forgetting can be influenced by historical self-forgetting, but is never caused by it. It is caused by my coming into being now in the context of embodiment, and by the immediate challenge this presents.

12. It follows that the self-perpetuating cycle of interpersonal hurt, while it is strongly reinforced by past history manifest as current habit, is not here and now primarily caused by it.

- Whatever cumulative destructive habits of interpersonal hurt I am locked into, what primarily feeds them and keeps them in place, is my ongoing present-time self-forgetting, my chosen absence from my continuous coming into being.
- The healing of these habits of hurt, while it needs deep resolution of past pain through emotional discharge and insight, has its foundation in continuously remembering and noticing now who I am and so resolving my current primary distress.

13. The basic form of interpersonal hurt is the victim-oppressor dynamic, and this dynamic is fundamentally always an exchange, a two-way process.

- No-one is ever purely a victim or an oppressor: each participates in the role of the other while being in their own primary role, and each can, to a greater or lesser degree, switch roles.
- Hence both roles are always imprinted in the primary victim, who will displace them both into further interpersonal hurt until there is resolution and healing.

14. A person, in the very act of coming into being now, is a co-creator of their being in their universe and their immediate setting.

- I am not just being made, I am co-involved in the act of making, I participate in the creative process.
- Furthermore, you and I are co-involved, we are all involved in the co-creating of being in our worlds. Hence the deep collaborative challenge of embodiment and hence the phenomena of widespread collective cosmic amnesia.

General application

The purpose of this section is to outline four broad areas for the application, the living, of the theory, four ways of putting it to the test of lived experience. I think all these four ways need to be concurrent, interweaving and supporting each other, and the first is the most basic, the foundation of the other three.

1. *Awakening to cosmic citizenship.* Choosing to remember who we are, opening up fully to our cosmopolitan status, our coming into being now, and dissolving primary distress.

- Turning about within ordinary consciousness to notice its great backdrop of cosmic consciousness, of universal free attention.
- Attending to the impact of archetypal imagery from within this cosmic field.
- Participating in immediate present experience, in the free attention and living presence of our world, and its wider context, in and through seeing, saying, hearing, touching and moving.
- Manifesting in expressive action our personal charismatic presence.
- Attuning to the life-prompts of the deep centre of divine potential within.

2. *Emerging with full self-esteem and interpersonal regard.* Healing face-to-face wounding and interrupting the self-perpetuating cycle of exchanging interpersonal hurt.

- Being self-appreciating, and validating and affirming others.
- Being open in relationship, with full emotional honesty; and negotiating choices based on a clear statement of personal preferences.
- Taking time out for healing the memories of interpersonal trauma through regression, catharsis and insight.
- Cognitively restructuring and revisioning our interpersonal past, present and future.

3. *Co-creating a self-generating culture.* Working in interrelated networks to generate alternative sub-cultures and to disperse the restrictive impact of conventional social taboos.

- Co-operatively inquiring, in overlapping networking groups, into transforming, through action, diverse aspects of everyday life-style.
- Progressively rewriting the scripts of each and every social role.
- Practising planetary consciousness, being both local and global in thinking and acting.
- Being ecologically caring, and symbiotic within the biosphere and physiosphere.

4. *Becoming an artist in living.* Choosing embodiment as a canvas for personal and shared symbolic expression of the meanings we give to, and find in, our co-created cosmos; and so recovering from the divisive, alienating use of language.

- Using everyday language to symbolize our participation in a seamless, subjective-objective world.
- In all areas of life and work, also using metaphor, analogy, pattern, to express our meanings, through the nondiscursive symbols of drawing, painting, movement, sound, film, and music; and using language in poetic and dramatic, as well as in prosaic, forms.

- Using ritual, ceremony and all social practices as symbolic forms to celebrate the ways we give meaning to, and find meaning in, our co-created worlds.
- Adopting a flexible, aperspectival outlook, being open to bracket our beliefs and reframe our worlds.

Application within co-creating sessions

Co-creating sessions are one-to-one, on a reciprocal basis, each person taking a turn both as the active creator and as the supportive co-creator.

1. *Participating in free attention.* This is the foundation practice for both creator and co-creator.

- Free attention is unrestricted consciousness, cosmic and abundant, not mine, not yours. It's everyone's and everything's. It is cosmopolitan awareness: each person participates in its vast scope and also focalizes it here and now.
- Unrestricted free attention can be accessed through feeling, and by distinguishing feeling from our emotions. Emotions are to do with the fulfilments and frustrations of our needs and interests. Feeling is to do with empathy, resonance, indwelling, being attuned to and participating in our immediate world, and in the universal awareness that is the continuous backdrop of our ordinary mind. When we feel, indwell the presence of our world, and this backdrop, we participate in abundant free attention. Feeling is the love of being.
- Co-creators can enter unrestricted consciousness by gently sustained and silent mutual gazing, noticing and accepting emotional states while not trying to do anything to them, and at the same time feeling each other's presence and opening to the wider reaches of awareness within which their communion is embraced. They can also do so by other methods: see item 10 below and Teaching point 1 below.

2. *The powers of free attention.* Unrestricted free attention that is everywhere appears to have at least four major powers, if given an opening by persons to do so. These are four powers to which both creator and co-creator, for their different purposes, can be responsive.

- It can release latent potential.
- It can discharge blocked energies.
- It can harmonize discordant or dissociated energies.
- It can transmute energies from one state into another.

3. *Human foci of free attention.* There appear to be at least three main foci or centres in the embodied person, where the four powers of unrestricted free attention can manifest in the creator to enhance and further his or her work.

- In the enteric brain, that is, in the belly: especially for releasing latent potential and discharging blocked energies. The enteric brain, the psychic and spiritual womb, the *hara* centre in Japanese tradition, just below the umbilicus, seems to be a locus of deep indwelling divine potential. It is a centre for life-prompts: how and when and where to unfold ourselves in space and time, when and how to come or stay or leave. It is a place for grounding the process of co-creating.

- In the region of the heart: especially for harmonizing discordant energies, or integrating the dissociated energies of head and belly. It seems to be a centre for feeling the living presence and abundant attention of our world in and through the process of perceiving, meeting and relating.
- In the head: especially for transmuting energies through imaging, revisioning and reframing. It seems to be a centre for turning about into our continuity with cosmic consciousness, and for receiving impressions and visions of its archetypal contents.

4. *Balance of awareness.* The creator's session seems to go well if there is a balance between expanded awareness, that is, being open to the wider reaches of unrestricted free attention, and focal awareness, that is, being open to how free attention is at work in one or more of the three main human foci.

5. *Four forms of awareness.* The creator in a session can be in four forms of awareness, two of them fruitful, two unfruitful. She or he can do creative work in a balance of the first two; but will be blocked in a coagulation of the second two.

- Expanded awareness in the wider reaches of unrestricted free attention.
- Focal awareness, where there is a sense of creative space around one or more of the human foci as free attention is at work within it.
- Primary contracted awareness, or self-forgetting, cosmic amnesia: manifest as a preoccupation with internal negative considering or outward restless activism.
- Secondary contracted awareness: being sunk in, or acting out, the unresolved pain of interpersonal hurt.

6. *The work of the creator.* Here are some suggestions about how you, the creator, might proceed with a session. Also before your work begins, choose what kind of contract you want with your co-creator and let him or her know. See 11 below, for the three contracts. Before your session begins, generate together with your co-creator a sacred space, a shared field for both of you in your different roles to access (see 1 above and Teaching point 1 below).

- First, keep open to the sacred space you have just co-created: self-remember, let go of cosmic amnesia, open up to unrestricted free attention.
- Second, let go of any secondary contraction, any agitation of old or current interpersonal hurt, which can be done by the next suggestion.
- Third, focus free attention in a relaxed body-mind space within the belly, around the *hara,* the psychic and spiritual womb, the inner wellspring, while still having a backdrop of expanded awareness. You create this focus just by feeling and imaging it. You may want to precede this simple focusing by any one or more of the following:
  - Deep, rapid breathing and body loosening.
  - Sounding, toning, glossolalia.

  - Explicit evocation of the divine potential within the *hara.* This can be elaborated into:
  - A simple ritual of opening to the divine life within.
- Fourth, go Dionysian, which simply means wait in the relaxed space around the belly-centre, in a completely open-ended way, without any preconceptions, for a spontaneous inner prompt about which field to open for the start of your creative work. Or go Apollonian, which means you take some pre-chosen topic for your work and you check in with the belly-centre for any prompt about how to (perhaps sometimes whether to) open it up. The soundness of a prompt is marked by the fact that it comes when you are inwardly relaxed, and is accompanied by an unmistakable subtle liberating release of energy.
- Fifth, enter the prompted field or way of opening, and proceed by following further inner belly-centre prompts, and by making your own creative choices, and by responding to your co-creator's suggestions (if that is the contract).
- Sixth, let the session unfold generously: be open to the range of fields (see no. 7 below), be open to the range of field skills (see no. 8 below), and be open to change the contract with your co-creator if and when it feels appropriate.
- Seventh, close the session after opening up to a felt affirmation in word, posture, gesture, movement, of your embodied presence as a cosmic and planetary citizen.

7. Co-creation fields. These are the different fields the creator can range over during a session. I call them co-creation fields since they are generated in the context of a co-creating contract. The creator is familiar with them for the purposes of self-direction and of openness to wide-ranging inner prompts. And the co-creator also, so that she or he can make relevant interventions, when that is the contract chosen by the creator. Both the creator, and the co-creator when making active suggestions, have in mind the field skills proposed in sections 8 and 9 below. What follows is a sketch: co-creators will elaborate it further in practice.

- 7.1. *Active presence.* This affirms the cosmopolitan person in active embodiment in a variety of ways, which can be variously combined. By the term 'sacred' below I mean connected to the whole (the Germanic root of 'holy' means 'whole') from centre to circumference. Active, charismatic presence is microcosmic: symbolizing archetypal forms and energies, and the expressive focus of divine potential deep within.
  - Sacred postures and gestures and movements and dance.
  - Sacred breathing.
  - Sacred toning, chanting, singing, glossolalia.
  - Vocal celebration, poetry, praise, diune prayer.
  - Sacred music.
  - Sacred drawing, painting, sculpture.
  - Sacred ritual, with the passive or active presence of the co-creator.

- 7.2. *Receptive presence.* This is opening in stillness to unrestricted free attention and the inner centre. Creators will have their own favourites. I offer four of mine. And they can be combined in various ways.
  - Opening to the divine ground, source, wellspring of my being in the belly, and feeling the gentle inflow of its life. I do this seated with eyes closed.
  - Feeling, and participating in, the living presence and abundant free attention of the world in the immediate process of seeing, hearing, touching and moving. The heart region seems to be a focus for this kind of participative awareness. I do this standing, out in nature, maybe moving a little.
  - Feeling a harmonizing figure-of-eight flow of energy through the heart, encompassing the belly in the lower loop and the head in the upper loop. I do this seated with eyes closed.
  - Turning about in the midst of the everyday organizing attention of ordinary consciousness to notice its continuity with the great backdrop of cosmic consciousness. I do this seated with eyes closed; and also, when I remember, in the midst of ordinary, everyday activities. This kind of opening seems to have its focus in the head region.
- 7.3. *Life-prompts.* This repeats the process for starting a session mentioned under 6 above, but for a different purpose. Focus free attention in a relaxed body-mind space within the belly, around the *hara,* the place of inner grounding, the soul's wellspring. Take to this place an issue, a concern, a decision to be made, that is engaging you in your daily life, and about which you are unclear. Hold the issue in the relaxed space and wait, without forcing it, for a given visual auditory, kinaesthetic or verbal image, which you shape and co-create as much as it shapes you.

As I said above, the soundness of a prompt is marked by the fact that it comes when you are inwardly relaxed, and is accompanied by an unmistakable subtle liberating release of energy. You may then want to reality-test the life-prompt and work out in a more rational way what seem to be its implications. The issue you take to this place will usually be quite specific, occasionally it may be very general. Be open to a response which says, effectively, 'It's up to you'.

- 7.4. *Regression.* This is the process of healing the memories of interpersonal hurt, freeing the soul of the victim-oppressor imprint which projects out distorted images, thoughts and choices and restricts the capacity for feeling resonance and attunement. Working in the field of regression seems to be fundamental for the full emergence of self-esteem, interpersonal regard and basic, human, emotional autonomy. This field is given very full attention in any training programme (see Training point 3 below).
  - The royal route is reliving the trauma, discharging the emotional pain, gathering in the insights and re-evaluations generated by the discharge. The two interacting ways of the royal route are through body work and through imagery work. These will be familiar to co-

counsellors and others who practise cathartic methods, and I will not go into details here. I believe the royal route provides the basic foundation way for healing memories of interpersonal pain.

- A supplementary route is via cognitive restructuring, which means revisioning and reconstruing painful memories so that the hurt within them is transmuted and transformed into benign emotion. See my *Helping the Client,* Chapter 8, (Heron 1990) for more details.

- 7.5. *Imaginal opening.* This is working with the visioning focus in the head region. Again, creators will have their own favourites. Here are some methods I have used.
  - Image-streaming: open the mind to an impromptu, improvised, spontaneous stream of imagery, which you continuously verbalize. Speaking it out in words keeps the stream flowing. Let the symbolism that emerges resonate within you. It may lead to a shift of field.
  - Thematic imaging: take a theme, such as your mission, calling or destiny, your cosmopolitan journey, an archetypal idea, and let it unfold through symbolic active imagination. This is image-streaming within a guiding idea.
  - Visualizing the future: empower your life now by visualizing in detail your abundant future in three, five, ten or fifteen years time; or by visualizing in detail the abundant future of planetary society in two, three or five hundred years time.
  - Idioretinal opening: with closed eyes, let after-images gradually fade away and then attend, without distraction, to ongoing vague retinal images, giving them a lot of attention until they open up and start to become windows for a deeper layer of inner seeing. Give every slight emerging glimpse the benefit of the doubt, feed it with attention, let it grow and go with it.
  - Opening consciousness into inner subtle spaces, visioning their powers and presences.

- 7.6. *Restructuring belief-systems.* Identify the underlying presuppositions of one's way of being in the world in general, or in some particular arena of living, weeding out those that are restrictive and deficient and replacing them and reprogramming oneself with ones that are liberating and abundant.

- 7.7. *Thinking and planning.* This is really two fields, traditionally called theoretical reason and practical reason. They are as important today as ever they were.
  - Creative thinking: bold reflection at the frontiers of your own knowledge and belief in any sphere; thinking through particular problems and questions, which may lead over into:
  - Action-planning: deliberating moral dilemmas and moral issues; deliberating choice options and their possible consequences; setting goals; selecting means; making specific plans; deciding what to do next.

8. *Field skills for the creator.* Here is a range of simple common sense skills for the creator when working with the different fields.

- Enjoy and feel a background awareness of all the fields while focused within any one of them; and balance working within a field with appropriate shifts between fields.
- Be open to unrestricted free attention to facilitate the work you do within each of the fields, with its powers of releasing potential, discharging blocks, harmonizing energies and transmuting energies.
- Be open to follow a sudden creative, spontaneous shift, or prompt to shift, from one field to another.
- Be open to making an intentional, experimental choice to shift from one field to another.
- Let go of overidentification with a field, using it as a defence against entering some other field that is beckoning.
- Interrupt premature closure of a field when deeper work within it beckons; similarly, interrupt sudden flight from the present field into another field, where the flight is a defence against getting deeper into the present one.
- Be open to keeping a balance between working in the main three foci of unrestricted free attention, the belly, the heart and the head.
- Ground the whole process by being open to prompts from the enteric brain, the *hara*, the psychic and spiritual womb, the belly-mind.

9. *Field skills for the co-creator.* These apply to the co-creator who has a contract to make suggestions to the client (for contracts, see 11 below).

- Be aware of the whole range of fields while the creator is busy within any one of them; and keep a balance between your facilitation of work within a field, and your facilitation of shifts from field to field.
- Be attentive to the cues which show how unrestricted free attention is facilitating the creator's work within each of the fields, with its powers of releasing potential, discharging blocks, harmonizing energies and transmuting energies; and suggest that client work with these cues when he or she misses them.
- Be attentive to cues indicating any sudden, creative spontaneous shift from one field to another, and encourage the creator to go with it.
- Suggest that the creator makes an experimental shift from the current field to another, when you have a strong sense that this would be fruitful.
- When you sense that another field is beckoning, and the creator is avoiding it by staying too long in the current field, suggest the relevant shift.
- Encourage the creator to stay with the current field and go deeper, when you sense he or she is prematurely closing it down, or is in flight from it by moving suddenly to another field.
- Make occasional suggestions which support the client keeping a balance between working in the main three foci of unrestricted free attention, the belly, the heart and the head.

- Ground your interventions by being open to prompts from your enteric brain, the *hara,* the psychic and spiritual womb, the belly-mind.

10. *The role of the co-creator.* The basic role of the co-creator is to generate and sustain, together with the creator, a shared field for accessing the four-fold power of universal, unrestricted free attention. This power is then focused both in the work of the creator and in the creative support, silent or spoken, of the co-creator.

- The co-creator and creator can together generate a shared field, a sacred space, for accessing the power of universal free attention by one or more of the following, for more details on which see Teaching point 1 below.
  - A period of mutual entrainment, with eyes closed.
  - A period of sustained mutual gazing (see also 1 above).
  - A period of impromptu active presence.
  - A conjoint invocation of unrestricted free attention, and a conjoint evocation of indwelling divine potential; which can be elaborated into a shared ritual.
- The co-creator sustains the shared field, while the creator is busy with his or her work, and focuses its unrestricted free attention through supportive presence for the creator, as revealed in gaze, posture, gesture, and, when appropriate, touch
  - This means enjoying the cosmic banquet, self-remembering, letting go of cosmic amnesia.
  - Dissociating from any twitches of secondary distress, old interpersonal hurt.
- The co-creator also focuses unrestricted free attention through appropriate interventions as in 9 above, if that is the contract.

11. *Co-creating contracts.* The creator chooses and states a contract for the co-creator's support, before starting his or her session. The creator may change the contract at any point in the session. There are three basic contracts.

- 11.1. *Presence contract.* The co-creator is asked to give supportive presence only, with no verbal suggestions, so the creator is entirely self-directing in her or his work. This gives scope for an uninterrupted personal journey of inquiry.
- 11.2. *Back-up contract.* The co-creator is asked to give supportive presence, with prompts to back-up the creator's self-direction. These are prompts about work within a field, and about moves between fields, which the creator has missed in self-directed working. This has the benefits of two creative, interacting perspectives at work.
  - Refinements of this contract are that the creator can ask for: within-field prompts only; moving-between-field prompts only; or both within-field and moving-between-field prompts.
- 11.3. *Leading contract.* The co-creator is asked to give supportive presence, with leading prompts. These are prompts which propose and sustain directions for the creator to take within a field or in moving from field to field. The creator may choose this contract with regard to some area of work where there is a lot of uncertainty, blockage, confusion.

Teaching points

When doing a training in co-creating, the following pointers seem to me to make good sense.

1. *Sacred space.* Offer plenty of exercises in creating a sacred space, a shared field for accessing the powers of unrestricted free attention. I would offer these exercises first of all for the whole group, where they are more powerful, and then invite people to try them out in pairs, as training for opening sacred space in one-to-one co-creating sessions.

- 1.1. *Mutual entrainment.* The group hold hands in a circle, close eyes, and attune to each other, feeling the presence of the group as a whole. When brain waves start to synchronize, there is a shared field of awareness opening out to the great mirror, the great backdrop of universal consciousness. An option here is to include synchronous breathing.
- 1.2. *Mutual participation.* The group hold hands in a circle, with open eyes, each person's eyes gently scanning everyone else's scanning eyes. Everyone participates in everyone's immediate living, manifest presence in and through seeing, touching and hearing. The group reveals itself as an embodiment of universal, unrestricted free attention.
- 1.3. *Impromptu active presence.* Group members individually improvise: sacred postures and gestures and movements and dance; sacred toning, chanting, singing, glossolalia; vocal celebration, poetry, praise, diune prayer; sacred music. The varied, spontaneous charismatic action opens up a strong shared field of unrestricted free attention.
- 1.4. *Interactive ritual.* By combining together simple, basic declarations with symbolic gestures and movements, done by everyone as a concerted whole, the group resonates with archetypal energies and opens up a strong shared field of unrestricted free attention.

2. *Fieldwork and inner prompts.* Offer several exercises in which people first learn the repertoire of fields and then learn to ground themselves in their enteric brain, the belly-mind, the psychic and spiritual womb below the umbilicus, and open to its prompts about working within a field and moving between fields.

- 2.1. *Presenting.* Describe to the group the seven fields, with wall charts and maps.
- 2.2. *Demonstrating.* Ask for volunteers one by one, and before the whole group, facilitate each volunteer to enter and work in different field. Ask people to volunteer for a named field.
- 2.1. *Mapping.* Invite everyone to draw their own map of the different fields with lines, colours, pictures, verbal labels. Give plenty of time for this, also time for people to talk about their maps in small groups.
- 2.2. *Invoking and imaging.* Invite people to work in pairs, five minutes each way, and take turns just to practise beginning a session with mentally and verbally invoking an image of the whole range of fields.
- 2.3. *Single field visits.* Offer a series of short sessions in pairs, say five

minutes each way. In each session, the creators take it in turn to work in just one field, which you specify. Specify a different field for each session.

- 2.4. *Multiple field visits.* This is a gymnastic, stretch exercise. Within a twenty minute each way session, creators are invited to touch base with each one of the seven fields for two or three minutes each. The co-creator keeps the creator gently on the move if he or she stays too long in a field.
- 2.5. *Belly opening.* Invite people to work in pairs, for ten minutes each way. The creator practises opening up to the belly centre, focusing free attention in a relaxed body-mind space around the *hara,* with a backdrop of expanded awareness and an image of the range of fields; and practises waiting for a liberating prompt about which field to work in, without actually starting to work in it. The creator can experiment with preceding the focusing by any one or more of the following:
  - Deep, rapid breathing and body loosening.
  - Sounding, toning, glossolalia.
  - Explicit evocation of the divine potential within the *hara.* This can be elaborated into:
  - A simple ritual of opening to the divine life within.
- 2.6. *Depth exercise.* Invite people to work in pairs for twenty minutes each way. The creator repeats 2.5, belly opening, this time going into the prompted field and being open to further prompts for deeper and deeper work in that field only.
- 2.7. *Organic exercise.* Invite people to work in pairs for forty minutes each way. The creator repeats 2.5, belly opening, goes into the prompted field, deepening into it through within-field prompts, and being also open to field-change prompts, following a sense of organic growth and wholeness in the session.
- 2.8. *Balance exercise.* Invite people to work in pairs for forty minutes each way. Repeat 2.7, organic exercise, but integrate with it making head choices about within and between field work, as well as following inner prompts.

3. *The regression field.* After exercises in fieldwork and inner prompts, I would have an in-depth training in regression, catharsis and spontaneous insight, for healing the memories of interpersonal hurt. Creators would be trained to be self-directing in this work, using back-up contracts from the co-creator. This would be a very important part of the training. And it would be set within the wider context of spiritual awakening and multiple fieldwork. For an account of cathartic methods, see Chapter 7 in my *Helping the Client* (Heron, 1990), always remembering that, in co-creating, these methods are primarily for creator self-direction and only secondarily for co-creator intervention. See also mine, and others', co-counselling manuals.

4. *The co-creating community.* I would propose that a co-creating community is not only a network of those who have co-creating sessions and attend local, national and international workshops. It is also at the same time a network of those

implementing together a self-generating culture. This I defined earlier as working to generate alternative sub-cultures and to disperse the restrictive impact of conventional social taboos.

- Co-operatively inquiring, in diverse networking groups, into transforming, through action, particular aspects of everyday life-style.
- Progressively rewriting the scripts of each and every social role.
- Practising planetary consciousness, being both local and global in thinking and acting.
- Being ecologically caring, and symbiotic within the biosphere and physiosphere.

5. *Political know-how.* A co-creating community would also be aware and imaginative about how its facilitators and organizers balance hierarchy (deciding for others), co-operation (deciding with others) and autonomy (people deciding for themselves) in its various meetings, workshops and activities.

6. *Inquiry reviews.* A co-creating community would also want to have periodic review meetings, locally, nationally and internationally, at which the theory and method of co-creating is confirmed and deepened, or disconfirmed and amended, in the light of ongoing experience of its use.

20

Coming into being

Report status: A story. **Place and year:** New Zealand, 1994-1997. **Spiritual focus:** Celebrating through improvised charismatic sound and movement our individual and interactive coming into being. **Subtle focus:** Exploring the range of subtle phenomena that support and enhance this celebration. **Social focus:** Affirming a group nucleus of holonomic spiritual activity and sustaining it within prevailing culture; injecting individual transpersonal activities into everyday culture; and creating a sub-culture of people intentionally inquiring into this kind of transpersonal social transformation.

The evolution of the wavy group

In late 1993, some months after the Scott's Landing event described in Chapter 13, I distributed flyer among interested persons in New Zealand. It proposed, for February through April, 1994, a four day journey of opening, a co-operative inquiry into transpersonal activities in everyday life, a training for co-operative inquiry initiators, and the start of an ongoing seed group. It presented these events as aspects of a self-generating culture. No fees were to be charged.

The three workshops all took place, and the second of them, about transpersonal activity in everyday life, has already been described in detail in Chapter 15. They proved to be links in a chain of events which started at Scott's Landing in March 1993, Chapter 13.

Eight people who had been at Scott's Landing met each month thereafter to check in with each other and share significant life events. They joined the transpersonal activities in everyday life inquiry, February to April 1994, and, enlarged by new members from that, continued on as a self-directing peer group after it closed and I had returned to Italy. This was the ongoing seed group, anticipated in the flyer. It continued to meet regularly throughout the southern winter of 1994-5, sharing personal and transpersonal experiences in a spirit of inquiry.

When I returned to New Zealand in early November 1994 I joined this ongoing group and we elected, over the summer of 1994-5, to focus our inquiry on the process of coming into being now. Each person adopted an idiosyncratic approach to this, choosing some of form of mantra, meditation, affirmation, inner opening, centering, postural alignment, continuous attunement, way of being present, ritual process, which attended to their continuous coming into being now.

> The theme adopted by the group was coming into being, affirming and celebrating this each day and observing the impact of this within our ordinary life. Over the years this

> has become a regular and powerful way of beginning my day and also a way of affirming myself within something new I am stepping into within ordinary life. So as a tool, a skill, I might say 'I affirm my coming into being in this world as a competent, skilful and balanced mediator and adjudicator', then tune in and evoke higher beings with these qualities and at the same time broaden my awareness with my eyes, to beyond this world, expand out the back and sides of my head, and feel into and breath in these qualities. (Barbara Langton)

We met every two weeks. The form of the meeting was variable, but usually contained these elements, including informal discussion of any of them:

- Settling in, and attuning to each other with hand contact, toning, mind-emptying and mutual resonance.
- This increasingly led over, after an early meeting in which we gave ourselves permission to become charismatically disinhibited, into an extended phase of improvised movement and toning. This was a slow, sacred, sinuous, interactive dance, with expressive gestures of the arms and hands, which established a potent field of subtle energy and spiritual presence. It was simultaneously empowered by co-ordinated harmonies of toning, with successive waves of crescendo and diminuendo. This combination seemed to well up out of our own coming to being now and to be both a charismatic expression and a celebration of it. It appeared to me to be marked by four phenomena:
    - A sense of numinous presence in our midst, as if each was open to and expressive of immanent spiritual life within each and every other, and between all.
    - A participative awareness of divine powers, archetypal energies of creation.
    - A participative awareness of unseen presences, refracting these powers.
    - Precision of beginning and ending: both the critical lift-off and the closure of the process were exactly timed, the qualitative shift of subtle energy being noted by all. They were not ours to command, but a matter of our co-operative openness and attunement to wider reaches of being and the movement of the spirit within.
- Each person shared their experience, over the previous two weeks, of using their way of attending to coming into being now, and the impact of this on their everyday life.
- Each person made a statement about how they intended to proceed for the next two weeks, whether using the same procedure, some modification of it, or some new procedure, or both.
- An act of closure, perhaps hand contact and silent attunement.

> The experience of the coming into being inquiry that lead into the formation of the wavy group was very strong for me. I remember at the time describing it as a spiritual awakening. The fortnightly participation in the group, linked by the daily practice of presencing, the experience of coming into being at every moment, at a daily morning meditation session, and throughout the day at random moments, seemed to open up a field that held

> me in a state of flow in relation to the world around me and the day to day work and relating I was engaged in. I had a strong sense of being held by something greater than me, a sense of spiritual family, or a class of friends who were learning together, that was very often with me during the day and while asleep. It was a felt presence of the other people involved as a container, or field of activity.
>
> The outcome in my life was a heightened sense of participating in an unfolding nature of being human in the world. The access into this awareness was assisted by the presence of, participation in, the field of inquiry held in place by myself and co-inquirers. (Rex McCann)

Because of its characteristic sinuous sacred dance, this group became known among its members as the wavy group. It met early one evening for the autumn equinox, in March1995, at the bottom of the grass-covered crater within the summit of One Tree Hill in the centre of Auckland. As some fifteen of us gathered, we spread far apart over the grass, deep in the crater, and stood scattered and silent for a while. Then, as if suddenly called, we moved slowly into the centre and entranced ourselves with moving and toning, until the equinoctial hour had had its expressive say.

The more formal inquiry phase, of planning and reporting back on individual practices used between group sessions, ended in April. The group continued to meet regularly throughout the southern winter and spring of 1995-6, to wave and weave together and otherwise interact.

> A consistent core group continues to meet fortnightly for some personal sharing and then what for me is the rich, deep, sometimes mysterious emergence of a varying mixture of toning, waving, stomping, growling, sounding instruments, silent attunement, co-creating and speaking out of resonance with an archetypal form, subtle energies of a planet or a seeming felt sense of the divine. (Barbara Langton)

It continued on as a distinct strand, with some of the same members as, and alongside, the empowerment in everyday life inquiry in the southern summer of 1996, Chapter 18.

> I particularly enjoyed the sessions where we all allowed ourselves to play with energy in a light and joyful way trying out different movements and sounds. It was as if we were tapping into a very potent energy source. During 1994-6 the energy of the group seemed to imbue the rest of my life and when I think back to it I can contact the energy now. It is timeless. (Dale Hunter)

When that ended in April 1996, it continued to meet regularly throughout the southern winter and spring of 1996, with many variations of format. For some weeks in the southern summer of 1996-7, it launched a gender inquiry in which the women met each fortnight in their own group, so too the men, and the combined groups met on the intervening weeks. The ongoing group continues to meet as I write.

> This ongoing group has continued to provide a rhythm of a grounded spiritual attunement, a creative emergent unfolding from a shared felt sense of appropriate timing, and a natural elegance of form and pattern. Its Dionysian style creates an expansive space when we gather. And I feel that it works because of our shared experience with a more Appollian formal co-operative inquiry, and because each individual is committed in their

own life both to emotional and to transpersonal process. The space is such that we seem free to share our personal ups and downs and life process as well as transpersonal space. And we do review our process periodically.

Another aspect that has interested me is the ability and flexibility of the group to expand and reduce in numbers without losing these special qualities. Only one year I noticed some resistance of mine, to opening up to a larger group after the smaller core group had had a close intimate time through one winter. Although perhaps losing some of the familiar intimacy, the richness of other people's energy and sharing easily balanced this for me. So it is as though a wider group who are part of it all for some months holds a container for the smaller group who meet more consistently throughout the year.

For me its value and importance is in outwardly acknowledging and having spiritual space, sharing this with others in a way I find empowering and grounded, and maintaining a form that is open, varied, flexible, emergent from the people present, spontaneously creative, disinhibited charismatically to varying degrees, deeply nourishing, light, warm, supportive and intimate. I find that it supports and enhances my own personal meditations and rituals. (Barbara Langton)

So four or six of us have been meeting, and it's a new configuration so it's not clear yet what is emerging. We may need to redefine what we're doing. Roberta staunchly resists anything that sounds like stultified effort or intentionality. She complained that we have evolved a predictable format: a bit of greeting chatter, a check-in round, some toning and /or movement, leading to some silent attunement. That's true of course, but it doesn't bother me too much, the shape of the container the juice comes in. But I know I take this business of alignment seriously, so I'm prey to all the distortions that come from over-identifying with spiritual effort. Richard thinks we are simply arguing out the tension between Apollonian and Dionysian approaches. I think appropriate effort is the central issue in all spiritual endeavours, and I know there have been times in our groups when we were functioning with an openness in which there is no distinction between spontaneity and intentionality. Where I get caught is in thinking of these states as the real goods, and subtly resisting or manipulating what is, in order to achieve what is not. I suspect that's where Roberta smells a rat. I spent our last meeting letting go of all sense of responsibility for the experience of anyone else present, and letting go of any desire to be collectively generating any particular state of being. It's a liberating expansion into the present. (Glenn McNicoll)

Evaluation

As I read it, the wavy group, in its several phases over the past four years, has been continuously inquiring, with highly flexible variations of format, into its own coming into being now. Its basic format is very Dionysian. It is more than adequate in terms of the broad sweep of its cyclic process, its total collaboration, its regular self-questioning (challenging uncritical subjectivity) and attention to emotional and interpersonal process. The inquiry is conducted in terms of a dynamic interplay between experiential knowing, presentational knowing, and practical knowing:

- The experiential knowing is of our coming into being now as persons in relation within the presence of Being and the surrounding field of interbeing.
- The presentational knowing is in symbolizing this radical knowing immediately in patterns of interactive sound and movement.

- The practical knowing, the knowing how, is twofold:
    - The skill, in the expressive use of interactive sound and movement, to symbolize and participate in the process of divine creation.
    - The very subtle skill in managing congruence between the three forms of knowing, so that no one of them takes off on its own alienated from the other two.

The fundamental research cycling is the continuous interplay between the three kinds of knowing. This is religious action inquiry. Conventional action inquiry involves thinking (propositional knowing) in the midst of action (practical knowing). This more basic kind entails skilled action (practical knowing) that symbolizes (presentational knowing) opening to our coming into being (experiential knowing). In this sort, the element of celebration, of ecstatic abundance, evident in skilled presentational expression is prior to, is wider and deeper than, the element of inquiry its symbolism embraces.

The research cycling becomes more complete when it is extended to include phases of conceptual reflection. There is a great deal of virtue in delaying this phase for a long while. This is partly because in our culture it is very easy for such reflection to become rapidly dissociated from its relevant experiential base, and thus to disregard, denigrate or deny it. It is also because the interplay of the other three kinds of knowing in religious action inquiry needs a substantial period of ripening and maturity before it can provide a stable foundation for reflective inquiry.

Epilogue to Part 2

Just a start

The short-term inquiries in Chapters 10-20 represent a first bathe in the spiritual inquiry pool. They are immersions to sample the potential of the method, to find out whether it can be done, and to see what people make of it. They are too short in length to provide more than an absolutely minimal warrant for their various kinds of stated, propositional outcome. Their outcomes in terms of transformations of being and transpersonal skills are a matter for each individual co-inquirer to declare. As I said at the opening of Part 2, I have found them deeply transformative in opening to the immanent spiritual life within, and in adopting forms of charismatic, expressive and interactive spiritual practice that constitute authentic transfiguration.

In these early days the overall impact of the method is for many people an important transformational outcome, as much as any particular outcome to do with the focus of a given inquiry, as is clear from the citations in Chapter 8. This impact is about spiritual self-discovery, about the affirmation of internal spiritual authority, of autonomous creativity in choosing and following a spiritual path. It is about the intimate connection between indwelling spirit and open inquiry, between inner liberation and mutually respectful, co-operative, spiritual exploration with other persons.

For me the impact of the method is an affirmation that spiritual authority is within, contextually located, maculate and self-revising, that it guides our spiritual path in liberal association with others, that it is inalienably central to human spirituality, and that it is indeed in its very nature a form of divine becoming. Spiritual transformation, as I now see it, is about creative spiritualization of the person and personalization of the spirit, in the context of collaboratively taking charge of our planetary estate within the cosmic whole.

Theological stripping

I think the method, applied to the spiritual field, presupposes and gives expression to a radical theology of the sort I have alluded to in Part 1 and explore further in Part 3. Others, however, may disagreee with this theology, while wanting to use and apply the method within their own framework of religious belief. By this kind of theological stripping and reclothing, the method can be taken into any spiritual school for long-term inquiry into its fundamental beliefs and practices.

What this process will challenge, of course, is any controlling, hierarchical authoritarianism within the school. Such authoritarianism, in my view, rests on an unacknowledged insecurity within the teacher about the validity of the beliefs and practices he teaches to others; or, to put it another way, on the projected denial of his own internal spiritual authority. Where such authoritarianism is intransigent, accomplished practitioners within the school can set up their own autonomous peer inquiry group.

Religious traditions do in fact have a slow, grinding, cautious, unacknowledged kind of inquiry going on, a 'living hermeneutic process' (Vroom, 1989), sometimes schismatic, in which new experiences and insights lead to revisions of doctrine and practice. My proposal is simply that this living hermeneutic process is made more explicit, intentional, focused, and liberated from the arbitrary constraints of reactionary conservatism.

Advantages and disadvantages

The methodological advantages of co-operative inquiry into the spiritual and the subtle, presented in Chapter 3, are that the co-inquirers are able to:

- Devise practices consonant with their inner light and life, and give form to their own original relation to creation.
- Elicit categories of understanding appropriate to their experience, without relapsing unawarely into traditional doctrines, new age euphoria, or culturally prevalent beliefs and values.
- Sustain critical subjectivity by the use of inquiry cycles and validity procedures.
- Clarify practical issues about entering and exiting from the experience.
- Winnow out criteria for distinguishing spiritual experience from purely psychological or subtle states.
- Manifest, as central to the inquiry process, charismatic transformation of everyday life: in personal behaviour, interpersonal relationships, organizational processes, and sociopolitical initiatives.

The primary disadvantage, as with co-operative inquiry in any field, is consensus collusion, that is, uncritical intersubjectivity: people unawarely conspiring together to sustain gratifying illusion, false premises, spurious method. This can be interwoven with research counter-transference: fear, triggered by the inquiry topic or process or both, is neither owned nor dispersed, and thus distorts what goes on in both the reflection and action phases. Consensus collusion needs to be confronted and interrupted by the sensitive and searching use of a devil's advocacy procedure at appropriate times. While research counter-transference calls for time out to deal intentionally, by agreed methods, with the emotional distress stirred up.

A particular disadvantage in the spiritual and subtle field is that short inquiries of a few days or a few weeks or a few months do not constitute any kind of sustained practice. Nor do they provide the ongoing support, fellowship and collegial spiritual power of an established school. One solution to this already exists for those who follow their own self-directed path of lived inquiry, where this includes selective, discriminating affiliation with one or more schools of practice. Another solution lies in establishing autonomous peer groups for long-term spiritual practice within the self-generating spiritual culture from which co-operative inquiry itself has emerged, as described in Chapter 20. Such groups are likely to have the following features:

- They are self-directed peer groups: there is no leader or long-term facilitator.
- They are clear and intentional about how they make decisions.
- They are founded on the practice of open inquiry: they work in the spirit of inquiry, without following formalized inquiry procedures.
- They attend to emotional and interpersonal processes as and when needed.
- They are vigilant about uncritical subjectivity: they periodically review their assumptions and procedures.
- They are innovative, risk-taking and disinhibited within the group: they are open to present impulses of immanent spiritual life, and present illuminations of transcendent spiritual consciousness.
- They are committed to transformative activities in everyday life outside the group.
- They engage once or twice a year in short-term formal and focused co-operative inquiries as a complement to their long-term practice.

This proposal for establishing such groups for long-term spiritual practice is not a lurch back into the old business of founding another authoritarian tradition. As I said in Chapter 3, neither I nor anyone else can set themselves up as an external authority who defines the nature of internal authority for other people. It is logically impossible to be authoritarian about the nature or the practice of internal authority, for by definition internal authority cannot be internal if it is commanded by someone else. No-one can practise internal authority, exclusively by following an external authority who prescribes what it is: self-direction cannot be other-directed. Autonomous people cannot dictate the nature of autonomy for others; they can only dialogue and co-operatively inquire with each about the naure of self-direction.

Any self-directed peer group, whose early destiny was grounded in the internal authority of its members, and whose future members start to ground it on appeals to the authoritative statements of the founding members, as disclosed in old records, has lost its way and stumbled into *mauvais foi*.

The great political advantage of transpersonal co-operative inquiries is the democratization of human spirituality, which has since recorded time been defined and controlled by the principle of authority. Human authority figures have, in the name of god or the gods or ancestors or the tribe or the church or the lineage or the tradition or the scriptures, told the rest of humanity what their spirituality is and how to express and develop it in practice. This is still the case today across the whole range of spiritual teachings from traditional religions, East and West, to channelled entities and new age gurus. As new cults, creeds and types of practice spring up today in great abundance, the founder of each immediately claims some form of authority to legitimate its teaching and win adherents.

Any spiritual school or tradition that claims any kind of authority for its spiritual teachings and practices will, as I stressed in Chapter 2, seduce, disregard or downgrade human autonomy and its internal authority expressed as critical subjectivity, independent judgement, individual discriminating practice, inner-directed unfoldment, personal freedom of spirit in defining spiritual reality and in choosing and shaping the spiritual path.

When human beings join together to support each other, and find collective power, in fully respecting each other's internal authority, then, I surmise, a radically new theology may well emerge. It may perhaps affirm, not the primacy of redemption or salvation or enlightenment or release or emptiness or god-realization, for all these things appear to have been promoted to maintain the mediating role of authority figures. It may celebrate, by contrast, the primacy of charismatic practice, of co-creative engagement with divine doing and becoming, found where autonomous humans co-operatively inquire into world-transforming skills within their universal estate. It may not be meditation and prayer that stand at the forefront of spiritual practice. The paramount path may be the creative work of the cosmic citizen, for which interior transfiguration hones the labouring blade.

Part 3: A participatory worldview

21

Participatory research

I have been much influenced by the modern tradition of experiential learning, in which the learner is directly in touch with the realities being studied. This holistic approach in higher and continuing education was promoted by John Dewey (1938). His account of the experiential learning cycle was transformed by Kurt Lewin (1952) into the inquiry cycle of systematic action research. These two strands, with many related influences, have given rise to fully participatory research.

One of the most developed forms of participatory research is co-operative inquiry (Heron, 1996a). The text below starts with a one page description of it. The remainder of the chapter goes in more depth into its underlying philosophy. It is an adaptation of a paper I co-wrote with Peter Reason, hence the authorial pronoun 'we'. In this version I have taken out technical discussions of constructivism and related matters, and I refer the reader who is interested in these things to the original paper (Heron and Reason: 1997).

One page description of co-operative inquiry

In traditional research on people, the roles of researcher and subject are mutually exclusive. The researcher only contributes the thinking that goes into the project, and the subjects only contribute the action to be studied. In co-operative inquiry these exclusive roles are replaced by a co-operative relationship of bilateral initiative and control, so that all those involved work together as co-researchers and as co-subjects. They *both* design, manage and draw conclusions from the inquiry, and they undergo the experience and action that is being explored. This is not research on people, but research *with* people.

Co-operative inquiry can be seen as cycling through four stages of reflection and action. In stage 1 a group of co-researchers come together to explore an agreed area of human activity. They may be professionals who wish to inquire into a particular area of practice; couples or families who wish to explore new styles of life; people who wish to examine in depth certain states of consciousness; members of an organization who want to research restructuring it; ill people who want to assess the impact of particular healing practices; and so on. In the first part of stage 1, they agree on the focus of their inquiry, and develop together a set of questions or propositions they wish to investigate. Then they plan a method for exploring this focal idea in action, through practical experience. Finally, in stage 1, they devise and agree a set of procedures for gathering and recording data from this experience.

In stage 2 the co-researchers now also become co-subjects: they engage in actions agreed; and observe and record the process and outcomes of their own and each other's experience. In particular, they are careful to notice the subtleties of experience, to hold lightly the conceptual frame from which they started so that they are able to see how practice does and does not conform to their original ideas.

Stage 3 is in some ways the touchstone of the inquiry method. It is a stage in which the co-subjects become full immersed in and engaged with their experience. They may develop a degree of openness to what is going on so free of preconceptions that they see it in a new way. They may deepen into the experience so that superficial understandings are elaborated and developed. Or it may lead them away from the original ideas into new fields, unpredicted action and creative insights. It is also possible that they may get so involved in what they are doing that they lose the awareness that they are part of an inquiry group: there may be a practical crisis, they may become enthralled, they may simply forget.

In stage 4, after an agreed period in stages 2 and 3, the co-researchers re-assemble to share the experiential data from these stages, and to consider their original ideas in the light of it. As a result they may develop or reframe these ideas; or reject them and pose new questions. They may choose, for the next cycle of action, to focus on the same or on different aspects of the overall inquiry. The group may also choose to amend or develop its inquiry procedures - forms of action, ways of gathering and recording data - in the light of experience.

This cycle between reflection and action is then repeated several times. Ideas and discoveries tentatively reached in early phases can be checked and developed; investigation of one aspect of the inquiry can be related to exploration of other parts; new skills can be acquired and monitored; experiential competences are realized; the group itself becomes more cohesive and self-critical, more skilled in its work.

Repeat cycling, balancing divergence and convergence, enhances the validity of the findings. Additional validity procedures are used during the inquiry: some of these counter unaware projection and consensus collusion; others monitor authentic collaboration, the balance between reflection and action, and between chaos and order.

Co-operative inquiry and its inquiry paradigm

Co-operative inquiry, as we have just seen, involves two or more people researching a topic through their own experience of it, using a series of cycles in which they move between this experience and reflecting together on it. Each inquirer is co-subject in the experience phases and co-researcher in the reflection phases. Persons are in reciprocal relation using the full range of their sensibilities to inquire together into any aspect of the human condition with which the transparent body-mind can engage.

Implicit in any such method of inquiry is an inquiry paradigm, a basic set of beliefs about the nature of reality and how it may be known (Guba and Lincoln, 1994). These philosophical beliefs are presupposed by the inquiry method, not established by it. Indeed the method itself gives expression to them. The beliefs are thrown into relief by four fundamental and interrelated questions.

- 'What is the form and nature of reality and what can be known about it?' This is the ontological question, about the nature of being.
- 'What is the relationship between the knower and what can be known?' This is the epistemological question, about the nature of knowledge.
- 'How can the inquirer go about finding out whatever it is that can be known?' This is the methodological question, about the nature of method.
- 'What sort of knowledge, if any, is intrinsically valuable?' This is the axiological question, about the nature of value.

These four questions are explored in the next four sections, respectively.

Reality as subjective-objective

Co-operative inquiry presupposes a participatory account of the nature of being. It holds that reality is subjective-objective. There is a given cosmos, a primordial reality, in which the mind actively participates, most immediately in the process of perception. Mind and the given cosmos are engaged in a co-creative dance, so that what emerges as reality is the fruit of an interaction of the given cosmos and the way perceiving mind engages with it. Mind actively participates in the cosmos, and it is through this active participation that we meet what is Other:

> Worlds and people are what we meet, but the meeting is shaped by our own terms of reference. (Heron, 1996a: 11)

The sceptic may ask how we can know we meet anything or anyone, if the meeting is always given our own shape. One answer is that when we open ourselves to meeting the given, the Other declares itself to us so that we resonate with its presence as the world.

> ... in so far as my hand knows hardness and softness, and my gaze knows the moon's light, it is as a certain way of linking up with the phenomena and communicating with it. Hardness and softness, roughness and smoothness, moonlight and sunlight, present themselves in our recollection not pre-eminently as sensory contents but as certain kinds of symbioses, certain ways the outside has of invading us and certain ways we have of meeting the invasion (Merleau-Ponty, 1962: 317)

This encounter is transactional, interactive perception. To touch, see or hear something or someone does not tell us either about our self all on its own, nor about a being out there all on its own. It tells us about a being in a state of interrelation and co-presence with us. Our subjectivity feels the participation of what is there, and is illuminated by it. Knowing a world is in this felt relation at the interactive interface between a subject and what is encountered. In the relation of meeting, my subjectivity becomes a perspectival window filled with a world which also transcends it. This ontology is thus subjective-objective:

> It is subjective because it is only known through the form the mind gives it; and it is objective because the mind interpenetrates the given cosmos which is shapes (Heron, 1996a: 11)

Or as Skolimowski puts it:

> Things become what our consciousness makes of them through the active participation of our mind (1994: 27-28).
>
> The cosmos or the universe is a primordial ontological datum, while the 'world' is an epistemological construct, a form of our understanding. (1994: 100)

Bateson makes the point that between the extremes of solipsism, in which 'I make it all up', and a purely external reality, in which I cease to exist, there is

> ... a region where you are partly blown by the winds of reality and partly an artist creating a composite out of inner and outer events. (in Brockman, 1977: 245)

From all this it follows that what can be known about the given cosmos is that it is always known as a subjectively articulated world, whose objectivity is relative to how it is shaped by the knower. But this is not all: its objectivity is also relative to how it is intersubjectively shaped. For there is the important if obvious point that knowers can only be knowers when known by other knowers: knowing presupposes mutual participative awareness. It presupposes participation, through meeting and dialogue, in a culture of shared art and shared language, shared values, norms and beliefs. And, deeper still, agreement about the rules of language, about how to use it, presupposes a tacit mutual experiential knowing and understanding between people that is the primary ground of all explicit forms of knowing. So any subjective-objective reality articulated by any one person is done so within an intersubjective field, a context of linguistic-cultural and experiential shared meanings.

The deep primary ground of language is not only a mutual participative knowing between humans, but also between humans and the more-than-human world of nature. Abram, following Merleau-Ponty (1962), affirms our ongoing reciprocity with the world, prior to, and as the ongoing ground of, all our verbal reflections. At the preconceptual level, our spontaneous sensorial engagement with phenomena is an experience of reciprocal encounter with dynamic presences that draw us into relation. To touch is to feel oneself being touched, to see is to feel oneself seen. The surroundings are experienced as sensate, attentive and watchful (Abram, 1996: 53-72).

The primary experiential ground, that is our embodied and embedded state, has both a defining boundary and a centre of reference relative to it. I never just perceive a world, I always perceive my being-in-a-world: a bounded field around my centre of reference. The boundary opens on to infinite horizons without. The centre of reference, the person, emerges from an infinitude within.

Every boundary, every finite limit to the seeing and hearing of my perceptual field, declares its latent infinity. Each limit in containing the known declares there is an unknown beyond it. It announces a series of limits that is unlimited, boundless. In one horizon we have tacit acquaintance with infinite horizons. The circumscription of our perceiving is fraught with the boundlessness of the given.

Likewise, my finite centre of reference has no ultimate centre, it is an infinitude within, an unlimited potential filling a space of no volume, the emptiness of any point. It is a pregnant void. Where the infinitude within, the void, first breaks into the manifest it appears as a finite locus, the centre of reference that is the distinct person (Heron, 1996a: 187-88).

Hence on the participatory account of reality, we may speak, like Karl Rahner, of 'unthematic experience' which in his theology is the inherent openness of the human being, prior to all education, to the infinite divine (Kelly, 1993). I return to participatory theology in the next chapter.

An extended and holistic epistemology

This participative worldview, with its notion of reality as subjective-objective, involves an extended account of the nature of knowledge. A knower participates in the known, articulates a world, in at least four interdependent ways: experiential, presentational, propositional and practical. These four forms of knowing constitute the manifold of our subjectivity, within which, it seems, we have enormous latitude both in acknowledging its components and in utilizing them in association with, or dissociation from, each other. This epistemology presents us as knowers with an interesting developmental challenge. We call this challenge critical subjectivity. It involves an awareness of the four ways of knowing, of how they are currently interacting, and of ways of changing the relations between them so that they articulate a reality that is unclouded by a restrictive and ill-disciplined subjectivity.

Experiential knowing means direct encounter, face-to-face meeting: feeling and imaging the presence of some energy, entity, person, place, process or thing. It is knowing through participative, empathic resonance with a being, so that as knower I feel both attuned with it and distinct from it. And it is also the creative shaping of a world through the transaction of imaging it, perceptually and in other ways. Experiential knowing thus articulates reality through inner resonance with what there is, and through perceptually enacting its forms of appearing (Varela et al, 1991). It delivers the lived-through 'pre-objective' world of immediate present experience, consciousness-world union (Merleau-Ponty, 1962). As such it relates us not only to particular beings, but at the same time to the field of interbeing, and the immediate here and now presence of Being, of which they are part

Presentational knowing emerges from and is grounded on experiential knowing. It is evident in an intuitive grasp of the significance of our resonance with and imaging of our world, as this grasp is symbolized in graphic, plastic, musical, vocal and verbal art-forms. It clothes our experiential knowing of the world in the metaphors of aesthetic creation, in expressive spatiotemporal forms of imagery. These forms symbolize both our felt attunement with the world and the primary meaning embedded in our enactment of its appearing.

Propositional knowing is knowing in conceptual terms that something is the case; knowledge by description of some energy, entity, person, place, process or thing. It is expressed in statements and theories that come with the mastery of concepts and classes that language bestows. Propositions themselves are carried by presentational forms—the sounds or visual shapes of the spoken or written word—and are ultimately grounded in our experiential articulation of a world.

Practical knowing is knowing how to do something, demonstrated in a skill or competence. We would argue that practical knowledge is in an important sense primary (Heron, 1996a; Reason, 1996). It presupposes a conceptual grasp of principles and standards of practice, presentational elegance, and experiential grounding in the situation within which the action occurs. It fulfils the three prior forms of knowing, brings them to fruition in purposive deeds, and consummates them with its autonomous celebration of excellent accomplishment.

As Macmurray (1957) pointed out, while you can divorce thought from action, you cannot divorce action in the world from thought. And we believe that what we learn about our world will be richer and deeper, if this descriptive knowledge is incidental to a primary intention to develop practical skills to change the world. This is the action paradox:

> We learn more profoundly about our worlds when we are more interested in enhancing them with excellence of action than in learning about them. (Heron, 1996a: 114)

Torbert underlines the pre-eminence of practical knowing with his view that what we need is an action inquiry useful to the actor and the point of action, rather than a reflective science about action. His account of action inquiry is that a person is conscious in the midst of action, seeing and correcting incongruities among the goal of the action and wider purposes within which it is nested, the strategic means, the immediate behaviour, and outcomes in the world. This, he holds, is an holistic and inclusive inquiry paradigm (Torbert, 1991: 221).

It is equally important that action not only consummates the prior forms of knowing, but is also grounded in them. It is in this congruence of the four aspects of the extended epistemology that lie claims to validity. This relationship can be shown as in figure 21.1.

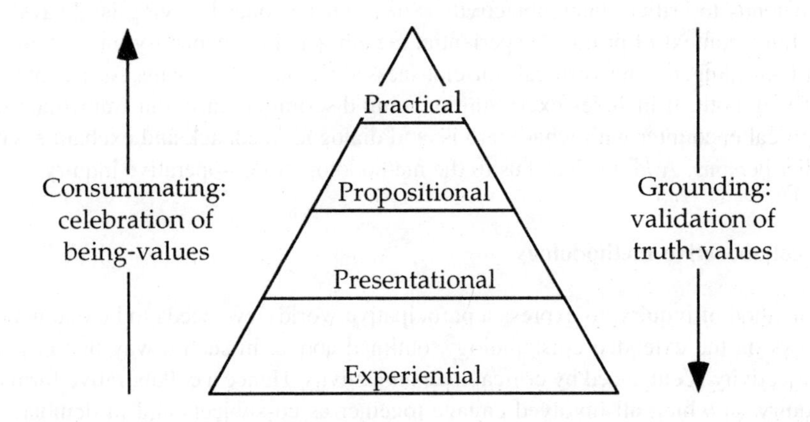

Figure 21.1

Critical subjectivity means that we attend both to the grounding relations between the forms of knowing, and also to their consummating relations. Thus it is a close relative of Torbert's 'consciousness in the midst of action' (1991: 221). Critical subjectivity means that we do not suppress our primary subjective experience but accept that it is our experiential articulation of being in a world, and as such is the ground of all our knowing. At the same time, we accept that, naively exercised, it is open to all the distortions of those defensive processes by which people collude to limit their understanding. So we attend to it with a critical consciousness, seeking to bring it into aware relation with the other three ways of knowing, so that they clarify and refine and elevate it at the same time as being more adequately grounded in it. This more general account of critical subjectivity complements the transpersonal account of it, given in Chapter 3, as inner spiritual discrimination.

In addition, since we accept that our knowing is from a perspective and that we are aware of that perspective, of its authentic value and of its restricting bias, we articulate this awareness in our communications. Critical subjectivity involves a self-reflexive attention to the ground on which one is standing. This is echoed in what Torbert calls 'a reframing mind' which 'continually overcomes itself, divesting itself of its own presuppositions' (1987: 211). It is related to what Bateson (1972) describes as Learning III, in which the mind can choose its premises of understanding and action, can detach itself from all frameworks to peer into and reflect on their presuppositions. It is Kegan's (1994) trans-paradigmatic fourth order consciousness; and Gebser's (1985) integral-aperspectival mind which grasps that no perspective is final, is transparent to the context of its own operation, is open to the context of that context; and so on. It also relates to those postmodern poststructuralists who do not deny truth and meaning as such, but hold that all truth and meaning are context-bound, and that context is boundless, infinitely extendable (Culler, 1982).

Critical subjectivity is not that of the dissociated Cartesian ego. It is subjectivity participating in the great web of interbeing, and within a shared human culture. So it extends to critical intersubjectivity. Since our personal knowing is always set within a context of primary experiential meaning and of secondary linguistic-cultural meaning, having a critical consciousness about our knowing necessarily means refining both. It includes exercising ongoing discrimination in our immediate reciprocal encounter with what there is, and dialogue, feedback and exchange with other persons. And this leads us to the methodology of co-operative inquiry.

A collaborative methodology

A method of inquiry, to express a participative worldview, needs to be one which draws on the extended epistemology, outlined above, in such a way that critical subjectivity is enhanced by critical intersubjectivity. Hence a collaborative form of inquiry, in which all involved engage together as co-subjects and in democratic dialogue as co-researchers (Reason and Heron, 1995; Heron, 1996a).

- People reflect together to define the questions they wish to explore and the methodology for that exploration (propositional knowing).
- Conjointly or singly they apply this methodology in the world of their practice (practical knowing).

- This leads to new forms of encounter with their world (experiential knowing).
- They find ways to represent this experience in significant patterns (presentational knowing) which feeds into a revised propositional understanding of the originating questions.

Co-researchers engage together in cycling several times through the four forms of knowing in order to enrich their congruence, that is, to refine the way they elevate and consummate each other, and to deepen the complementary way they are grounded in each other.

Research cycling is itself a fundamental discipline which leads toward critical subjectivity and a primary way of enhancing the validity of inquirers' claims to articulate a subjective-objective reality. There are also a range of further of procedures which develop this effect. These include: managing divergence and convergence within and between cycles; securing authentic collaboration; challenging uncritical subjectivity and intersubjectivity; managing unaware projections and displaced anxiety; balancing reflection and action; attending to the dynamic interplay of chaos and order. For a full discussion of these, together with a set of radical skills of being and doing required during the action phases of the inquiry, see Heron (1996a).

Co-operative inquiry is closely related to other forms of participative inquiry such as action science (Argyris and Schon, 1974; Schon, 1983; Argyris et al, 1985), action inquiry (Torbert, 1991), participatory action research (Fals-Borda and Rahman, 1991), and some forms of feminist inquiry (Mies, 1993). Fals-Borda reports that some 35 varieties of participative action inquiry have been identified worldwide.

Practical flourishing an end in itself

The fourth fundamental question is about what sort of knowledge is intrinsically worthwhile, valuable as an end in itself, not as a means to anything else. An essential feature of any inquiry paradigm is whether it regards knowing the truth in propositional form as an end in itself, and as the only end in itself. This was the position of Aristotle for whom intellectual excellence was the highest end of man (but not woman).

If knowing propositional truths is the one and only intrinsically worthwhile state of affairs, *then* ultimately this legitimates all kinds of mayhem on the way to acquiring it. Hence the view of Bacon that nature must be tortured to wrest her secrets from her. Hence the modern propensity to educate the intellect in damaging dissociation from feeling, imagination and action. Since universities are the home of inquiry paradigms and since they are largely Aristotelian institutions in their commitment to intellectual excellence, we need to know, as a defining feature of it, where each paradigm stands on this fundamental issue.

The participatory paradigm answers the value question in terms of human flourishing, conceived as an end in itself. Such flourishing is construed as an enabling balance within and between people of hierarchy, co-operation and autonomy. On this view, social practices and institutions need to enhance human association by an appropriate integration of these three principles: deciding for others, deciding with others, and deciding for oneself (Heron, 1989; 1993). Hierarchy provides appropriate direction by those with greater vision, skill and experience (Torbert, 1991); it is authentic when it seeks the developmental emergence of autonomy and co-operation in those who are being directed. Collaboration roots the individual within a community of peers, offering basic support and the creative and corrective feedback of other views and possibilities (Randall and Southgate, 1980). Autonomy expresses the creative, self-creating and self-transfiguring potential of the person (Heron, 1992).

The shadow face of authority is authoritarianism; that of collaboration peer pressure and conformity; that of autonomy narcissism, wilfulness and isolation. The challenge is to design institutions which manifest valid forms of these principles; and to finds ways in which they can be maintained in self-correcting and creative tension.

This kind of flourishing is practical knowing: knowing how to choose and act - hierarchically, co-operatively, autonomously - to enhance personal and social fulfilment and that of the eco-networks of which we are a part. Such human fulfilment is consummated in the very process of choosing and acting. So in the participatory paradigm, we believe that practical knowing is an end in itself; and intellectual knowing is of instrumental value in supporting practical excellence.

The value question can also be put in terms of the ultimate purpose of human inquiry, since any ultimate purpose is an end-in-itself, is intrinsically valuable. In the participatory worldview the account of reality as subjective-objective, as co-created with the given cosmos, leads over into the value question. For what purposes do we co-create reality? The answer to this is put quite simply by Fals-Borda: to change the world (Fals-Borda, 1996); or as Skolimowski points out, *participation* implies *engagement* which implies *responsibility*. The participative worldview is necessarily leads to an action orientation; not an impulsive action which, as Bateson (1972) describes it, cuts through the circuits of that natural world, but a reflective action, a praxis, grounded in our being in reciprocal engagement with the given.

So within the participative worldview the primary purpose of human inquiry is practical: our inquiry is our action in the service of human flourishing. Our knowing of the world is consummated as our doing in the world and participatory research is thus essentially transformative. While some inquiry projects may be primarily informational and result in propositional knowing, transformational projects are primary (Heron, 1996a).

Reason (1993, 1994a) has suggested that a significant purpose of inquiry in our times is to heal the split that characterises modern existence, and suggests that such healing practice will have a sacred dimension:

> To heal means to make whole: we can only understand our world as a whole if we are part of it; as soon as we attempt to stand outside, we divide and separate. In contrast, making whole necessarily implies participation: one characteristic of a participative worldview is that the individual person is restored to the circle of community and the human community to the context of the wider natural world. To make whole also means

> to make holy: another characteristic of a participatory worldview is that meaning and mystery are restored to human experience, so that the world is once again experienced as a sacred place (Reason, 1994a: 10).

This means expressing living knowledge in practical service to peoples' lives (Reason, 1996). This active participation in community, which makes holy, is also a political process (Bookchin, 1991; Bachrach and Botwinick, 1992). It honours the basic right of people to have a say in forms of decision-making, in every social context, which affect their flourishing in any way. This includes, most importantly, the right to be involved in the knowledge creation processes that affect their lives.

Furthermore, the purpose of inquiry is not only the relief of oppression. As Skolimowski puts it, we need to find again ways in which the human mind can be celebrated, we need to take the courage to imagine and reach for our fullest capabilities. It is argued that humanity is 'nature rendered self-conscious' (Bookchin, 1991 :313), that human beings are a part of the cosmos capable of self awareness and self-reflection (Swimme, 1984). We hold that humans consummate such self-awareness as creative agents, whose practical inquiry is a celebration of the flowering of humanity and of the co-creating cosmos, and as part of a sacred science is an expression of the beauty and joy of active existence.

There is a urgent need to re-vision our view of ourselves as co-inhabitants of the planet. As many of us have asserted, with greater or lesser degrees of concern, the current Western worldview has come to the end of its useful life, and, as well as some remarkable achievements in material well-being and human possibility, has left us with a legacy of human alienation and ecological devastation.

The participatory worldview, with its emphasis on the person as an embodied experiencing subject in reciprocal engagement with other presences, human and more-than-human, its assertion of the living cosmos we co-create, and its emphasis on the consummation of knowing in action, is more satisfying. It responds creatively to the emerging mood of our times, overturns the mechanical metaphor which underpins positivism, provides models for action inquiry and above all offers humanity a more satisfying vision to live by.

A self-generating culture

If humanity were to live by it, then we can envisage a society whose members are in a continuous process of co-operative learning and development, and whose forms are consciously adopted, periodically reviewed and altered in the light of experience, reflection and deeper vision. It is a society whose participants continually recreate it through cycles of collaborative living inquiry (Heron, 1993, 1997b). Such a society is a self-generating culture. It has several strands.

1. Decision-making Exploring the use of three basic modes of decision-making - deciding autonomously by oneself, deciding co-operatively with others, and deciding hierarchically for others, so that in different sorts of association - from the family to the regional assembly - we can combine and balance them in different forms. These forms are adopted intentionally, subject to periodic review, with an accepted procedure for changing them. This same conscious learning process is equally applicable to all the points that follow.

2. Association Exploring forms of association in living and working, to find ways of balancing the claims of doing things: alone, with others, or alongside others.

3. Habitation Exploring the where and how of housing: private dwellings in the existing urban and rural set-up; private dwellings in a communal village; co-habitation in a communal building. Exploring different forms of ownership and rights of use.

4. Roles Exploring new behaviours in, and beliefs about, a wide range of social roles: woman, man, parent, child, teenager, adult, aged, friend, citizen, and many more.

5. Economics Exploring forms of economic organization, and of job definition, in order to choose awarely different ways of distributing and combining the roles of owner, manager and worker; and different forms of income and wealth distribution, and of economic analysis to accommodate a wider range of values than classical economics.

6. Ecology Exploring ways of caring for the planetary environment, sustaining and enhancing its dynamic eco-system: covering energy, technology, agriculture, pollution, etc. As part of this enterprise, researching the structure and processes in this world in the context of their interrelation with the structure and processes in subtle dimensions of being.

7. Education Exploring forms of providing for children and young people of all ages: how they are to be cared for, raised and educated, and by whom. Also exploring forms of education and training for the personal and professional development of adults, which include methods for dealing with individual and social overload of emotional distress, and for deep levels of pain and suffering.

8. Intimacy Exploring ways of giving social form to spiritual, emotional and physical intimacy, to nurturance, sexuality and family. Any such form - whether it is open bonding, closed bonding, celibate bonding, serial bonding, one parent family, two parent family, multi-parent family, or any other - is chosen awarely in the presence of others, there is a support network for it, and there is an acknowledged social process for changing the form.

9. Conflict Exploring forms of conflict resolution: different ways of dealing with hostility and tension, irrational outbursts, irreconcilable opinions, broken agreements, confusion of purpose. People devise such forms, have them ready, and learn to use them when relevant.

10. Rituals Exploring and improvising rituals, special events, holidays and feast-days, to celebrate, mark, or mourn the great recurring themes of individual, social and planetary life: birth, coming of age, relationships, graduations, visits, arrivals and departures, beginnings and endings, the seasons, solar and lunar cycles, death, and so on. Exploring rituals and other forms of inquiry: to foster our inward, occult and spiritual development; to interact with the subtle worlds, their powers and presences; and in communion together to attune to the divine within and beyond, and present as, creation.

22

Participatory theology and cosmology

This concluding chapter sketches out a speculative theology and cosmology embracing a participatory and dipolar worldview, and the spirituality of personhood and embodiment.

God and what there is

A central problem about god is the relation of god to what there is. If god does not include absolutely everything, then there is something greater than god, to wit, god and what is not included in god. If, on the other hand, everything without exception is included in god, then my unawareness of and alienation from god is at the same time god: bits of god are unaware of god, a part of god is also apart from god.

This is the classic theological dilemma. One horn, that there is something outside god, has an explicit dualism that makes god less than the whole, and presupposes a tacit monism, the unnamed and unacknowledged totality of being that includes god and what is outside god. The other horn, that god includes everything, has an explicit monism that includes a tacit irreconcilable dualism of what is simultaneously god and not-god.

Christian theology in general tries to make some headway with the dualistic horn. It propounds a relative dualism in which god creates the universe out of nothing, sustains it and is immanent within it, but its manifest fabric is not included in god. Creation is a relatively autonomous zone of being that is separated out from the god who makes it and upholds it.

> Christian thought reflects a qualified dualism between god and the creation, whereby an irreducible difference is related through an indissoluble bond. (Rouner, 1983: 166)

This still leaves unanswered the question, 'What is the unacknowledged something that includes both god and god's extruded, irreducibly different, creation?'

Oriental religious thinkers and western absolute idealists like Schelling and Hegel try to make something of the monistic horn. Everything that exists is a form of one absolute everpresent spirit. What appears to be not spirit and apart from spirit is illusory and therefore does not exist. The occurrence of such illusion is due to the fact that spirit becomes estranged from itself (Hegel's *Entfremdung*), forgets itself, falls asleep, loses itself in creation and progressively through the unfolding history of creation returns to full awareness of itself as absolute spirit. This ostensibly monistic view propounds the bizarre, incoherent dualism of the simultaneous co-existence both of an absolute all-knowing, all-inclusive spirit and of its massive self-forgetfulness.

The Christian account of an 'irreducible difference' between the human creature and the creator leaves human experience and action outside god, intrinsically alienated, and leads inescapably to the whole theology of divine incarnaton and atonement, to petitionary prayer and an intercessionary priesthood. The oriental account of ultimate oneness makes human experience and action an illusory play of spirit, and leads to the theology of total self-dissolution and of the end state of absolute enlightenment, to human divinization and guru-worship.

The Christian created self exists. It is always on the road to, but can never get to, god and needs the mediation of Christ and his priests to bridge the gulf. The oriental self doesn't really exist. Its illusory status is transcended in once-and-for-all god-consciousness, to achieve which the aspirant needs to surrender to, and identify with, an enlightened one who has attained.

Participatory theology

A participatory theology stands in contrast with both these positions. It holds, speculatively, that:

- All manifestation is included in divine being. It is divine temporal process, divine becoming. The divine also indwells, is immanent in, all manifestation as spiritual life; and transcends it as spiritual consciousness.
- Persons in relation with each other and their immediate world are our experiential locus of divine becoming, our here and now present being of the divine.
- They participate in each other and in their immediate world. Each person's participation is transactional, co-creative with divine being in shaping what there is, in articulating a subjective-objective reality. Person's participating in each other shape an intersubjective reality.
- The distinctness of each person is inseparable from their participative engagement with wider unities of being.
- The critical self-determining subjectivity of persons is a vital component of the innovative thrust of divine becoming.
- The participation of persons in the experiential being of the divine waxes and wanes. It is never totally absent. It is always to some degree explicit as a necessary condition of being in a world. It oscillates, above this necessary ground state, between fully intentional participative openness to immediate present experience, and blind alienated contraction within a closed egocentric self.
- The explicit participation is always contextual, within the immediate here and now field of present experience, a context with permeable boundaries. Such participation is never complete or absolute, and is capable of further and indefinite outreach to the manifest, inreach to the immanent, and upreach to the transcendent.
- Persons participate tacitly, potentially, in all other manifestations of the divine, in the spiritual life indwelling all manifestation, and in the spiritual consciousness transcending all manifestation.

- A person's tacit, potential participation in the divine is infinite and is the everpresent ground of their unfolding explicit, actual participation. The infinitude of the divine is fully in each actualized person as their potential.

The infinitude of divine being thus includes many distinct manifestations of becoming, participating ever more richly in divine fullness. The infinitude of divine wholeness manifests as innumerable unfolding divine partialities. They are not irreducibly different from the divine: they are distinct, developing epiphanies. They are not illusory forms of divine self-forgetfulness which dismantle in divine self-remembering. They are the flowering of the Many on the ground of the One. The analogue is the creative novelist who generates images of people whose destinies and characters unfold within the total field of his or her imagination.

How does this view cope with the monistic horn of the dilemma, which has the problematic consequence that the one all-inclusive god includes parts that are apart from god? I doubt whether it resolves it fully, but it manages it rather better, perhaps, than the Christian and oriental approaches. Firstly, it holds that each person is always to some necessary baseline degree explicitly participating in divine being, and is tacitly participating *in toto*. Secondly, it holds that the process of becoming, the progressive flowering of the many, is part of manifest divine being; that this becoming is not a play of illusion, but a real profusion of infinite potentiality unfurling into actuality. The infinite necessarily includes as an aspect of its nature the indefinite unfoldment of endless variations of the finite.

It still has a person, one of the divine Many, who can get identified with illusory, egoic and contracted states. Thus there is a part of a part of god quite unaware of god. The analogue of the story writer is again helpful. The persons in the story are entirely included in the writer's imagination, yet can be conceived as having no aware internal dialogue with the author at all: their conscious process is entirely contained within the parameters of character and plot devised by the writer. Equally, it is possible for the writer to imagine people who, within these limits, turn about to dialogue with their author about their state of being and their fate.

The theology of embodiment

I hold, then, persons are always to some degree explicitly participating in immediate divine being, and are fully participating, tacitly, in the wider reaches of divine being. By immediate divine being I mean the experiential world in which every person is immersed by virtue of their embodiment. The experiential world has interdependent dipolar aspects: there is feeling the presence of the world and there is imaging being in a world. These aspects lead us, respectively, into presence-as-such and consciousness-as-such, the dipolar spiritual nature of the divine, which is manifest in immediate present experience, and consummated in transformative action in relation with self, the other and the world.

Feeling the presence of the world

Concomitant with participative imaginal shaping of a world is feeling at one with presence of the world being shaped. In *Feeling and Personhood,* I distinguish between emotion and feeling, as follows:

> By the term 'emotion' I mean the intense, localized affect that arises from the fulfilment or the frustration of individual deeds and interests. This is the domain of joy, love, surprise, satisfaction, zest, fear, grief, anger, and so on. Thus defined, emotion is an index of motivational states. By 'feeling' I refer, with special usage to the capacity of the psyche to participate in wider unities of being, to become at one with the differential content of a whole field of experience, to indwell what is present through attunement and resonance, and to know its distinctness while unified with the differentiated other. This is the domain of empathy, indwelling, participation, presence, resonance, and such like. (Heron, 1992: 16)

Participative engagement with what there is includes a vital component of empathic resonance. This is a living intersubjective communion with the presence of whatever we perceive, from another person to a solid rock. This is a communion with her, his or its experiential way of being in its world. More widely, it is feeling an interconnected web of discrete, interacting presences of many kinds and at many levels, within the all-encompassing inclusive and unitive presence of the cosmos as a whole.

To feel my own presence is to feel the spatiotemporal fulness of my being embodied in a world. It is to feel my embodied being emerge empowered from its indwelling immanent spiritual life. Just so, to feel your presence is to feel the fullness of your personal embodiment welling up from, and presented by, this same immanent spiritual life, which indwells you as it indwells me. When we attend to each other's presence, then there is a mutuality of presence, a relational presence, the go-between divinity of empowering life. The presence of Being is there where there is a mutual presence of being with being.

Just as we participate in the form of whole of the cosmos, through the imaginal process of explicit and tacit perception, so we participate in the presence of the whole cosmos through the affective process of explicit and tacit resonance. When we enter explicitly the mutual presencing of beings within our immediate context, we also at the same time have tacit acquaintance with the great orchestration of mutual presencing that wells up from immanent spiritual life within other beings at the very boundary of that context. And this mututal presencing extends as a numinous cloud of unknowing involving other beings far beyond our context. So there is the explicit presence of Being revealed by the interbeing relations within our immediate context, and there is the tacit presence of Being latent within contexts as yet unknown to us

The concept of presence

The term 'presence' comes from the Latin *prae* and *esse,* so it means literally to be in front of, before. The Latin verb *praesse* meant 'to be at hand'. The English word 'presence' has a range of uses all of which have a bearing on the meanings I give 'presence'. In ordinary usage, it refers to:

- The state or fact of being present; being there; the state of being before or in the same place with a person or thing; current existence or occurrence; the place where a person is; the existence in space and time of a person or a thing; immediate proximity in time or space.

- The place or space in front of, or immediately surrounding, a person; the area immediately surrounding a great personage, especially a sovereign;
- A person who is physically present.
  - A person's bearing, especially when it commands respectful attention; impressive appearance and demeanour, or force of personality.
  - The quality of self-assurance and effectiveness that permits a performer to achieve a rapport with the audience: *stage presence.*
- A divine, spiritual or incorporeal being or influence felt or conceived as present; a present being.
- The diplomatic, political, or military influence of a nation in a foreign country, especially as evidenced by the posting of its diplomats or its troops there.

Presence-as-such

I give the term 'presence-as-such' an all-inclusive generic meaning which both subsumes all ordinary meanings and is far more extensive. Presence-as-such is the immediate domain of any and every experiential transaction among distinct presences. It is resonant empathy of each with each and each with all and all with each.

Local. It is here in this neighbourhood, where the experiential transaction is. It is here where co-presencing is. It is the domain of felt transactions among distinct beings.

Immanent. It is not identical with, or reducible to, the content of immediate experience. It includes that content and is also within it, indwelling it. It is immanent within each distinct presence, and within all experiential transactions, in a given domain. It is immanent as indwelling spiritual life, whence each presence emerges into embodied being, and whence the relations between presences emerge into embodied transactions. Immanence is the infinitude within, infinite potential.

Finite. Presence-as-such manifests as actual finite mutual experience, set within a boundary, a limited context, beyond which is the cloud of potential presence and presences unknown, yet of deep tacit acquaintance.

Experiential. It is the domain of the lived-through world: of encounter, meeting, face-to-face relationship, communion, being with who and what is there, feeling attunement with present entities of all kinds.

Particular. It is the domain of the specific, the particular, the individualized and the idiosyncratic.

Transactional. It involves the mutual non-separate participation, interfusion, interpenetration, of the several distinct presences of an experiential domain. Presence-as-such is the set of all transactional relations between the participating presences of any given domain.

Temporal. It unfurls, unravels, unfolds in time and its component presences are each compounded of multiple interacting temporal rhythms. It manifests as interdependent rhythmic patterns.

Inclusive. It is one with many faces, including all actual domains of immediate experience

Dramatic. It has, in all its manifestations, physical and subtle, striking appearances, forceful qualities, aesthetic impact.

Multiple. It is a manifold. In any immediate experiential domain presence-as-such abides within and includes many distinct presences and the relations between them. And there are innumerable domains of immediate experience.

Existential. It is actuality. It is immediate existence, the very presence of what is here.

Emergent It is continuously generative. As manifest presence it emerges from its immanent depths of spiritual life, the infinitude within each participating presence and within the transactions between all the presences of a given domain.

Vitally exciting. It is living, energetic, motile, sensational, erotic, emotional.

Protopersonal. It is the ground, the source of the soul and of emergent personhood.

Imaging being in a world

Conscious embodiment is the experience of imaging my being in a world kinaesthetically, tactually, visually, aurally. This imaging is not separate from my consciousness and is not separate from what it images, which for convenience I will call the world. By the process of perceptual imaging my consciousness participates in the world. Perceiving is a continuous enactment of a consciousness-world union within a local context. At the same time, both my consciousness and the world transcend the imaging which conjoins them. When I am conjoined with the being I call a tree by visually imaging it, both I and the being transcend the imaging process.

My kinaesthetic and tactual body, that is, my experiential body, the felt sense from within of my body and its immediate engagement with its world, is the central figure 1 of which the circumambient ground 1 is my visual and aural world, extending around my body. My immediate world of visual and aural perceiving, as a whole, is figure 2 to a vague wider world, ground 2, which my visual-aural imagination shapes around it. As soon as I imagine that ground 2 has some explicit perceptual shape, it becomes figure 3 to an inchoate ground 3. And so on.

Now the world of perceiving is inseparable from the world of imagining: to see a perspectivally oval plate is at the same time to imagine its circularity; to see one side of a mountain is also to imagine somwhat the other side of it. Perceiving a world is also and at the same time imagining a world, and the imagining is necessarily more extensive than the perceiving. Perceiving a world depends on imagining more of it than we perceive. This process involves primary imagination: not the secondary imagination of inventing a phantasy world, but the grounding imagination that makes the perceived world real.

Consciousness for us humans is inseparable from perceptual imaging, which is inseparable from primary imagining, and all three are inseparable from the world as thus imaged and imagined. Furthermore, the primary imagining of the perceptual world is inseparable from the primary imagining of the world beyond perceptual reach. My consciousness thus participates explicitly in the perceptual world, penumbrally in the world just beyond the reach of my perceiving, and subliminally or tacitly in the entirety of whatever there is way beyond my perceptual reach, the infinite horizons of grounds that are figures to further grounds that are figures, and so on. Below the threshold of immediate perceiving, primary imagination is co-extensive with, and engages us with, the infinite totality of what there is: we tacitly participate in the very present creating of the total body of the divine.

If my mind at some level participates in everything, is in union with everything, engages with infinite horizons, we can also and more appropriately say that my explicit consciousness is a local, limited and partial outcrop of an omnipresent, limitless, cosmic, primary imagination that is the coherent ground of all manifestation, all actuality. Once I say I participate in the infinite, I can with more vigour say that infinite mind, consciousness-as-such, has a finite locus that is my explicit perceptual consciousness.

There are two important corollaries of this view. The first is that my consciousness, because in one aspect it is inseparable from perceptually imaging and primarily imagining a world, is also in that respect spatial. Images are forms of space, and thus the spatial form of consciousness. The second is that my spatial consciousness has impact upon, influences and modifies the world it images and shapes. This influence is most obvious in the kinaesthetic imaging of my body, which, as motor imaging, moves my body, and can influence its shape and state. Also in tactual imaging of its interaction with its world, for this can influence the shape and state of the immediately bounding world. It is not obvious in visual and auditory perceptual imaging, but by virtue of their participatory engagement with what there is, we can assume a subtle energetic effect.

Consciousness-as-such

I postulate that the inclusive consciousness, in which we are local experiential finite foci, is cosmic, transcendent, infinite, imaginal, general, intelligible, spatial, multidimensional, multivalent, unitive, hierarchical, emanative, ecstatic, and hyperpersonal. And that it is dipolar to presence-as-such, which has correlative interdependent properties, outlined above.

Cosmic. It includes all that there is, all that exists or subsists in any mode of being on any level of being. The universe in every respect, potential or actual, ideal or real, is the content of consciousness-as-such. This content is not reducible to consciousness-as-such, since it is interdepedent with presence-as-such, see below.

Transcendent. It is not identical with it contents. It is more than them: it transcends them in the sense that it is aware of them. Consciousness is always consciousness of some content. This consciousness of is the basic form of transcendence. Consciousness is always beyond what it is conscious of.

Infinite. It is limitless, without boundaries, boundless in two senses. There is no limit to the extent to which it transcends its contents. And there is no limit to the extent of its contents: a limit to any range or set or sample of its contents by definition points to what is beyond the limit. But there can be relative and provisional limits set to any selected range of its contents.

Imaginal. Its contents are imaginal in form. They can be co-imaged by any finite consciousness in terms of perceptual imagery and various other kinds of imagery.

General. It informs its contents with archetypes which relate to what is general and universal in the cosmos.

Intelligible. Its contents and their interrelations are the repositories of meaning and information.

Spatial. Since its contents are imaginal, can be refracted as perceptual and other kinds of imagery, they are inherently spatial. Imaginal space is the general form of consciousness-as-such.

Multidimensional. It includes different kinds and degrees of imaginal space. We know of memory image space, imagination space, dream space, perceptual space, many dimensions of extrasensory perceptual space.

Multivalent. It has the power to combine these different kinds and degrees of imaginal space with each other in multitudinous ways.

Unitive. It is one. There is one ineffable, boundless transcendent consciousness of limitless and varied contents. Its contents, too, are a unitive, interdependent, interpenetrating and interactive system.

Hierarchical. It illuminates its contents; its archetypal light pours down upon them; it is a descent process.

Emanative. It is continuously imaginally creating its contents, both sustaining what there is as it is, changing what there is into innovative forms, and adding entirely new content.

Ecstatic. In its ineffable, boundless transcendence of its contents, it stands outside them, at the same time as including them. This standing-outside-what-is-also-included is ecstatic.

Hyperpersonal. It is the one and only infinite hyperperson and utters the primary originating speech 'I am', where 'I' is the transcendent consciousness and 'am' relates to the totality of the contents of that consciousness.

Immediate present experience and the theology of action

In imaging our world and feeling resonance with what is present, we abide in local divinity, where transcendent spiritual consciousness and immanent spiritual life are revealed here and now in the phenomenal and subtle content of our experience, and are consummated in transformative actions to transfigure our human estate. For the theology of action, humans are co-creators on the crest of divine becoming.

Inquiry into Being

I use the term 'Being' here to mean the divine, or god/dess. I believe in Being because Being is always present in my attention. 'Ever presence' is one way of naming Being. It is not that the presence of Being claims my attention: this could imply that there is a gap between my attention and Being, and that I am attending to Being. But there is no gap, and Being is not an object of my attention.

Indeed Being is present just because there is no gap between me, my attention and any object of it. There is a seamless whole with three apparent distinctions in it. It is this seamlessness which is Being, ever presence.

I don't attend to the seamlessness. I attend within it. I participate in it. I am being within it. I feel it as the one and only and inclusive ground of my attending to what is here.

In a wider sense, I already am the seamlessness. This I am in the statement 'I am the seamlessness' is an inclusive I am: it is more than the I who attends to objects. The subject, the I who attends to things, just because it is part of a seamless subject-attention-object whole is continuous with the I am who is that seamless whole. I am in this inclusive sense is another way of naming Being.

Put it this way: attention is inseparable from its content, they are seamless, there is no gap. The content has apparent limits, but these limits are in reality a penumbra of unspecified endlessness. Correlatively, attention has apparent limits but in reality dissolves into a very subtle unending awareness of nonspecific unlimited content. And I who direct attention seem to have very evident limits, but not in reality, since to notice any such apparent limits is to do so with an I that is beyond them. So my local subjective I seems to be included in an infinite I am that is seamless with a limitless awareness of unlimited content.

I don't generate or create the seamless I am of present experience, I just enter and leave it as my local attention comes and goes with waking and sleeping. It is ever present because, in one obvious and minimal sense, whenever I am around it is present. In a deeper sense it is ever present since its total transcendence of the apparent limits of my local experience makes it independent of the presence or absence of that experience.

I can't attend to, direct my consciousness to, the ever present, since this misconstrues it as a limiting and limited object, and leads to a fruitless search. Indeed, I can't search for it at all since I am already participating in it. I can't notice it or become aware of it, since all such locutions suppose that I close a gap between me and it, and there is no gap to close. I simply participate in it, do what I am already doing, and be as I am already being. I don't practise the presence of Being as some spiritual activity supervenient upon my ordinary consciousness. My ordinary consciousness is now, as always, in the presence of Being.

Of course it seems that I get cut off from the ever present because I become so preoccupied with my subjectivity and with the objects of its concern that subject and object seem to be separate from each other and both seem to be separate from my attention. I can end this preoccupation, stop the illusory avoidance of seamlessness, and simply be as I actually am a participant in the ever presence of Being.

Participatory cosmology: a conjecture

Suppose, by virtue of a principle of intrinsic signature, each entity in the cosmos has a relative autonomy of both form-process and presence that makes it distinct but not separate from every other entitity. Suppose also that each relatively autonomous entity in the cosmos has a tacit acquaintance with the form-process and the presence of every other entity, that is, tacitly knows how it is being both morphologically and experientially. Suppose that, via this principle of tacit acquaintance, each entity has some impact, however minimal, on every other entity. So every entity is all the time influencing every other entity.

Suppose further that this influence is increased by the principle of homology, correspondence of form-process between one entity and another, and correspondence of felt experience between one entity and another, and that the greater the correspondence in either or both respects the greater the influence.

Suppose there is another dimension of influence manifest through the holonomic principle, whereby the whole of each more comprehensive, composite entity is coded in some distinctive patterned way in each of its component entities and partially controls each of them by virtue of this resident code.

The holonomic principle is a special case of the homologic principle. The whole influences the part, and part responds to and acts on the whole by virtue of the whole having a representative pattern of itself within the part, and by virtue of each having a felt sense of the experiential status of the other.

Suppose, finally, a principle of innovative co-creation. Each entity has the potential to influence every other in a manner that goes beyond, and can modify, either intrinsic signature or tacit acquaintance, and either holonomy or homology. Such influence, when made actual by persons, arises from an intentional co-creative engagement with their infinite indwelling potential.

In a participatory universe, on this hypothetical model, there are thus five basic forms of influence. Each and every entity, being relatively autonomous, will have a self-organizing influence on itself. Corresponding entities on the same level of being will have significant reciprocal peer influence on each other. Wholes will have a down-hierarchy influence on their component parts. Parts will have an up-hierarchy influence on their containing wholes. Each and every entity, being potentially co-creative, can have transformative impact on the four prior forms of influence.

Immediate present experience will manifest via autonomy and parity, with self-determining influence and reciprocal co-operative influence. Transcendent spiritual consciousness will manifest via down-hierarchy, with influence from whole to part. Immanent spiritual life will manifest via up-hierarchy, with influence from part to whole. Charismatic action in persons, the comsummation of immediate present experience in multivalent transformations, will manifest via intentional co-creation, modifying autonomy, parity, down-hierarchy and up-hierarchy.

These conjectures may, or may not, have some relevance to shaping the agenda of some future co-operative inquiry. And, whether such speculations are pertinent or not, may inquiries to come flourish.

References

Abram, D. (1996) *The Spell of the Sensuous*. New York: Vintage Books.

Allione, T. (1984) *Women of Wisdom*. New York: Arcana.

Almaas, A.H. (1996) *The Point of Existence*. Berkeley, CA: Diamond Books.

Apffel-Marglin, F. (1994) 'Development or decolonization in the Andes', *Daybreak*, 4(3): 6-10.

Argyris, C. & Schon, D. (1974) *Theory in Practice: Increasing Professional Effectiveness*. San Francisco: Jossey-Bass.

Argyris, C., Putman, R. and Smith, M.C. (1985) *Action Science: Concepts, Methods, and Skills for Research and Intervention*. San Francisco: Jossey-Bass.

Asante, M.K. (1984) 'The African American mode of transcendence', *Journal of Transpersonal Psychology*, 16(2): 167-177.

Assagioli, R. (1965) *Psychosynthesis*. Baltimore: Penguin Books.

Aurobindo, Sri (1970) *The Life Divine*. Pondicherry, India: Sri Aurobindo Ashram.

Bachrach, P. & Botwinick, A. (1992) *Power and Empowerment: A Radical Theory of Participatory Democracy*. Philadelphia: Temple University Press.

Bateson, G. (1972) *Steps to an Ecology of Mind*. San Francisco: Jossey-Bass.

Bateson, G. (1979) *Mind and Nature: A Necessary Unity*. New York: Dutton.

Battista, J.R. (1996) 'Offensive spirituality and spiritual defenses', in B.W. Sutton, A.B. Chinen and J.R. Battista (eds) *Textbook of Transpersonal Psychiatry and Psychology*. New York: Basic Books.

Berdyaev, N. (1937) *The Destiny of Man*. London.

Bertalanffy, L. von (1968) *General System Theory*. New York: Braziller.

Bleakley, A. (1996) 'Motes', *Collaborative Inquiry*, 19: 7-12.

Bohm, D. (1980) *Wholeness and the Implicate Order*. London: Routledge and Kegan Paul.

Bookchin, M. (1991) *The Ecology of Freedom: The Emergence and Dissolution of Hierarchy*. Montreal: Black Rose Books.

Bortoft, H. (1986) *Goethe's Scientific Consciousness*. Tunbridge Wells: Institute for Cultural Research.

Boud, D. (1988) (ed) *Developing Student Autonomy in Learning*. London: Kogan Page.

Boud, D. and Miller, N. (1996) (eds) *Working with Experience: Animating Learning*. London: Routledge.

Brockman, J. (1977) (ed) *About Bateson*. New York: E.P. Dutton.

Buber, M. (1937) *I and Thou*. Edinburgh: Clark.

Camphausen, R.C. (1992) *The Divine Library: A Comprehensive Reference Guide to the Scared Texts and Spiritual Literature of the World*. Vermont: Inner Traditions International.

Capra, F. (1983) *The Turning Point*. London: Fontana.

Childress, D.H. (1995) (ed) *Anti-Gravity and the World Grid*. Stelle, IL: Adventures Unlimited Press.

Christ, C. (1980) *Diving Deep and Surfacing*. Boston: Beacon Press.

Coan, R. (1989) 'Alternative views of the evolution of consciousness', *Journal of Humanistic Psychology*, 29(2): 167-199.

Coomaraswamy, A.K. (1943) *Hinduism and Buddhism*. New York: Philosophical Library.

Cortright, B. (1997) *Psychotherapy and Spirit: Theory and Practice of Transpersonal Psychotherapy*. Albany, NY: SUNY Press.

Crook, J. (1996) 'Authenticity and the practice of Zen', *New Ch'an Forum*, 13: 15-30.

Culler, J. (1982) *On Deconstruction*. Ithaca, NY: Cornell University Press.

Cummins, G. (1967) *The Road to Immortality*. London: Psychic Press.

Cunningham, I. (1988) 'Interactive holistic research: researching self-managed learning', in P. Reason (ed) *Human Inquiry in Action*. London: Sage.

Da Avabhasa (1992) *The Knee of Listening*. Clearlake, CA: The Dawn Horse Press.

Dalai Lama (1996) *The Good Heart*. Boston: Wisdom Publications.

Daly, M. (1991) *Gyn/Ecology: The Metaethics of Radical Feminism*. London: The Women's Press.

De Wit, H.F. (1991) *Contemplative Psychology*. Pittsburgh, PE: Duquesne University Press.

Dean, T. (1984) 'Primordial tradition or postmodern hermeneutics?', *Philosophy East and West*, 34(2): 211-226.

Denzin, N.K. & Lincoln, Y.S. (eds) *Handbook of Qualitative Research*. Thousand Oaks, CA: Sage.

Dewey, J. (1929) *The Quest for Certainty*.

Dewey, J. (1938) *Experience and Education*. Kappa Delta Pi.

diZerega, G. (1996) 'A critique of Ken Wilber's account of deep ecology and nature religions', *The Trumpeter Journal of Ecosophy*, 13(2): 52-70.

Fals-Borda, O. & Rahman, M.A. (1991) *Action and Knowledge: Breaking the Monopoly with Participatory Action Research*. New York: Intermediate Technology/Apex.

Fals-Borda, O. (1996) *Remarks on Participatory Research at the Conference Quality in Human Inquiry*. Centre for Action Research in Professional Practice, University of Bath. Transcript published in *Collaborative Inquiry*, 19(2).

Fenton, J.Y. (1995) 'Mystical experience as a bridge for cross-cultural philosophy of religion: a critique', in T. Dean (ed) *Religious Pluralism and Truth. Eassays on Cross-Cultural Philosophy of Religion*. Albany, NY: SUNY Press.

Ferguson, M. (1980) *The Aquarian Conspiracy*. Los Angeles: Tarcher.

Ferrer, J. (1998a) 'Teoría transpersonal y filosofía perenne: una evaluación crítica', in M. Almendro (ed) *Psicología y Conciencia*. Barcelona: Kairos. English version in *Transpersonal Knowledge*. Manuscript in preparation.

Ferrer, J. (1998b) 'Speak now or forever hold your peace: an essay on Ken Wilber's *The Marriage of Sense and Soul: Integrating Science and Religion*', *The Quest*, forthcoming.

Ferrer, J. (1998c) 'Conocimiento transpersonal: una aproximacion epistemica a la transpersonalidad', in F. Rodriguez (ed) *Psicologia y Psicoterapia Transpersonales*. Barcelona: La Liebre de Marzo. English version in *Transpersonal Knowledge*. Manuscript in preparation.

Ferrer, J. (1998d) Personal communication.

Ferrer, J. (1998e) 'Beyond absolutism and relativism in transpersonal evolutionary theory', *World Futures: The Journal of General Evolution*, forthcoming.

Fox, G. (1694) *Journal*.

Fox, M. (1983) *Original Blessing*. Santa Fe, NM: Bear and Company.

Friedman, N. (1994) *Bridging Science and the Spirit*. St Louis, MO: Living Lakes Books.

Gadamer, H.G. (1976) *Philosophical Hermeneutics*. Berkeley: University of California Press.

Gebser, J. (1985) *The Ever Present Origin*. Athens: Ohio University Press.

Gendlin, E. (1981) *Focusing*. London: Bantam Press.

Gerber, R. (1988) *Vibrational Medicine: New Choices for Healing Ourselves*. Santa Fe, NM: Bear.

Gilligan, C. (1982) *In a Different Voice: Psychological Theory and Women's Identity*. Cambridge, MA: Harvard University Press.

Gimello, R. (1983) 'Mysticism in its contexts', in S. Katz (ed) *Mysticism and Religious Traditions*. New York : Oxford University Press.

Goldenberg, N. (1979) *The Changing of the Gods*. Boston: Beacon Press.

Goleman, D. (1988) *The Meditative Mind*. Los Angeles: Tarcher.

Govinda, Lama Anagarika (1960) *The Foundations of Tibetan Mysticism*. London: Rider.

Grof, S. (1976) *Realms of the Human Unconscious*. New York: Dutton.

Grof, S. (1985) *Beyond the Brain*. Albany, NY: SUNY Press.

Grof, S. (1988) *The Adventures of Self-Discovery*. Albany, NY: SUNY Press.

Guba, E.G. & Lincoln, Y.S. (1994) 'Competing paradigms in qualitative research', in N.K. Denzin & Y.S. Lincoln (eds) *Handbook of Qualitative Research*. Thousand Oaks, CA: Sage.

Guenon, R. (1945) *Man and His Becoming According to the Vedanta*. London: Luzac and Company.

Hanegraaff, W.J. (1998) *New Age Religion and Western Culture: Esotericisim in the Mirror of Secular Thought*. Albany, NY: SUNY Press.

Hartshorne, C. and Reese, W. (1953) *Philosophers Speak of God*. Chicago: University of Chicago Press.

Heidegger, M. (1962) *Being and Time*. New York: Harper and Row.

Heron, J. (1975) *Practical Methods in Transpersonal Psychology*. Human Potential Research Project: University of Surrey.

Heron, J. (1987) *Confessions of a Janus-Brain*. London: Endymion Press.
Heron, J. (1988) *Cosmic Psychology*. London: Endymion Press.
Heron, J. (1989) *The Facilitators' Handbook*. London: Kogan Page.
Heron, J. (1990) *Helping the Client: A Creative, Practical Guide*. London: Sage.
Heron, J. (1992) *Feeling and Personhood: Psychology in Another Key*. London: Sage.
Heron, J. (1993) *Group Facilitation: Theories and Models for Practice*. London: Kogan Page.
Heron, J. (1996a) *Co-operative Inquiry: Research into the Human Condition*. London: Sage.
Heron, J. (1996b) 'Spiritual inquiry: a critique of Wilber', *Collaborative Inquiry*, 18: 2-10.
Heron, J. (1997a) 'A way out for Wilberians', http: //www.sirt.pisa.it/icci/WilbErrs.htm
Heron, J. (1997b) 'A self-generating practitioner community', in R. House and N. Totton (eds) *Implausible Professions: Arguments for Pluralism and Autonomy in Psychotherapy and Counselling*. Ross-on-Wye: PCCS Books.
Heron, J. and Reason, P. (1997) 'A participatory inquiry paradigm', *Qualitative Inquiry*, 3(3): 274-294.
Hick, J. (1973) *God and the Universe of Faiths*. Oxford: Oneworld Publications.
Houston, J. (1987) *The Search for the Beloved*. Los Angeles: Tarcher.
Hunt, H. (1995) 'Some developmental issues in transpersonal experiences', *Journal of Mind and Behaviour*, 16(2): 115-134.
Huxley, A. (1945) *The Perennial Philosophy*. New York: Harper & Row.
Hyde, L. (1949) *The Nameless Faith*. London: Rider.
Isenberg, S.R. & Thursby, G.R. (1985) 'A perennial philosophy perspective on Richard Rorty's neo-pragmatism', *International Journal for Philosophy of Religion*, 17: 41-65.
Jantzen, G.M. (1994) 'Feminists, philosophers, and mystics', *Hypatia*, 9(4): 203-4.
Jones, K. (1996) 'Movements in British Buddhism: a cautionary note', *New Ch'an Forum*, 13: 7-8.
Jung, C. (1936) 'Yoga and the west', in *Collected Works*, volume 2, second edition, Princeton, NJ: Princeton University Press, 1969.
Katz, S.T. (1978) 'Language, epistemology, and mysticism', in S. Katz (ed) *Mysticism and Philosophical Analysis*. New York: Oxford University Press.
Kegan, R. (1994) *In Over Our Heads: The Mental Demands of Modern Life*. Cambridge, MA: Harvard University Press.
Kelly, G.B. (1993) *Karl Rahner: Theologian of the Graced Search for Meaning*. Edinburgh: Clark.
Kelly, S. (1998a) 'Revisioning the mandala of consciousness: a critical appraisal of Wilber's holarchical paradigm', in D. Rothberg and S. Kelly (eds) *Ken Wilber in Dialogue: Conversations with Leading Transpersonal Thinkers*. Wheaton, IL: Theosophical Publishing House.
Kelly, S. (1998b) 'Breaks in the chain', in D. Rothberg and S. Kelly (eds) *Ken Wilber in Dialogue: Conversations with Leading Transpersonal Thinkers*. Wheaton, IL: Theosophical Publishing House.
Kemmis, S. and McTaggart, R. (eds) (1988) *The Action Research Planner*. Victoria: Deakin University Press.
Kharitidi, O. (1997) *Entering the Circle*. London: Thorsons.
King, R.H. (1940) *George Fox and the Light Within*.
Kitselman, A.L. (1953) *E-Therapy*. New York: Institute of Integration.
Klee, R. (1997) *Introduction to the Philosophy of Science*. New York: Oxford University Press.
Klimo, J. (1988) *Channeling*. Los Angeles: Tarcher.
Kornfield, J. (1989) 'Obstacles and vicissitudes in spiritual practice', in S. Grof & C. Grof (eds) *Spiritual Emergency: When Personal Transformation Becomes a Crisis*. Los Angeles: Tarcher.
Kornfield, J. (1990) *Buddhist Meditation and Consciousness Research*. Sausalito, CA: Institute of Noetic Sciences.
Kremer, J. (1992a) 'The dark night of the scholar', *Re Vision*, 14(4): 169-178.
Kremer, J. (1992b) 'Whither dark night of the scholar', *Re Vision*, 15(1):4-12.
Kremer, J. (1994) *Looking for Dame Yggdrasil*. Red Bluff, CA: Falkenflug Press.
Kremer, J. (1996a) 'The shadow of evolutionary thinking', *Re Vision*, 19(1): 41-48.
Kremer, J. (1996b) 'Evolving into what, and for whose purposes? Reading Bateson', *Re Vision*, 18(3): 27-36.
Kremer, J. (1997) 'Are there indigenous epistemologies'. Unpublished manuscript.
LaBerge, S. (1985) *Lucid Dreaming*. New York: Ballantine.
Lacey, A.R. (1986) *A Dictionary of Philosophy*. London: Routledge and Kegan Paul
Lachs, S. (1994) 'A slice of Zen in America', *New Ch'an Forum*, 10.

Lewin, K. (1952) *Field Theory in Social Science.* London: Tavistock.
Lilly, J. (1972) *Center of the Cyclone.* New York: Julian Press.
Lincoln, Y.S. and Denzin, N.K. (1994) 'The fifth moment', in N.K. Denzin and Y.S. Lincoln (eds) *Handbook of Qualitative Research.* Thousand Oaks, CA: Sage.
Lyotard, J. (1984) *The Post-modern Condition: A Report on Knowledge.* Minneapolis, MN: University of Minnesota Press.
Macmurray, J. (1957) *The Self as Agent.* London: Faber and Faber.
Maslow, A. (1970) *Motivation and Personality.* New York: Harper & Row.
McDermott, R. (1988) 'Philosophy as spiritual discipline', *Towards,* 3(2): 31-39.
McDermott, R. (1993) 'Transpersonal worldviews: historical and philosophical reflections', in R. Walsh and F. Vaughan (eds) *Paths Beyond Ego.* Los Angeles: Tarcher.
McMahon, E. and Campbell, P. (1991) *The Focusing Steps.* Kansas City, MO: Sheed and Ward.
Merleau-Ponty, M. (1962) *Phenomenology of Perception.* London: Routledge and Kegan Paul.
Mies, M. (1993) 'Feminist Research: Science, Violence and Responsibility', in M. Mies and V. Shiva (eds) *Ecofeminism.* London: Zed Books.
Miller-McLemore, B. (1985) 'Epistemology or bust: a maternal feminist knowledge of knowing', *The Journal of Religion,* 72: 229-247.
Minnich, B. (1990) *Transforming Knowledge.* Philadelphia: Temple University Press.
Monroe, R.A. (1972) *Journeys Out of the Body.* London: Souvenir Press.
Moody, R. (1977) *Life After Life.* Atlanta: Mockingbird Books.
Moody, R. (1993) *Reunions: Visionary Encounters with Departed Loved Ones.* New York: Villard Books.
Moss, R. (1986) *The Black Butterfly: An Invitation to Radical Aliveness.* Berkeley, CA: Celestial Arts.
Mudge, L.S. (1983) 'Hermeneutics', in A. Richardson and J. Bowden (eds) *A New Dictionary of Christian Theology.* London: SCM Press.
Nasr, S.H. (1981) *Knowledge and the Scared.* New York: Crossroad.
Noyes, R. (1980) 'Attitude changes following near-death experiences', *Psychiatry,* 43: 234-41.
Olson, A. and Rouner, L. (1981) (eds) *Transcendence and the Sacred.* Notre Dame: University of Notre Dame Press.
Patrides, C.A. (1980) (ed) *The Cambridge Platonists.*
Perkins, M. (1971) 'Matter, sensation and understanding', *American Philosophical Quarterly,* 8: 1-12.
Peters, R.S. (1966) *Ethics and Education.* London: Allen & Unwin.
Rahula, W. (1974) *What the Buddha Taught.* New York: Random House.
Randall, R. and Southgate, J. (1980) *Co-operative and Community Group Dynamics... Or Your Meetings Needn't Be So Appalling.* London: Barefoot Books.
Raphael, M. (1994) 'Feminism, constructivism and numinous experience', *Religious Studies,* 30: 511-526.
Reason, P. (1988) (ed) *Human Inquiry in Action.* London: Sage.
Reason, P. (1993) 'Reflections on sacred experience and sacred science', *Journal of Management Inquiry,* 2(3): 273-283.
Reason, P. (1994a) (ed) *Participation in Human Inquiry.* London: Sage.
Reason, P. (1994b) 'Co-operative inquiry, participatory action research and action inquiry', in N.K. Denzin & Y.S. Lincoln (eds) *Handbook of Qualitative Research.* Thousand Oaks, CA: Sage.
Reason, P. (1996) 'Reflections on the purposes of human inquiry', *Qualitative Inquiry,* 2(1):15-28.
Reason, P. and Heron, J. (1995) 'Co-operative inquiry', in J.A. Smith, R. Harre and L.Van Langenhove (eds) *Rethinking Methods in Psychology.* London: Sage.
Reason, P. and Rowan, J. (1981) 'Issues of validity in new paradigm research', in P. Reason and J. Rowan (eds) *Human Inquiry: A Sourcebook of New Paradigm Research.* Chichester: Wiley.
Ring, K. (1984) 'The nature of personal identity in the near-death experience', *Anabiosis,* 40(1): 3-20.
Rogers, C. (1959) 'A theory of therapy, personality, and interpersonal relationships, as developed in the client-centred framework', in S. Koch (ed) *Psychology: A Study of a Science,* Vol 3. New York: Penguin.
Rogers, C. (1980) *A Way of Being.* Boston: Houghton Mifflin.
Rosenthal, G. (1987) 'Inflated by the spirit', in D. Anthony, B. Ecker, and K. Wilber (eds) *Spiritual Choices: The Problem of Recognizing Authentic Paths to Inner Transformation.* New York: Paragon House.
Rothberg, D. (1986) 'Philosophical foundations of transpersonal psychology: an introduction to some basic issues', *Journal of Transpersonal Psychology,* 18(1): 1-34.
Rothberg, D. (1994) 'Spiritual inquiry', *Re Vision,* 17(2): 2-12.
Rothberg, D. (1996) 'How straight is the spiritual path', *Re Vision,* 19(1): 25-40.

Rouner, L.S. (1983) 'Dualism', in A. Richardson and J. Bowden (eds) *A New Dictionary of Christian Theology.* London: SCM Press.
Saiving, V. (1976) 'Androcentrism in religious studies', *The Journal of Religion,* 56: 177-197.
Saiving, V. (1992) 'The human situation: a feminine view', in C.P. Christ and J. Plaskow (eds) *Womenspirit Rising.* San Francisco: Harper.
Schon, D. (1983) *The Reflective Practitioner.* New York: Basic Books.
Schroedinger, E. (1964) *My View of the World.* London: Cambridge University Press.
Schroedinger, E. (1969) *What is Life? and Mind and Matter.* London: Cambridge University Press.
Schuon, F. (1984) *The Transcendent Unity of Religions.* Wheaton, IL: Theosophical Publishing House.
Scotton, B.W., Chinen A.B. & Battista, J.R. (1996) (eds) *Textbook of Transpersonal Psychiatry and Psychology.* New York: Basic Books.
Sheldrake, R. (1981) *A New Science of Life.* London: Blond & Briggs.
Sinclair, L. (1986) 'Women and religion', in M.I.Duley and M.I. Edwards (eds) *The Cross-Cultural Study of Women.* New York: Feminist Press.
Skolimowski, H. (1985) *The co-creative mind as a partner of the creative evolution.* Paper read at the First International Conference on Mind-Matter Interaction. Universidada Estadual De Campinas, Brazil.
Skolimowski, H. (1994) *The Participatory Mind.* London: Arkana.
Smith, H. (1976) *Forgotten Truth.* New York: Harper and Row.
Smith, H. (1982) *Beyond the Post-modern Mind.* New York: Crossroad.
Spretnak, C. (1991) *States of Grace: The Recovery of Meaning in the Postmodern Age.* San Francisco: Harper-Collins.
Spretnak, C. (1995) 'Embodied, embedded philosophy', *Open Eye,* California Institute for Integral Studies, 12(1): 4-5.
Stace, W.T. (1961) *Mysticism and Philosophy.* London: Macmillan.
Stcherbatsky, T. (1962) *Buddhist Logic.* New York: Dover.
Stevenson, I. (1966) *Twenty Cases Suggestive of Reincarnation.*
Swimme, B. (1984) *The Universe is a Green Dragon.* Santa Fe, NM: Bear.
Teilhard de Chardin, P. (1961) *The Phenomenon of Man.* New York: Harper Torchbooks.
Tillich, P. (1951 63) *Systematic Theology,* 3 vols. Chicago: University of Chicago Press.
Torbert, W.R. (1987) *Managing the Corporate Dream: Restructuring for Long-Term Success.* Homewood, IL: Dow Jones-Irwin.
Torbert, W.R. (1991) *The Power of Balance: Transforming Self, Society and Scientific Inquiry.* Newbury Park, CA: Sage.
Trungpa, C. (1986) *Shambhala: The Sacred Path of the Warrior.* London: Bantam Books.
Underhill, E. (1927) *Man and the Supernatural.* London: Methuen.
Varela, F. J., Thompson, E. and Rosch, E. (1991) *The Embodied Mind: Cognitive Science and Human Experience.* Cambridge, MA: MIT Press.
Vroom, H.M. (1989) *Religions and the Truth.* Grand Rapids, MI: William B. Eerdmans.
Wahl, J. (1953) *Traité de Métaphysique.* Paris: Payot.
Walker, S. (1987) (ed) *Speaking of Silence: Christians and Buddhists on the Contemplative Way.* New York: Paulist Press.
Washburn, M. (1995) *The Ego and the Dynamic Ground: A Transpersonal Theory of Human Development.* Albany, NY: SUNY Press.
Wenger, W. (1991) *How to Image-stream.* Gathersburg: Psychegenics Press.
Whitehead, A.N. (1929) *Process and Reality.* Cambridge: Cambridge University Press.
Wilber, K. (1977) *The Spectrum of Consciousness.* Wheaton, IL: Theosophical Publishing House.
Wilber, K. (1980) *The Atman Project: A Transpersonal View of Human Development.* Wheaton, IL: The Theosophical Publication House.
Wilber, K. (1982) 'Odyssey: a personal inquiry into humanistic and transpersonal psychology', *Journal of Humanistic Psychology,* 22(1): 57-90.
Wilber, K. (1983) *Up from Eden.* London: Routledge and Kegan Paul.
Wilber, K. (1986) 'The spectrum of psychopathology', in K. Wilber, J. Engler and D.P. Brown (eds) *Transformations of Consciousness: Conventional and Contemplative Perspectives on Development.* Boston: Shambhala.
Wilber, K. (1990) *Eye to Eye: The Quest fo the New Paradigm.* Boston: Shambhala.
Wilber, K. (1995) *Sex, Ecology, Spirituality: The Spirit of Evolution.* Boston: Shambhala.
Wilber, K. (1997) *The Eye of the Spirit.* Boston: Shambhala.

Wilber,K. (1998) *The Marriage of Sense and Soul: Integrating Science and Religion.* New York: Random House.

Wilber, K., Engler, J., and Brown, D. (1986) *Transformations of Consciousness.* Boston: Shambhala.

Winkelman, M. (1993) 'The evolution of consciousness? Transpersonal theories in light of cultural relativism', *Anthropology of Consciousness,* 4(3): 3-9.

Wright, P. (1995) 'Bringing women's voices to transpersonal psychology', *Re Vision,* 17(3): 3-10.

Zaehner, R.C. (1957) *Mysticism Sacred and Profane.*

Zaehner, R.C. (1958) *At Sundry Times.*

Zukav, G. (1979) *The Dancing Wu Li Masters.* New York: William Morrow.

Index